Transforming Ourselves, Transforming the World

Transforming Ourselves, Transforming the World

JUSTICE IN JESUIT HIGHER EDUCATION

Edited by Mary Beth Combs
and Patricia Ruggiano Schmidt

FORDHAM UNIVERSITY PRESS
New York   2013

Fordham University Press has no responsibility for the persistence
or accuracy of URLs for external or third-party Internet websites
referred to in this publication and does not guarantee that any
content on such websites is, or will remain, accurate or appropriate.

Fordham University Press also publishes its books in a variety of
electronic formats. Some content that appears in print may not be
available in electronic books.

Library of Congress Cataloging-in-Publication Data is available from
the publisher.

Printed in the United States of America
15 14 13   5 4 3 2 1
First edition

For Jesuits past and present, and for their work for justice throughout the world.

For my parents, Thomas D. Combs Jr. and Mary E. Combs. Thank you for my Jesuit education at Fairfield University, for supporting my decision to join the Jesuit Volunteer Corps, and for teaching me, by example, to care about the wider community and to work for justice.—*Mary Beth Combs*

It is a privilege to dedicate this book to the Jesuits who inspired and set me on a course of action for justice: Rev. Donald Maldari, Rev. John Breslin, Rev. Charles Beirne, Rev. Donald J. Kirby, Rev. Joseph Marina, Donald Zewe, SJ, and Rev. Louis Sogliuzzo. My life was transformed, as were the lives of many of our students.—*Patricia Ruggiano Schmidt*

Contents

Acknowledgments

The chapters that constitute this book include essays submitted in response to an international call for contributions on the topic of justice in Jesuit higher education, and also are based on papers presented at the Association of Jesuit Colleges and Universities (AJCU) Commitment to Justice in Jesuit Higher Education conference held at Fairfield University in Fairfield, Connecticut, June 18–21, 2009. The idea for this book evolved from discussions among members of the AJCU Commitment to Justice in Jesuit Higher Education National Steering Committee, and the editors would like to thank their colleagues on the 2009 national steering committee for their generous support throughout the publication process: Juniper Ellis (Loyola University Maryland) served as chair. June's dedicated leadership and friendship inspired us and also guided the book's development. Other members of the committee include Kurt Denk, SJ (Kramer Levin Naftalis and Frankel LLP), Keenan Grenell (Colgate University), David McMenamin (Boston College), Kathleen Orange (Spring Hill College), Nicholas Santilli (Notre Dame College of Ohio), Winston Tellis (Fairfield University), and Georgie Weatherby (Gonzaga University). They cheerfully encouraged the process at every turn and advised us in numerous invaluable ways. The editors also would like to thank the participants and discussants at the 2009 Commitment to Justice in Jesuit Higher Education conference for their comments and advice on the papers presented at that time, as well as Fairfield University for hosting the conference. We also gratefully acknowledge generous summer research funding from Fordham University that supported our work editing the book.

Editing this book has been a rewarding experience despite the challenges posed by working with editors, reviewers, and authors separated by time zones and by justice work in other countries and continents. The book's national review board organized a diverse review team whose fields of expertise ran the gamut of academic disciplines, and we are grateful for the work of the national review board: Roger Bergman (Creighton University), Jean Wahl Harris (Scranton University), Kent Koth (Seattle University), Rev. Jonathan Lawrence (Canisius College), Betsy Linehan (St. Joseph's University), Mary Roche (College of the Holy Cross), and Steven Saum (Santa Clara University). We also would like to thank the members of the review team for their generosity in reading all of the submissions and for carefully critiquing two sets of revisions for each of the chapters. The review team included Niyati Ahujan, Eileen Angelini, Paul Aspan, Gregory Baker, Racquel Bergen, Roger Bergman, Frank Bernt, Melissa Boyle, Sr. Patricia Brady, Jay Buss, Fr. Luis Calero, Stephen Casey, Judith Chapman, Patricia Christian, Judith Chubb, William Clark, SJ, Ricardo Dobles, Joseph Dreisbach, Matthew Eggemeier, Mary Elsbernd, Patricia Erickson, John Farnsworth, Jane Fisher, Fred E. Foldvary, Mary Anne Foley, Nancy Fox, Beth Furlong, Janine P. Geske, Ann Green, Patricia Griffin, Dennis Hamm, Jean Wahl Harris, James Hayes, SJ, David Henry, SJ, Irene Hodgson, Le Xuan Hy, Steven Jones, Virginia Johnson, Carol Kelly, Tom Kelly, Victoria Kill, Kevin Krycka, Kristin Kusanovich, Laurie Laird, Jonathan Lawrence, Benjamin Liebman, Betsy Linehan, Tanya Loughead, Madeline Lovell, Maria Marsilio, Gordon Mayer, Michael McCann, Julie McDonald, David McFadden, Sharon Meagher, Jean Molesky-Poz, Robert Moore, Susan Mountin, Rebecca Murray, Anil Nathan, Laura Nichols, Peter Norberg, Kevin Nordberg, Joe Orlando, Jeff Peak, Thomas G. Plante, Tom Purcell, Janet Quillian, Ken Reed-Bouley, Meghan Ashlin Rich, Erin Robinson, Nancy Rourke, Fr. Stephen Rowntree, SJ, Robert Shannon, Michelle Sharp, Alice Smith, Karen Snetselaar, William J. Stover, John Suggs, Justin Svec, Daniel Sweeney, SJ, Jennifer Tilghman-Havens, Joe Vinson, Ron Volkmer, Keith Douglass Warner, OFM, Georgie Weatherby, Jos Welie, Loreen Wolfer, Amy Wolfson, Ann Wright, and Wayne Young. We would like to thank our contributors for responding constructively to sometimes voluminous editorial comments and frequent requests for information. We are indebted to them for their good-humored patience while we completed the manuscript. We also would like to thank the members of the editorial board at Fordham University Press, and Robert Oppedisano, who commissioned this book on behalf of Fordham University

Press. Finally, we would like to thank Fredric Nachbaur, who came to the Press as director once the book was already in progress, and whose friendly stewardship, encouragement, and patience helped us to complete it.

Introduction

A Fruitful New Branch

DEAN BRACKLEY, SJ

A few years ago a young man shared with me his enthusiasm about starting as a teacher in one of our Jesuit schools. Although he realized that he would be teaching privileged students, he said he welcomed the opportunity to form leaders who would occupy important posts in society and exercise their professional responsibilities with integrity, a final point that stood out in my hearing.

His comment percolated in my subconscious and later resurfaced in the form of a question: Did the new teacher realize how bad things are?

> Poverty, the most lethal weapon of mass destruction, kills more people each day than die from terrorism in an entire year.
> Over 5 million people have died in Central Africa's recent wars, mostly from sickness and hunger, and the world barely notices.
> At least 150 governments currently practice torture.
> Our environment is in crisis, our ecosystems under siege.
> The US prison system is the largest in the world, warehousing 2.3 million people, most of them black and brown men from poor communities.

Faced with facts like these, can we limit the mission of Jesuit-sponsored higher education to forming competent, honest professionals for societies as they are? The contributions to this book assume we cannot. They assume that the mission is education for both personal *and* social transformation.

Some of these essays have their origin in the Conference on Commitment to Justice in Higher Education held at Fairfield University in June 2009. Others were submitted in response to a national call for contributions for this book. All of the essays share research, reflections, and best practices as part of an ongoing response to the challenge posed by Peter-Hans Kolvenbach, SJ, in his October 6, 2000, address at Santa Clara, "The Service of Faith and the Promotion of Justice in American Jesuit Higher Education." This collection of essays celebrates the tenth anniversary of that historic address, in which the superior general of the Jesuits called on Jesuit colleges and universities to form students in a "well-educated solidarity" and to engage the social problems of our time.

Far from simply repeating what was said in the past, the contributions to this book demonstrate a new maturity and depth, the fruits of experience. They cover a rich variety of topics: engaged pedagogy; the roots of our mission in Ignatian spirituality and Catholic tradition; local and international immersion experiences; curriculum redesign in nursing, language study and law; transformational poetry and music; race; nonviolence; the environment; and justice within Jesuit institutions. The topics are grouped into three parts: Formation and Learning, Research and Teaching, and Our Way of Proceeding (or institutional practice), although many chapters reach beyond their assigned category.

The education for transformation of which these essays speak draws on a venerable legacy of Jesuit Catholic education. That tradition is diverse and dynamic, spacious and welcoming. It is also distinctive. Much as we admire the most prestigious secular colleges and universities, we do not simply strive to imitate them. At the same time, neither do we want our institutions to devolve into confessional enclaves. When we are feeling pretentious, we claim to have higher standards. More modestly, we hold ourselves to a more comprehensive set of criteria for academic excellence.

In the Jesuit Catholic tradition, education is more than information; it is formation of the whole person. Education seeks wisdom. It is not just about being a success as a professional but about being a success as a human being as Steven Privett, SJ, remarks. That includes struggling to understand the meaning of life and growing in moral sensitivity and practical reasoning and judgment. Maturing in practical wisdom is not a complementary "pastoral" add-on, but an essential dimension of academic excellence, integrally considered. Any education worth the name will help us learn how to size up what is at stake morally in situations and respond appropriately.

Not everyone sees it quite this way. In today's academy, a major current of discourse separates facts and values, intelligence and morals. In this view, values and moral commitments are ultimately matters of personal preference, not of reason, which is itself reduced to the analytical rationality of the natural sciences. Faced with this perspective, it can be tempting—even for people who want to educate minds and hearts—to line up head and facts on one side (academic excellence) and heart and values on the other; or, through ambiguity, to give the impression that we buy into that split. We do not. While we distinguish these elements, we also integrate them. We affirm scientific rationality but also practical (moral) reason as indispensable for understanding reality and therefore as essential for academic excellence. You cannot properly educate the head without the heart, and vice versa.

The "value-free" challenge can take another form. In the Catholic outlook that inspires Jesuit education, truth is "objective" and we should strive to realize "objective" goods in the world, such as life, peace, justice, and love. Doesn't this view of things constrain academic freedom? The answer is a resounding "No"; it ought not. The conviction that what is true and right cannot be reduced to human convention goes hand in hand with the recognition that the splendor of the truth is too marvelous for any individual or group to grasp once and for all. The truth shines forth in diverse ways, in a multiplicity of cultures and in a manner that depends on times and places. Only free inquiry, coming from different directions, can adequately approach its glorious fullness. In our age of insuperable pluralism, above all, the Jesuit Catholic outlook forbids imposing one's views in the academy and instead demands humility and utter seriousness in the search for what is true and right. It further affirms that faith and reason, rather than conflicting, complement each other in the service of many splendored truth.

Education is about maturing in intelligence which in the Jesuit tradition means intelligence integrally considered—that is, taken in its several related dimensions. Human intelligence is embodied; it is a sentient, feeling intelligence. It is intelligence nourished by imagination. Its exercise is inextricably intertwined with volition and interest. It is shared intelligence, the product of socialization into a particular culture and its traditions. Being serious about education requires taking all this into account. That, too, poses challenges that, when faced up to, enrich the educational adventure!

Our intelligence is embedded in interests and affectivity, just as it is shaped by the cultures of which we are a part. These are the necessary matrix of knowledge. They provide the grid (or paradigm, as one contributor puts it) by which we interpret experience. However, they also limit and even distort our perception. In particular, those who populate Jesuit-sponsored colleges and universities in the United States are, for the most part, well-off; they live and they educate (and are educated) in the world's richest country and sole superpower. While this context is fertile ground for education, it is also fertile ground for shared prejudice and blind spots.

The unconscious assumptions that underlie interpretive grids are rooted in people's desires and commitments. Understanding is further shaped by a public discourse that is interested and partly distorted. This makes education more than a matter of pushing back the frontiers of ignorance. It is also "cognitive hygiene," even "cognitive liberation." Learning must include exercises that help free us from prejudice and unmask the public lies that shore up the status quo. This is all the more necessary insofar as distortion is rooted in sin. I use this language to indicate how pervasive and deep-seated distortion is and therefore how radical the solution must be. Sin is an analogous concept; that is, sin takes various forms. There are personal sins and sinful habits, but also original "sin" and structural sin. Sin generates personal, habitual, original, and structural distortion, which education must strive to overcome. Not that the victims of distortion—all of us—are always culpable for it. (People are not culpable for original "sin" and structural sin in the same way as for personal sin.) Even so, many biases are anchored in stubborn commitments and disordered desire. Ignatian spirituality and pedagogy address this challenge, inviting us to a personal transformation that orders our affections, liberates our imagination, erodes prejudice, and expands our horizon.

Engaging other perspectives helps do that. It surfaces questions that otherwise fail to arise. This book offers examples of engaged pedagogy designed for that purpose: insertion programs, community-based learning, study abroad, internships, clinical placements, and other forms of interacting with the poor and with cultures other than our own. Most of these exercises expose students and teachers to unfamiliar situations and viewpoints that provoke the kind of salutary disorientation that helps free the understanding, rendering it more "flexible." Although some might consider these exercises to be frills, or even a threat to academic rigor, the opposite is true. Without methodical and sustained efforts of this kind, we are lacking in our pursuit of academic excellence, integrally considered. Engaged pedagogy fits squarely in the tradition of Jesuit pedagogy. However, today we recognize the need for it more readily, thanks to a new appreciation both of widespread injustice and of personal and collective cover-ups.

More than in the past, we stress that and insist on education for *social* transformation. This is a new branch, sprouting organically from the old tree of Jesuit Catholic education. The Jesuit way of proceeding has always emphasized responding to the real world and its needs. In his meditation on the Incarnation in the Spiritual Exercises, Saint Ignatius portrays God taking in the whole world, observing how people labor, how they love and hate, are born and die. The Trinity then decides to respond to suffering humanity by sending Jesus. Jesus in turn calls everyone to respond, with God, to help heal a broken world.

Today we recognize, more than our forebears, that this same world is in constant change and that it is configured in profoundly unjust ways that we can and must address. In part, this is hardly new. Consciousness of historical change has spread ever since the Renaissance. But, in another way it is new. Awareness of the global scale of human suffering and its structural causes has only become widespread since the second half of the twentieth century—in the wake of two world wars, the advent of atomic weaponry, massive decolonization, widespread international travel, and the information explosion. Until recently, knowledge of this type was shared mostly by elites. However, today the mass of humanity is exposed to singular horrors and to the institutional mechanisms that generate injustice on an unprecedented scale. This new awareness has led Christian churches, and other religious bodies as well, to rediscover the centrality of justice in their scriptures and traditions. The Catholic Church expressed this new awareness in Vatican II's *Constitution on the Church in the Modern World*

(*Gaudium et spes,* 1965) and in many subsequent statements and actions in response to the signs of the times. Jesuit-sponsored education for social transformation is part of that response.

As superior general of his order from 1965–83, the charismatic Pedro Arrupe helped the Jesuits recognize that the innocent victims of structural injustice are a principal, if not *the* principal sign of our times. He inspired his brother Jesuits to reconceive their mission as the service of faith and the promotion of justice. Arrupe had ministered to the sick and dying at the Jesuit novitiate outside Nagasaki after its atomic obliteration in 1945. He was a man marked by the horrors and promise of his time. His 1973 address, "Men and Women for Others" (Arrupe himself later endorsed the more inclusive title), articulates a new vision for Jesuit education in response to a world torn by injustice and violence. Peter-Hans Kolvenbach further developed that vision for higher education at Santa Clara. The essays in this book represent further growth of this green branch on the living tree of the Jesuit educational tradition, one that promises abundant fruit in the future.

The contributors to this book harbor no illusions that they have completed the task. Their work poses many challenges that will occupy educators for a long time to come. Here I list some of those challenges, most of them formulated explicitly in the pages that follow:

Does our institution have a social-justice program that addresses structural issues, or are programs limited to service? Is historical-social analysis part of the core curriculum?

How can we help students manage the anger, guilt, and frustration— which their encounters with unjust misery frequently induce— and grow into a sustained, compassionate commitment?

How can we better address issues of race in our teaching and learning?

Are we educating in nonviolence?

How can teachers be fair-minded and avoid demagoguery, without according undeserved attention to sophistic arguments that seek to shore up privilege and cover up injustice?

How can our institutions better support and train faculty in engaged pedagogies and community-based learning?

How can we evoke a desire for the faith that does justice?

How can we increase the number of students from low-income households at our institutions, as well as the number of students, faculty, and administrators from underrepresented groups?

What costly academic and athletic programs, of limited benefit to the university community, might be curtailed to free up resources for need-based scholarships?

How to promote a simpler campus lifestyle? What luxury services should go?

How can colleges or universities exercise a prophetic role in the wider society? How can the institution protect those members of its community who exercise such a role within or beyond the campus?

How can we make colleges or universities "greener"?

Is it appropriate to house ROTC programs on campus? Would it be more appropriate for ROTC students to receive military training elsewhere? Should criteria be spelled out concerning research for the Department of Defense?

Is a college or university's investment portfolio subject to criteria of social and environmental responsibility?

How can we help trustees better appreciate and share the vision of transformative education?

How can we collaborate more effectively with colleagues in Jesuit institutions, especially in poor countries, to promote justice and defend the environment? How can we better share library resources and research technology with them?

The current Jesuit superior general, Adolfo Nicolás, SJ, developed this final point in his recent address to presidents of Jesuit colleges and universities and their colleagues who had gathered in Mexico from around the world ("Depth, Universality, and Learned Ministry: Challenges to Jesuit Higher Education today," April 23, 2010). He pointed to the new website, www.jesuitcommons.org, as a promising resource for future networking among Jesuit institutions.

Conditions are much worse in the world than most people suppose. And even though we can know how bad things are, we are prone to ignore that or forget it, aided and abetted by messages that distract and cover up. At the same time, the bad news is not the whole story, much less the last word. In recent decades, inspiring initiatives and social movements have been multiplying around the globe. Groups of people are struggling, perhaps more than ever, to fashion a more habitable world. This book bears witness to one example of this. The renewal of Jesuit higher education is part of an evolving awareness of and response to the crises of our times. Nourished by their Jesuit heritage and poised to collaborate on a global scale, they are in a privileged position to respond to the real problems of our time. Our students are a particular source of inspiration. They are tired of meaningless materialism. They want to learn, not just how to make money, but how to make sense of their lives. They hunger for a spirituality that can satisfy their longing for God, one that will help them make their way amid a cacophony of surrounding messages. They want to belong to a community that supports and challenges them as they discover their vocation. They know that they are part of a global human family to which they want to contribute. They want to help change the world. Jesuit higher education responds to these needs. Among the many wonderful things going on today, we have to suspect, with Peter-Hans Kolvenbach, that Jesuit higher education has the potential to transform us and equip us to transform a broken world.

Part I: Formation and Learning

Introduction

DAVID J. O'BRIEN

> Tomorrow's "whole person" cannot be whole without an educated awareness of society and culture with which to contribute socially, generously, in the real world. Tomorrow's whole person must have, in brief, a well-educated solidarity. . . . Students, in the course of their formation, must let the gritty reality of this world into their lives, so they can learn to feel it, think about it critically, respond to its suffering and engage it constructively. They should learn to perceive, think, judge and act for the rights of others, especially the disadvantaged and the oppressed.
>
> —Fr. Peter-Hans Kolvenbach

These words from Father Kolvenbach's historic 2000 address at Santa Clara University to leaders of US Jesuit higher education, "The Service of Faith and the Promotion of Justice in American Jesuit Higher Education," headed the invitation for contributions to this part of the book. The committee invited proposals describing the "kinds of learning" that would "create a 'well-educated solidarity'" and "sustain that formation." The passage and the invitation pointed to central challenges arising from three decades of efforts to implement the call of the 32nd General Congregation of the Society of Jesus. At that time colleges and universities were asked to renew Jesuit education for the service of faith and promotion of justice in the context of the option for the poor. Since then solidarity, affirmation of the unity of the human family and commitment to the common good has emerged as a central theme.

In responding to this call Jesuit colleges and universities for over thirty years have devoted academic attention to social analysis and social ethics and expanded programs of community service and service learning. More and more courses incorporate consideration of Catholic social teaching while cocurricular experiences of encounter with the poor utilize action-reflection methods that change hearts and minds. Often these projects were handled separately in classroom and campus ministry, but now it is clear that "learning and formation" must go hand in hand.

In the period immediately following the 32nd General Congregation in 1974, when many faculty and staff were still reeling from national conflicts over racism and the Vietnam War, programs may have emphasized encountering the "nitty-gritty" of poverty and violence, thinking about injustice critically, and working to raise consciousness through agitation and education. Today programs may still feature experience and critical awakening in facing those persistent realities, but perhaps with more attention to responding constructively. There may be less need to persuade ourselves and our students that injustice exists, more need to encourage one another to believe that change is possible and we can help bring it about. That constructive turn is now an essential element of "justice and peace" education. Perhaps in earlier years social education was often centered in campus ministry and religious studies. The constructive turn opens the way to renewed attention to justice seeking and peace building in all disciplines, departments, and schools.

These chapters provide evidence that faculty and staff at Jesuit colleges and universities are facing these challenges in many academic areas with the realism and generosity Father Kolvenbach called for. John F. Freie and Susan M. Behuniak describe how one Political Science Department set out "to teach for social justice in the real world." To achieve the kind of "transformation" of students into the "active democratic citizens" they believe Jesuit education requires, they dealt with pedagogy, curriculum, and "student culture." Their "pedagogies of engagement" raise important questions about power in the classroom as well as society, suggesting attention to the politics of knowledge. And they warn that there must be support across institutions if individual and departmental innovations are to be successful.

Advocates of education for justice often stumble when asked how it is to be incorporated into specific departments, including the arts. Christopher Pramuk has a compelling response from music. "Beauty

Limned in Violence" is the title arising from his experiments with "protest music in the Ignatian classroom." The chapter opens imaginations to the idea that good liberal arts education is formation for "well educated solidarity." In fact the story of this class about protest music takes one directly to solidarity, Father Kolvenbach's central virtue. Here music and mysticism embody dreams of the beloved community as the actual goal of history—think of Martin Luther King's most famous speech on the Washington Mall and his last speech in Memphis—the goal grounded in faith in a God who is "a friend of human beings."

Another response is found in Carol Kelly's report, "Teaching Poverty in America through the Arts." Teaching an interdisciplinary social science course on poverty in America, the author found ways to engage students through poetry, theater, and dance. This helps break through "paradigms" that prevent people from seeing poverty around them, a necessary first step to "transformational education." The chapter makes a convincing case that using the arts instills "intellectual flexibility" needed to inspire students "to become people who seek and act for justice."

Tom Kelly, writing about Creighton University's "commitment to education for transformation," describes a single remarkable immersion project in the Dominican Republic. The story of this project illustrates how one "immersion-based community-learning foreign study program" effectively humanized "the reality of social injustice." Applying a community-based learning approach to an overseas immersion experience, the authors hope that Encuentro Dominicano will enable students to make choices and commitments to a life for others, the heart of Jesuit educational aspirations.

Gary K. Perry and Madeline Lovell of Seattle University describe an immersion experience in New Orleans after hurricane Katrina. Their emphasis is on teaching social analysis through its practice. It is interesting that they were only able to carry out the course after persuading authorities to allow them to use the format from overseas immersion in a domestic setting. The students studied the history and culture of the city and the responses of official and grass roots organizations to the disaster. They assessed the groups benefitting from redevelopment, and consulted the experience of artists, organizers, and survivors. This was a good example of the new interest in community-based research.

After reading these reports by faculty, all hoping to inspire students to live a "well-educated solidarity," one recalls the invitation's reference to "sustaining" such formation. The immersion programs in a special way suggest the need for a greater realism about living out the commitment to justice in the world as it is. Political options are not always adequate, given the realities of power and privilege, nor are the churches and other communities of conscience always supportive of serious civic engagement. When students leave school, fired by a deeper faith and awakened social conscience, where are they to go to find communities of shared faith, mutual support and common commitment; the kind of community they might have enjoyed at school or on a summer or overseas service project? Will they find pastoral care appropriate not just to acts of mercy and justice, but also to a lifetime oriented toward service to the human family? Similar questions arise about political life. Political parties are often part of the problem, public interest lobbies are hard to find, and prevailing ideas of citizenship are thin, centered almost exclusively on voting. Many voluntary associations and national and international nongovernmental organizations help deal with one cause or another, but few seem adequate to the level of responsibility we and our students come to experience through education for justice. Thus the question of sustaining commitment to solidarity arises, a question not just for students but for all of us who work in Jesuit higher education.

1   Beauty Limned in Violence

Experimenting with Protest Music in the Ignatian Classroom

CHRISTOPHER PRAMUK

Ah but in such an ugly time as this, the true protest is beauty.

—Phil Ochs, liner notes to *Pleasures of the Harbor*

Good art must be hard, as hard as nails, as hard as the heart of the artist.

—Henry James, *The Crooked Corridor*

The title of this book, *Transforming Ourselves, Transforming the World*, implies a costly and sometimes terrible grace that we may not readily wish upon ourselves or our students—the grace of solidarity and sacrifice, even the grace of martyrdom. As the lives of St. Ignatius and his companions, the Jesuit martyrs, and a host of saints (Christian and non-Christian) teach us, to be transformed by the world is to let our hearts be broken by the sufferings of others; it is to *suffer with* others, with strangers beyond our usual horizon, and not, at the end of the day, to restrict our compassion and commitments to merely "our own." In an Ignatian context, to be transformed by the world implies the willingness, as in the First Week of the Spiritual Exercises, to fix our gaze on Jesus who is still being crucified, and from that place at the foot of the cross, to ask ourselves: "What have I done for Christ? What am I doing for Christ? What ought I to do for Christ?" (Ignatius 1991, 138).

I have often wondered at this remarkable colloquy of the First Week, which directs the retreatant to "imagine Christ our Lord suspended on the cross before you," and from this darkly imaginative place of communion to "converse with him," yet to do so "in the way one friend speaks to another" (ibid.). Note here the haunting convergence of beauty and violence, friendship and desire. The Christ whom Ignatius invites us to contemplate on the cross is unquestionably beautiful, both divinely and humanly beautiful, yet here we are confronted with a terrible paradox: "How is it that he has passed from eternal life to death here in time, and to die in this way for my sins?" (ibid.). Ignatius wants us to linger in the belly of this paradox, a piercing narrative that has no parallel in the religious world. For Ignatius, the fact that the Creator and Lord who is Infinite Goodness would choose to die *in this way* for my sins and for all the world reveals something crucial about the nature of God, above all, the boundless scope of God's desire. Like a lover who "gives and communicates to the beloved what he or she has" (ibid., 176), God holds nothing back in the Incarnation.

But the colloquy is also meant to awaken something crucial and unquestionably beautiful in the nature of humanity and in the heart of the receptive retreatant: namely, our deepest desire and capacity to "do something" in return for God, whose friendship for the world has shown no bounds. Here are the seeds of a wondrous, but unmistakably cruciform, spirituality. To ask "What ought I to do?" for the crucified Christ implies, in the first place, that I *can* do something for him; second, that I would *desire* to do so as his friend, regardless of personal cost; and third, that Christ himself desires that I would do so. Even more, it is one of the distinctive geniuses of the Spiritual Exercises to gently render this desire to do something for the crucified Christ as a drama, an ongoing discernment, that plays itself out in friendship and solidarity with "all the world"—especially with those who suffer, like Jesus, the ignominities of an impoverished, violent, and anonymous death. Jesuit Jon Sobrino (1994) is right to insist that today, the climactic question of the First Week becomes this: "What must I do to help take the crucified peoples down from the cross?"[1]

In this essay I explore just one way I have tried to provoke and awaken this question, which is the question of justice and solidarity, in the hearts and imaginations of my undergraduate theology students. How to stir in our students in an imaginative and evocative way both the wondrous desire and graced capacity to "transform the world and be transformed" that limns the cruciform heart of Ignatian spirituality? As a lifelong musician, my own spirituality or way of being in the world has been profoundly shaped by music, and especially its capacity through all the senses to carry me outside myself, as it were, and into communion with the mysterious, transcendent dimension of reality. But certain songs, in my experience, do much more potentially than carry us beyond ourselves; in particular, certain songs from the venerable tradition of protest music have the capacity to break through reflexive defenses, open our eyes, and convict us with the darker dimensions of reality, the painfully cruciform visage of suffering that we would rather not see. At its best, protest music not only plunges us into the reality of unjust suffering in the world; by doing so it forces us to ask ourselves, as individuals and as a society: *What do you intend to do about it?*

Phil Ochs, the extraordinarily gifted songwriter of the civil rights era, once described an effective protest song (with characteristic flourish) as "a song that's so specific that you cannot mistake it for bullshit."[2] Ochs's passion as an artist was history, "to instigate changes in history"; he saw his songs as "subversive in the best sense of the word. They are intended to overthrow as much idiocy as possible."[3] In the context of a world and especially a nation that has committed itself to so much idiocy, the art of the protest singer is, at the very least, the art of "aesthetic rebellion"[4] against the status quo. In a world that has so perfected the art of selective remembering, protest music dares to tell the stories we would rather forget, memories that irritate the ruling consciousness and challenge collective myths. Yet what fascinates me most about protest music, and the intuition I most wish to explore here, is the way it evokes something beautiful, even while interrupting our reflexive assumptions about beauty. Here something beautiful "breaks through," but not without delivering a painful revelatory sting. In this way protest music shares something crucial, even sacramental, with the Ignatian imagination, where an appreciation for beauty is leavened by a strong sense for the tragic and ironic—that is, the paradoxical realization that beauty often finds us in the valley of the shadow of death, lying at the foot of the cross, buried in layers of horror, guilt, and violence.

In what follows my aim is to get inside the narrative and aesthetic landscape of three songs that have long haunted my own religious imagination, songs that are subversive in the best sense of the word. I have shared these songs with my students, and believe other Jesuit educators might fruitfully experiment with doing so as well. Where highly discursive approaches to teaching theology risk falling on deaf ears, music has a way of breaking through to students—especially those not favorably inclined toward traditional religiosity or explicitly theological discourse—in powerful and unpredictable ways. Such listening exercises, like the Spiritual Exercises themselves, comprise a kind of brief but intense immersion experience inside the classroom, and are always a risk. Yet I have found that the risk is nearly always worth taking, helping to awaken in my students, and rekindle in myself, the desire to do something for a world shot through with unspeakable injustice and violence, and above all, the desire and commitment to help take the crucified peoples down from the cross.[5]

Remembrance and Resistance

I begin with what is arguably the mother of all protest songs, "Strange Fruit," recorded by Billie Holiday in 1939 and sung until her death in 1959. Hailed in December 1999 by *Time* magazine as the "Best Song of the Century,"[6] the title "Most Disturbing" might have been more apt. Opening with the image of "southern trees" that bear a "strange fruit," the song confronts the listener with a series of shocking juxtapositions in which a bucolic scene of beautiful magnolia trees, "sweet and fresh," is transformed, with the "sudden smell of burning flesh,"[7] into a lynching site.

The printed word cannot do justice to Holiday's 1939 recording, much less to her devastating embodiment of the song in live performances, which extended over a period of twenty years. To be sure, the song's revelatory power, whether past or present, hinges considerably on the empathy, receptiveness, and no doubt the lived experience of the listener, to say nothing of the social dynamics of a particular performance. Yet when I have shared the recording or video footage of the song with my students, I have been amazed and humbled, indeed, sometimes troubled, by the range of responses evoked by Holiday's rendering, which, for many listeners, still reverberates darkly into the present situation of race relations in the United States.[8]

The late jazz writer Leonard Feather called "Strange Fruit" "the first significant protest in words and music, the first unmuted cry against racism" (Margolick 2000, 17). Drummer Max Roach referred to Holiday's 1939 recording as "revolutionary," and record producer Ahmet Ertegum called it "a declaration of war . . . the beginning of the civil rights movement" (21).[9] Jazz musicians everywhere still speak of the song with a mixture of awe and fear. Perhaps the highest praise came from Samuel Grafton, a columnist for the *New York Post*, who described the record as "a fantastically perfect work of art, one which reversed the usual relationship between a black entertainer and her white audience: 'I have been entertaining you,' she seems to say, 'now you just listen to me.' The polite conventions between race and race are gone. It is as if we heard what was spoken in the cabins, after the night riders had clattered by" (75). Mal Waldron, the pianist who accompanied Holiday in her last years, was more pointed in his appraisal: "It's like rubbing people's noses in their own shit" (21).

It is no wonder that the first time Billie Holiday sang "Strange Fruit" in public she thought it was a mistake. It was February of 1939, at New York City's Café Society, and as she remembers it, "There wasn't even a patter of applause when I finished. Then a lone person began to clap nervously. Then suddenly everyone was clapping" (16). The song quickly became a signature part of her repertoire. Whenever Billie sang "Strange Fruit," all service in the club stopped, and the room was darkened, save for a pin of light trained on her face. When the song ended, the light was extinguished. No matter what kind of applause followed, the band would play no encores. These rituals—which strike me as almost liturgical in their precision and regularity—were insisted upon by the club's owner, Barney Josephson, who says he wanted people "to remember 'Strange Fruit,' get their insides burned with it" (50).[10] Holiday herself would often be in tears after performing the song, and require considerable time before she could pull herself together for the next set.

The song worked, in part, because of the stark contrast between Holiday's beauty and elegance on stage and the song's implicit anger. With her voice accentuating imagery of trees that "bear," and "fruit" that is "plucked," it was clear that she understood the sexual motives unleashed in many acts of lynching, acts that frequently involved the accusation of rape, and mutilation or removal of the victim's genitals. "I am a race woman," she often said, with the integrity and force of a woman who had herself known the blows of racism (O'Meally 2000, 136).

We are not too far here, I wish to suggest, from the eschatological confrontation mediated by the colloquy with Christ on the cross during the First Week of the Spiritual Exercises. Indeed, for Christians shaped by the liturgical remembrance of Jesus' passion and death, "Strange Fruit" cannot help but resonate in the same "negative space" as the haunting Negro spiritual, "Were You There When They Crucified My Lord?" Like the spiritual, "Strange Fruit" functions in the first place as a locus of a "negative contrast experience," revelatory in the first place of *what should not be*.[11] But what makes both songs so disturbing, and at once so potentially transforming, is their capacity to draw us into communion with a living history, a real presence. Not only *were* we there, by entering into the song we *are* there. As one woman said of "Strange Fruit," "When Billie sings [that song], you feel as if you're at the foot of the tree."[12] This kind of remembering, in other words, is more than just a memory of something that "happened" in the past; it is more akin to what the Catholic mystagogical tradition calls *anamnesis*: "It is *an epiphanic calling forth*" (Evdokimov 1990, 166).[13]

Of course it would be tempting for even the most empathetic listener to conclude that there is nothing beautiful in either song, nothing redemptive. On this point I would like to interject a comment from one of my students, a young white woman, who is a survivor of sexual abuse and of many desolate years working in the sex industry in northern Ohio. In response to a question about "Strange Fruit" on an exam, she wrote: "The song itself does not give us anything to be hopeful for, but the act of singing it does." This wise insight—surely grounded in and intensified by her own experience of sexual objectification and violence—may be reframed in terms of our thesis: the singular cry of protest and resistance is not only holy, sharing in God's own protest against injustice and lament for the dead; it is also beautiful, evoking wonder, renewed energy, and hope against hope in the responsive community.

And yet, as my student added, with a wisdom once again limned in her own pain: "this kind of 'dangerous memory' is a double-edged sword, because it can lead to remembering with vengeance, instead of remembering with hope. . . . Only hope brings an end to the suffering."[14]

Confronting the Violence in Ourselves

Clearly the longing for justice and the impulse toward revenge walk a precariously thin line, balanced on the knife's edge of memory, the memory of unjust suffering. Protest music lives on this dangerous fault line between righteous anger and resistance, on the one hand, and the bitterness that would seek to cleanse itself by returning violence for violence, on the other. Indeed, the power of many an effective protest song lay precisely here, in the artist's refusal to simply resolve the tension, with the turn of a lyric, on one side or the other.

Nowhere is this tensive dynamic better realized than in Canadian singer-songwriter Bruce Cockburn's devastating recording of 1984, "If I had a Rocket Launcher," a song written after the artist had spent several days visiting Guatemalan refugee camps in the border region of Chiapas, Mexico. In early 1983, at the invitation of the world hunger organization OXFAM, Cockburn and a group of other Canadian artists had spent several weeks in Nicaragua and other Central American countries that were being devastated by years of conflict and so-called low-intensity warfare, a war financed and more or less directed by the United States government. A day after leaving the camps, where the refugees he met "were starved, denied medical care, and were still subjected to [brutal, cross-border] attacks by the Guatemalan army," Cockburn sat in his tiny hotel room, and "over tears and a bottle of Bell's [scotch]" (McGregor 1990), set down his experience in song.

Set darkly over a hypnotic guitar riff, verse one paints a scene of descending dread as a helicopter gunship approaches the refugee camp, "second time today," while "everybody scatters and hopes it goes away." Verse two voices contempt for the men who unleash the blind fury of the gunships, the generals, and "their stinking torture states." Verse three raises a piercing lament for the people of Guatemala, "with a corpse in every gate," and verse four looks almost desperately to the future, as the singer confesses his determination "to raise every voice, at least I've got to try." The refrain, pulsing mantra-like after every verse, warns anybody who will listen, everybody and nobody at once, "If I had a rocket launcher/some son of a bitch would die."[15]

Though Cockburn had serious reservations about recording "Rocket Launcher," for fear of misinterpretation, much to his surprise the song became a worldwide hit, even while many radio stations in the United States refused to air it. In the twenty-five years since its release, the artist, an avowed Christian, has been repeatedly asked to justify the motives that gave rise to the song.[16] He is always quick to point out that the lyrics reflect his own very raw and personal experience of the camps: "I can't imagine writing it under any other conditions" (Harrington 1984). At the same time, he gestures to something more in the music, something universal: "Aside from airing my own experience, which is where the songs always start, if we're ever going to find a solution for this ongoing passion for wasting each other, we have to start [by confronting] the rage [within ourselves] that knows no impediments, an uncivilized rage that says it's okay to go out and shoot some one" (ibid.).

Here Cockburn puts his finger squarely on the luminous and darkly revelatory power of protest music at its best. For those who have ears to hear and eyes to see, especially for citizens of the United States, the artist holds an unforgiving mirror up to our faces, forcing us to confront horrors still perpetrated throughout the world in our name, and allegedly in the service of our best ideals. But Cockburn's revulsion cuts still deeper, turning the mirror back toward his own face, and recognizing with much horror how his own righteous anger, his visceral impulse to defend life, has morphed into explosive contempt and the urge to return violence for violence. In his notebooks from the camps, alongside the names and stories of the survivors, Cockburn had scribbled: "I understand now why people want to kill."[17]

Much like "Strange Fruit," it would be tempting to conclude that there is nothing beautiful in the song, nothing redemptive, and to be sure, many of Cockburn's otherwise loyal Christian fans still chafe at the mention of "If I Had a Rocket Launcher." In my own listening, however, the song reverberates with sacramental power in at least two ways. First, there is a terrible beauty in the song's devastating honesty, its raw portrait of a soul that recognizes, in the words of Reinhold Niebuhr (1949, 101), that "the profoundest enigma of existence [lay] not in the evil surrounding it *but in itself.*" This troubling realization, says Niebuhr, is precisely where the discomfiting "good news" of revelation takes root: in the heart of those who *know what they are*, who have come to recognize, in fear and trembling, the evil they are capable of, the rage they have, in fact, unleashed into history. Note again how closely this realization corresponds with the purgative contemplations during the First Week of the Exercises, not least the colloquy with the crucified Christ and vivid meditation on the fires of hell—all culminating in fearful wonder (and gratitude) that the earth "has not opened to swallow me up" in my guilt, that the Angels who bear "the sword of Divine Justice" have in fact "endured me, and guarded me, and prayed for me" (Ignatius 1991, 139).

The human predicament expressed in "Rocket Launcher" recalls in some ways the youthful Inigo de Loyola, whose "hidalgo" personality— loyal, impetuous, passionate, fearless—led him on at least one occasion to the brink of murder.[18] Indeed, the Jesuit bent toward action more than words, the mobilization of energies and resources toward a single-minded purpose, can be seductive and flatly dangerous if not grounded in humility and relentlessly honest self-examination, the way of discernment Inigo would learn later, during his tortured months at Manresa. By the grace of God, Inigo gradually learned to harness and redirect his passions toward the service of God and others, now patterning his affections by a new norm, a new *love,* who is Jesus. What results in the Spiritual Exercises, as Monika Hellwig (2008, 57) observes, is a spirituality that is "countercultural and revolutionary in a nonviolent way." In particular, meditation on the passion and death of Jesus "invites attention not only to what Jesus suffered physically, but to the discernment process that Jesus went through and the action to which it led—which in turn provoked bitter persecution" (ibid., 58).[19] At its truest, Ignatian spirituality cultivates a Christ-haunted paradox: deep passion for life in all its forms and the passionate commitment to its defense, but also the kind of vulnerability, "detachment from self-interest" (ibid., 57) and readiness to serve that leads, in places where life is most vulnerable and threatened, to martyrdom.

This brings us back to Cockburn's piercing lament from the refugee camps. Note how the artist's cry of protest is not for himself or his own kind, but for the forgotten ones, those robbed of any "real presence" on the world stage, robbed even of a footnote in the history books. By remembering the victims of history, Cockburn calls them forth epiphanically, as it were, into our midst; like the Hebrew prophets of old, the artist forces us to *see* the hidden ones who still suffer by what we have done, or what we have failed to do. Indeed, it is this stubborn commitment to *memory* that marks protest music at its best with something like a liturgical character. By remembering the forgotten dead, songs like "Strange Fruit" and "Rocket Launcher" implicitly express "the love God has for them, and, as a first act of reparation, aims to prevent 'a monumental scandal: the silence that closes over them in our world'" (Sobrino 2003, 21). Even more, as Jesuit theologian Jon Sobrino insists, to remember the dead is *for us* an act of faith. "It means not only conferring 'dignity' on the dead but seeing a saving power in them: they summon to conversion, bring light and salvation" (ibid.).[20] During liturgies in El Salvador, after every name invoked in the litany of missing and murdered human beings, the gathered assembly shouts out, *Presente!* Who can deny the power of this calling forth as an act of hope, galvanizing our commitment to transform and be transformed by the world?

On tour in the United States some years ago, Cockburn reintroduced "If I Had a Rocket Launcher" into his live show after a self-imposed hiatus of several years following the terrorist attacks of September 11, 2001. On his reasons for pulling the song after 9/11, he said: "I think it's the wrong emotional climate, especially in the U[nited] S[tates] right now. People will hear it the wrong way, and I don't want to run the risk of feeding a body of emotion that I don't want to [stir] up" (Griwkowsky 2002). The sentiment recalls his feelings back in 1984, when the song had just been released. Cockburn wants his audience to see, but to see finally *with love*, and not to strike out in revenge: "The thing is, there are people in [the helicopters, too], you know? The weird thing about it is they stop looking like people because of what they're doing. I guess that's what makes it so easy to want to shoot them down because . . . they make you feel like they forfeited their humanity somehow. But they're pawns in it. . . . Anyway . . . the one thing I must stress in case anybody's under any delusion . . . is that this is not a call to arms. This is a cry, this is a cry."[21]

"You Can't Blow Out a Fire"

In 1980 the British pop artist Peter Gabriel recorded a spare but extraordinarily powerful song entitled "Biko,"[22] in honor of Stephen Biko, the student leader and antiapartheid activist who was tortured and killed while in police custody in Soweto, South Africa. Few songs in my experience have the capacity to generate more interest and spirited dialogue among students today than this one, especially when the lyrics are studied in conjunction with historical material on Biko and the South African freedom struggle, and video of live performances, available via the Internet. The effect of Gabriel's spare poetic mastery is chilling: while the world turns, "Port Elizabeth weather fine," people are dying, people like Biko, unknown and unsung, in hidden places everywhere.

If my students' reactions are any indicator, the song resonates as much today as it did thirty years ago, rebelling against a world that divides itself in "black and white," where torture is "business as usual," a sad but "necessary" adaptation to the War on Terror (in the way cockroaches, for example, adapt to new toxins in the environment), and where far too many children imagine their future in "only one color dead." Yet in the context of such a world—our world—protest music galvanizes resistance, and turns the responsive community toward another possible dawn, the birth of new hope. As the song closes, Gabriel seems to suggest that those who deal in death cannot have the final say, wherever hope, our capacity to imagine something other than more of the same, has been ignited. "And the eyes of the world are watching now, watching now."

But there is more. For every invocation of Biko's name in the song, every cry of lament—*the man is dead, the man is dead*—there is another cry, *Yihla Moja, Yihla Moja*, which means, "Come Spirit, Come Spirit." In other words: the man is dead, the man is *not dead*, the man is dead, the man is *not dead*. Here the cry of protest, the very act of naming and calling forth the dead, transforms into the cry of resurrection hope, the conviction that death is not the final word for Biko, or any person unjustly cut down in history. Why? Because God's desire for life is more powerful, more "present" even, than the seemingly intractable waves of senseless death in which our history is plunged. Thus the Fourth

Week of the Spiritual Exercises bears us through crucifixion into the wonder of an empty tomb, a mystery that enfolds all things in the presence of the risen Christ, the Spirit of God who promises to be with us, both now and in the hour of our death, and one day, to deliver us from every evil.

During a concert in 1986 marking the end of a worldwide Amnesty International Tour dedicated to ending apartheid, Peter Gabriel led a crowd of several hundred thousand people from all over the world in singing "Biko."[23] The moment, I wish to suggest, was not only artistically electrifying, it was liturgically efficacious in almost every sense of the phrase. As the kick-drum pulsed relentlessly like a heartbeat, and bagpipes pierced the air in a searing lament, the artist stood onstage like a priest gathering and raising the prayers of the people, all invoking a living presence, a single man, a cloud of witnesses. As Gabriel left the stage he proclaimed to the wondrously mosaic congregation, still singing and waving banners, "The rest is up to you! The rest is up to you!" Less than ten years later, under enormous internal pressures and with protests rising from every corner of the earth, apartheid was formally dismantled and free elections were held in South Africa.[24]

Justice Education as Education in Wisdom

Against all lights of practical reason, Christian theology and spirituality, to say nothing of Christian art, has always claimed a certain beauty, albeit an ironic beauty, in the wisdom and foolishness of the cross. Thus in a Christian and certainly in an Ignatian context, education for justice is education in wisdom, yet a dangerously cruciform wisdom, which makes no end-runs around the ambiguities and contradictions of the human condition. Here Sts. Paul and Ignatius and a host of other saints would be in full agreement: We must not fear to accompany our students directly into that condition and that struggle which Jesus himself never deigned to avoid, a way of being in the world that freely takes into itself darkness and light, longing and fulfillment, absence and presence, suffering and joy. It is this unexpected coexistence, even to the point of identity, of certain contraries in the human experience that prompted Jesuit scholar William Lynch (1973, 101) to speak of "the irony of Christ," and to assert that "the irony of Christ is Christ himself":

> The irony of Christ is unique. It involves mastery of the world, spiritual freedom . . . ; it works through death and weakness; it therefore dethrones every other pretentious idea and establishes the movement through the human condition, and the total human condition (not the human condition of the beautiful people) as the way. Weakness becomes one of the great forms of power. Age, sickness, and death lose their power over man and take on another form of power.[25]

For Lynch, a Catholic and Jesuit education could hold no higher purpose than to form students under this paradoxical wisdom, or what he termed an educated Christian irony. To grow in such a wisdom is to learn—through ever deeper immersion in and reflection on the human world—that it is only in realizing and suffering our ignorance that we find ourselves on the path to deeper truth; only by tasting illness and mortality that we can truly begin to live as compassionate human beings; only by embracing our own poverty that we are able to embrace those whom we call "the poor"; and only by passing through the many smaller deaths in our lives that we may face physical suffering and death in peace. Here, of course, Lynch not only evokes the teachings of Jesus but also Jesus' life and the nature of his very being in the world *as Christ*: "the poor man who is the Incarnation of God; the messiah born in a stable; the king who entered Jerusalem on a donkey; the teacher who embraced lepers, ate with sinners, and proclaimed freedom for prisoners; the imprisoned and executed one who was raised and exalted as Lord" (Kane 2009).[26]

To "transform the world and be transformed" is to "put on the mind of Christ" (Phil. 2:5), to be formed, transformed, and inspired under the pattern of humility, compassion, and service that marks Jesus' own earthly pilgrimage in grace. It is, as Pedro Arrupe suggests, to fall in love with God, and thus, to fall in love with God's world. This is the genius and greater glory of the Spiritual Exercises; it is the genius of the *Ratio Studiorum*, with its bringing together of the sciences integrally with the humanities; and it is the genius of good art, art infused with the contemplative eye of love. There is and will always be a crucial place for such art in our classrooms and on our Jesuit campuses.[27] As Jesuit patristic scholar Brian Daley (1988, 16) has observed, there is "an inner affinity between the Christian pedagogy or mystagogy of the *Spiritual Exercises* . . . and the effect on the human person of liberal studies at their best." Both seek "to lead the human mind from praise to reverence to service: to set up the conditions in which that mind will fall in love with beauty and goodness, will find 'joy in the truth,' so that it might be freed from fear and illusion, might acknowledge the truth for what it is and allow its love of that truth to bear fruit for others."[28]

Conclusion

In a 1965 interview for *Broadside* magazine, Phil Ochs articulated his understanding of "transforming the world and being transformed" as an artist, to being saved, as it were, by beauty. His words reflect a wisdom well beyond his twenty-five years: "It's not enough to know the world is absurd and restrict yourself merely to pointing out that fact. . . . It is wrong to expect a reward for your struggles. The reward is the act of struggle itself, not what you win. Even though you can't expect to defeat the absurdity of the world, you must make the attempt. That's morality, that's religion, that's art, that's life."[29] Not to put too fine a point on these reflections, but it seems to me that there is something quite Ignatian in Ochs's expressly secular but hard-bought vision of things. Perhaps beauty is found, after all—or finds us most ready to receive it—not in what we win but in "the act of struggle itself," the willingness to immerse ourselves body and soul in the history we have been given, and thus to be drawn into that same horizon of grace that rendered Jesus' own struggle unspeakably beautiful, even where it plunges into violence and death on a cross.

Like the Spiritual Exercises, art infused with the contemplative eye of love not only dares to plunge us into the paradoxical and sometimes horrific mystery of the human condition; in doing so, it can help us to *bridge the gap* between the horrors we witness and the more humane and unfathomably beautiful future into which God draws the whole creation, the beloved community toward which we struggle in grace. Intuitively the artist understands what theology sometimes forgets:

There is no path to the reign of God save through Jerusalem, no way to Easter save through Good Friday. And in that drama each of us en-fleshes, at different moments of our lives, a wide range of possible roles: I am Peter, fleeing the violence and ugliness of the cross; I am Mary, weeping at the bloodied feet of her son; I am Joseph, anointing the body with oils, and returning it with infinite care to the earth; I am Jesus, alone in the hell of God's terrifying silence.

In sum, the accent in protest music on finding beauty and grace in the struggle itself corresponds closely with what German theologian Johann Baptist Metz (1997, 163) calls "a mysticism of open eyes," a spirituality which evokes the mysticism of Jesus himself as dramatized in the synoptic Gospels. Metz writes: "In the end Jesus did not teach an ascending mysticism of closed eyes, but rather a God-mysticism with an increased readiness for perceiving, a mysticism of open eyes, which sees more and not less. It is a mysticism that especially makes visible all invisible and inconvenient suffering, and—convenient or not—pays attention to it and takes responsibility for it, for the sake of a God who is a friend to human beings" (ibid.).[30] What I have described in the best of protest music as an open-eyed commitment to reality, to memory, and to responsibility and hope for those who suffer, reverberates deeply with an Ignatian manner of educating for justice that dares to place itself at the foot of the world's crosses, and to ask not only "What is God waiting for?" but also "What are *we* waiting for?" What must we do to help the crucified peoples down from the cross?

Awakening this question both in and beyond our classrooms is but a first step, of course, in the grace of transformation. The real challenge comes in helping our students, one by one, discern their own vocation in solidarity with the world's joys and sorrows. Such discernment is the labor of a lifetime, a truism I think we model best by sharing with students our own stories, our own struggles to do something beautiful for Christ, with all the hopes, failures, and unexpected graces that mark these human journeys.[31] For my own part, I pray to grow in the courage I have not yet found: to live my life more authentically, indeed, more artistically, under the paradoxical wisdom and beauty of the cross. To make my own the words of Bruce Cockburn: "The world is getting worse. The poor are getting poorer. Tension is increasing. For most of us in the developed world, we have a choice. And we can exercise that choice with wisdom. That's what I stand for" (Griwkowsky 2002).[32]

2 Teaching Poverty in America through the Arts

CAROL E. KELLY

During the final moments of Suzan Lori-Parks's Pulitzer Prize–winning play *Topdog/Underdog*, the audience is holding its breath. As the stage lights come down and the house lights go up, there is no immediate burst of applause—there is silence, a confused, disturbed, and stunning silence. Even after the formal response to the play has been offered through enthusiastic—though palpably serious—applause, the audience remains dazed; they wander off into the night reeling from the experience. As one student put it, "It felt like I just saw my brother die."

Technically, Lori-Parks has produced this effect in her audience by manipulating the plot, or form, of her work in the same way that Ibsen had done a century earlier. There is no denouement, no period of adjustment during which the audience and the characters can process, in this case, a brutal fratricide. Ibsen's goal was no less than a transformation of the social and public arena. He sought to inspire action. And so, following his lead and relying on the inherent power of art, I let the work of Lori-Parks and others do what statistics and dogma cannot do—bring about a transformation of the spirit. Father Kolvenbach (2000) is clear: "Fostering the virtue of justice . . . is not enough." The sort of justice we should be seeking as educators is a justice that "requires an action-oriented commitment to the poor."

I tell my students that over the first warm summer weekend last year in Chicago there were thirty-six shootings, seven of them fatal. Or, closer to home, escalating gang violence in the past year resulted in the shooting death of a student at a public high school that is within easy walking distance of our campus. The students take note in the same dutiful manner that they have copied the statistics from the overhead. But they are not transformed; they are not compelled to action. In his address at Santa Clara, Father Kolvenbach tells us that the heart must be touched by direct experience. As educators, we can provide formalized direct experience through service learning opportunities, and certainly that is a vital (and "not too optional" [Kolvenbach 2000]) component of my Poverty in America course. But, even then we may not be able to meet the measure set forth by Father Kolvenbach. Service learning provides our students with something to "do," not necessarily producing the long-term effect of who they will become. What we wish is for them to become the sort of people who have "the will to change the sinful structures afflicting our world" (Kolvenbach 2000) In order for that to happen, Father Kolvenbach admonishes that a spiritual conversion is required.

Kieran Egan (1998) has written extensively about the way in which standardized education systems contribute to desensitize the adult learner. He advocates using the arts across the curriculum to prolong the sensitive nature inherent in the child. He writes about how music can be used to teach history, or movement used to teach the sciences. Pertinent to teaching at the college level, Egan's observations offer information about the way in which art allows the adult learner to fully experience the world and its stimuli, observing that the feeling of fear and pity, experienced by adults through drama, is a remembrance and reawakening of the purity of their feelings as children. He quotes Victor Shklovsky: "Art exists to help us recover the sensation of life, to make us feel things, to make the stone *stony*" (227). The arts can prepare hearts for spiritual conversion and they provide the requisite direct contact when geography, class, social barriers, pedagogy, and basic practical safety make that contact impossible. Joseph L. Badaracco Jr. (2006) writes about his experience teaching MBA candidates at Harvard over a period of ten years. He uses dramatic literature to teach leadership, employing the likes of Shakespeare and Miller in lieu of case studies. He writes that drama allows us to see into the human person in a way that facts or external observations do not. His students are studying ethics, learning to develop qualities of character. For Badaracco, Willy Loman has more to offer about the power of vision than does a corporate executive, and Antigone has more to offer about sound reflection than does the study of balance sheets. I am inclined to agree. To crudely paraphrase my student's comment, art can make you feel what it is like to lose your brother to gun violence. Inaction becomes unacceptable after that.

I have been teaching Poverty in America at the university level for many years. It is one of just a handful of interdisciplinary social sciences classes on campus. Since students are required, as part of our core program, to take five credits of such courses, my student cohorts are made up of students from every corner of the university. The vast majority of them do not choose to study poverty in America as a result of personal interest or inclination. And even though there are those who have personal experience at one or another end of the economic spectrum, the majority of my students come from somewhat moderate wealth.[1] Engaging these students on a level that is commensurate with that espoused by Father Kolvenbach in his speech at Santa Clara is a challenging undertaking. This paper addresses aspects of challenges directly and explores the way in which the arts can be used to meet those challenges. Most specifically, the paper is concerned with the manner in which collectively held paradigms relative to the poor influence student learning and development, and the ways in which an interdisciplinary curriculum, relying heavily on the arts, can be used to create a learning experience that is potentially transformative. It should be made clear that the arts are used not as a compliment to the curriculum, but as a central component of a curriculum that includes sociology, economics, and philosophy in order to examine a subject that is often taught through the lens of only one of these disciplines at a time. This centrality of the arts to the curriculum sometimes surprises students who discover, on the first day of class, that their study of poverty in America is going to include two trips to the local repertory theatre, a dance performance, and spoken-word poetry finals. Clearly, this methodology functions most optimally when live performance opportunities are widely available to the instructor. But, even in the absence of such opportunities, there are ways to get, if you will, a play "off the page and onto the stage."

"I learned so much in this class—way more than I could have by just watching Rush [Limbaugh]." This comment is taken from a student evaluation of Poverty in America. Another student writes, "I didn't realize how many people are really that poor in America." For a brief period in this country, during the genesis of the war on poverty, the poorest neighborhoods, hidden in the urban core of prosperous American cities, flickered into visibility. In Michael Harrington's (1962) seminal work "The Other America," he describes poverty in America as an "invisible land." He notes that the poor in America were so far beneath the average American's radar, that when Galbraith published his own work, "The Affluent Society," people misinterpreted the meaning and thought that Galbraith's book was about the way in which the prosperity of the 1950s had created a decent standard of life for everyone. Four decades later, Katrina became another beam of light, illuminating the humanity behind the statistics and begging the questions: "What is acceptable within our own borders? What is the nature of the human person—of human dignity? Are we, or are we not, our brother's keeper? Can we ask, anymore, whether our actions reveal or destroy our claim to being an honorable people?" It is questions such as these that lead to the development of Father Kolvenbach's "well-educated" student who maintains, in her very being, solidarity with the poor. Why is it then, that despite the stubbornly static poverty line, Americans express surprise when that poverty is momentarily in the national spotlight?

In "Monkey See, Monkey Do," David Shipler (2006) notes that coverage of Katrina was widely referred to as having "revealed" the deep poverty of the region. Had poverty become, as Harrington worried it might, invisible again? In "Come Hell or High Water: Hurricane Katrina and the Color of Disaster," Michael Erin Dysan (2010) notes that poor citizens living in the Delta had been "largely ignored, rendered invisible, officially forgotten." In "Seeing and Not Seeing: Complicity in Surprise," Virginia R. Dominguez (2006) worries that the surprise people felt at seeing the level of poverty, and the implications of social inequalities associated with it, led people to quickly adopt the description of the situation as "Third World." She believes that this is out of a need to remove conditions of extreme poverty from an American context. Noting the element of surprise at such poverty on the part of many Americans, she quotes President Obama: "There seemed to be a sense that this other America was somehow not on people's radar screen." She wonders: "Where do we all think those 37 million [poor] people live?" Dominguez notes that there is plenty of statistical, sociological, and historical information available about poverty in America.

Yet people still just don't see it. This inability to *see* is the effect of errantly held paradigms relative to poverty in America.

Understanding the philosophy of paradigms, especially the way errant paradigms literally blind people from seeing (understanding and accepting) facts, is one of the keys to meeting the challenges of teaching Poverty in America. Futurists such as "Bicks Bickson" (a consultant who advises Microsoft, Guiness Stout, and other companies about the effects of paradigms on business strategies) and the more well-known writer and speaker Joel Barker (1992) define paradigms as ideological regulations through which one filters incoming data. If the filter is too strong—the paradigm too closely held—one can be blinded, literally and figuratively, to incoming data no matter how compelling it may be. Barker is fond of telling "paradigm stories." A couple of these stories are worth repeating here to show the power that paradigms hold over our ability to perceive information. Barker recounts how the Swiss watch making industry executives could not see that the future of watch making was the digital watch, which had been invented by their own researchers. Their *blindness*, and subsequent refusal to develop (or patent) the new watch prototype, resulted in an almost complete reversal of their former success in the industry. The Swiss paradigm for watch making mandated the inclusion of a mainspring and bearings, none of which are required in the oscillating quartz watch. In another example, gastroenterologists refused to—or could not—see data that confirmed, without doubt, that bacteria in the stomach lining cause certain stomach ulcers. Bacteria existing within the stomach did not fit their paradigm. The Nobel Prize for medicine was awarded some twenty years later to the cardiology students who discovered the bacteria and promptly cured the patients by administering common antibiotics. With hot button topics such as poverty in America, paradigms are strongly held because they are influenced by opinions that too often are not based on fact. As I ask my students: "Have you ever had an argument with someone about politics or a social issue, backing yourself up with facts and statistics, and felt compelled to tell the person with whom you were arguing that they just did not see what you were saying?" I tell my students that their instincts were correct. The person *didn't* see. In all likelihood, the filter of their paradigm blinded them to the facts of the argument.

Sadly, events such as Katrina make seeing the poor in America easier because their plight is fleetingly unmasked. But dislodging an errant paradigm requires more than sporadic bursts of contact and even more than several months of coverage by the media. Shipler (2006) says that although the "bright searchlight of [media] attention focuses for a while," it swings away too quickly for the kind of consistent coverage that might change a paradigm. He offers that one might "imagine that reporters and editors who spend months on a series would grow attuned to issues that would then seep into daily coverage [but that] big projects seem isolated from the flow of other reporting." He reports that although he has spent years "exploring race and poverty throughout the country, [he has] rarely felt a sensation of familiarity, as if [he had] read this somewhere or heard that before."

The present economic crisis brings with it the potential to focus national attention on poverty in America once more. The media offers a random sampling of stories about increased demand at food banks and about how applications are on the rise for the bare minimum in public assistance. The focus of most of these stories is on coping; the stories aim to reveal how those who are new to economic duress are managing. Those who were already at the bottom of our economic ladder, and the many more for whom the bottom rungs of the ladder have been sawed off, remain mostly outside our focus—as usual— hidden discretely behind our collectively held paradigms about what it means to be poor in America. For even as students struggle to develop the intellectual flexibility that will allow them to see the poor, other paradigms blind them to facts about who the poor are, and why their lives are marked by poverty. These paradigms are so strongly held that they become myths, governing people's attitudes about whether or not even the most basic safety net should be provided for those living at the bottom of the economic ladder. These are myths that will have to be dispelled if our students are to, as Father Kolvenbach directed in his address at Santa Clara University, "let the gritty reality of [the] world into their own lives."

In "See Poverty, Be the Difference," Dr. Donna Beegle (2007) introduces her discussion of poverty myths by quoting from J. F. Kennedy's inaugural address: "The great enemy of the truth is not very often the lie—deliberate, contrived, and dishonest—but the myth—persistent, persuasive, and unrealistic." Myths that many Americans believe—paradigms that blind Americans to the truth about poverty in their nation—are familiar enough to my students that during the first days of class they are able to rattle them off with great ease. I ask them to answer some basic questions about the poor in America. Sometimes, I allow them the protection provided by anonymity, asking them to tell me the way they think that "other people"—a cross section of Americans—would likely respond to my questions. Either way, student responses recount the mythology with disturbing consistency to the myths listed by poverty analysts such as John Iceland (2003). For example, I ask my students who they think make up the majority of the poor in America. They respond that the majority of the poor are blacks who live in ghettos in cities. Both Beegle and Iceland report that this is a common misconception and that it is factually incorrect. Poor blacks comprise only about one fourth of the total poverty population. Occasionally, students respond that the majority of the poor are homeless. This is also untrue, but the myth is perpetuated by the visibility of the homeless, which reinforces the errant paradigm in defiance of readily available facts. I ask my students why people are poor, and they respond that it is because the poor don't work. Beegle notes that it is a common belief that people are able to escape poverty through hard work. The implication is that their poverty is the result of laziness. My student response is consistent with this general misconception among the public. The facts show that almost half of those living at or below the poverty line in America work at least part time—and many more, according to Barbara Ehrenreich's (2001) research for *Nickle and Dimed* work multiple jobs. Six years teaching this course, asking these questions every quarter to section after section of students, receiving virtually the same responses, reveals that the errant paradigms are fully functioning as filters to the truth about poverty in America—filters that must be removed before one can even hope to approach transformational education.

The genesis of these errant paradigms is found in the earliest days of our nation's history. In accordance with our Anglican roots, poverty was thought to be a result of a flaw within the individual, rather than any external structural factors. Poorhouses were institutions that sought to correct these flaws—to fix the "defects" in the "inmates" that were supposedly prohibiting them from succeeding financially. Michael Katz (2003) describes how this way of thinking about the poor as defective, dependent, and delinquent, became the legacy of thought about the poor. This legacy of thought is apparent when one considers the following quotes:

> We cannot, for our own comfort, let people starve and freeze on our streets, but we resent their accepting our largesse while indulging in counterproductive habits, that we know would decrease our own productivity and well-being, if we so indulged. (Levitan 1998, 225)

> All of the evils attributable to the current system of poor relief [can] be traced to the same root: The difficulty of discriminating between the able poor and the impotent poor. (Katz 2003, 236)

> The idle will beg in preference to working: relief is extended to them without suitable discrimination. They are not left to feel the just consequences of their idleness. (Ibid.)

I use the comparison of these quotes to show students how collectively held social and economic paradigms have impacted attitudes about poverty over the course of two hundred years in our nation's history. There has been very little in the way of intellectual flexibility over this time. Myths about poverty being a result of poor character, indolence, and willful error continue to inform public debate about assistance. The first quote is from 1998, post–welfare reform. The second is from the Quincy Report in 1821; and the third dates back to the mid-nineteenth century. The quotes illustrate the ongoing tension that exists between *compassion and deterrence* as we, as a nation, consider whether to provide assistance to those who fall beneath the rungs of the economic ladder. It has been noted by researchers at the Economic Policy Institute and other antipoverty policy analysts, that this sort of tension—between wanting to provide help but wishing also to guarantee that we don't help too much—was the major factor contributing to the Personal Responsibility and Work Opportunity Act that eliminated "welfare as we know it." If one must work to receive assistance, then—at the very least—perhaps we might admit that he or she is not lazy.

What we seek to foster in the minds and hearts of our students is a thirst for justice. Yet our national discourse cautions us against being "too" just, as though we must guard ourselves against being too lenient with our compassion. How can we expect our students to keep an open mind about the nature of poverty—what it means to live under the crushing burden of poverty in the wealthiest nation on earth—when our public debate is strangled by the perpetuation of myth, especially when, for many of our students, the poor in their own country are hiding in plain site?

What I have discovered is that this legacy of thinking about poverty, this "poorhouse mentality" (i.e., that the poor are somehow "defective, dependent, or delinquent" [Gans, 1995]) seems to be almost genetically encoded in the minds of many students. And, as noted, statistics convince few and certainly do not seem to have risen to a level that can dependably prompt action for justice. This includes even the most compelling and basic of statistics: One in five children live in poverty in America; three quarters of all single parent households have incomes that fall below federal subsistence levels—a very low bar indeed. Even when one paints a mental picture of the hardship that the poor face, students can be unmoved. They can be told that in our urban centers parents are afraid when their children go off to school, and that households in urban centers recycle discarded appliances for use as barriers against stray bullets on exterior walls. In some neighborhoods, the infant mortality rate is higher than anywhere else in the industrialized world, garbage isn't picked up regularly, and emergency response is slow, if it comes at all. This isn't Iraq or Palestine. There are many such places in the United States. One of them is twelve blocks from the White House. It is called Shaw. It is within walking distance of the power center of our country. It turns out that one needn't travel to the other side of the planet to have an epiphany about the poor. And yet, even armed with this irrefutable information, something more is needed. As Father Kolvenbach notes, this something more is direct contact, which can be provided by a curriculum that utilizes the arts. And so, I begin by asking my students another simple question: "Are You Having A Good Day?"

When I first ask my students about the ways in which they define what is a good day for them, their answers are predictable, occasionally, though rarely surprising, and always illuminating for our discussion of paradigms. For most students, a good day involves being prepared and on time for classes, or, even better, *not* having to go to class; having coffee with friends; not having to go to work, or getting off work early. It seems that a lack of activity is the mark of "goodness" in a day. Sleeping late is always a winning bet. In the spring term at my university, the most commonly offered answer about what contributes to a good day involves whether or not one has had a donut. A great deal of fund raising for summer study abroad is done on our campus through the selling of Krispy Kreme donuts. Very rarely, a student will provide a divergent answer, such as the student who was a recovering alcoholic. His eyes focused squarely on mine, and, when asked what would be a good day for him, replied, "any day I stay sober." But the truth is that almost all the responses reference a life free from trauma, one in which a good day means not even having to perform tasks that much of the world might consider luxuries: school, study, and productive social engagement.

The model we hold for a good day is, of course, a paradigm. After informally polling my students, I show them an alternative paradigm for a good day, expressed in artistic form in the following lyrics by Ice Cube:

> Just waking up in the morning, gotta thank God
> I don't know but today seems kinda odd . . .
> Hooked up on it later as I hit the do'
> Thinking will I live another twenty-fo'
> I got to say, today was a good day.
> Plus nobody I know got killed in South Central LA.
> Today I didn't even have to use my AK.[2]

I explain the concept of paradigms to my students in much the same way as I have done above, showing them how a paradigm can be thought of as a model, a set of rules or regulations through which one filters incoming data. Paradigms can be good, as they make our world intelligible to us. They enable us to process information by acting as a screen through which we perceive information that is thereby ascribed context and meaning. For some, the paradigm of what constitutes a good day involves Krispy Kreme donuts. For others, a good day is one in which one didn't require the use of his automatic weapon, a day during which one is somehow still alive to experience another twenty-four hours of life. Those for whom this alternative paradigm exists dwell in an America where children routinely suffer from untreated posttraumatic stress disorder, where a war zone is not on the other side of the planet, but is across the block, down the street, or in the front yard.

Intellectual filters, paradigms, fed by generations of thinking about the poor govern the tension between compassion and deterrence, and render students blind to the paralyzing effects of poverty in America. This is why students find it possible to be intellectually flexible about the poor on the other side of the planet, while remaining intellectu-ally—and I would add emotionally—cold to the poor on the other side of town. This is America, after all. Everyone can make it if they only try hard enough. And, so long as there is a single example of success that defeats the odds, a single example out of hundreds of thousands, the paradigm retains its strength. But see the world through the eyes of others, through *their* paradigm for a good day, and then you are on your way toward solidarity with them.

Paradigms govern not only an individual's perceptions, but collectively held paradigms govern, as we know, the thinking and perception patterns of large groups of people. When the filters of these paradigms paralyze the intellectual flexibility of the group, they give birth to myths and misperceptions such as have already been described. The process is startling in its simplicity. If the group, for example, accepts that anyone can achieve financial success through "hard work"—never defining, of course, what hard work might practically and logistically mean, or whether access to work even exists—then it follows that anyone who is not financially successful must be lazy. Cause and correlation become indistinguishable, and logic is surpassed by the efficiency of myth and rationalization. The myths and the ill-conceived opinions serve as a sort of false framework for belief, until the collective population comes to accept, as fact, things that are blatantly false. Then, as if that were not enough, we must deal with information-overload that desensitizes students.

Think of the world in which we live—our super-paced daily life— metaphorically: think of our perception of this world as a spinning crystal, suspended in midair, its multifaceted surface whirling so rapidly that one cannot clearly see the individual planes. Think of each plane on the crystal as one element, one issue, or one aspect of our collective world. The spinning crystal exemplifies information overload, revealing the complicated processes of navigating through even a single day as it whirs by. Here is yet another reason to employ the arts. Art has the capacity to freeze the crystal. Engagement with a work of art can allow one to see, with great clarity, an individual plane on the crystal, and to further use that plane to refract the illuminating light of understanding. Art enables us to focus, uniting us with the deepest sensibilities of the human person. This is especially true in the case of performance art. As one student during the recent quarter put it, after having attended a piece of live theatre: "The audience is at one moment laughing uncontrollably, and looking around themselves in uneasy silence the next as a dose of cold, hard reality about race relations is delivered without warning." And another students notes: "The second act is . . . in an abstract form: the actors utilize their bodies and vocals to bring to life the streets of an inner city, an inner city family, and a prison cell . . . the actors become humanized, and the audience is able to empathize with the inner and external struggles being presented on stage."

Art connects with us on a "pre-paradigm" level and can be authentically utilized across the full curriculum of course units: the means of production and the matter of wealth; race, class, and issues of economic mobility; the faces of the working poor; and America's future and the global economics of poverty. My students are typical of those at Jesuit universities nationally, representing the variant religious, cultural, and political sectors of American life. In order to foster an educational environment that will utilize the diversity inherent in my student cohort, I implement experiential learning strategies that are grounded in the arts, role play in a welfare simulation, for example, in order to bring students inside the thoughts, dreams, emotions, and sensibilities of those who struggle with the disabling hardship of poverty in America.

As stated earlier, the arts are not meant to be used merely as reference materials. In order for a truly interdisciplinary approach to work, and in order for the artistic pieces to act as a catalyst for a transformative educational experience, at least basic aesthetic and critical analysis must be used in the same way in which one would apply such analysis in an arts class. Accordingly, I teach my students in Poverty in America how to analyze the form of a piece of art in order to further their own understanding of the artist's intent. Form is the significant arrangement of parts of the whole, the part-to-part, parts-to-the-whole relationships that together convey the artist's intent. I ask my students to listen to "All That I Got is You," by the hip-hop artist Ghostface Killah.[3] I instruct them to listen for whatever stands out for them in the words, but to also consider the music's structure, the form of the piece in total. What one initially hears in the piece are the raw dynamics of hip-hop lyrics, delivered in staccato rhythms and harsh rapid-fire cadences, conveying a tangible feeling of the brutality of inner-city life. The listener is confronted by the crushing reality of what it is like to live in a blighted urban neighborhood: this is a world that is "in your face" all the time. The lyrics rest on top of, or better said, are delivered in tension against, a 1, 5 over 7, 6m, 3m chord structure. The chord structure is short, reliable, dependable, and reassuring. The stability of such chord structures is familiar in contemporary western music. The chord structure provides an aesthetic experience that is at once reassuring and familiar. These chords support the smooth melodic line of the chorus as the singer, Mary J. Blige, repeats the phrase "All That I Got Is You." The lyrics reveal the seeming impossibility of survival. The chord structure and the melodic line of the chorus, the *form*, communicate *how* those who live in these environments manage to survive at all.

Many of my students listen to hip-hop music on what Aaron Copland described as the sensual plane of listening in which one allows the music to wash through his or her audio environment without really focusing on the musical or expressive elements. I ask my students to examine what the music is really communicating, and to listen critically by analyzing the form. The art takes them on the other side of the paradigm, if you will, to an authentic confrontation with the grim reality of what life is like for others of their own generation whose accident of birth was less fortunate. The myth of meritocracy is difficult to retain when the art connects us to real human experience: arriving for school, as it is your day to wear the pair of pants; having spent the night in the same bed with your incontinent brother; having picked roaches out of your cereal—if you had some this morning—and no milk, you use sugar water; having used a newspaper in lieu of toilet paper; shivering without a coat; eyes having been wiped with your mom's saliva because you don't have a nice warm shower: *This is not the same experience as arriving in your warm suburban, sack lunch in hand, wearing your down parka!*

I ask my students: "If this were you, how would you do that day in school? What would you expect on your return home? What is it like to try to buckle down on the homework to get ahead in such an environment, especially if you had never actually met a single person—never known anyone—who managed to get out? "How do people survive in such a life?" The answer is in the music. The social relationships of the poor are complex, finely textured, they allow for survival against all odds. The relationships are conveyed in the music's chord structure. The crystal plane begins to refract, allowing one to see the world through the eyes of another. My students begin to understand the power of paradigms. The middle class talks school, college, and success. That is their paradigm. The poor talk survival. One student who performed his service learning in a juvenile detention facility reported that the analysis of this piece of hip-hop music is what enabled him to better understand the "in your face" attitudes of the young men incarcerated in the facility.

Throughout the first week of class, students learn how to analyze a work of art so that it may act as a catalyst for the learning process of I intend for my Poverty in America course. Eventually, the class will attend full-length plays, using them as tools to illuminate economic and sociological concepts. The plays function to bring students of my course inside the lives of those whose struggles have informed these interdisciplinary concepts. Admittedly, one is at the mercy of the local artistic scene when planning such a course curriculum. In our community, theatre, dance, and musical events are easily accessible and relatively numerous, and, because the course structure is broad enough, artistic pieces have a way of fitting themselves into the curriculum. For example, in the course unit entitled "America's Future and the Global Economics of Poverty," students learn the facts about the plight of undocumented workers through the explicit connection with economic, political, and sociological data. When Lisa Loomer's play *Living Out* was produced, it was included to provide an implicit connection with the human persons at the heart of that data. In the course unit on

"The Means of Production and the Matter of Wealth" students read August Wilson's play, "Radio Golf," which provides a lens through which to examine "Winner Take All Systems" (Frank 2003), The students are also exposed to *The Shipment*, by Young Jean Lee, which is performed by the Young Jean Lee Theatre company, and which directly challenges the audience to confront their own paradigms about race and cultural relationships. A piece such as this, which includes extensive movement and a structure designed to create the effect of a variety show, is only effective if seen live. Student comments about this performance reveal the power of its unusual structure. One student writes: "The unusual structure of the piece caused the audience to feel excitement, mystery, and surprise." Noting the "asymmetrical" structure of the play, the student continued:

> I realized that the humor [inherent in many sections of the piece] must be incorporated in order for people to solve racism and accept that it still exists. Young Jean Lee successfully pushed the audience to laugh at the plight of racism while also making us reflect on the devastating situation we live in . . . Racism directly contributes to poverty; if people ignore that racism exists in America, then they are ignoring that poverty exists.

One of the most powerful dramatic resources that I have used is Suzan-Lori Parks's Pulitzer prize-winning play, *Topdog/Underdog* (2001), which provides the introduction to this paper. In the play Parks creates a world where the pressures of structural factors on the poor, and the disparity between the ideal of meritocracy and the reality of economic immobility due to random socio-economic status, are viscerally, and ultimately violently, lived out. The power of the play as a tool for teaching Poverty in America is so strong that I include the play in class as a regular part of the reading. Performance of another live piece will almost certainly be available, and that other piece will serve double-duty, offering insight on its own as a part of the curriculum, and enabling students to conceptualize the impact that other works, such as *Topdog/Underdog*, would have in a live performance.

Topdog/Underdog is included in the section of the course unit that focuses attention on the black underclass and on the distinctions between the formal and informal urban economies. Discussion of the play is centered on the artistic device of the metaphor, which is the connective tissue of the form of the play. An example of Parks's use of metaphor connects to the course unit on economics. As part of an ongoing and evolving definition of poverty, my students have been introduced to Adam Smith's definition of poverty as being a lack of "necessaries" [as the experience of being unable to consume] "not only the commodities which are indispensably necessary for the support of life, but whatever the custom of the country renders it indecent for creditable people, even of the lowest order, to be without" (1976, 351–52). The play features two brothers, Lincoln and Booth. Yes, their names are metaphors. When dividing their meager earnings, which are barely enough to pay for the single room occupancy hotel in which they live, Booth insists that they pay the phone bill. Why is it so important to him to do this? The brothers have been without phone service, and they are certainly not in a financial position to consider adding on obligations. Booth explains that owning a phone establishes the following:

> 1) You got a home, that is, you ain't no smooth talking smooth dressing homeless joe; 2) that you is in possession of a telephone and a working telephone number which is to say that you got thuh cash and thuh wherewithal to acquire for yr own self the worlds most revolutionary communication apparatus and you together enough to pay yr bills! . . . [And] 3) you ain't got no wife or wife approximation on the premises.

Booth is saying that a phone allows one to exhibit financial viability. The person who can pay the phone bill has achieved a level of social reliability that moves him or her into the respected middle class by illustrating a capability to maintain bourgeois norms. Having a phone shows the world that you have managed to secure a dwelling, beyond a homeless shelter, as a phone line means that you have a permanent address. And, should a man give his phone number to a woman, a man proves that he is morally ethical, that he can be trusted. In essence, owning a telephone is what is requisite for a person, even of the lowest order, to have in order that to be considered a creditable person.

Booth's dialogue provides a metaphor for a twenty-first-century version of Adam Smith's definition of poverty.

The metaphor that anchors the plot is the game of three-card monty. Together with the play's title, the card game alludes to economic stratification and class subordination. Lincoln, the eldest brother, is a master of the game, but has given it up in favor of a "sit down job with benefits." Lincoln works in an arcade where he wears white face and an Abe Lincoln costume. Tourists assassinate him for the price of entrance. We know that, despite his relentless hard work and extraordinary displays of merit (he practices dying at home), his pay is less than his white predecessor, and he expects to loose his job to a wax dummy. Meritocracy is a myth for Lincoln. He gave up three-card monty because the game is illegal and dangerous, even though Lincoln's mastery of the game had ensured him financial success. Three-card monty can be seen as a metaphor for the drug trade that hammers our urban backwaters, providing the only certain financial security in the absence of opportunities in the formal economy. Park's play explores the fascinating nature of one game. But both games (cards and drugs) involve skill, hierarchy, street savvy, sophistication, and death. Using three-card monty as a metaphor for the drug trade is essential, because the standard audience demographic has paradigms about urban violence and economic decay which prevent them from caring, or make it impossible for them to see, how the drug business is, for many, the only available connection to the global economy. Paradigms about drug "thugs" render the general population immune to the pain experienced by mothers who watch their sons die in the streets as a result of gang warfare. Caught off-guard, watching the relatively benign game of three-card monty, we find that we grow to love the characters as human beings; we are able to forgive their poor choices. Without dismissing them as thugs, we understand the plight of those who have no access to the formal economy, we feel loss at their death, and we find ourselves grieving. We experience a bit of the pain that is all too real for those mothers.

I start the discussion of the play by encouraging the students to look at the play's form. In *Topdog/Underdog*, the conflict builds unrelentingly, pausing through brief moments of satire, which exacerbate the conflict. The climactic moment of the play is a shooting—Booth shoots

Lincoln. In some plays, the audience and the characters onstage are given time to recuperate from whatever has occurred in the climax. There is a period of adjustment, a denouement. Not here. The dialogue is rapid-fire. We hear that Booth has "popped" Grace, his supposed girlfriend, though we never meet her. There is a quick debate between the brothers. A shot rings out and Lincoln is dead. The stage lights go dark as we hear Booth's keening wail, and the house lights go up. The audience is left to stumble off into the night. Recognizing that the form of the play, the plot, includes a pointed lack of denouement that is critical to understanding Suzan-Lori Parks's message. As the discussion of the play evolves, students are encouraged to keep this recognition of the form in mind.

In this final scene of the play, Booth challenges Lincoln to test him in a game of three-card monty. They gamble for Booth's inheritance, as he calls it. This inheritance is purported to be five hundred dollars, knotted at the bottom of a nylon stocking. Booth has never opened the stocking which his mother gave to him when she left. He was eleven then.

The game plays out just as it would on the street. Booth wins the first time, just as the duped tourist might in lower Manhattan. But Lincoln is a master of the game and its associated showmanship. They play a second round, and Booth picks the wrong card. The inheritance is lost.[4]

Booth's inheritance serves as a metaphor for the hope and the possibility of a better future, a future that is largely dictated by one's financial and genetic inheritance. The image of the stage prop—the balled-up stocking—is metaphorically linked to the character's diminished internal resources. As a result of his socio-economic status, Booth has no emotional or spiritual resource. The inheritance is so tightly wound up, literally and figuratively, that only Lincoln's knife can penetrate the knot in order to visualize and release its potential. Booth has no concept of how to develop financial assets, and he has not been bequeathed with even the modicum of the external resources of education, support systems, role models, and social skills. Instead, he has the meager seed money, which he can only gamble away, hoping that somehow fate will allow him to win just this one time. When fate fails to provide, yet again, he does not have the emotional resource to deal with the blow.

His response is deadly. Violence kills both the hope that the inheritance might have provided, and the only family he has.

The act of fratricide and our reactions to it, heightened by the form of the piece, are analogous to what our actions *should* be at the news that, on any given summer month, there are more murders than there have been days in our nation's poorest neighborhoods. There are brothers killing brothers, violent death infecting the minds and hearts of children growing up in blighted neighborhoods, and there are hard structural factors that lock hopelessness into everyone's worldview. This morning, it is all too likely that a mother weeps, her son's blood staining the asphalt.

When we refuse to see individuals within a population, when we divorce ourselves from their humanity, we need not bother with solutions to their situation. Believing that their situation is self-made, that it does not have anything to do with us, and that our perspective about these people is safely couched in politically correct ideology, our relationship to them as members of a collective community is successfully severed. We might learn about the sociological and economic realities that support Wm. Julius Wilson's (1997) theories of out-migration, but we find it difficult to be moved to any action. Parks's play counters the impersonal by bringing us into relationship with Lincoln and Booth. She reveals the humanity of Booth and Lincoln through a connected web of metaphors so that our prejudices can be held at bay long enough to allow our relationship with the characters to develop. And the form she employs keeps us from complacency. As my students find, it becomes unacceptable to do nothing.

Conclusion

This essay has focused on the use of contemporary music and drama as tools for teaching the subject of poverty in America. Other pedagogical methodologies incorporate the arts through experiential learning. These include a welfare simulation, during which students participate in role play as professionals and applicants in the Temporary Assistance to Needy Families program; an ongoing socio-economic status card game, in which students unwittingly feel the very real effects of living at the bottom of our economic and social ladders; and a cost of living research project (COLP), which I designed so that students would have a context for all statistical data relative to poverty and wealth in the United States. The COLP uses the city as the learning environment, and students become mobile and active agents of their own understanding. The combined effect of these methodologies is transformative because it is active, and because the arts draw students into a relationship with those who inform the statistical tallies.

Evidence that using the arts contributes to an educational experience that has the ability to be transformational is clear in both the statistical ratings of the course overall and in the student comments on class evaluation forms. What is most striking is how clearly student responses differ between terms when arts events were more plentiful relative to terms when they were not. Overall ratings for the course which average response to questions about the course as a whole, the instructor, and the level of stimulation toward active learning are always above 4.0 out of a scale of 5.0, with a majority of terms scoring in the range of 4.30 to 4.70. Scores are consistently higher during terms when attendances at outside performance events are included. Individual scores calculating students' evaluations of their own learning, in particular, is markedly higher when live performance opportunities usable toward the service of the curriculum are available. A score of 4.75 is not uncommon in the single area regarding the stimulation of active learning, which is the better indicator of the course toward the purpose of moving students to action. Students in the course consistently serve more than the required number of hours at service learning assignments, as well, many performing over twenty hours of service when only sixteen have been required. One of the more compelling points in terms of student outcome is that during the most recent term, students had the option of attending an outside event, a play, and those who chose to attend were the students whose service learning hours were voluntarily increased. Neither the increase of service hours or the option to attend the play affected the student grades—these were student choices. Student comments directly referencing the interdisciplinary structure of the course are common, as are comments specifically referencing the use of arts across the curriculum. A sampling of such student comments follows:

The series of simulations (involving role play) made the material more accessible.

This interdisciplinary course was the only class I found rewarding.

This course was authentically interdisciplinary . . . I could use information from it in all of my other classes and in my daily life.

The plays gave me a visual representation of the content I was learning.

Course was more interesting with . . . more creative active learning.

The cross-disciplinary learning [was what was most enjoyed about the class].

The course made me go beyond the academic aspect. I was encouraged to analyze different cultures . . . which really led me to eye-opening experiences.

It was always interesting . . . incorporating other material such as plays.

Very different from other courses—there was a lot of interaction involved.

Very interdisciplinary—loved the arts aspects.

This class will let me use the knowledge I have obtained and hopefully with my business degree I can help change poverty. This class actually meant something to me.

It was very interactive and allowed me to broaden my horizons on the poorest populations.

The professor was adamant about educating and engaging us on many levels, such as through literature, music, theatre, film, and active learning. Every class was stimulating.

The literature and drama. [In response to what student felt most contributed to their learning.]

The arrangement of multimedia learning and activities were enhancing to my learning experience.

Education that promotes justice, compassion, empathy, and action demands that the student have an open mind, demands that the student practice intellectual flexibility. The filtering mechanism in one's closely held paradigms can effectively blind one to seeing the world through another's eyes, be it to see a war zone in an urban neighborhood, a genocide in the relocation of the Navajo Nation, or to understand injustice in the plight of the dad who must juggle two low-wage jobs just to pay for the most basic of shelter for his family. In order to understand the crippling effects of being poor amidst great wealth, in order to fully comprehend what the statistics ultimately *mean* and why they demand acting for justice, students must gain freedom from the paradigms about poverty in America that promote errant ideas and falsehoods. It is my conviction that using the arts as part of an interdisciplinary pedagogy is the most effective means by which to instill intellectual flexibility in the minds of our students, and to thereby move them to become people who seek and act for justice.

3 Encuentro Dominicano

Creighton University's Commitment to Education for Transformation

TOM KELLY

> Through my weekly service site, giving love and dignity to orphaned children with developmental disabilities and our campo stays, living with wonderful, instantly accepting host families, my world was transformed.
>
> —Becca Harvey, Encuentro Dominicano alumna[1]

In March 2007 fifteen students from Encuentro Dominicano, Creighton University's study abroad program in the Dominican Republic, had been immersed in a small rural and very poor community called Ocho de los Caballeros (Eight of the Gentleman). It is a small fishing community squatting illegally on the shore of a very large inland lake called Lake Hatillo in the Dominican Republic. Comprised of about thirty-five families, the population suffered from a variety of water-born diseases including skin fungus, parasites, and eye problems.

Our educational goal was to try to understand the poverty and structural difficulties of the rural Dominican poor by entering into and sharing their lives for a short time. Our project with the community was to build an aqueduct so they could have clean, fresh, running water for bathing, cooking, and consumption. This project was chosen by the community after a Creighton chemistry professor tested their local "clean" water source which registered 1,600 parts fecal matter. Eleven parts fecal matter would be considered unsafe in the United States. That immersion was one of our best. The students established strong connections with their families and the families really cared for the students. The project was a great success as well, and for the first time in their lives, the villagers had clean running water. Students left their families in tears, and many returned throughout the semester as well

csk

as years later, to visit and spend time with those who had been so hospitable to them.

Encuentro Dominicano tries to instill in its students the commitment that real solidarity extends into their time back in the United States. Solidarity does not end when one boards the flight home to resume a life briefly left behind. I am not always sure that I believed we had succeeded in instilling this commitment of solidarity—until the tropical storm that destroyed Ocho de Los Caballeros.

In December 2007 tropical storm Noel hit the Dominican Republic and caused sustained flooding, heavy loss of life, and severe strain on the infrastructure of a country that could ill afford it. I received an e-mail at Creighton from the ILAC Mission with photographs of Lake Hatillo clearly spilling over its banks. We were told that Ocho, the same community that our students had immersed in, was twelve feet under water. I immediately e-mailed these photos to the group of students who had lived and worked there but didn't really know how they would respond. Thirty minutes later the first knock on my door came with a student in tears asking about the health of her family? Her brother? Her sister? Her Mom and Dad? I said I didn't know, it was too early to tell. Before I knew it my office was full of students wanting to know how their families were, The entire time only relational terms were used (Mom, Dad, brother, sister, etc.)—at no time did anyone ask how the Dominicans were doing in Ocho de los Caballeros.

When the full extent of what had occurred at Ocho became known, the students who had immersed there organized and began fundraising to rebuild the homes of "their families." Aided by a local priest in the Dominican Republic named Father Neno, the community received a piece of land acquired on their behalf by the government and began to rebuild with funds from the government and various faith communities in Spain and the United States. Creighton students raised nearly $18,000 in three weeks for this effort. Some students called Father Neno and asked whether they should fly down there to be with the community as they rebuilt or should they donate the money they would have used on flights for the rebuilding? Father Neno said the community would prefer their presence to any donation, so three students flew down to accompany this community for over a week. Over the years nearly all students who immersed in Ocho de Los Caballeros have returned at some point to visit their families—and many say those relationships have kept the experience of Encuentro Dominicano alive in their hearts and souls.

Although anecdotal, this story illustrates that an immersion-based community-learning foreign study program that cultivates relationships can be an effective means of personalizing and, thus humanizing, the reality of social injustice. Ocho existed, nearly forgotten, at the end of a dirt road. It was populated by people with no rights or claim to the land they lived on. It was destroyed because of the lack of good infrastructure in a country with a GDP that grew every year. Its people had become family for our students.

Encuentro Dominicano

> Encuentro truly helped me experience and be with people who live in the unacceptable conditions that the majority of the world lives in. For us Americans, we are constantly in our own little "bubble" only caring about our busy lives and never knowing other perspectives besides our own. However, going to the Dominican Republic and building relationships with the people of our world who are in a sense forgotten, truly opened my mind and changed me forever.[2]

It is not always easy living and studying in the Dominican Republic. Our students will tell you this without hesitation. At the same time they will tell you they have grown and changed in ways they never expected. When they saw people suffering from easily preventable and treatable diseases, massive systemic injustice, widespread unemployment and underemployment and living conditions that most only see on infomercials for international charities—you are going to change and change drastically. The key to this transformational process is a commitment to academic rigor in the context of community-based learning, and an emphasis on building relationships and spiritual reflection through a commitment to a faith that does justice.

In a talk given at Santa Clara University on October 6, 2000, the Father General of the Jesuits, Peter-Hans Kolvenbach (2000), proposed that these two deliberately open words may be interpreted as meaning respectively, "the service of faith . . . [by bringing] the counter-cultural gift of Christ to the world," and the "justice of the Gospel which embodies God's love and saving mercy." Kolvenbach emphasizes Ignatius' desire to combine words with deeds. Social action in the name of the justice of the Gospel must be combined, he proposes, with much analysis and reflection (ibid.). In 2001 Kolvenbach added the gloss that the promotion of justice needs to combine academic rigor with social activism.[3] In applying these principles to contemporary higher education in Jesuit universities, Kolvenbach (2000) proposes that students be educated in "solidarity for the real world," and "solidarity is learned through contact rather than through concepts [only]." "When the heart is touched by direct experience, the mind may be challenged to change. Personal involvement with innocent suffering, with the injustice others suffer, is the catalyst for solidarity which then gives rise to intellectual inquiry and moral reflection" (ibid.). Kolvenbach adds that "students, in the course of their formation, must let the gritty reality of the world into their lives, so they can learn to feel it, think about it critically, respond to its suffering and engage it constructively." Finally, he proposes that "insertion programs," "off-campus contacts," and "hands-on courses" at Jesuit universities should not be "too optional and peripheral, but at the core of every Jesuit university's program of studies" (ibid.).

Encuentro Dominicano has tried to apply these goals articulated by Father Kolvenbach directly to the curriculum and formation that is an integral part of the program. Students are housed just outside of Santiago at the Centro de Educación para Salud Integral (Center for Integral Health and Education—the ILAC Mission). During their four-month stay, students take twelve to fifteen hours of coursework, immerse in local communities for three weeks, and engage in community-based learning twice a week in Santiago. The program is a mix between the traditional approach to study abroad (living together, studying, and traveling) and an immersion component that puts them in direct and prolonged contact with marginal communities who survive on subsistence farming and occasional outside employment. The ILAC Mission has built relationships in these communities, called *campos*, for over thirty-five years. In short, Creighton students have been afforded the opportunity and privilege of living in some of these communities in order to experience and understand life in the developing world in a unique way.

Encuentro Dominicano has three main priorities that flow through all its programming and coursework: to make concrete connections between academic learning and lived experience in the context of the developing world; to reveal the complexity and responsibility of living in a global community; to integrate this new knowledge and experience in a spirituality of faith and justice. What we hope for is an integral Jesuit education, one that combines the best of academic resources with immersions in communities suffering from systemic injustice.

ILAC Mission: Context and Community

> The workers here watch out for us: Miguelina has acted as a moth-erly figure for us when we go out at night, the security guard Antonio shines his flashlight up the stairs when we walk up to our rooms in the dark of an *apagon* (a power-outage) after a long night of studying, and Elfi is always there to offer us his goofy smile and a big teddy bear hug. It is this ILAC that we have come to love and the relation-ships that we have built here not only in our group but also with the workers that will truly leave an impact on our hearts forever.[4]

Creighton University's mission statement emphasizes: "The ILAC Center in the Dominican Republic is an international, Catholic, Ignatian-inspired, collaborative health care and educational organiza-tion that exists to promote the integral well-being and spiritual growth of all participants. It is built upon the values of Ignatius of Loyola, Founder of the Jesuits (Society of Jesus)."[5] There are two components that comprise this vision. The first is the ILAC Mission in the Domini-can Republic, staffed by thirty-five Dominican employees and active in health, education, agricultural, and spirituality initiatives. The second is the ILAC office at Creighton University which serves as a bridge between groups in the United States and the needs of communities served by the ILAC Center in the DR. "All of Creighton's ILAC pro-grams emphasize the importance of global vision and understanding in the process of educating well-rounded individuals. To this end it offers dental, medical, nursing, pharmacy, law, physical therapy and occupational therapy, undergraduate and high school students, and also to faculty-led groups, medical/surgical teams and other colleges the opportunity for service learning and immersion experiences in the rural Dominican Republic."[6]

Encuentro Dominicano, an initiative of Creighton's College of Arts and Sciences, partners with both the Division of Student Services at Creighton and the ILAC Mission in the Dominion Republic to implement its vision of education for transformation. The ILAC Mission in the Dominican Republic has a clearly stated vision: "To cultivate growing human integration in harmony with faith and the development of society."[7] The mission proposes to do this through three "institutional norms" or action items which include: promoting the faith for integral development of the person, generating a love of service, solidarity and fairness; empowering persons to be their own agents of a higher quality of life; and strengthening the institution by consolidating its sustainability, efficiency and efficacy to carry out its own vision.[8] Each of the three major divisions within the ILAC Mission realizes these institutional norms in different ways and to varying degrees.

Within the Health Division of the Mission there are a variety of approaches. This division welcomes occupational therapy groups, physical therapy groups, and surgery teams (eye, bone, hernia, etc.) from the United States and makes their services available to those who would never have the opportunity to benefit from a First World level of health care. In the summer, entire medical teams from Creighton University's Schools of Medicine, Dentistry, Pharmacy and Nursing descend upon five to six different rural communities, immerse with those communities, and respond to the health needs of those communities in all manners possible. But perhaps the most effective overall health initiative supported by the ILAC Mission in the Dominican Republic is the program called *Cooperadores de Salud*. It is here in their Health Collaborator program where Encuentro Dominicano, as an academic program, meets and integrates with the vision of the ILAC Mission.

Health Collaborators with the ILAC Mission are usually women (and some men) who are first recognized as leaders within their own communities. They live a life for and with others, participate in the faith life of their villages, and usually have the personality and leadership traits that "call" them to greater service. When a community in relationship with the ILAC Mission puts forward their candidate for health collaborator, an intense period of preparation lasting three years ensues, during which the candidate is carefully trained in basic preventative health care practices, a spirituality of service, and the services made available by the ILAC Mission to assist their communities. Health collaborators are not paid a salary. They answer a call to serve their communities by making their time and energy (and, sometimes financial resources) available to meet the health needs of their communities. I have seen extraordinarily self-sacrificial acts of service on behalf of health collaborators including feeding twenty to thirty people out of the back of their homes on a regular basis as well as giving up days and weeks with family to accompany the sick and infirm on trips to the mission to seek the care they need.

There should be

Because the ILAC Mission serves over one hundred rural communities, the point of contact with those communities, the health collaborator, is a very important position. This person functions as a bridge between the needs of rural communities and the various services (spiritual, health, educative, agricultural) provided by the ILAC Mission. When Encuentro Dominicano sought ways to immerse our students in rural communities, health collaborators were essential to our encounters with some of the Dominican Republic's poorest people. Without them, what we try to do would be impossible.

Building a Program in Another Culture

Each day of service Kali and Zach shadowed a variety of FONDESA employees to see firsthand the process of microfinance at its finest. A typical day would be putting together the *horario de calle* (the street schedule), going to meet the clients at their *empresas* (businesses), and assisting with paper work for the approval process, collections, and client credit histories. They visited a variety of microenterprises, including *colmados* (small, neighborhood grocery stores), a meat processing factory, a plastic recycling center, and florists. They were given tours and explanations of how these businesses work to expand their business horizons.[9]

In a relationship-based society, the outsider is hard-pressed to make entry. For the majority of foreigners in the Dominican Republic, that is not a concern. Most visitors only see the Dominican Republic from the perspective of its polished north coast resorts and casinos, or from the depths of its entrenched and very lucrative sex-tourism business. To get into rural communities and *not* be treated as tourists is a real challenge—one that was overcome through our partnership with the ILAC Mission. Because we did not have established relationships with the rural poor in the Dominican Republic, we attached to an organization of those who did.

Each successive administrative director of Encuentro Dominicano has had to learn first how to work in harmony within the ILAC Mission. By carefully building relationships and showing an interest in all the mission does (not just our narrow interests), trust is developed and connections are made. Having a local and respected Catholic mission to provide for the logistics, transportation, housing, and academic space for our program has been absolutely essential. There can be no replacement for local expertise both in terms of cultural education and appropriate resource allocation. Extended immersions in marginal communities were possible only because the ILAC Mission had established long-term relationships with these communities and were trusted by them. The relationship is mutually beneficial. Financial resources from students living and learning at the ILAC Mission helps the mission extend its reach and improve its services. Relationships with marginal communities the mission has cultivated for decades are shared with us. This allowed us entry into a world that for most North Americans is simply inaccessible.

Students in Encuentro Dominicano engage in a rigorous course of study that includes material on the history, sociology, and economics of the Dominican Republic considered not only from the various perspectives on international development but also through the lens of a faith that does justice. When designing the Encuentro program, the question became, how can we personalize this academic knowledge? How can we humanize this learning? How can this academic material become transformational knowledge? We proposed both a weekly community-based learning service commitment and an immersion component to the program. It was important that the immersion was long enough to build relationships that could humanize the learning in the classroom. The keys to both these components are the relationships the ILAC Mission has built with various communities over the past thirty-five years. These communities became accessible to us through the health collaborator.

When the administrative director of Encuentro Dominicano first meets a possible Dominican host community open to an immersion, a delicate negotiation takes place where both means and motives are plainly laid out. Those involved in this initial encounter include the administrative directors of the ILAC Mission, the academic director of Encuentro Dominicano, and the health collaborator of the rural village. The first step we take is to answer the question of why we want our students to live in this village for the next ten days. The answer is usually a variation on this theme: we are trying to teach students about how most of the world lives and what their responsibilities to the world are in light of this knowledge and their faith. We have studied this reality in our classroom, but without a direct experience of your lives (of the *campesinos*); the learning will not be successful. Would you be willing to serve as our teachers for these students in the classroom of your lives, here in the campo? Will you teach them how to wash their own clothes by hand, sleep in *mosquiteros*, work with their hands, and be part of your family even though they can't always communicate very well? We would be grateful for this hospitality, and in return we have some resources we would like to use in order to benefit the community as a whole. If the response to this entreaty is positive, which it always has been, we move to the second step.

The second step is to ask for a community meeting with the same initiators, as well as the leadership of the village. In this meeting we listen to the needs of the community, discover what they lack, what they feel they need, and what we can do given our available resources. By the conclusion of this meeting, the community has usually identified a project, which always includes the students working with Dominicans toward a concrete improvement of their community. Past projects have included bridges, aqueducts, housing, and latrines. The goal for the relationship between Encuentro Dominicano and every community with whom we immerse is mutual service for and with each other.

Emphasizing Connections to Lived Experiences

> Through my time in the Dominican Republic this past fall, I was able
> to engage with the poor and see true poverty with my own eyes. It
> was not something easy to do, but I believe that through the constant
> challenge of seeing poverty and consequently challenging it through
> questioning the situation, I was able to experience something that
> no other program could offer.[10]

While traditional academic learning is invaluable in our culture,
Encuentro Dominicano emphasizes academic learning's connection to
lived experience. It is one thing to study the reign of the late Dominican
dictator Rafael Trujillo, and it is another thing to listen to a Dominican
campesino reminisce back to times when things got done because someone was in charge. It surprises many of our students when typical Dominicans communicate a preference for a dictator over democracy, a
development that is more and more common in Latin America. When
one gets inside Dominican society and begins to see the frustration,
corruption and inefficiency of political life, the other perspective
becomes more plausible. It is one thing to study *machismo*, the cultural
dominance of men in Latin America, and another thing to experience
it while immersing themselves in one of the *campos*. It is eye opening
for our young women to observe and experience the lives of their Dominican counterparts not only through the difficult and tiring work they
do everyday but also through the inferior social position in which many
of them find themselves.. When female students are gently told that
women don't use shovels or build homes, it is interesting to see what
responses that engenders and the mutual learning that occurs for both
Dominicans and US students. It is one thing to study Haitian immigration to the Dominican Republic and listen to representatives of the
Jesuit Refugee Service document human rights abuses and it is another
thing to see a Dominican border guard quietly put away his whip as our
students arrive at the bridge that separates Haiti from the Dominican
Republic.

Students encounter situations that require them to synthesize and
integrate their new knowledge, cultural understanding, and personal
reflection in real time. Can or will students confront these issues
beyond the structured classroom setting? Will students recognize that

newly befriended Dominicans are treated differently than themselves when they are out dancing merengue, salsa, and bachata in the city—and that this different treatment is due in part to skin color? Will they confront the machismo they experience in the campo, and if so, how? We hope that through many hours of preparation and course work, as well as careful student life mentoring and community building, students are well prepared to handle situations that might conflict with their individual ethics and past cultural experience.

Experiential, community-based learning without the comforts and normalcy of the traditional university setting can be disturbing and frustrating for Creighton students. Simply cramming for exams, or reading just enough to get through the next class session before heading back to the apartment on campus to play video games does not work in this learning environment. Successful classroom work is instead viewed as preparatory. If done well, it can build the knowledge base they need to successfully participate in the experiential learning and travel opportunities, which the program provides. Grounding the program in community-based learning is essential if we intend for our students to learn about the poverty they will inevitably encounter in the context of the Dominican Republic.

A central aspect of the program concerns how students learn about poverty. We study statistics, we see flow charts on unemployment, and we study how the GDP of the Dominican Republic has risen every year for the past twenty years while the percentage of its people in poverty has only increased. We read about the struggles of those in poverty, but until we experience the life of those who live in poverty—at least as a visitor—our knowledge is incomplete.

The immersions we require as part of our core class for the program are usually what allow for such life experiences. Mari saw her "little sister" in the campo suffer from an ear infection for days because the family could afford neither the cost of ibuprofen nor the trip to a pharmacy. The child lay on the cement floor for seven days because it was the only way to keep cool while her fever raged. Erin watched her "father" suffer from simple ailments that she could have remedied back in Santiago with a quick trip to the corner pharmacy. Joel, a business major, saw his father load his harvest on the back of a donkey and walk it the eight miles to a market, amazed that anyone could make a profit when one's production and distribution system is so primitive. Students witnessed children throughout the campo drinking unsanitary water which caused parasites and worse simply because they didn't know better. John and Andy worked on farms with their host parents. Sweaty and exhausted at the end of the day—they knew their "fathers" had worked all day for the equivalent of a mere six dollars. Caitlin and Joey listened to their father explain his life while working for two years in a free zone factory near Santiago and why their family preferred the life of a struggling fisherman squatting on land he does not own. Personal stories such as these don't come in textbooks.

When we meet with every community prior to our students' immersion, we emphasize that *they* are the teachers of their way of life—and when they welcome a student like a member of their family, they can teach some invaluable lessons. Students help cook, clean clothes, care for animals, and share meals with their families. Others work on farms planting corn, picking yucca, and carting bananas. Some pre-med students accompany rural physicians as they serve those with little or no access to decent health care. Most students bathe with buckets of water on a daily basis and nearly everyone goes to sleep at 8 PM because there is no electricity. Slowly, slowly, they begin to realize what poverty really is. Poverty is not so much the lack of iPods and air conditioning; rather it is a kind of vulnerability—in all aspects of life—which comes from a complex set of factors beyond the control of those who suffer from them. This vulnerability cannot be taught in a classroom, but it can be briefly glimpsed in the campo. Prior to our departure from one campo, a student asked me to drive to the pharmacy (ten kilometers away) to buy some cold medicine for them. I asked him, "What would a *campesino* do if they had what you have right now." He answered, "They would lie down and wait to get better." I said, "Have a nice rest."

Understanding Global Complexity

The service sites and course material broadened my worldview and gave me new insight into many fields of study. I learned how to examine psychological processes cross-culturally with actual field research in Multicultural Psychology and determined root causes of international economic inequality in EDP 361.[11]

Upon their arrival to Santiago and their new home, the ILAC Center, the students have a difficult time understanding Dominican reality. "Why don't people work here?" they ask. Their first response is, "If they just try hard, it will pay off and they can climb the economic ladder like everyone else." This, of course, presupposes a particular reality where success is both expected and possible and hope is normal. Breaking through preconceived notions brought by North American students is often one of the great challenges of educating in a developing world context.

What difference does it make that this country was conquered by Spanish, French, American, and Haitian forces and that an oligarchy has always dominated social, cultural, political, and economic life? Can those on the bottom of the socio-economic ladder think in terms of upward mobility? Is our perspective that "if people simply work hard they will succeed" a product of our own cultural upbringing that does not translate into other contexts? What psychic barriers exist in a country where the wealthy have always controlled access to opportunity and possibilities of improvement?

Soon, students learn that reality is very complex. *Campesinos* work hard in their fields but cannot compete with dairy and corn products from the heavily subsidized and highly technical US market that have flooded the country following trade agreements like CAFTA. Electricity is expensive and never steady because of government corruption that results in much electricity being stolen. This same corruption has its sociological roots in the survival mechanisms employed by peasants. The 300-year colonial occupation of the island taught them to take care of their own interests and the interests of their relatives by serving those in power. There is no common good, only my individual good.

"Why don't companies take better care of their workers?" students often ask. Business students learn here through "internship" opportunities with major multinational companies that such a question is very complicated. Some companies refuse to pay more in salary and benefits because if they do, manufacturers will simply open factories in China or Honduras and produce the same product for much less. Students are confronted by an increasingly complex world where subsidies in the United States or the lack of workers rights in China directly impact the standard of living in the Dominican Republic. Globalization can be partly understood in books, but it can be more deeply grasped through relationships.

Providing both the intellectual and experiential components of understanding a complex global reality is central to the goals of Encuentro Dominicano—and much easier said than done. What is certain is that First World responses to seemingly simple problems are almost never sufficient. One learns to delay judgment and try to understand the multiple dimensions, both proximate and distant, to a given problem. This "delay" is often frustrating for First World "fixers," those for whom problems have always been fairly easy to understand and solve.

Committing to Faith and Justice

The Creighton University mission states: "Our Jesuit vision commits us to form women and men of competence, conscience and compassion who have learned from reflecting upon their experiences of being for and with others. We do this in a service of a faith that does justice." I can think of no program in the university that better exemplifies this than Encuentro Dominicano.[12]

Perhaps what is most important in the approach of Encuentro Dominicano—through its curriculum, its living-learning community, and its retreat component—is a spiritual dimension that underlies everything we do and gives this program its unique identity as Catholic and Jesuit. Encuentro Dominicano has tried to apply the goals outlined by Kolvenbach at Santa Clara directly to the curriculum and formation that is an integral part of the program. Orientation begins with the academic director and student life director modeling ways to reflect and integrate the enormous amount of information and experience that students are exposed to. Texts in the core class focus not only on sociology, history, and economics but also on discernment, faith, and solidarity. This is supplemented by student life organized reflection sessions where students reflect upon and articulate their ongoing struggles to understand. We realize that students come to us from many backgrounds, but we insist that there be a spiritual dimension to personal development and experiential learning—in fact, it is essential. One of the key texts in the core course states,

I do know that the world needs a critical mass of people who will respond to suffering, who are ready to make a long-term commitment, and who will make wise choices along the way. Without such 'new human beings,' I doubt any amount of money, sophisticated strategies, or even structural change will make our world much more human. . . . Sustaining a life of generous service requires a spirituality. (Brackley 2004, 3)

What does this mean for a program emerging from a university that is both Catholic and Jesuit? We propose "that to live means to seek and find God everywhere, in order to collaborate with God in service to others" (ibid., 5) Part of this "everywhere" of course, must include the world in which we find ourselves—even if it is a home in the midst of a landfill. Another aspect of this occurs through the relationships that form and sustain us, and yet still another part is in God's movement in our hearts and souls while we are buffeted by the challenges and suffering in this world. This is why following each immersion we retreat as a group for two days to discern how to integrate our experience into a vision for our life that may challenge deeply held presuppositions and beliefs. This integrating aspect of the program is essential if the knowledge gained and the experiences lived are to mean anything in the future. "Responding to massive injustice according to each one's calling is the price of being human, and Christian today. Those looking for a privatized spirituality to shelter them from a violent world have come to the wrong place" (ibid. 7).

Conclusion

The curriculum of Encuentro Dominicano gave each one of us a base for understanding more about the world we live in. It made us more aware, challenged us to think differently, and empowered us to promote change in many social justice issues.[13]

The question remains though, are we successful in integrally educating our students for a faith that does justice? While various assessment efforts are in process, there are anecdotal indications that what we are teaching is taking root. The story of Ocho de Los Caballeros is one of

those. In addition, we actively assess the learning in Encuentro as it
passes through the phases of a given semester and beyond. The first
way is the required weekly journal that all students hand in on Friday
afternoons. Students are taught during orientation week that a journal
is not a personal diary; it is a place where they are encouraged to make
connections between the academic material they learn in the classroom
and the lived experience of the people and culture. It is extraordinary
how their capacity to reflect upon lived reality and classroom material
matures and progresses over a semester. To evaluate whether someone
understands a book explaining the role of race in the Dominican
Republic (Haitian-Dominican relationships are defined by race) is quite
different than witnessing an army truck round up and deport Haitians
and their children (or those who appear to be Haitian) right off a main
street in downtown Santiago. The purpose of the Encuentro program is
to make the connection between these two different kinds of knowledge and experience, in light of a faith that does justice. In addition to
the community-based learning journals received weekly throughout the
semester, we assign a lengthy "integration" paper which asks the student to combine a rigorous academic exploration of a topic emerging
from the core course (which covers economics, sociology, and history)
with an experiential reflection on the same. Finally, when students
return to Creighton following their semester, an extensive fifteen-page
assessment is filled out at the reorientation retreat. Every aspect of the
program is covered in this assessment including program preparation,
academics, language training and acquisition, service learning and
site assessment, the ILAC Center, extracurricular activities, a self-
evaluation, faith and spirituality opportunities, and personal growth
and change. This assessment mechanism gives us constant feedback
from participants of the program and allows us to make needed adjustments as necessary.

Ultimately, Encuentro Dominicano will only be successful if our students make choices and commitments in the future that distinguish
them from a world where material accumulation, self-interest, and
individualism reigns supreme. Now that the program is completing its
fifth year, we are beginning to track our graduates to determine
whether participation in Encuentro has informed their chosen paths.

Anecdotal evidence is very strong that it has made a significant differ-ence. We hope that exposure to the reality of a developing country will open hearts and minds to the responsibility that we have to care for others, especially the "least among us."

Social responsibility can and should take varying forms—business leaders who care about more than simply the bottom line, teachers who truly want to form and serve students, doctors who connect with their patients in their own language, government and civic leaders who have a preferential option for the common good over self-advancement. Will we be successful? Only time will tell. In the meantime, we do every-thing we can in the Dominican Republic to teach students how 70 percent of the world lives day to day. We hope they leave us committed to a life for others.

4 Teaching Social Analysis through Academic Immersion

GARY K. PERRY AND MADELINE LOVELL

It has been a couple years since I have made contact with you. I continually come back to my experience in New Orleans, through the class you provided, and feel touched by the opportunity and experience that were created while we were there. I am e-mailing you to keep in touch as I find myself with a unique opportunity. I am moving to Geneva, Switzerland. As a result, I will be giving up my job and searching for work in one of the international organizations. As I fill in my resume, I find myself continually citing my experience while in post-Katrina New Orleans. We were offered such a valuable opportunity and I just wanted to thank you

—Student e-mail, February 18, 2010

The above comments reflect the transformative impact that a unique academic immersion experience in post–Hurricane Katrina New Orleans had on twenty-three college students. Although it has been over seven years since the aftermath of Hurricane Katrina transformed the environmental, social, and cultural landscapes of the US Gulf Coast, the recovery effort is still ongoing. The recovery of the US Gulf Coast requires that we move beyond a framework of charity and develop a spirit of service that is rooted in social justice. On June 21, 2008, we took this directive to heart and led a group of twenty-three undergraduate students from Seattle University to post-Katrina New Orleans for a ten-day academic immersion experience. This chapter reports on the extent to which our study-away course allowed our students to be in service for social justice as they developed a social analysis of the aftermath facing post-Katrina New Orleans.

Teaching undergraduates to do social analysis offers both challenges and opportunities. Many are young with limited life experience. Such students may have led sheltered lives with little direct experience of injustice or difference across class and race. Classroom-based learning provides theoretical frameworks for understanding inequality. However, such frameworks often seem distant from students' lived experience. Linking an intensive service-based immersion to the application of theory offers the opportunity to engage fully the student in the study of injustice as it is manifested in society and how it might be addressed.

The Role of Social Analysis

What does social justice look like in an academic immersion experience? A justice-oriented approach to immersion-based education requires the integration of social analysis into the core objectives of the learning experience. When conceptualizing the learning aims of our academic immersion experience, we found Catholic social thought and our training in the social sciences to be fundamental to the course design process.

Joe Holland and Peter Henriot, SJ, outline a convincing model for linking the core tenets of social justice to faith: Faith is defined both in a religious tradition and, moreover as a means of service to populations disproportionately impacted by the social ills facing a globalizing world (Holland and Henriot 1983). It is our hope as educators in the Jesuit tradition of "a faith that does justice," to give students the tools to create a better world for the glory of God. Social justice, therefore, manifests itself in faith through critical social analysis. The relevance of social analysis—as a method of inquiry and a tool for social change— exceeds the realm of pastoral service. It is a means of discerning all of the factors involved in a social problem so that right and ethical responses may be chosen.

Social analysis is at the foundation of justice-oriented education (Butin 2007; Holland and Henriot 1983; Oakes, Rogers, and Lipton 2006). Social analysis requires an engaged pedagogy that is committed to equity, transformation, and liberation. Holland and Henriot (1983, 4) define social analysis as "the effort to obtain a more complete picture of a social situation by exploring its *historical and structural relationships*." Social analysis first requires that we clearly identify the social situation. Social phenomena (for example, poverty, racism, war, and climate change) exist within the interplay of historical and structural contexts. Our ability to define critically a social situation will often shape our approach to analyzing the social phenomenon.

But defining a social situation is only the initial stage of social analysis. Effective social analysis carries with it an underlying investment in getting to the root of the issue. What are the causes of poverty? Why are certain demographic populations more likely to be harmed by global capitalism? How is racism maintained? How do we end poverty? Who will suffer most from global warming? These questions demand that we not only assess individual choices but that we interrogate social systems—within which all individuals must exist—as a method of getting to the root issues associated with these social phenomena.

In other words, social analysis requires that we focus on social systems (i.e, economic, political, social, cultural, and so on) as we seek to form a more holistic understanding of social phenomena and social realities. Toward that end, we must analyze how various social structures or social institutions (i.e., schooling, multinational corporations, government, religion, and so on) operate within these distinct yet interrelated social systems. Social analyses must be situated within and across a given time and space. It presupposes that by interrogating social systems we may radically challenge the social structures that shape the social situations or social realities that individuals encounter. This is not to say, however, that individual behavior is determined by social systems. Rather, individuals' choices and behaviors are interrelated with these social systems. Ultimately, social analysis is not achieved through an intellectual labor of solely describing social systems but by the transformation of the human condition, which is dependent on human agency and collective action.

The primary tool we used to facilitate the development to examine the interplay between individuals and social systems was participatory action research (PAR). PAR is an ideal method both for facilitating student learning about post-Katrina New Orleans and for assisting students with conducting a social analysis concerning a social phenomenon of interest to them (McIntyre 2007). Students identified an area of interest for their project before leaving for New Orleans. They were then placed in a service setting related to their interest. For example, if a student was interested in examining post-Katrina New Orleans through the lens of education, he or she was placed in a school setting. Participation in service informs social analysis while at the same time contributing skills and knowledge to community partners. To this end we established a working agreement between our students and their community partners that concretized that the central purpose of the students' volunteerism was to deepen their awareness of how their respective research issues interfaced with the work and lives of the people at their given service site.

We expected the students to draw from a range of data sources while developing these reports: scholarly literature, empirical evidence, policy documents, mass media, their field experiences, and their personal and group reflections. All PAR reports were required to have the following five sections: (1) a statement of the issue, which was to inform the reader about why he or she should care about the student's research issue; (2) a review of the literature, which was to provide the reader with a cogent summary of the existing research or scholarship on the student's research issue; (3) a summary of the PAR process, which was to provide the reader with a synopsis of how the student conducted her or his social analysis; (4) a report of the emergent findings, which was to illustrate for the reader the key lessons the student learned as a result of both her or his social analysis and the overall academic immersion experience; and (5) a discussion of the study implications, or a statement about the meaning of the student's social analysis to the lives and work of their community partners and the recovery efforts in post-Katrina New Orleans.

Course Structure

Our academic immersion course or our academic immersion experience (we use both terms interchangeable throughout this chapter) was titled New Orleans: The Legacy of Katrina. Our course grew out of our respective personal interests, scholarly agendas, and service commitments with the aftermath of post-Katrina New Orleans. Although the nature of our relationships to New Orleans, as well as the Gulf Coast, differs, we were personally affected by the inhumanity of the aftermath. The personal did become political and in the winter of 2006 we began having conversations about how the two of us could respond to this catastrophe.

Global Education

We wanted to create a course that allowed for a rigorous academic preparation in social analysis that was situated in an immersion experience. However, there was no format in our College of Arts and Sciences that would facilitate a credit-bearing academic course that is designed to function as a study-abroad course but whose focus and destination is a US domestic city. In order for this course to be approved as a new course offering, by our College of Arts and Sciences curriculum committee, we were informed that we would have to apply for approval under the aegis of the Seattle University Office for Education Abroad.

Given that this course was not really abroad (and the problematic nature of identifying post-Katrina New Orleans as "foreign"), we proposed that it be considered under a broader rubric of global education. From its inception, our course applied a global perspective to conceptualize the aftermath; therefore, when we were asked to operate our course through the Education Abroad Office, it was mainly to gain access to staff to handle administrative details, salary for faculty, handling of student fees as well as scholarship assistance for students. In addition, we recognized that the culture of New Orleans is different from that experienced by the majority of Seattle University students. Nearly all of the twenty-three students enrolled in our academic immersion course had grown up in the Pacific Northwest (Washington, Idaho, or Montana). While eight were nonwhite students, or students of color (African-American and Latina), they too had lived their lives in the Pacific Northwest. For a student population whose lived experiences and worldview are rooted in the Pacific Northwest, the journey to post-Katrina New Orleans was an encounter with difference.

Learning Objectives

By taking students to post-Katrina New Orleans, we were able to create a learning experience that embodied the crosscutting themes of global justice education. Our course had five core learning objectives: (1) to explore the social history and culture of New Orleans; (2) to evaluate how government and grassroots organizations respond to natural disasters; (3) to identify who is benefiting from the New Orleans redevelopment; (4) to learn from organizers, artists, and survivors in New Orleans; and (5) to devise ethical and just responses for how society and communities should respond to natural disasters.

Course Design

How did we design our course to meet these learning objectives? We developed a two-phased approach to meeting the learning outcomes for this course. First, there was an on-campus component, which involved five three-hour class sessions that were held in spring 2008. These five sessions addressed the following: the socio-historical context of South Louisiana, the politics of natural disasters, grassroots movements in post-Katrina New Orleans, the right to return movement, and conducting PAR.

Phase two of our course was the ten-day immersion experience in New Orleans. In short, this segment of the two-phased course brought to life the textbook knowledge that students were acquiring in the pre-academic immersion experience. It is important to note that our students worked in small groups as they volunteered with community partners related to their research interest. Because of the time constraints placed on any academic service learning course it is vital that faculty instructors be meticulous in the planning of the service learning experience and pragmatic when establishing the learning outcomes.

The students' time in post-Katrina New Orleans involved a range of service, research, and cultural immersion activities. These activities included tours of historical landmarks in post-Katrina New Orleans, a very emotional assessment of the state of the Ninth Ward, and site visits to the remnants of post-Katrina New Orleans's public housing industry. Each day's events was followed by a debriefing and a period of reflection as well as time for students to journal about their day's experiences.

After the students' first day of service, we met as planned to debrief and reflect. As we listened to the majority of our students speak with great excitement about their first day of service. The students were excited to know that they had been placed with community partners that had great relevancy given their research interest and their respective reasons for enrolling in this academic immersion experience. As instructors of the course, we were delighted to know that we had identified community partners that allowed students to align the course's learning objectives with their own personal ambitions.

Assessment Procedures

In order to assess the students' learning and the impact of this course on promoting social justice, we reviewed feedback from three key sources: (1) the student evaluations of the course, (2) the students' reflections in their journals as well as in their reflections during our daily debriefings, and (3) the students' PAR reports. Our process for reviewing these data sources was collaborative. Our assessment strategy was to surmise how the students processed their experiences with the course and how the course equipped them to meet the core learning objectives we identified for this academic immersion experience. We plan to conduct a more detailed and empirical assessment of how our community partners viewed, and possibly benefited from, the academic immersion course at a later date.

Enhanced Learning through Student Experiences

Our academic immersion course had a profound impact on our students' learning about post-Katrina New Orleans. If our numerical course evaluation is any indication of the impact and success of this course (4.5 on a 5-point scale), our students were transformed by their involvement in this academic experience. Quantitative feedback on a course evaluation; however, can only reveal so much, and we found the students' reflections in their field journals, their conversations during our group debriefings, and their analysis in their final reports to be immensely informative to our understanding of the students' experiences with the course.

Although we never had illusions that our students would affect systemic social transformation, as part of their academic immersion experience, our students did accomplish many tasks. These tasks, furthermore, were pivotal in assisting community partners in their recovery efforts. In addition to the direct service activities that some students conducted, students also wrote grant applications, prepared a community assessment, gave class presentations to encourage children to dream of college, and so on. Our students completed their service commitments with rich and varied academic as well as personal experiences. The breadth and depth of our students' experiences in post-Katrina New Orleans are captured by their student reflections on the academic immersion experience. Are review of the students' reflections allowed us to identify the following six thematic areas: making the connections, dealing with difference, bridge building, becoming a stakeholder, transformation through personal stories, faith and justice, and student experience through the lens of race.

Making the Connections

We wanted students to be able to see links or intersections between the types of social issues they were confronting and the personal implications on both their community partners and themselves. One student who worked with a charter school reflected on how her service experience intersected with a tour the class took of the public housing crisis in post-Katrina New Orleans. We were drawn to this student's reflection because it epitomizes much of what we had hoped students would gain from the overall academic immersion experience. The student, who we will refer to as Amber, wrote the following in her reflection journal: "I was surprised to learn how housing and owning a home/property influences and rules others systems, such as education. . . . Education is my passion and I really want to close the achievement gap, and [I] want to help students and schools that are behind or underperforming. Now, I know to keep a close eye on the politics of housing" (student journal entry, June 28, 2008)."

Two of our students who were majors in environmental studies had the opportunity to work with a grassroots organization in the Ninth Ward. Although these two students spent their service days working on a variety of highly relevant projects (e.g., developing a community farm in the Lower Ninth Ward, restoring a wetland near the Mississippi River Delta, and removing black mold from damaged homes), their greatest learning seemed to stem from their personal challenges. These challenges, moreover, were the result of the sheer magnitude of the recovery effort and the limitations of their community partner to address this problem in its entirety. The following passage from the reflection journal of one of the students, who we will call Beth, aptly captures both the frustration and the students' personal growth in these moments of difficulty.

> I left today's [service task] feeling relatively unsatisfied. I felt as though despite all the work we had done and seen done today it was all nowhere near enough; not even a dent in the damage Hurricane Katrina had left behind. . . . It is especially daunting because at this point the [community partner] seems to be entirely at the mercy and generosity of the public and private investment. . . . If individual people or companies do not take an interest in the wetlands, then there will be no money with which to deal with any of the problems: at this point very few seems to care. (Student journal entry, June 30, 2008)

It was common for our students to have feelings of frustration and doubt, as demonstrated by the previous excerpt, throughout their time in post-Katrina New Orleans.

Dealing with Difference

We felt it was our responsibility to remind constantly the students of their reasons or intentions for embarking on this academic immersion experience. Are we here to save the people of post-Katrina New Orleans? On the other hand, will the social change we desire come from our ability to heed the lessons of your service and immersion experiences? The former question led students to recognize and to question their cultural assumptions about the people of New Orleans—especially its poor and its racial minority communities. Students began to see that a model of service rooted in saving people assumes that the people you are working with are helpless, incapable, and culturally deficient. Beyond the unspoken assumptions that underlie this question is a taken-for-granted power dynamic wherein students are seen as all-powerful and their community partners are consequentially dependent upon their benevolence.

For a group of our social work students, who volunteered at a day-care center for low-income families, the need to go beyond their good intentions was a difficult process. The students who worked at this placement site had also had prior experience working in daycares back in Seattle. The students initially brought their experiences with the Seattle daycare centers and their well-honed theories of child development to their service experience. The students would discuss and write about the "problems" they observed in the daycare center with certitude and self-righteous judgment. The students were not so quick to disabuse themselves of their ethnocentrism. One of the students, who we will refer to as Casey, happened to be a child psychology major. Casey provided an account of her service learning experience at the daycare that illustrates the tensions and the contradictions that some students struggled with when confronting difference.

> Some things I noticed [at the daycare] were very different from the daycare I work at in Seattle. . . . One thing I learned about were foster grandmothers. I had never heard of them before. They were older women who come spend time in each room [with the children] and act as a grandmother would. . . . The experiences at the daycare was such a cultural shock; it is just so different then the daycare system in Seattle. As I left [the daycare], I wondered if this is how all daycares are in New Orleans or just at [my service site]. (Student journal entry, June 22, 2008)

Casey's comparison between her service experience and her daycare experience back in Seattle was a constant refrain in her reflexive process. She went on to write:

> We [she and her group members] wanted to hold the babies, or at least interact with them because it seems as if the people who worked [at the service site] don't really interact with the babies at all. They just feed them, burp them, and then put them in a swing or back to bed. There doesn't seem to be much schedule to it; the babies eat when they want and sleep when they want and for as long as they want. This is very different from the daycares I am familiar with back home. (Student journal entry, June 22, 2008)

Although valid concerns for child safety were voiced, these students were seldom self-reflexive about why they had such visceral reactions to how the staff operated the daycare. Upon deeper reflection and through a more personable interaction with the daycare staff; however, the students soon came to question their own cultural stereotypes. Nevertheless, Casey's reflections still remind us that when some students encounter difference they have the potential either to be transformed by the experience or to become more invested in their cultural stereotypes about the other—as indicated by her concluding remarks on her overall academic immersion experience:

> It was very evident that African Americans have their own culture in the South. Their culture is what guides everything else . . . even at [the service site] there seemed to be a culture that was based on lack of motivation and understanding. The staff could care less. It seemed as if the daycare teachers hated their jobs. They also did a lot of unsafe, unsanitary and in general unhealthy things. . . . I think it was because they didn't have the knowledge. (Student journal entry, July 1, 2008)

Although we were both pained and puzzled by Casey's overall assessment, we believe it is a brutal and necessary reminder that even our best intentions may not lead to the anticipated outcomes we would have liked.

Building Bridges

The importance of bridge building was a common social justice implication that emerged out of the student reports. We noticed that many of our students were able to translate their service into a blueprint for how their home academic institution (i.e., Seattle University) could remain connected with their community partners. A student, who we will refer to as Dawn, worked with a low-income housing advocacy group in post-Katrina New Orleans put forth the following vision for bridge building:

> Seattle University has the opportunity to invest in and continue a relationship with [my service site]. This relationship would provide

students with real-world experience to combat racial discrimination in the housing sector of New Orleans. My service site is also very focused in fighting for public housing, which is an area of interest for many Seattle University students concerned for social justice . . . potential information learned from this interaction can be used here, at home, in Seattle University's relationship with our own low-income housing community of Yesler Terrace. There is much to be learned from [my service site] on Seattle University's part on how to successfully and positively interact with low-income communities. (Student journal entry, June 27, 2008)

Building effective and sustainable bridges between a community partner and an academic institution is a social justice issue. Furthermore, it is contingent upon how we engage with our community partners. When debriefing with some of our community partners they were quick to thank us for not patronizing them or assuming that they had nothing of value to offer for our students' intellectual and personal growth. Because we prepared our students to conduct themselves as social justice workers, we stressed that it is important to be mindful of our impact on the community. Humility matters and is part of social justice in action. When thinking about the role that humility plays when doing social justice work, we were reminded of the following passage from a student we will refer to as Erica. Erica, who worked with staff and students at one of the growing number of charter schools in post-Katrina New Orleans, demonstrated her social justice training when making the following observation in her PAR report.

Our seemingly menial task of painting the stairways in the school was greatly appreciated by everyone who walked by. I believe that our simple presence in the school was beneficial to [my service site]. Being there and showing that we care about them and want to take the time to come and get to know the school, the students, and the staff was very beneficial to the spirit of the school. Finally, I believe that being able to talk with and get to know some of the children while they helped us paint or while we taught a class helped them to learn about different places and get exposed to new things that they otherwise might have not been exposed to. My group members and

I were able to create strong relationships with the students and faculty at our partner site and a relationship between [my service site] and Seattle University will be easily sustained. (PAR report, August 1, 2008)

Becoming a Stakeholder

A central component both to the students' PAR project and to the academic immersion experience was for students to imagine themselves as key stakeholders. We fought against any desire for students to accept a more detached standpoint or to position themselves as tourists of other people's suffering and struggle.

While volunteering at a charter school, a group of our students encountered numerous opportunities to become key stakeholders. One student, who we will refer to as Felicia, described in her PAR report how she witnessed one of the highly inexperienced teachers at the school lose control of her class on multiple occasions. Felecia recalled how she worked as a student mentor back in Seattle. When an opportunity presented itself for Felicia to show leadership, while also being mindful that she did not usurp the authority of the teacher, she did. Felicia explains that experience as follows:

> While my student and I sat in the hallway, three other students were put out of the class by [the teacher]. Those students were allowed to return to class after several minutes. One of the students was a girl whom I had observed being exceptionally responsive and respectful during class. I asked her why she was sent out and she said it was because she did not have her workbook. This student was in the midst of looking for it when [the teacher] called her out for not having it. Just when the girl started to explain to [the teacher] why she did not have her workbook out, [the teacher] sent her out. This student stood in the hallway, next to the classroom door, for at least fifteen minutes. While we sat in the hallway, she pulled out her workbook and we worked on a few pages of it together. (PAR report, August 1, 2008)

From this excerpt, we learn that Felicia had a choice. She could have ignored this student as to not interfere with the teacher's punishment;

however, Felicia realized that an opportunity presented itself for her to show initiative and leadership by intervening in the life of a child who was otherwise distraught by her treatment.

It would have been easy to label this teacher as a bad teacher, but Felicia brought an analytical eye to the situation. In her PAR report, she goes beyond a common perception of many public school teachers as bad teachers. Felicia was able to see the teacher and the situation in a broader socio-political context. She was aware of the absence of experienced and credentialed educators in the post-Katrina New Orleans school system. Felicia made the following astute social analysis of the situation:

> The need for teachers in the schools creates a sort of catch-22. There are not enough qualified teachers who want to teach in low-income, failing schools, where the district has at-will contracts (seen in most charter schools) and has eliminated the teacher's union, so the schools are desperate to take what they can get. In New Orleans unqualified teachers are even more problematic due to the loss of school records during the hurricane. Information about special education students and their specialized curriculum have been lost. Counselors and school psychologists, another resource that the schools are lacking, are needed to re-evaluate students and create Individualized Education Programs. Without this information, teachers are at a disadvantage to implement the most effective teaching methods, and students are at a loss of a quality education. (PAR report, August 1, 2008)

Transformation through Personal Stories

We did not know that personal stories of Hurricane Katrina survivors would be such a powerful force to radicalize or call our students to action. In a number of the students' PAR reports, we saw references to how encounters with different survivors—some planned and some by chance—shaped the students' view of social justice.

As case in point, Mr. Harris (a lifelong resident of the Tremé neighborhood in New Orleans) talked with his students about how his community came together in the 1970s to fight to prevent the city from destroying its beloved and most historic community in the name of urban development. He went on to share that this spirit of fighting is not rare in New Orleans and that it is with such spirit that he and other survivors plan to rebuild their city. Our students' thinking about social justice was impacted by accounts from survivors like Mr. Harris. Gina, as we refer to her, was one of those students, and she wrote the following in her journal: "As I reflect, the more I realize how important protests are. Not necessarily a physical protest, but a political protest. By this I mean that people with power and resources need to use them. They need to take advantage of them in a very real way—like a protest" (student reflection journal, June 21, 2008)." Gina's ability to articulate how grassroots folks spoke truth to power is further indication of how this academic immersion experience enhanced student learning and their commitment to using social analysis as a method for social justice. Her call for social change recognizes the need for everyday people to be part of the process.

Harriet is another student whose thinking about social justice was influenced by her experience with Mr. Harris. Harriet was particularly attracted to Mr. Harris's passion for social justice. She expressed her admiration as follows: "Our first tour, with Mr. Harris of Tremé, was so full of life and *fight*—he's been fighting his whole life for this town. Seeing Congo Square and hearing its history really gave me a better idea of why so many people feel a personal, historical connection to this city" (student journal reflection, June 21, 2008). It was that sense of personal and political connection to post-Katrina New Orleans that we were most hoping for our students. A type of connection, moreover, that would allow them to have empathy for the conditions that continue to plague the city and the desire to want to fight for a more just and humane society.

Faith and Justice

For some of our students the vision of a more just and humane post-Katrina New Orleans was supported by their faith traditions. The Catholic heritage of New Orleans is evident throughout this city's history, culture, architecture and people. One of our students, who we will refer to as Ina, would often reflect on her experiences through the prism of her faith. The following excerpt from Ina's journal eloquently captures the intersection of faith and social analysis:

> Today I went to St. Louis Cathedral for mass. . . . This cathedral has played an important role in New Orleans. . . . At the beginning of mass, the Archbishop welcomed all parishioners, those who are from parishes who have not yet been rebuilt, as well as a special welcome to those who have come to help New Orleans rebuild. I also thought it was interesting that they televise the mass for those in prison and in the hospital. It seems as if the church is trying to play a large role in the city after the storm . . . and from what I have witnessed so far, the church has been helping its parishioners, parishes, and schools rebuild. (Student journal entry, June 29, 2008)

Student Experiences through the Lens of Race

As we assessed student feedback from the course, we soon realized that the impact of the course on the students and on their level of social justice was filtered through the students' diverse racial locations. Our white students often engaged with and processed the academic immersion experience in different ways than our nonwhite students. It would not be until the seventh day of the academic immersion experience that we would realize the effects of the students' varying levels of race awareness.

A critical race moment in the academic-immersion experience came when our students attended a workshop on undoing racism, which was organized by a community partner. Because this organization has an international reputation for its powerful antiracism workshops, we felt this opportunity would be a rich supplement to course readings and the students' experiences while in post-Katrina New Orleans. Many of our white students, however, were shocked by the workshop's definition of racism. The workshop facilitators defined racism as racial prejudice plus power (i.e., white privilege). Based on this definition, the workshop presenters argued that only and all white people are racist, because only and all white people have power (or racial privilege). This argument enraged some of our white students. They refused to participate during the workshop and some even came to resent that they were obligated to take part in the workshop. While reflecting back on her discomfort with the workshop, one of our white students—who we will refer to as Jessica—wrote the following in her journal: "At this point [in the workshop] I feel incredibly helpless. I just don't see how this *static* definition is a step forward at all. All it does for me is separate, and the point of undoing racism is to stop separation. . . . All white people are racist, and Blacks can't be? What is the point of this?" (student reflection journal, June 28, 2008).

Even though some of our white students were angered by the workshop's framework for racism, the majority of the nonwhite students and some of the other white students had a very different reaction. One white female student, who we will refer to as Karen, had a different sensibility about the workshop and she even critiqued some of the reactions of her white peers.

> I understand people's frustrations about the format and decorum of the workshop, but I also feel that they [the White students] focused too much on that while discussing the experience. . . . I think it was just the specific word "racist" that was upsetting to them. It was just a small part of the presentation, and they [the White students] should have been focusing on the institutional issues that [the workshop facilitators] talked a lot more about. (Student reflection journal, June 28, 2008)

Many of the white students felt attacked and unsafe during the workshop. According to one white student, who we will refer to as Lauren, "It took me a while to get ready to write this journal entry. Today we went to an undoing racism workshop . . . It was one of the most difficult, trying, and uncomfortable days ever" (student reflection journal, June 28, 2008). Lauren's comments might give one the impression that the nonwhite students felt safe during the workshop. However, a number of our nonwhite students also expressed strong feelings of disappointment and frustration with their white peers. For example, Melanie, as we will refer to her, was a nonwhite student who made the following observation:

> Frankly, I was embarrassed to be part of our class. Even in the van, leaving the workshop, students were being sarcastic. . . . I felt like

this showed they didn't listen. . . . As I thought about our debriefing
. . . one of the things I found most disgusting about it was that many
of the White students in our class admitted that they did not think
racism occurred in Seattle, and were not able to draw connections
between New Orleans and things happening in Seattle. When we
[i.e., some non-White students] told them that there was racism,
they tried to explain to us why we were wrong and that just pissed
me off. I thought some of the comments made were ridiculous, igno-
rant, offensive, and just plain stupid. (Student reflection journal,
June 28, 2008)

As instructors, it was never our intention to make students feel unsafe.
We spent much time debriefing this experience both in groups and
with individuals modeling interracial dialogue between ourselves (one
instructor is African American and one is white). Although extremely
challenging, the workshop experience provided an invaluable opportunity for us to remind the students about how our racial locations impact
our interpretation of what happened in the aftermath of Hurricane
Katrina. Ultimately, this workshop reminded us that we need to cultivate brave spaces or courageous conversations about race, opposed to
the more palatable format associated with safe spaces, if we are to
prepare students to engage with the racial realities of post-Katrina New
Orleans.

Conclusion

Our assessment of the students' feedback indicates that our academic
immersion course was very successful in meeting its five learning
objectives.

First, students left this experience with a more comprehensive and
firsthand understanding of the social history and culture of New
Orleans. They toured the city, learned from local experts about the
history and cultural heritage of the city and region, and saw firsthand
the devastation and rebuilding efforts. This provided the historical and
structural foundation for a more complete understanding of the realities of post-Katrina New Orleans.

Second, our students were able to analyze critically key social issues
related to the recovery of post-Katrina New Orleans. Through their

service work, their reflections, and their PAR projects, they were led to seek the root causes of the social dilemmas they encountered and to evaluate the societal response to Katrina as they processed their own role and responsibility in the recovery efforts. Through readings, lectures, and service they examined how varying levels of social institutions have contributed to or tried to respond to the problems the city faces.

Third, as students explored the impacts of the storm and rebuilding efforts, they were driven to examine who was really benefiting for redevelopment efforts. Such interrogation of social systems must guide any challenge to social structures. For example, students were strongly impacted by the tour of public housing projects where they saw locked and empty buildings full of owners' possessions three years later even though there had been no storm or flood damage. They were called to question the amount of money spent to keep such buildings closed. They wondered why the inhabitants had not been allowed to gather their belongings from undamaged buildings and where those persons were now. Would they be allowed to live in the new housing being very gradually built? Would such housing be affordable? What role did race and social class have in the demolition of public housing units?

Fourth, learning from organizers, artists, and survivors in post-Katrina New Orleans proved to be a significant modality for the group's intellectual and personal growth. As evidenced in the student reflections quoted above, certain experiences stood out in this regard. Many noted that Mr. Harris's personal narrative of social action was particularly inspiring. However, he was only one of many who challenged them to think differently about the world.

Finally, we were impressed with our students' ability to devise ethical and just responses to the aftermath based on their academic service experience. The development of a critical social analysis of the plight of post-Katrina New Orleans was always central to our course. The PAR reports provided the most meaningful feedback with which to answer the fifth learning objective. Unlike the more process-oriented and spontaneous feedback our students provided us in their group discussions and journal reflections, these called upon a more reasoned response to many of the systemic and societal issues students encountered. Their suggestions regarding the more equitable allocation of resources to financial, housing, educational, neighborhood, and health/mental health needs were grounded in theory and in practice.

Nonetheless, pedagogical challenges did arise and we would offer the following suggestions to others who seek to develop similar courses. It became clear that an academic pretrip discussion of race and racism was insufficient preparation for some of our students given their life experience. In the future, we would explore how to better assess student cultural competency and if necessary offer experientially based learning such as the racism workshop prior to the trip when students would have more time to process and struggle with the information offered.

At the end of the day, our students brought more than their good intentions to post-Katrina New Orleans. Over the course of their academic-immersion experience, our students were able to identify who is gaining and who is losing in the new New Orleans. Our students were able to do this social justice work, and to be transformed in the process, because of their ability to apply the foundational concepts of social analysis when engaging with distressed communities in post-Katrina New Orleans.

5   Adopting the Mission of Social Justice in a Political Science Department

JOHN F. FREIE AND SUSAN M. BEHUNIAK

As members of a political science department at a Jesuit college, we have asked ourselves many times: What is our mission and what does it mean for us?

The answers, for indeed there are several, have not come easily.

The five full-time faculty have been constantly pulled in different directions by such practical considerations as marketing concerns, teaching philosophies, our standing as a noncore department, and the practices and content of our very discipline. However, committed to the belief that Jesuit education must infuse our departmental mission to the extent that we be distinctive from other political science departments, we turned for guidance to the principles of Jesuit higher education as summarized in Le Moyne College's mission statement. The words were inspiring, but their meaning for our educational practices were unclear. How exactly to give life to the terms such as diverse learning community, academic excellence, whole person, search for meaning and value, leadership, service, and promotion of "a more just society." Could we simply choose to employ rigorous standards and call it a day, or did we need to address each feature and check it off as if it were part of a to-do list?

What follows, then, is the story of how one department transformed itself in order to encourage the transformation of others. It is our department's story of the interpretation of the Jesuit concept of participatory citizenship related to significant events in Central America (Calero 1994; Ellacuría 1982). It is a somewhat surprising story because forming consensus turned out to be easier concerning what we perceived as the larger issues, demonstrating the wisdom of the adage that the devil is in the details.

Taking the Jesuit Mission to Heart

The department's 1992 evaluation by the Faculty Senate Curriculum Committee was the impetus for the changes that would unfold over the coming years. In particular, one of our outside evaluators noted that although we claimed to follow a traditional political science curriculum, we often substituted it with special topics courses on contemporary issues, and although the college articulated a commitment to Jesuit mission, we were silent about how we connected with it. So although the review noted that we were working at a flat-out run, it also questioned whether we were finding the space to do the teaching that we wanted to do, using the pedagogies we thought best, and connecting to the Jesuit mission in ways other than intellectual rigor. The report concluded bluntly: Despite our work ethic and dedication to teaching, we were not meeting our obligations to our students.

As much as this conclusion stung, what made it easier to accept was the path proposed to rectify the situation: explore how our orientation toward teaching politics rather than political science and our leanings toward the use of engaged pedagogies over lecturing were compatible with Jesuit educational philosophy. This avenue for change was viewed as promising by each of us in the department, although not for identical reasons. Some of us were most attracted to the pedagogical possibilities; some to connecting with Jesuit values; and some to developing an outside the mainstream curriculum. So, there was easy agreement on the direction we would go, but we still had little idea of how to get there or even where it was we hoped to arrive.

It soon became clear that we had to begin by educating ourselves as to what comprised Jesuit education. Through reading, discussion, conference participation, and reflection, a central theme emerged. What spoke to us most clearly was the Jesuit commitment to educate students about social justice issues by not simply informing them, but by encouraging them to act to transform themselves and their world. We were particularly struck by the words of Ignacio Ellacuría, SJ, who seven years before his 1989 assassination in El Salvador, gave the commencement address at Santa Clara University in which he challenged educators to use their unique talents and resources in the pursuit of social justice:

The university must carry out this general commitment with the means uniquely at its disposal: we as an intellectual community must analyze causes; use imagination and creativity together to discover the remedies to our problems; communicate to our constituencies a consciousness that inspires the freedom of self-determination; educate professionals with a conscience, who will be the immediate instruments of such a transformation; and constantly hone an educational institution that is both academically excellent and ethically oriented. (Ellacuría 1982)

This theme was one that our diverse department—Catholic or not, activist or not, male or not, feminist or not, conservative or not, tenured or not—could support. Later, we would find further inspiration in a speech of the then superior general of the Society of Jesus Peter-Hans Kolvenbach, given again at Santa Clara, that articulated what a social justice orientation could mean for our students:

Students, in the course of their formation, must let the gritty reality of this world into their lives, so they can learn to feel it, think about it critically, respond to its suffering, and engage it constructively. They should learn to perceive, think, judge, choose, and act for the rights of others, especially the disadvantaged and the oppressed. (Kolvenbach 2001, 155)

So, we accepted the challenges presented by Ellacuría and Kolvenbach to teach for social justice in the real world through participatory citizenship. With a better understanding of what our role could be as a political science department at a Jesuit institution, we returned to the observations and questions noted in our 1992 departmental review: first, whether our adoption of the standard political science curriculum limited us in our ability to teach about social justice; and second, whether pedagogies could be deliberately developed to inject "gritty reality" into the lives of our students.

In tackling these two issues, we soon found it necessary to face a third: the relationship between a department transformation and the larger context of the college as a whole. Our efforts to change, then, would also have to weigh if not actually confront a variety of factors: student culture, other academic departments, the college core, and the entire administrative organization. Transformative change, we discovered, implicates the very institution itself.

The Discipline of Political Science

Was political science getting in the way of teaching about politics? Our answer was a qualified, yes and no. As is true of most academic disciplines, political science is primarily concerned with explaining phenomena, in our case political behavior. While an important strain of the academic literature deals with normative issues including social justice, the dominant part of the discipline stresses scientific explanation, "professional detachment," and empirical studies that create data, analyze them, and build theories based on the data. The scientific study of politics, although challenged, continues to dominate the publications of the first-tier political science journals, the education of the professoriate, and less directly, the teaching of political science in undergraduate programs.

Our curriculum reflected this detached orientation. In addition to requiring an introductory course on American Politics, we also required majors to take a course on the Scope of Political Science and another on the Methods of Political Science (which was supplemented by a four-credit statistics course.) Upper-level American Politics courses emphasized the usual national players: Congress, president, Supreme Court, state politics, interest groups, and electoral behavior. (One exception was a course on Women and Politics that had been taught for years as a law course.) In addition, we had one course each on Public Administration and Public Policy. Within Public Law were two courses on Constitutional Law and one on Judicial Systems. Political Theory courses were divided from each other by either chronology (e.g., ancient versus medieval) or location (e.g., American). There was an introductory course to Comparative Politics and some regional course offerings, and a cluster of upper-level International Relations courses. We supplemented the college core by requiring majors to take two courses in a foreign language, two in American history, and three from the other social sciences. But of greater significance than the topics of the courses we taught was the uneasy feeling we all had about our discipline—that it had "become increasingly detached and irrelevant to political practice" (Davis 2005, 2). Yet, it would have been difficult to differentiate us from any other political science department or to point to something that owed itself to the Jesuit mission of the college. So the answer appeared to be yes, political science was limiting us.

But why were we accepting these limitations? Although the curriculum in some disciplines is regulated by external accrediting organizations and others may be more tightly controlled because of their presence in the college core, we were restricted by neither of these considerations. Our only parameters were those that were internal—a result of being socialized into our discipline. But if the curriculum is to be used to enhance Jesuit education, faculty in every discipline must struggle with what is possible given their particular position both within their discipline as well as at their college or university. In the curricular discussions that followed, we deliberately stepped outside the boundaries of mainstream political science to ask how teaching in the Jesuit tradition should affect what we taught and how. Melding the challenge of Jesuit education to what we believed should be the central focus of our discipline—politics—we concluded that in order for students to lead lives sensitive to issues of social justice they must come to view themselves as active democratic citizens who embrace participatory citizenship. This is citizenship that demonstrates an active interest and is capable of initiating or participating in various developments in the nation and the world.

Citizenship, then, became the touchstone that linked us as political scientists to Jesuit education. The call to citizenship involves more than simply voting, paying taxes, or obeying the law; by necessity it calls students to a participatory orientation that is along the lines sketched out by Benjamin Barber (1984, 117) in his book *Strong Democracy*: "It rests on the idea of a self-governing community of citizens who are united less by homogeneous interests than by civic education and who are made capable of common purpose and mutual action by virtue of their civic attitudes and participatory institutions rather than their altruism or their good nature."

Although the citizenship focus made sense to us, we also knew it came with risks. While most of our discipline would be addressing politics from the top down through the study of political elites, we would be challenging this orientation by a bottom-up approach that made ordinary citizens the starting point for analysis. Such a departure from the mainstream of one's discipline could result in some negative consequences: Would we too closely resemble a high school "civics" program? Were there appropriate textbooks available? Would this approach make us less marketable in the future or (perhaps worse) less publishable? (And any department that receives outside certification would most likely have even more perilous concerns.) In the end, our decision was easier than would be expected because it came down to the fact that this was something we wanted to do and even agreed was important to do. An unexpected result was that the theme of citizenship gave our department more purpose than just the teaching of political science; now we were engaged in a joint effort to teach our discipline in a way to promote something we believed in—social justice.

Transforming the Curriculum

Therefore, our first step in educating for participatory citizenship was to revise our curriculum accordingly. To do that, in 1993 we invited to our campus Benjamin Barber, a political theorist who was at that time director of the Walt Whitman Center for Culture and Politics of Democracy at Rutgers. With his help we began to conceptualize how the citizenship theme could reshape our curriculum. These revisions would eventually test our pedagogies and which elements of the academic environment were in place or were needed to sustain them.

Citizenship theme. The most obvious starting point for introducing the citizenship theme was in the 101 course, Introduction to American Politics. This course is now organized around the theme of an ongoing debate that exists in the United States between elite democracy and popular democracy (Miroff et al. 2010). Some of our other courses would see no change in title but would now contain a reoriented perspective: Congress would focus on the significance of representation; the meaning of "justice" would animate study of the Supreme Court; and Modern Political Theory would thematically question the use of power (i.e., who has it, who does not, how is it used, and for whom) rather than wading through a historical list of great philosophers. No matter what we were teaching, we all committed to incorporate some aspect of citizenship within our courses whether it be questions, literature, or data about participation, rights, responsibilities, theory, conflicts, or values.

Revision of Scope. Perhaps the best example of change within a prior existing course is how the Scope of Political Science course was thoroughly revised to respond to our new department commitments. The essence of what comprises the discipline is still very much a part of the course, but three additional components were added: a week-long study of Jesuit education, our departmental response to it, and guest presentations by each of the five of us about how we attempt to synthesize our professional activities within the discipline with our commitment to Jesuit education. Students are encouraged to become a part of this ongoing reflection; in fact, by course end they write a paper in which they situate themselves within the discipline in light of the department's educational vision.

Unique courses. Elective courses often mirror the research interests of particular faculty members. Why not, then, create courses that mirrored the mission of the department? Therefore, another aspect of our approach was to create new courses that would directly address issues relevant to social justice and participatory citizenship. Thus, we have developed courses such as Social Activism, Environmental Politics, International Human Rights, and a course offered at no other school, Student Rights. The subject matter of these courses directly touches upon aspects of Jesuit education while emphasizing the responsibilities of citizens to be attentive to issues and to effectuate change. And although a shift in content was necessary, these courses are still true to the discipline of political science. Democratic theorists agree. Forming students who will engage in politics means developing "foundational knowledge of democratic principles and an understanding of complex social, legal, and political structures and institutions" (Colby et al. 2003, 111). We believe that the best way to teach foundational knowledge is to embed it in courses that connect with social justice issues with the everyday interests of students. This resulted in the most dramatic change regarding our offerings in political theory. With a retirement, we deliberately sought and hired a new political theorist who had a vision of how to replace our chronological courses with concept courses such as War, Peace, and Violence, Democracy and its Critics, and Power and Justice. Political theory traditionally serves as the backbone of political science, but as revised, it also serves as the foundation for social activism.

Requirements. Popular democratic theory has taught us the value of creating spaces or opportunities for political engagement. Knowledge about participation is not enough; there have to be settings conducive to participation. Kolvenbach, using the words of Pope John Paul II, reminds us that solidarity with those who suffer under injustice is learned "through 'contact' rather than through 'concepts'" (2001, 155). The imperative that we must move beyond abstraction to action is one echoed by Colby et al. (2003) in their comprehensive study of civic education. These scholars note that programs that foster generic analytical capacities are insufficient. Engaged citizenship requires something more than rhetoric—it requires first, that education be rooted in commitments to both social justice and activism; and second, that this form of engaged citizenship education must be built upon a knowledge of politics. Service learning (SL) is often promoted as a way of teaching about social justice and civic activism by putting students engaged in the "gritty reality" of the world (Barber and Battistoni 1993). This led us to initiate a requirement of three one-credit SL courses (attached to several of our three-credit courses) for all of our majors.[1]

When a course is offered with the SL credit, all students who register for the three-credit course must also register for the one-credit SL. Although we get complaints and petitions that exceptions be made, we have held firm on this universal rule, and although awkward, it has benefits. First, the SL credit is graded separately and so we can maintain more quality control for the on-site supervisors, encouraging students to perform better than we could if the service was embedded within a four-credit course (i.e., they can fail SL while passing the course.) Second, the SL credit appears on the transcript, denoting its presence and importance as a distinct accomplishment.

Although a separate credit, the value of the SL experience comes from how effectively it is integrated within the course (Markus, Howard, and King 1993). Integration of the SL experience has taken several forms in different courses at different times: separate paper assignments that are tied to course concepts and literature but that incorporate the first-hand experience; class times devoted to discussing student experiences and observations; comparison of SL experiences vis-à-vis the text; additional readings or research about the service site; in-class panels or guest speakers from the host sites; student presentations based on the SL experience; attendance at extracurricular events connected with the site or the issue; and class projects connected to following up on the experience (e.g., a tutoring experience that led students to do fundraising for the program even though they had completed their required number of hours).

Each of our department's members have experienced wonderful moments when students have brought something unexpected back into the classroom based on the SL experience. For example, one semester the Intro students were placed in sites that would bring them into close contact with people who lived in poverty; meanwhile, they read *Class Matters* by correspondents of the *New York Times* (2005), a book that explores how class distinctions powerfully shape education, health care, occupations, and political power. The students were open to this critique of the American dream, but not entirely sympathetic, much less convinced. It was then that one student introduced a story from his service at a soup kitchen: he had been confronted by a homeless man who challenged him about the T-shirt he was wearing. On the T-shirt it said "Charlie's Angels" in reference to the president of the college whose first name was Charlie. The homeless man accused the student of wearing the T-shirt to avoid being confused with those being served: "If you're an angel, then what does that make me?" The shaken student told this story to the class in the voice of a person aggrieved; someone whose good work had not been received with gratitude. This led to a class discussion that was uncomfortable but also unforgettable: Why should the poor show gratitude? Do college students and the poor have stereotypes about each other? What are the expectations of those who serve and those who receive? Whose perceptions about charity inform public policy? And, what would Kolvenbach's notion of solidarity with the poor mean in this specific circumstance?

Rough edges to this program remain, but we persevere in the belief that the experiences connect our students with people in the community who they would not ordinarily meet, that the exchange of learning for service benefits everyone, and that student learning is enhanced when theory can meet practice. Still, SL is not the panacea to the problem of how to engage students in "gritty reality." As we discuss in the next section, it is a useful pedagogy, but it neither can nor should be the only route to attentive citizenship.

The Pedagogy of Politics and the Politics of Pedagogy

Looking back now, it seems like a natural progression in that the question of what we should teach led us to more consciously assess how we teach. Perhaps because of our discipline, we easily accepted the view of classrooms as political environments that contain power relationships. Consequently, we were conscious of and concerned about the pedagogical strategies we employed. Since our goal was to encourage active citizenship, it made sense that the skills of citizens be honed in the classroom. Indeed, it was difficult to imagine how we would encourage students to examine values, question authority, and put beliefs into practice if we demanded that they sit passively taking notes about what we said. Political scientists have argued that positive orientations toward civic activism are learned as a result of both attitudinal change as well as behavioral change and the two often cannot be meaningfully separated (Pateman 1970; Finkel 1985). This is because positive attitudes toward activism often lead to action, but activism itself also often leads to attitudes supportive of those behaviors. Thus, we realized the important link between curricular and pedagogical approaches designed to explore civic activism.

If asking faculty to teach content related to a specific theme is enough to raise eyebrows about academic freedom, suggesting to them how best to teach sets off five alarm sirens. Knowing this, we agreed to disagree. Although our department has broad general agreement on our goals, we also give each professor the latitude to employ pedagogical approaches he or she believes are most effective given the content of the courses, the particular objectives in the course, and the individual level of comfort and skill at using pedagogical techniques. This not only allows each of us to tap into our strengths in teaching, but it also recognizes that students themselves have different learning styles that they can then match with the different professors. Thus, while working within a general framework of an agreed upon theme of active citizenship, we were guided in our diverse teaching approaches by two pedagogical orientations: employing pedagogies of engagement and creating an ethical classroom.

Pedagogies of engagement. Although a majority of college courses are taught primarily relying on lecturing (Shedd 2002), educators who are concerned about teaching for civic activism more commonly employ a variety of pedagogies of engagement (Colby et al. 2003). Pedagogies of engagement adopt the perspective that learning is an active, constructive process in which students struggle to work through problems and connect new ideas with what they already know while faculty support students in these efforts (see, for example, Freire 1970; Hooks 1994; Palmer 2007; Crabtree et al. 2009). Consequently, learning starts by identifying student interests and then developing pedagogies that integrate learning, as much as possible, into the contexts where the ideas will be applied.

As might be expected, we employ a wide variety of student-centered pedagogical techniques. At various times in various courses faculty have used simulations, role-playing, moot courts, debates, field research, collaborative learning, service learning, and individual learning contracts. Student assignments have included: academic journals, video-production, poster sessions, group research projects that focus on campus problems, research undertaken for conference presentation, analytical essays, college-wide panel presentations, presentations to the board of trustees, policy statements, and even the writing and performing of a song and an original play. Several things unite these diverse approaches and activities: they are engaging in that they make students care about what is being studied, they connect students with real-world controversies, they encourage students to assess their own values and make decisions, and they remind students that their choices have real consequences for real people.

Jesuit education calls upon us to treat students as whole individuals, people who feel as well as think. While emotional excitement is possible in the traditional classroom, too often that connection is made by the professor rather than by the students (Finkel 2000). Pedagogies of engagement are based on the premise that learning is enhanced if students are actively and emotionally engaged in their work, so we viewed such approaches as a way of integrating emotion into the classroom. Student-centered pedagogies provide an atmosphere where emotions are often expressed and where teachers can use those emotions to enhance the educational process. Ideally, the professor should design activities and create an environment whereby students feel safe to tackle the difficult task of making sense of what they read and experience, think and feel.

Nevertheless, while there is agreement in our department about the goal of actively engaging students in the learning process, there is disagreement on precisely how to achieve it. For example, while virtually all pedagogies of engagement highlight the importance of discussion, how do we best encourage it? Discussion skills—listening, articulating one's position, developing a persuasive argument, empathizing with others, being able to compromise, and so on—are important skills to learn in college because they are skills that are critical for active democratic citizenship. While our majors are considered by many other faculty as among the most active in classroom discussions, we do not have agreement on the best pedagogical approaches for achieving those results.

For example, on the specific topic of how to improve skills of persuasion, we disagree about the use of debates. Some of us incorporate formal debates into our courses with the intention of teaching research, argumentation, and quick thinking skills. Others of us eschew debates as divisive, and disingenuous as participants are not in fact open to persuasion—that is, open to the possibility that they may be wrong and be willing to change their perspective if that proves to be the case. One pedagogy encourages authority and confidence; the other inquiry and intellectual humility. We do not believe that it is necessary as a department to resolve these differences and we have left the issue to be decided by each individual professor, but we do believe that it is important to remain focused on the overall objective and to continue exploring what pedagogies of engagement mean for us as teachers.

The ethical classroom. Those who write about the "ethical classroom" maintain that students learn not just the subject matter of the course, but they also learn, usually subconsciously, from the manner in which

the class is taught. Educators in elementary and secondary schools tend
to be more concerned about the "hidden curriculum" than are most
college teachers and as a result there is more research and more interest in creating ethical classrooms in these grades than occurs in higher
education (see McClurg 1998; Charney 2002; Lane-Garon 2002). As
we confronted how we could be sensitive to the messages sent in the
hidden curriculum we asked ourselves a number of questions. Can we
ask our students to treat others ethically and reasonably if we are
authoritarian and unreasonable in the classroom? Can we teach active
citizenship but create classroom environments that encourage students
to act as passive receptacles? What are the professor's areas of legitimate authority and what areas of authority should students have control
over? Should rules that regulate discussions in the classroom be established and, if so, who should establish them? Who should create rules
that govern the operation of the class (e.g., due dates for assignments,
penalties for late papers) and what procedures should be followed to
reconsider those rules? These, and other similar questions, were not
questions we had previously considered, but once we started on the
path toward teaching our students to be active democratic citizens by
practicing citizenship they were inevitable. Still, the answers we arrived
at were not universal as each professor responded in his or her unique
fashion to the hidden curriculum.

The Institutional Context

The transformation of a single department can add to the strength of
the Jesuit mission but cannot support the demands of it alone. Transformative education must be guided by a compelling educational philosophy that is implemented throughout the college. What any single
academic program, let alone a single course, can do to teach for social
transformation is limited. Restricted to those who enroll in our courses,
by the extent of our control of the student environment, and by some
administrative decisions, ours remain modest contributions to what
must be a college-wide effort. Among the many different factors, three
areas in particular most affect our effectiveness: other departments,
student life, and the administration.

Other departments. Although we believe that we can be and have been successful at teaching our majors to be active, engaged citizens who will work for social justice, our impact is largely limited to the students who take our courses and participate in our programs. We would like to believe that we are a part of a coordinated college-wide effort to reinterpret ourselves in light of the multiple goals of Jesuit education, but the reality is that few programs or departments have actually done that. Instead, most (and especially the older departments) remain replicas of similar programs found at most other schools, and most of our colleagues remain where we started—unable to explain exactly how they relate to Jesuit education, let alone how they relate to preparing students to transform the world. This suggests, then, the value of interdisciplinary teaching, departmental evaluations, work-shops, campus institutes, and other opportunities for faculty across the campus to discuss, share, and explore their connections to mission and to each other.

Student life. When college graduates look back on their undergraduate years, most first remember their relationships with friends, the extracurricular activities they participated in, and the general feel of being in college (Colby et al. 2003). This area, collectively called "student life," therefore, needs to be consciously addressed by academic departments. The objective should be to link with student life so that it supports what happens in courses; otherwise college culture can undermine academic work by being viewed as oppositional.

Yet, because of the organization of institutions of higher learning, professors usually have little input into how student life is structured. The separation of academic affairs and student life often functions to undermine the Jesuit mission of teaching the whole person as few schools, even Jesuit schools, utilize the arena of student life to shape character. Instead of using student life as a space to extend and supplement academic programs it is viewed as a way of recruiting students. Consequently, millions of dollars are spent not to link student life with courses, but to build luxury dorms, climbing walls, hot tubs, and the like. What's more, professional administrators can resent what is seen as "interference" of faculty into "their" area of responsibility. Our institution is no different.

Nevertheless, things can be done. Student groups that are "spin-offs" from academic departments can be created and extracurricular activities tied into courses can be developed. What's more, classes can sometimes be created that use aspects of the student culture itself as the subject matter of the course, or parts of the course. For example, our department embraced the idea that in order to create active citizens who will transform the world we had to provide a space for active students who will work to transform their campus. Consequently, we very deliberately work with students by supporting them in student organizations, encouraging them to critically examine and to try to change campus culture—including extracurricular components into some of our classes—and offering a unique certificate program that encourages student leadership.

For example, a course titled Student Rights focuses directly on the political position of students in college. The course provides an analytical framework for students to understand the politics of higher education as both a process and as an organization, and even more specifically, their position in this structure. Consistent with the theme of active citizenship for social justice, topics of study emerge from students' experiences, course activities are designed to allow students to critically assess the political and social nature of the college, and students can substitute traditional research projects with those that initiate changes where they believe changes are appropriate. Other courses, such as Environmental Politics, have included service learning components that focused on implementing programs and changing physical structures to make the campus more green. In short, the classroom can be extended to aspects of student life. By doing this, education is no longer viewed by students as something they are being prepared for in the future; students begin to see themselves as citizens who can act to change things now. Eric Gorham (2000, 170) also makes the case for this approach: "A university or college which permits students to appear as citizens is one that offers these adults a chance to participate in its governance, as a part of the *pedagogical* task of those universities."

In addition, we have further institutionalized the linkage between the academic nature of the department and student life by creating a program that encourages student leadership on and off campus, as well as reflection about those experiences. Entitled the Leadership Experience for Activism Program (LEAP), the program requires that students take three courses that include service learning, that they participate in an internship at a nonprofit organization, that they become a leader of a campus group, and that they write a senior research paper about democratic leadership. LEAP provides an important symbolic statement about the department's commitment to producing graduates who will work in organizations committed to social justice as well as providing the major with a small group of students (LEAPers) who will provide leadership on campus in a variety of student-run organizations. To further emphasize our commitment to activism we present a graduation award to the senior, not with the highest grade point average, but with the most outstanding record of service to the community.

As much as we believe that these activities promote the formation of students for others, we as faculty pay a price for this. The major downside to our involvement in student life concerns the issue of time and how ours is eaten up by this work. The more time we spend with students on clubs and planning trips, speakers, and policy initiatives, the less time for our own class preparations, grading, research, and writing—much less for our own lives. And as the college moves to more significantly tie our pay to meritorious performance (usually interpreted as publishing), we wonder about the financial repercussions of our commitment and whether this commitment will weaken should our paychecks suffer. There also seems to be movement toward diverting resources away from teaching and programmatic issues and toward research. Three examples: (1) the college allows faculty to apply for a reduced teaching load (of six instead of seven three-credit courses) in order to pursue a research agenda, but not for developing a course, or for extraordinary service; (2) rank and tenure requirements are being revised to formalize outside reviews of faculty publications, yet changing our student evaluation instrument that assumes we are all lecturers is not on the agenda; and (3) the Center for Faculty Excellence, a one-person operation devoted to the enhancement of teaching, has been eliminated.

Another issue, (but one that admittedly makes us smile), is that quite understandably, administrators become uneasy when students become politically active. Our students cause trouble. They have created their own college newspaper when they believed the campus paper had been "captured" by the administration; they have held informational sessions in the dorms advising residents about their rights regarding warrantless searches and seizures; they researched, obtained cost estimates, and proposed improved dormitory safety measures; and they challenged the legality of Resident Life's attempt to tie the distribution of wristbands (that gave them entrée to a popular student social event) to proof that they had filled out a US census form.

A recent struggle that we as a department have faced is that many students expect the college itself to run according to democratic principles and practices, when in reality and like most businesses, it does so only in particular and agreed upon areas (e.g., the purviews of the student and faculty senates). Instead of democracy, there are people entrusted with making decisions unimpeded by any obligation to follow the will of the majority. Layered on this bureaucratic structure is the fact that neither is the Catholic Church a democracy and there are some stances on social justice that are set in stone. Therefore, that the teaching and practice of active citizenship can clash with this culture comes as no surprise.

Usually, inclinations toward democracy and deference to authority coexist, but there are occasions when students (and even more frequently, faculty) balk. A case in point was when the faculty attempted but failed to garner a three-quarter vote to override the provost's veto of a measure that would have extended health care benefits to the partners of homosexual employees.[2] Some of our students were vocal about their disappointment and urged us as faculty to "continue the battle." They viewed the issue in terms of social justice and promoting equality for a group of people excluded from health care. Yet there was no possibility that the college would change its policy given the positions of the board of trustees, the local bishop, or the Vatican. In this case, individual students and faculty were frustrated by the fact that the meaning of social justice would be set by those bodies alone. Other issues regarding sexuality have raised similar conflicts: the distribution of condoms on campus; abortion and birth control counseling; and a performance of the "Vagina Monologues." When tensions involving social justice, Church authority, college identity, academic freedom, and democratic citizenship emerge, there is indeed a "teachable moment" to explore these dynamics with students, but we also need to acknowledge that this can be dangerous terrain for both students and faculty. Student groups can lose funding; individuals can be denied awards; faculty can face negative evaluations. Work for social justice can appear deceptively easy when the issues are safe issues like being against poverty or for improved public education. What, however, are our responsibilities when our students want to take a path that is fraught with controversy? And what are the administration's responsibilities when these issues arise?

Administration. In order to develop a coordinated, college-wide effort, aggressive and committed leadership is required from administrators and from faculty governance committees such as the curriculum committee. Yet, in academia today administrators are far more focused on maintaining the economic viability of the institution than they are in preparing students who will work for social justice, and many a curriculum committee drowns in paperwork concerning catalog changes, new programs, and departmental evaluations. What's more, the reputation of the college or university is achieved by encouraging and supporting faculty research in their disciplines, and not by encouraging faculty to prepare students for public service (in low paying jobs no less). In sum, even a department that is willing to dramatically change its theme, its course offerings, its pedagogy, and its connection to student life, must find that this effort is supported and reinforced across the college, rather than find itself isolated, disparaged or even punished.

Conclusion

We believe that our political science department has been transformed. Our curriculum, course content, pedagogies, requirements, and student programming have noticeably moved away from disjointed individual endeavors toward a shared mission underpinned by Jesuit educational philosophy. We realize, however, that the true measure of our efforts is not how we are transformed but how our students are transformed. They are, after all, the reason for it all. So now we are working with the college-wide Student Learning Assessment director in gathering data about what, if anything, has changed. The initial findings are encouraging. For example, at senior exit interviews, our students can articulate not only the mission of the department, not only what Jesuit education means, but even more importantly, what their educational experiences have meant to them as undergrads and how they plan to incorporate this in their futures. They speak in terms of "growing not only as students but as people"; they weigh how they will use their skills to be "valuable to society"; they recall the value of service in an "unfamiliar community"; and they speak of themselves as "citizens" who are "engaged," "critical thinkers," "intellectually aggressive," and "confident enough to put our views forward, defend them, and to participate."

For all of us, then, this taking of the Jesuit mission to heart is not a single decision or action, but an ongoing process. Even with a common goal in sight, the path that takes us from where we were to where we are going is an uncertain journey each academic year as the landscape around us continues to change: college leadership, new faculty colleagues, student demographics, cultural expectations, economic forces, our individual interests, and even what emerges as the pressing social justice issues of the day. We progress, make false starts, take a step back, but keep moving. On the way, we have learned that we can transform some things but that there are also other factors over which we have little control. Our power to transform can only extend so far. But just as our mission is to support our students in the formation of "who they become" (Kolvenbach 2001, 156), so this mission requires of us to identify what we as a political science department at a Jesuit college are and what we should continue to strive to become.

———

Since this article was written, the political science department at Le Moyne College has changed its focus, prompting professors Susan Behuniak and John Freie to retire from their positions at the college.

Part II: Research and Teaching

Introduction

LISA SOWLE CAHILL

The most obvious, traditional, and defining mission of institutions of higher education is the cultivation and dissemination of knowledge, captured in the phrase "research and teaching." The virtues of the university are the virtues of speculative reason that lead to contemplation of the truth: wisdom, science, and understanding. The intellectual accomplishments of faculty, manifest in their publications and scholarly reputations, are the main attraction to prospective students and the primary factor establishing the standing of each institution nationally and internationally. Research and teaching are the two primary criteria for tenure and promotion of faculty, and for enlisting new faculty in the enterprise of any university or college.

At the same time, however, virtually every institution of higher education values service of faculty and students to the institution itself, and within larger communities. In fact, collegiality and service also serve as important criteria for admitting students and recognizing faculty, administrators and staff. This is particularly true of religiously affiliated institutions, not least of all Catholic ones. The value of service is famously captured in the Jesuit motto, "men and women for others."

This part of the book is dedicated to the integral connection among the following aspects of the mission of higher education: research, teaching, and service. Speculative reason and practical reason are interrelated, especially when it comes to understanding and doing justice. The chapters included here exhibit clearly the reasons both why intellectual inquiry is never truly "abstract," in the sense of independent from its practical and social environment, and why in Jesuit institutions the practical commitments to spiritual depth and service to others are profoundly interdependent with the intellectual enterprise.

This introduction will develop four points about the interdependent relationships that are stated or implied by the chapters in this part: the

transformation of knowledge by practical work for justice, the connection of knowledge and practice to ongoing commitment to justice, the
transformation of institutions as well as persons to embody justice, and
theological resources to back the hope that work for justice will bring
tangible results.

Transformation of Knowledge by Practices

Often educators think of the connection of their knowledge and their
teaching to justice and social change as a relation of cause and effect.
We know about Jesus' ministry to the poor, Catholic social teaching or
the witness of Jesuit leaders and we translate that into a responsibility
to share this wisdom with our students, and encourage them to act on
it. Likewise, students see service projects in which they participate as
the application of knowledge about justice and injustice that they learn
in the classroom and from invested professors. This cause-effect model
of knowledge and service is not incorrect, but it is only half of the
picture.

Equally important are the insights gained into reality, truth, and
obligation from the practices in which we engage. To be in a classroom
or do research is already a practice; the style of learning and teaching
may communicate the message that knowledge is about technical professional competence, theoretical publications, or academic excellence.
Indeed these types of formation and results are important in their own
right. Yet the essays in this part attest to a more complete model of
Jesuit education. At a first level, as Mary Zampini and Joan Kerley state
with regard to the foreign language classroom, an important goal is
"personal and social transformation." But beyond this, as these chapters
imply, transformation is a two-way street. Engagement in transformative practices in turn transforms the originating knowledge. Those who
engage in service and work for social justice come to see more clearly
what actually constitutes justice and injustice; what it means to be a
good, virtuous, or religiously committed person; what it means to live
with dignity; and what are the characteristics of a good society. As
Zampini and Kerley quote Father Kolvenbach's 2000 address at Santa
Clara University, "Personal involvement with innocent suffering, with

the injustice that others suffer, is the catalyst for solidarity which then gives rise to intellectual inquiry and moral reflection."

Encouraging critical intellectual inquiry is a key aim of justice education. In the context of study of the Spanish language, student and faculty experience in a preschool program for immigrant children stimulated intellectual reflection on the difference between charity and justice and on the implications for justice of realities such as political abductions in Argentina and Chile; voting practices in South America; the murder of Oscar Romero; and events in the history of Spain, such as the expulsions of Moors and Jews. In a somewhat different way, Susan Jackels et al. show how work with coffee farmers in Nicaragua led to a better understanding of the chemical processes involved in fermenting coffee. A commitment to "fair trade" marketing led professors and students to study an area of the field of chemistry that was relevant to their practical goals. New intellectual understanding then in turn redounds to greater commitment to more practical work for justice.

Similarly, addressing nursing education, Suzanne Hetzel Campbell et al. show how involvement with vulnerable populations, including substance abusers, leads clinicians into a better appreciation of the medical impact of "social determinants of health," including poverty, cultural marginality, and stigma. Working with nursing home residents, students gain both practical and intellectual knowledge of the role of autonomy (or lack thereof) in the ethics of health care. From their own powerlessness to ameliorate residents' situations, students better understand how institutions function, and how change can or cannot be effected within them.

A most crucial sphere of intellectual understanding that is enhanced by practical exposure to justice and injustice is defining what justice itself is. Zampini and Kerley express some reservations about whether it is even a good idea to try to define justice, given that its practical requirements will vary considerably with circumstances and options. It is certainly true that no uniform "system" of justice could ever be devised that would cover every practical application. Nevertheless, these essays together do point to the essentials of a definition, a definition that is coherent not only with Jesuit educational ideals, but with the tradition of Catholic social teaching (comprising Vatican II and papal encyclicals since the late nineteenth century).

In contemporary Catholic and Jesuit perspective, justice has at least four characteristics. First, it concerns both the common good and the dignity of the individual. Justice cannot be reduced to "the greatest good for the greatest number" (utilitarianism), to the demands of communal roles and obligations (communitarianism), or to individual freedom and autonomy (liberalism). In the Jesuit perspective, justice always includes the common good, since persons are inherently social; but it also includes the right of every person to share in the basic benefits of the common good, as well as his or her duty and right to participate in society and make a contribution.

Second, justice goes beyond personal virtue and commitment. It also refers the fairness of institutions and institutional behavior. To be a just person and to treat others fairly is necessary but not enough. Hence the importance of educating the person to be actively committed to others, not only those whom we meet personally, but also those well-being we can affect through social institutions, laws, voting, economic policies, and so on.

Third, justice in Catholic and Jesuit perspective requires a "preferential option for the poor." Variations on this phrase, originated by liberation theology, appear in the works of Paul VI, John Paul II, and Benedict VI. Justice goes beyond liberal equality or equality of opportunity. Justice requires more than legal requirements of nondiscrimination and free choice. Justice demands that the playing field be leveled so that those constrained by limits on basic freedom and self-determination—such as poverty, lack of education, racism, or entrenched gender subordination—enjoy a genuine chance at human flourishing and happiness.

Fourth, justice is both local and global. Since the 1960s, popes have recognized that justice includes responsibility for "the universal common good." The international nature of Jesuit education, and alliances among colleges and universities in more privileged and still "developing" areas of the world illustrate the necessarily global scope of the commitment to justice. As Zampini and Kerley point out, our students are usually familiar with the idea that they personally should share, serve, and donate. Jesuit education has the additional role of introducing them to "systemic questions about why certain groups are marginalized," "how our actions in the United States affect other parts of the world," and what "really benefits the poor in the long run." With a critical consciousness of the causes of injustice, students are equipped and motivated to make changes.

Ongoing Commitment to Justice

According to David Koelsch, for instance, Jesuit law schools aim to produce lawyers who, having practiced the Spiritual Exercises and devoted time and energy to legal aid clinics, will not only maintain their personal integrity and morale but also serve justice in their profession and in society. But habituation in personal and social virtue takes time and consistent formation. Zampini and Kerley lament that while Jesuit institutions strive to prepare their graduates for personal and professional commitment to the building of a more just society, "true transformation . . . requires a lasting commitment," and the long-term effects of the experience of service learning are unknown. When courses and a degree program end, so may engagement for justice.

In fact, Molly B. Pepper, Raymond Reyes, and Linda Tredennick show that even our Jesuit universities are not necessarily the incubators of justice we hope. A study at Gonzaga University produced results that could probably be replicated on many other campuses. White, male heterosexual students rated the importance of diversity and of celebrating it lower than did other students, but they perceived it as in fact more valued and celebrated on campus. AHANA students (racial and ethnic minorities) reported more negative experiences with diversity than did white students, female more than male, and GLBT (gay, lesbian, bisexual, transgender) students more than straight. Most students see the university as falling below their own assessment of the importance of diversity. Moreover, most students report having had negative experiences around their socioeconomic status regardless of other factors, indicating perhaps that economic and class differences govern campus interactions more than students think they should. Commendably, Gonzaga has since instituted a number of measures to help improve understanding and relationships on campus, including workshops for both students and faculty. Pepper, Reyes, and Tredennick note that shared actions and joint practices are essential to building trust that endures over the long haul, and even in the face of setbacks and rejection.

All of these chapters show in different ways how faculty can model long-term engagement and induct students into practices of justice as integral to professional identity. The bottom line is that long-term results require more than personal conviction; they require opportunities to participate in transformative work for change, in institutions that enable and sustain partnerships for justice.

Institutions

Pepper, Reyes, and Tredennick provide the data to show that even Catholic Jesuit institutions can be disappointing when it comes to habituation in the virtue of justice. Koelsch offers the equally dispiriting probability that students and faculty in Jesuit law schools, as well as Catholic lawyers, are little or no more exempt from the stresses, dysfunctions, and erosions of integrity that beset law students and lawyers in general.

But while most of the authors in this section train their sights most explicitly on the conversion and moral formation of students, as well as students' increased understanding of what justice means in theory and practice, it is also quite evident that the authors all also have much more extensive changes in mind. And they are putting those changes into practice—in their own institutions, in their professions, in professional and liberal arts education, and even in international networks of NGOs, corporations, governments, and religious denominations.

Jackels et al., for example, mention collaboration not only between international Jesuit universities and Nicaraguan coffee cooperatives, but with justice-minded roasting companies, Catholic Relief Services, USAID, academic associations of chemists and chemistry conferences, and science journals showcasing research related to fair trade coffee. Jackels et al. point to global groups and factors that have helped create the economic crisis among coffee growers—bankrupt banks, rising unemployment and hunger, and urban migration—and imply that changes are needed.

The proposal for nursing education by Campbell et al. looks explicitly at institutional changes aimed at the entire profession of nursing. Her "ecological model of health looks at socioeconomic determinants of health on a global scale, and cites Benedict XVI's 2009 encyclical, *Caritas in veritate* to validate global health justice as a proper and necessary aim of Catholic agents, institutions, and education. All health care delivery systems must aim to integrate justice in access to care, resource allocation, and recognition of "health care as a societal right." Nurses see it as their distinctive mission to be the voice of the most vulnerable, including poor women, immigrants, and the elderly; and to combat human rights violations, third-world debt, racism, and gender discrimination, not only as nurses, but as world citizens responsible for the common good. The priority of justice for the global poor, and the need to work within networked institutions and alliances to accomplish that aim, is a salient theme in the chapters by Jackels et al., Campbell et al., and Zampini and Kerley. As Zampini and Kerley state, Jesuit educators lead students "along a path of personal transformation so that they may in turn work toward transforming the world in the promotion of a more just society."

Christian Faith, Theology, and Hope

Koelsch provides perhaps the most explicit invocation of the resources of faith and spirituality to sustain personal integrity and virtue; inspire social solidarity; and hold up practical work for justice as a Christian, Catholic, Jesuit responsibility. Zampini and Kerley probably express a feeling common to many who wholeheartedly share in the justice mission of Jesuit schools, but do not have scholarly, educational, or professional expertise in theology, Catholic social teaching, or Ignatian spirituality; or in the complexities of global economics, politics, and government: "How can the professor who has expertise in teaching a foreign language (or some other course of study) be expected to also have expertise in the area of the promotion of justice in today's society?"

One of the most ready resources for faculty with diverse backgrounds will be Catholic social teaching. The key concepts of universal humanity, common good, human dignity, mutual rights and responsibilities, solidarity, and even "preferential option for the poor" will make sense from many viewpoints and within different religious traditions. But Christians also have biblical and theological resources so back commitment to justice, some shared with Jews and Muslims by virtue of our common scriptures. They include creation, the making of humanity in the "image of God," the historical presence of God to humanity, human sinfulness and the need for repentance, liberation from oppression, covenant community, the prophets' denunciations of social injustice, and calls for communal reform, Jesus' inclusive ministry of the kingdom or reign of God, the need to sacrifice in order to be faithful to one's mission, the solidarity of God with human suffering, the possibility of resurrection life through divine power, the empowering of believers by the Spirit of God, and the eschatological action of God to renew the earth and its inhabitants, action in which by God's grace humans can share.

An especially important religious and theological theme is hope—hope that because in our actions and those of our communities we experience renewal, our action can also renew the societies in which we participate. It is often said that the "theological virtues" of faith, hope and charity are "infused" by God, not acquired by human effort and practice like the cardinal moral virtues, prudence, justice, fortitude, and temperance. All these essays show just how important practice or habituation is in forming a lasting commitment to justice. But although hope is indeed a gift of God, it is not disconnected from practice either, precisely because God is present to us in history, in relationships, in community, and when together we do works of love and justice.

In his 2007 encyclical on hope, *Spe salvi*, Benedict XVI repeats at least three times that the gospel is not only "informative," it is "performative." If we really hear the Christian message, we will take action. When we act for justice's sake, we not only gain knowledge, we see that living in a different way is possible, and our confidence and efforts are nourished. This is why, according to *Spe salvi*, Christian hope is "an active hope."

Hope that change is real and possible comes in large part from actions that create change, from shared practices of solidarity and transformation. Hope does not require assurance that our action can end all racism, sexism, violence, and poverty. It simply requires that we courageously lend a hand in solidarity, and pursue the changes that lie within our power. Forming alliances to act increases social power and inspires future, even more effective action across broader networks of people. *Spe salvi* even goes so far as to claim, "All serious and upright human conduct is hope in action."

The following chapters about research and teaching are eloquent witnesses to the interdependence of intellectual inquiry and practical engagement; they also show how the pairing of knowledge and service in Jesuit education can cultivate the virtue of justice and display the virtue of hope.

6 Social Justice Themes in the Foreign Language Classroom

MARY L. ZAMPINI AND JOAN KERLEY

In recent years, many institutions, including Jesuit ones, have incorporated a service learning component within their foreign language courses. The pedagogical benefits of providing students with an opportunity to interact with native speakers through community service projects have received some attention in the literature (e.g., Beebe and DeCosta 1993; Hellebrandt and Varona 1999). To date, however, we are unaware of any significant discussion among Jesuit foreign language programs regarding the role that such activities play in the promotion of social justice and the development of a "well-educated solidarity," as urged by Fr. Peter-Hans Kolvenbach in his address at Santa Clara University in October 2000. This chapter examines the integration of social justice in the second language classroom through a consideration of the role that service learning has played in Spanish at Le Moyne College.

In order to address these issues, we first describe Le Moyne College's service learning requirement for Spanish and discuss the positive outcomes and challenges that the students and instructor faced. This serves as a point of departure to examine a broader range of themes related to the promotion of social justice in the foreign language classroom, including the challenge of facilitating a developmental shift from charity to social justice within our students. Such a shift is critical in order to reach the goals of personal and societal transformation. Finally, we propose that the Spiritual Exercises of St. Ignatius of Loyola provide a useful framework for guiding instructors and students along the path toward this developmental shift and for creating more effective reflection assignments. In addition, because the Spiritual Exercises are compatible with theories of intercultural competence, they may play a beneficial and naturally complementary role in the Jesuit foreign language classroom.

Spanish Service Learning Requirement

Le Moyne College is a small liberal arts institution in Syracuse, New York, with an undergraduate population of approximately 2,800 students, including 25 Spanish majors and 15 to 20 Spanish minors. The Spanish courses that require service learning are intermediate-level classes (Spanish Conversation and Composition I and II) that serve as a bridge between the lower levels of language instruction and upper division coursework in literature, composition, and conversation. The student make-up of these classes tends to be quite varied and includes Spanish majors and minors, as well as students from other disciplines who need to fulfill a language requirement. They also include students at all stages of their academic career, from freshmen to seniors.

The primary focus of the Spanish Conversation and Composition course is to review major grammatical structures as students work to develop more sophisticated speaking and writing skills in Spanish. Another goal is to deepen knowledge of and appreciation for Spanish-speaking cultures. Historically, this latter goal has been addressed through readings that focus on individual, and sometimes unrelated, aspects of Hispanic culture; that is, students read snippets of information about the Spanish-speaking world but fail to study cultural themes in depth. As a result, they may learn bits of trivia, but they often fail to gain any meaningful understanding of Hispanic cultures.

To address the lack of cultural integration and opportunities for real-world experiences, the instructor of the Spanish Conversation and Composition course (Mary Zampini) incorporated a service learning component in 2007 with two primary objectives: first, to provide students with opportunities to use their Spanish outside the classroom and interact with native speakers on a regular basis; and second, to join the service learning initiatives of Le Moyne College in order to more fully implement its mission of "educating the whole person." Admittedly, however, a desire to promote social justice issues was not among the initial goals of the instructor. As such, she became very much like the students as she began to grapple with the wider implications of our role in the community and to reflect upon the notions of social justice and a well-educated solidarity as applied to the Spanish-language classroom.

The description of the service learning requirement here focuses on the 2007/2008 academic year, the first year of its implementation, although the basic requirements have changed little since then. First, the professor required all students enrolled in Spanish Conversation and Composition I, II to complete eighteen hours of community service each semester (two hours per week for nine weeks); there were no nonservice sections of the course available.[1] Hence, students who may have been uninterested in service could not opt out of the requirement. Most students worked at the MANOS Early Education Dual Language program, a bilingual preschool program for children aged eighteen months to four years housed in a local elementary school within the Syracuse city school district. The majority of the MANOS children come from families who have recently immigrated to the United States from Spanish-speaking countries, primarily the Caribbean. The MANOS teachers are all native speakers of Spanish, as well, and the parents of the MANOS children must take classes at a local adult education center, where they study English, work toward their GED, or receive job training. The Le Moyne College (LMC) students played with the children, read to them, and assisted the teachers with various projects and learning activities. LMC students that could not make a weekly site commitment due to scheduling or job conflicts worked throughout the semester to prepare a book reading and lesson plan for the MANOS children and went for one two-hour session toward the end of the semester. From spring 2007 through the end of spring 2009, 115 students contributed 1,967 hours assisting in the MANOS classrooms.

In addition to the required site visits, LMC students wrote weekly journal reflections that described their community service work. In order to relate their service experience with class content, the journal assignments incorporated the grammatical structures and vocabulary covered in class. Grammatical and semantic accuracy, the student's ability to describe his or her weekly activities, and the degree to which the student fulfilled the particular assignment all contributed to the student's grade. At the end of the semester, students submitted a longer reflective essay in Spanish in which they discussed what they learned from the experience and considered the benefits and challenges of community service. The essay received a grade according to a rubric that gave equal weight to overall content, organization, vocabulary, and language (grammatical accuracy). The average grade for all service-related work constituted 20 percent of the final average for the course. During the last week of classes, students also completed a survey from the Office of Service Learning that asked them to evaluate the program, their experiences, and their reactions to service learning through a series of Likert scale questions with room for additional comments.

Positive Outcomes of the Spanish Service Learning Requirement

The service learning component of the Spanish Conversation and Composition classes has proven quite successful. LMC students tend to respond positively to the experience, and the Le Moyne faculty have developed a friendly and productive working relationship with the teachers and administrators of the MANOS program. The MANOS teachers value and appreciate the LMC students' help, and the students quickly warm up to the children under their charge. In their final Spanish essays, many students reported that their speaking and listening comprehension skills in Spanish improved over the course of the semester, as did their confidence in using the language to communicate with native speakers. Such positive effects have been reported elsewhere as well (e.g., Eyler et al. 2003; Hellebrandt and Varona 1999).[2]

In addition, the Office of Service Learning surveys revealed that many LMC students recognized benefits other than linguistic gains to their service experiences. Of the approximately thirty Spanish students that participated in 2007/2008 academic year, the surveys found that:

> 46 percent strongly agreed and 41 percent agreed that "I am comfortable working with cultures other than my own."
>
> 12 percent strongly agreed and 25 percent agreed that "Service work has helped me clarify my major in college."
>
> 28 percent strongly agreed and 50 percent agreed that "Service in a local community has helped me to identify personal strengths and weaknesses."
>
> 52 percent strongly agreed and 34 percent agreed that "Service helps me prepare for leadership and service in my professional life."
>
> 35 percent strongly agreed and 56 percent agreed that "Service is an integral part of Jesuit education."

This latter finding is particularly relevant in that it shows that the students recognize the role that service learning plays in characterizing and promoting the mission of the Jesuit institution. Furthermore, since participation in service learning was a requirement for all, these results do not merely reflect the opinions of a subset of students who may have been independently interested in and appreciative of the benefits of community service or service learning.

Perhaps the most positive outcome occurred during Spring 2008, in which involvement with the MANOS children transformed some students' commitment to one that extended beyond the course requirements. After reading a newspaper report that the bilingual program had lost its funding and might have to close the classroom for the youngest children (eighteen months to two years), the LMC students organized a fundraising campaign. They held several events on campus, including a bake sale, pancake supper, collection at Mass, and gift raffle. In addition, they contacted a local TV station to increase public awareness and promote their fundraising efforts. As a result, they raised over $2,000 that helped keep the classroom open for the rest of the year.

While the students' commitment to the children produced an immediate reaction of charity in some (e.g., "Let's do something to raise money!"), it produced questions of more systemic justice issues in others (e.g., "Why does this program have to beg for money to survive while programs in other nearby areas have plenty?"). Capitalizing on this "teachable" moment, the instructor gave an assignment that provided students with a guided opportunity for a reflection on their motives in the fundraising efforts vis-à-vis the notions of charity and social justice. The students wrote an essay in English, in which they were asked to define in their own words both "charity" and "social justice" and to describe the difference between the two concepts. They were also asked to reflect on what motivated them to become involved once they heard that the MANOS program had lost its funding.[3]

Although the degree of participation in the fundraising activities varied among individual students, their overall efforts and reaction to the news of the imminent closing of a MANOS classroom clearly demonstrated the beginnings of a mental shift from charity to social justice. As such, this experience exemplified the words of Father Kolvenbach

(2000) in a very real way: "Personal involvement with innocent suffering, with the injustice that others suffer, is the catalyst for solidarity which then gives rise to intellectual inquiry and moral reflection." This is precisely the type of shift that members of Jesuit institutions are called to promote.

The student response also reflects the beginnings of the kind of personal transformation that we as Jesuit institutions hope to inspire in our students. The relationship that the LMC students developed with the MANOS teachers and children not only opened their eyes to a world that few had previously experienced, but also made them a part of that world. They became partners in helping to prepare the children for their future scholastic endeavors and felt invested in their well-being. The LMC students' actions likewise transformed the world of the MANOS participants by allowing the program to continue for the remainder of the year.

Student Challenges

Despite the overall success of the service learning requirement in Spanish, several obstacles remain for students, faculty, and the institution. First, an initial student challenge was the location of the MANOS program in a bilingual inner city school and, as some of them described it, a "bad neighborhood." Many students initially felt nervous about going there, but they quickly warmed up to the children. The MANOS teachers and staff also made them feel welcome and safe. While most students adjusted well, it remained a challenge for others throughout the semester. For example, one student noted in the service learning survey: "Service helped me see other parts of Syracuse and I enjoyed being around the children. . . . However, I felt somewhat out of place because the teachers spoke Spanish and the neighborhood intimidated me."

Second, the time commitment was demanding; in order to use the college's shuttle service to go to MANOS, for example, students had to carve out a three-hour block of time in their schedule. A few students commented that, because of the extra work involved, the course should be worth four credits, rather than three. This is a legitimate concern (see also Bringle and Hatcher 1996) and leads to a larger institutional one, since increasing the number of credit hours assigned to the course

increases the number of credits needed to fulfill the language requirement or to complete the Spanish major or minor. Given the curricular
demands placed upon students within their own disciplines, many
departments are unwilling to support such an increase.

Third, the journal assignments used to process their service learning
experiences also presented challenges. Many students lacked the
required linguistic ability in Spanish to opine or reflect in depth on
issues related to service learning. As a result, their journal reflections
often contained very simplified or superficial statements in Spanish,
such as: "I was nervous at first, but now I am not." "I had a lot of fun
at MANOS." "It is important to help others." Because these difficulties
became quickly apparent, the instructor changed the format of the journals to be less *reflective* (on issues of social justice, for example) and
more *descriptive* (e.g., describing what happened on a particular day).
As mentioned above, the journal assignments also incorporated grammatical structures covered in class. For example, while studying the
preterit and imperfect past tenses, students described what happened
during the service visits by focusing on the narration of background
information versus completed events. While studying the future tense,
students chose one child in the MANOS program and described in
detail that child's life in twenty years. Assignments of this type, however, do not lend themselves to a thorough reflection of service learning
and issues of social justice, and the true intention of using the journals
for substantive reflection is diminished or obscured. This is a challenge
that is somewhat unique to the foreign language classroom, especially
if students write journal reflections in the target language.

Finally, service learning may have the unintended consequence of
reinforcing perceived stereotypes among students, rather than breaking
down cultural barriers.[4] Instructors must remain cognizant of this
potential difficulty and be ready to discuss these issues with the class.
While we cannot recall a specific instance of this happening in the
course at hand, a different type of misconception became apparent
through some of the journal assignments: many students seemed to
have a very optimistic (and perhaps naïve) view of the students' future.
For example, in the assignment on the description of a child's life in
twenty years, the journals were mostly quite positive and projected a
bright and successful future for the children. The fact that the children

were in a bilingual program led many LMC students to believe that their educational success was somehow assured, simply because they were learning both Spanish and English. The LMC students sometimes forgot the economic and social reality of the children's lives outside the classroom. The challenge for the instructor, then, is to find a way to temper naïve optimism with a more realistic viewpoint without reinforcing stereotypical perceptions and generalizations.

Instructor Challenges

Faculty members must likewise confront and overcome several challenges as they work to provide effective service learning opportunities for their students.

Time

First, developing and overseeing the service learning experience entails a significant investment of time and effort. Hence, part of the "praxis" (cf. Freire 2000) is discerning how much time one can devote to redesigning a course given competing demands and obligations. Even after preparing the course, faculty must spend time throughout the semester ensuring that the program runs smoothly and dealing with problems as they arise. Moreover, several researchers (e.g., Hellebrandt and Varona 1999; Osborn 2006) have argued that the instructor must participate alongside the students and learn with them in order for service learning to be truly effective. As Eyler and Giles (1999, 191) assert, "If instructors are going to do a good job of integrating service and learning, they need to have an understanding of the students' experience, and this may entail continuous effort and on-site presence." The demands on time are thus significant, especially for junior faculty members working toward tenure. Unless the institution is willing to reward faculty for this type of pedagogy (e.g., within the rank and tenure process), the time needed to design effective and meaningful service learning opportunities and to engage students in an academic discussion that leads them to a deeper understanding of social justice issues will inhibit and discourage faculty participation (see also Bloomgarden and O'Meara

2007; Abes, Jackson, and Jones 2002; Battistoni 2002; Eyler and Giles 1999).

Incorporation of Social Justice into the Foreign Language Classroom

A second challenge for instructors, especially those at Jesuit institutions, concerns the incorporation of social justice themes into the foreign language curriculum, beginning with a consideration of what social justice is. As noted above, the LMC students' response to the economic precariousness of the MANOS program led to a guided reflection on the notions of charity and social justice. Asking students to define social justice, however, led us to consider whether there had been discussion among Jesuit institutions regarding our own definition. One is offered by Hollenbach, found in Battistoni (2002, 22), who states that social justice "refers to the obligations of all citizens to aid in the creation of patterns of social organization and activity that are essential both for the protection of minimal human rights and for the creation of mutuality and participation by all in social life." Other authors describe social justice, but they stop short of defining it. Osborn (2006, 16–17) even resists the notion of defining social justice, for in doing so he says "I [am] borrowing unconsciously from others in academe, as filtered through my own experiences and privilege, and subject to the influences of my own life. In my own human craving for order, I too have made choices to preserve certain features and devalue others." It may be, then, that a given discipline will find a particular interpretation of social justice more appropriate to the goals, research agenda, and pedagogical endeavors of its field than others.

The difficulty of incorporating social justice issues into the curriculum goes far beyond that of an acceptable working definition, however. Kolvenbach (2000) challenges Jesuit colleges and universities to implement the promotion of justice "in who our students become, in what our faculty do and in how our universities proceed." Noting that our students are in a period of formation, he states: "Tomorrow's 'whole person' cannot be whole without an educated awareness of society and culture with which to contribute socially, generously, in the real world . . . the students need close involvement with the poor and the marginal now, in order to learn about reality and become adults of solidarity in the future." As foreign language educators, however, we struggle to provide students with sufficient opportunities for skills development in the four areas of language learning (speaking, listening, reading, and writing). Thus, a fair question asks whether or not the teaching of social justice is an appropriate use of time in a language course that may already have too much material to cover. In order to overcome this challenge, one must examine class activities and homework assignments in a new light in order to determine how to effectively integrate social justice themes with the existing course content. As Osborn (2006, 60) exhorts, language educators must "focus on grammar and vocabulary in a way that enables us to . . . talk about values, continue the inquiry with students and community, learn to listen to the stories in the community and classroom, connect to social movements, and move into conflict."

In addition, the selection of appropriate cultural topics may provide another means of integrating social justice issues into the language curriculum. The textbook used in the course described here, for example, contains cultural readings on (among other things) the *desaparecidos* (or "disappeared") of Argentina and Chile; Archbishop Óscar Romero of El Salvador; the Moorish invasion and domination of the Iberian peninsula; the expulsion of the Moors and Jews from Spain; and the Spanish Civil War and dictatorship of Francisco Franco. These topics lend themselves well to a discussion of social justice issues, but it took the instructor a while to feel comfortable in doing so and to learn how to effectively present them in such a way so as to allow students to reflect upon their broader implications, rather than simply acquire basic factual information. In designing the curriculum, therefore, we must strive to incorporate topics that are relevant to the acquisition of Spanish language skills and that furthermore introduce students to the realities of the world in which they live but, perhaps, have never encountered: discrimination, the rights of immigrants, differing cultural expectations, the politics of war, and so on. In this way, we can help our students achieve the "well-educated solidarity" that Kolvenbach (2000) believes is essential.

Teacher Preparation

Finally, the integration of social justice themes in the classroom has at its root another critical challenge for faculty engaged in service learning: teacher preparation. Faculty teach and do research in their respective fields of expertise, but those fields may not necessarily include social justice themes. Moreover, few instructors receive training in teaching social justice as it relates to their discipline. Yet the Jesuit ideal of forming "men and women for others" who will be "leaders" in their chosen fields challenges us to look for ways to incorporate justice themes. It thus becomes the same type of "praxis experience," as Freire (2000) calls it, for the instructor as it does for the students.

In addition, the challenge of moving students away from a model based solely on charity toward a model that examines the systems and structures that contribute to injustice is critical to the success of any service learning endeavor. This challenge is both daunting and developmental. From a young age, our schools and society encourage students to share with each other, participate in service projects, and contribute to endeavors that assist the less fortunate. However, we often fail to introduce children and adolescents to more profound and systemic questions of why certain groups are marginalized, how our actions in the United States affect other parts of the world, and whether or not their charity really benefits the needy in the long run. We as educators in the Jesuit tradition must help our students move from a charitable stance to a justice one, but it is unclear how we may best achieve this goal. Therefore, more focused research and training opportunities that will allow us to better understand how to meet this challenge are essential.

Future Directions

Foreign language instructors thus face a number of practical and theoretical challenges as they search for ways to successfully incorporate service learning into the foreign language curriculum. Moreover, instructors at Jesuit institutions face the additional challenge of leading their students along a path of personal transformation so that they may in turn work toward transforming the world in the promotion of a more just society, as encouraged by the Jesuit mission. Since this challenge is somewhat unique to the faculty of Jesuit institutions, this section will focus on that issue and will examine ways in which instructors may reflect on the relationship between their academic discipline and issues of social justice. In particular, we propose that instructors may use the methodology of the Spiritual Exercises of St. Ignatius of Loyola in guiding their own actions, as well as those of their students, through the service learning experience.

The Spiritual Exercises of St. Ignatius of Loyola

Some of the methodology used in the meditations of the Spiritual Exercises of St. Ignatius of Loyola could move the service learning reflection process forward in a way that is truer to the Ignatian tradition. The director in the Exercises constantly encourages the directee to go deeper in a particular meditation if there is something more to be discovered there. Our process in writing this article provides an example of how we applied this principle. First, we reflected on how the journals had been structured and how they might have been structured differently based on the first author's reflection as the professor of the course, as well as the second author's experience with both directing the Spiritual Exercises of St. Ignatius and participating in the service learning process as an auditor in the course. As we shared these reflections, we noticed the feelings of consolation/desolation that led us to a deeper insight and a desire to explore how we could restructure the journal writing experience. This led to a commitment to design a journal model that would help the students look at issues of justice in their own lives, using the principles of the Spiritual Exercises to guide us, something that we had not done previously. In this way we began to model for ourselves a process that the professor might incorporate into the students' journal assignments.[5]

The Jesuit ideal of social justice is firmly rooted in the spirituality and worldview of the Spiritual Exercises (Arrupe 1973; Kolvenbach 2000; Brackley 2004, 2005). As one progresses through the Exercises, one becomes more adept at identifying underlying motivations and examining previously unconsidered assumptions, biases, or values by which one had lived. The goal in doing so is to find one's true vocation. Brackley (2005, 6) states:

> Engaging suffering people and injustice frequently awakens in students the crucial question: What am I doing with my life? . . . Education of the whole person, in the Ignatian style (as Paul Crowley says), helps students discover their vocation in life, above all their *vocation to love and serve*. . . . That vocation might be to raise kids, to discover galaxies, to drive a truck—or a combination of these. Whatever it is concretely, faith and reason point to a deeper *human calling* that we all share: namely, to spend ourselves in love.

Some comments from the service learning surveys illustrate how this experience led students to reflect on their own vocation. For example:

> The experience helped me realize I want to work with kids.

> Now I am even more motivated to double major in Spanish and continue with it.

> The experience helped me to find my strengths and weaknesses in working with children, and I was able to give these children a new face to talk to.

> It helped me a lot with my future career as an adolescent therapist.

As seen, the LMC students' experiences with the MANOS children awakened in them precisely the question posed by Brackley and the goal of the Spiritual Exercises: finding one's true vocation.

Another key element of the Spiritual Exercises is that of discernment, a process that assists the person in making decisions by paying attention to times of "consolation" and "desolation" (cf. Rules of Discernment in the Spiritual Exercises, numbers 313–36). According to Brackley (2004, 48–49), consolation leads to peace, joy, and a desire to commit oneself in service, while desolation leads us to focus on ourselves in sadness or unease. In their service learning experience, students encounter people and situations that may differ radically from their own life experiences. Helping them to notice these differences and to identify their feelings and reactions to them can become the beginning of a discernment process. For example, one student wrote: "I tried my hardest to participate and help, but many times I felt lost." Another commented: "It allowed me to feel more comfortable talking with people who are native speakers. I feel it really will help me be more comfortable when I go abroad." Instructors should therefore structure journal reflections in such a way so as to encourage students to continue exploring their feelings vis-à-vis their assumptions, values, and prior experiences in order to lead them to a deeper insight. This may prove difficult in a second language class in which students have not mastered the language of instruction; however, instructors can nevertheless allow some reflections in the native language without compromising the linguistic goals and objectives of the course.

Brackley (2004, 170) also offers a schema that could further aid instructors in designing a journal format, namely the three poles of discernment: "one subjective (i.e., myself) and two objective . . . (i.e., concrete reality and the word or *logos* about reality)." He believes that the objective side "embraces culture, including all the means by which we interpret reality: the symbols and languages we use to make sense of the world . . . the values, virtues, and norms that govern behavior" (ibid.). Thus, by challenging our students to examine their familiar world vis-à-vis the world of the other as experienced in their service learning activities, we can remain faithful to the reflective process of the Spiritual Exercises. The discernment process also allows instructors to encourage students to find their true vocation, their heart's desire, and their way of being of service in the world. Indeed, the following quotes form the service learning surveys reveal that the service learning process became a transformative one for some LMC students:

Service learning is a good way to be involved in the community and celebrate all cultures.

Service learning helped me to see Spanish used in a real life situation and helped me to appreciate many things. The experience was eye opening and fun.

The experience made me become aware of the situations of some families (especially those who have a language barrier).

These reactions evolved independently of knowledge of the Spiritual Exercises and suggest that, through a more systematic application of the process of discernment (e.g., specific journal assignments), we may enhance students' personal growth, deepen their understanding of social justice issues, and guide them along their path toward finding their vocation in a uniquely Jesuit way.

Intercultural Competence

In addition to the Spiritual Exercises, the literature on intercultural competence (e.g., Savicki 2008; Tonkin 2004; Galura et al. 2004) can help foreign language instructors improve students' ability to reflect on issues of social justice. Moreover, knowledge of the components of intercultural competence can inform the discernment process of the Spiritual Exercises discussed above. To give an example, Bennet (2008, 16–17) discusses five principles for developing intercultural competence. Among these, she states that cultural knowledge and contact do not necessarily lead to either cultural competence or a significant reduction in stereotypes. In addition, culture learning suggests that disequilibrium need not lead to dissatisfaction. An awareness of these principles can assist instructors in guiding their students toward a more reflective stance and a deeper understanding of the world in which we live. They may accomplish this through a process of discernment and a "praxis" model of action (Freire 2000) that involves *action*, followed by *critical reflection* on that action, followed by *new action* based on the critical reflection.

In addition to intercultural competence, Bennet (2008, 18–21) discusses cognitive, behavioral, and affective competencies that are necessary to help study abroad students succeed. Besides cultural knowledge and self-awareness, she lists "the ability to empathize, gather appropriate information, listen, perceive accurately, adapt, initiate and maintain relationships, resolve conflict and manage social interactions and anxiety" as vital behavioral skills (ibid., 19). The same may be true for language students who perform community service; that is, service learning in a different cultural environment within one's own community can also produce stages of culture shock. Instructors should therefore engage their students in using some of the skills mentioned by

Bennet by the way they structure reflection questions. Having students discuss an experience that involved culture shock or feelings of discomfort may also be part of a discernment process that will help prepare them to make the shift from cultural awareness to cultural understanding, and later, from an awareness of the social injustice to a deeper reflection of its ramifications and one's reactions to it.

Finally, Bennet states: "As the keystone of intercultural competence, curiosity shapes the study abroad experience as no other skill or characteristic does" (20). Curiosity is a hallmark of a good discernment process, as well. When a person begins to notice his or her actions and corresponding feelings, as well as how and when they change, a true process of self-knowledge and self-discovery vis-à-vis the other can begin, not in a judgmental way, but in a way that acknowledges differences. In terms of teaching justice, part of that will involve the realization that sometimes things are not the way that they should be, and we, as global citizens and Jesuit educators and students, are called to address those injustices. Insights such as these, therefore, may assist foreign language students in processing their service learning experiences and help fulfill the cultural course objectives at the same time. They may also teach students to become more critical thinkers, who can then begin to incorporate the ideals of the "service of faith in the promotion of justice" into their lives. This is a necessary step on the road to personal transformation and one that will strengthen our efforts in encouraging and preparing students to transform the world in which they live.

Conclusion

To conclude, service learning and the study of foreign languages can be naturally compatible and mutually enhancing endeavors due to their communicative and interactive nature. This often serves as the primary motivation for the incorporation of service learning into the foreign language curriculum as instructors look for meaningful ways to contribute to the development of linguistic skills and enhance cross-cultural understanding. The responsibility for members of Jesuit institutions does not stop there, however, as instructors are called to foster a "well-educated solidarity" and to educate their students to be leaders in the service of others. Service learning presents an ideal means for doing so. As shown here, for example, students' experience with, and commitment to, the children in their care during their participation in service learning helped them develop a social justice stance as they faced the potential closing of one of the preschool classrooms. True transformation, however, requires a lasting commitment, as well as continued reflection. This goal is more difficult to achieve, as well as to measure. For most students, service learning ends once the course ends, and the lasting effects of their experiences are unknown (see also Abbott and Lear 2010 for similar discussion). As Jesuit institutions, we cannot be content if transformation (or the beginnings of transformation) ends when the course ends or on graduation day. While it is good and appropriate to celebrate the transformative behavior that comes about as an immediate and direct result of participation in service learning, we must also search for ways to encourage a more permanent commitment to the Jesuit ideals of social justice.

As an initial step to achieving this goal, we have proposed that the Spiritual Exercises of St. Ignatius of Loyola provide a framework for leading instructors and students through a process of discernment that may help them more fully understand and embrace their responsibilities to confront the social injustice in our world. We have outlined possible applications of the Spiritual Exercises that offer instructors a uniquely Jesuit approach to guiding students through the reflection process and that, moreover, complement theories of intercultural competence. This is just a first step, however, and we hope that this study will provoke additional reflection, inquiry, and research on the ways in which we can most effectively prepare our faculty to address social justice themes in the classroom, as well as ways in which we can best promote the developmental shift from charity to social justice within our students. In this way, we will come closer to achieving the goal of personal transformation, and we will be better equipped to prepare our students to work toward transforming our world to create a more just society.

7   Coffee for Justice

SUSAN C. JACKELS, CHARLES F. JACKELS,
CARLOS VALLEJOS, AND MICHAEL MARSOLEK

Pedro Pablo Ortiz and his wife Marta and their five children live on a coffee farm in Matagalpa, Nicaragua situated on a mountaintop at an altitude of 1,250 meters (4,100 feet). The farm has a little over three acres of lush coffee plants grown under ideal conditions. Pedro belongs to the cooperative *La Fe de las Nubes* (Faith of the Clouds), which itself is a member of a second order cooperative, CECO-SEMAC ("Aroma of Coffee" Union of Multiple-Service Cooperatives) and has just received word that the cooperative has received Fair Trade certification. Through the cooperative, he receives support to help him farm coffee by traditional artisan methods. His farm is also in transition for organic certification, having one more year remaining in a three-year transition period. Achieving organic certification is a natural step for Pedro's family because they have never been able to afford agrochemicals of any kind. Asked what he would do if the farm were to sell coffee and thereby realize a profit (he has yet to do this), Pedro immediately replies with his plans to obtain a loan from the cooperative and improve his *beneficio* or wet mill for coffee processing. This he says would help improve the quality of coffee that he can produce.

This chapter describes how academic scientists and engineers have joined on a journey with families like Pedro's in Nicaragua as they strive to escape the cruel economics of the coffee crisis, enter the organic and Fair Trade specialty coffee markets, and sell coffee in the United States through a network of companies and Catholic Relief Services (CRS). If successful, Pedro's family would approximately double their income, from forty cents to about eighty cents per day per person (2008 data). The Coffee for Justice project, initiated in 2003, aimed to use the group's scientific expertise and appropriate technology in order to study the questions of the artisan coffee farmers and put into their hands

FIGURE 7-1. Pedro Ortiz and family. (Photo courtesy of Susan Jackels.)

simple methods for improvement of coffee quality that could aid them in gaining access to the specialty coffee market.

Background

Nicaragua is the largest country in Central America, with 5.4 million people in an area about the size of the state of New York. It is the second poorest country in the Western hemisphere with a GDP per capita of $750, with half of the population living below the poverty line, and one-third of all adults over age fifteen being illiterate (United Nations Development Programme [UNDP] 2002). The distribution of income in Nicaragua is among the most disproportionate in the world, with the wealthiest 10 percent of the population receiving over one-half of the nation's income. The highest concentrations of poverty and illiteracy are found in Nicaragua's rural areas where there is also the greatest rate of population growth. This situation, combined with Nicaragua's history of political turmoil, foreign intervention, and natural disasters, such as the earthquake that leveled Managua in 1972 and Hurricane Mitch that caused one billion dollars in damage in the rural areas in 1998, has created many hardships. However, the people of Nicaragua have become resilient and strong, however, as they struggle with the issues of poverty and sustainability. Thus, Nicaragua is a potent example of the need for global solidarity, and it provides a great opportunity for service-related research and activities in collaboration with impoverished people.

The political, economic, and environmental problems of Nicaragua have now been aggravated by the coffee crisis. By 2001 the collapsing world coffee market yielded the lowest inflation-adjusted prices in one hundred years, only one-quarter of the 1960 level (Oxfam International 2003). According to Brown (2004) and Bacon (2005), this collapse—caused by global oversupply from increased coffee production, falling coffee demand, and an abundance of low-quality coffee—has given rise to serious economic, social, environmental, and health problems in all of the coffee-producing nations.

The coffee crisis was particularly acute in Nicaragua because the labor and finance sectors were disproportionately dependent upon revenues from coffee, the nation's major export (International Coffee Organization 2003). Thus, beginning in 2000, Nicaraguan rural incomes fell, hunger indices rose, large coffee farms and the banks that financed them went bankrupt, and unemployment rose dramatically. By 2001 an estimated 200,000 people in the agricultural sector were unemployed. Smallholder farmers were unable to sell their crops, and many abandoned their farms and migrated with their families to urban areas, where they often became desperate urban poor.

In response to this crisis, CRS/Nicaragua distributed food to families dependent on coffee production. This emergency relief response evolved into a longer-term ongoing development project focused on helping Nicaraguan farmers escape the coffee crisis. This was to be accomplished through strengthening cooperatives, diversifying small-scale farming, improving and maintaining coffee quality standards, supporting farmers in obtaining organic and Fair Trade certifications, and developing access and linkages to specialty coffee markets in the United States. The first phase of the CRS project, called "Coffee Quality Improvement and Fair Trade," was funded by United States Agency for

International Development (2003, 5) and helped lay the groundwork for improving the well-being of three hundred small-scale farm families. In 2003 CRS initiated a Fair Trade campaign in the United States aimed at creating a market for an "alternative system of international trade rooted in right relationships—relationships that respect human dignity, promote economic justice and cultivate global solidarity" (Catholic Relief Services 2009). Thus, opportunities for socially conscious consumers were to be created in the United States even as the coffee producers readied an improved coffee product for sale to buyers in a CRS Fair Trade Network, currently consisting of fifteen socially conscious roaster companies (www.crsfairtrade.org/coffee/). Over the past several years, Bacon (2005) has studied and recognized as effective the strategy to help Nicaraguan smallholder coffee producers through coffee quality improvement and access to specialty coffee markets. This approach, which works through the farmers' agricultural cooperatives, is also suggested by the success of the small-scale organic coffee sector in Chiapas, Mexico in mitigating the effects of the coffee crisis and economic neoliberalization (Martinez-Torres 2006).

Susan Jackels's involvement in the Nicaraguan coffee crisis came about through the meetings of an academic association of chemists from Jesuit universities called ISJACHEM, the International Jesuit Association of Chemistry and Chemical Engineering Universities and Schools (www.isjachem.org). ISJACHEM had its first meeting in 1996 in Barcelona, Spain, and in 2011 held its thirteenth meeting in Madrid, Spain, at the Universidad Pontificia Comillas. These meetings bring together faculty and administrators from more than twenty Jesuit universities worldwide, including Seattle University (SU) and the University of Central America Managua. Although originally focusing on chemistry and chemical engineering, ISJACHEM has subsequently broadened to include all of the natural sciences and engineering. The members of ISJACHEM have overcome language and cultural barriers to focus on their common Jesuit mission, to help each other improve teaching of science and engineering, and to engage in interdisciplinary projects involving collaborations between their colleagues from more-developed and less-developed countries. In conversations with her counterparts from Jesuit universities in Central and Latin America, but especially Nicaragua, Susan Jackels was informed about the coffee crisis and was challenged to apply her expertise in chemistry to help the Nicaraguan coffee producers (CRS 2006, 15).

Response to this challenge also presented a potentially rich educational opportunity for students and faculty from both developed and developing countries to work together with those most directly affected by the coffee crisis. A RAND study (Wagner, Brahmakulam, Jackson, Wong, and Harlow 2001, xiv) found that in most cases international scientific collaboration is initiated as the result of person-to-person meetings at research sites or international conferences, suggesting that groups and conferences such as ISJACHEM are critical in facilitating this type of activity.

During a trip to Nicaragua in March 2003, Susan learned of the CRS Coffee Quality Improvement and Fair Trade Project from Ms. Lara Puglielli, then country director of CRS/Nicaragua, In further discussions, she found that there was a match between the issues of coffee quality improvement in which she was developing an interest and the needs of CRS/Nicaragua and their Nicaraguan agricultural NGO partners, Association for Development and Diversification of Agricultural Communities (ADDAC) and Caritas Matagalpa (now CECOSEMAC). During these meetings, it also became clear that in order for the research questions to be relevant, they had to be formulated jointly with Nicaraguan partners, addressing the specific needs of the small-scale coffee producers of ADDAC and Caritas. It also became clear that Spanish language facility and an understanding of the basics of international development by nongovernmental organizations (NGOs) were needed in order to facilitate the project.

During the same exploratory trip, Susan visited the University of Central America Managua (UCA Managua) and met Dr. Vera Amanda Solis—then dean of the Faculty of Science, Technology, and the Environment—and Mr. Carlos Vallejos, professor of chemistry. She learned that the mission of the UCA Managua in science is much broader than basic education and includes a strong mandate to serve civil society (*proyección social*). In chemistry, this service mission was envisioned as a laboratory that could offer Nicaraguan customers affordable certified analyses for agricultural and environmental samples, while also serving the educational needs of UCA students. The idea of such a laboratory where students from Nicaragua and the United States could work together and learn professional practices of applied chemistry in service to society was exciting. Opportunities were also envisioned for students from both institutions to have valuable educational field experiences arising from participation with the CRS/Nicaragua coffee quality improvement project and the Nicaraguan coffee cooperatives. However, this vision could not become reality without institutional support. Thus, the exploratory trip culminated in a meeting of officials from SU, CRS/Nicaragua and UCA Managua where all of the issues were discussed, and the partnership for coffee quality improvement and the UCA laboratory was officially begun in March 2003.

After this trip, Susan and her husband, Charles Jackels, also a chemist and faculty member at University of Washington Bothell, applied for sabbatical leaves to spend time at CRS/Nicaragua and UCA Managua to formulate the research and to work on the projects. Together, they applied to CRS/Nicaragua as volunteers, with a proposal for a field study of the fermentation step in coffee processing on smallholder farms. CRS/Nicaragua provided essential support that included: identification of places to stay; facilitation of contact with the cooperatives and their technical staffs; identification of a group of leadership coffee producers who were receptive to visits on their farms; translation when needed on the farms; and transportation to the remote farms over rugged mountainous terrain.

To prepare for the sabbatical, Susan joined a seminar on international development and took more than a year of Spanish classes. Essential background included Nicaraguan history and economic development, the socio-economics of the coffee crisis, and the function and organization of international NGOs, in addition to a survival-level fluency in Spanish. With these initial steps began a program of study and application that has been ongoing for over nine years. Involving four faculty and twenty-one students from SU and UCA Managua, the project has included field studies near Matagalpa and laboratory studies in both Seattle and Managua. These studies have resulted in a patent publication, academic publications and presentations, capstone/thesis projects for students, and professional development for faculty, but *most importantly*, they resulted in knowledge and training for Nicaraguan coffee farmers that may have assisted them in improving their situation.

It became apparent that support and involvement of the project partners from the development community and agricultural cooperatives would be essential not only for project feasibility, but also to ensure that the knowledge and training would become widely available and sustained. In this way the project would be contributing not only to the capacity and success of a number of individual producers, but to the accumulation of "social capital" by the agricultural communities, a resource found to be most important in a similar context in Mexico (Martinez-Torres 2006). As an example, the cooperative CECOSEMAC sought the Coffee for Justice team's collaboration and advice in designing and funding a coffee-processing mill for a remote community (details follow). Although this engineering project was considerably different than the previous science-based ones, CECOSEMAC's confidence in and experience with our team permitted this project to go forward with great success. The remainder of this chapter describes these projects and their outcomes.

Initial Field Study of Coffee Fermentation

In conversations with the coffee producers, the question asked by them most often was how to avoid "over fermentation," since this was generally thought to lower the taste quality of the coffee when it was subsequently dried and roasted. Conversations with United States Agency for International Development staff confirmed this observation. The fermentation step of coffee processing enables the coffee beans to be washed clean of the sweet mucilage that clings to them after the skin and fruit have been mechanically removed. A batch is considered "over fermented" if that process is allowed to continue beyond the time needed to loosen the mucilage. While the producers had a simple tactile test for fermentation completion, they desired to know if that test was trustworthy and what degree of over-fermentation would make a measurable difference in coffee quality.[1] In other words, they desired a better understanding of the quality control issues in this process and a mechanism for effectively managing it. Our goal, then, was to study the process on the small farms, find a chemical species that could serve as an indicator of the fermentation process, and find a simple field test that producers could use themselves to diagnose the fermentation on their farms.

Prior to their deployment on the coffee farms, appropriate testing methods and experiments needed to be developed and tested in the laboratory. This step was crucial, because once the equipment and personnel were deployed in Nicaragua, there would be neither sufficient time nor resources to redesign the methods during the visit. Since fresh coffee cherries cannot be routinely obtained in the United States, a model system was needed in order to develop the chemistry in the SU laboratory before departure. A literature search revealed that mango fruit has somewhat similar composition to coffee fruit mucilage (Olle, Lozano, and Brillouet 1996; Avallone et al. 2000), so yeast was added to chunks of mango fruit and the resulting "fermentation" was monitored using a simple testing system marketed for field work in the food industry for products like yogurt, wine, and beer. The EM Science Reflectoquant system, a battery-operated quantitative reader for color sensitive test strips, uses reagent-coated plastic strips that react with simple biochemicals—such as hydrogen ion (pH), ethanol, glucose, or lactic acid—to measure their concentrations by colors that are quantitatively measured by a small battery-operated, hand-held reflectometer. A digital thermometer also was used to track the temperature of the fermenting mass. In this way, the tests and experiments were perfected on the mango chunk model. Subsequently, a "mobile laboratory" was assembled containing all the equipment necessary to monitor fermenting coffee-bean mucilage on the farms in Nicaragua. This laboratory had to be fully functional for several days without supplies of pure water or electrical power and had to be compact enough to be carried for approximately one kilometer by an assistant.

Despite having never been tested on coffee in the field, the experiments and equipment worked well, enabling time-profile concentrations of four chemicals to be collected during coffee fermentation. In January 2004, at the peak of the harvest season, seven fermentation batches were studied under differing conditions on three small-scale farms and one large-scale gourmet coffee farm in Nicaragua in runs lasting from twelve to twenty-four hours. It was found that there were similar patterns in the time-profiles of the chemical indicators, despite the differences in location, altitude, coffee plant variety, rainfall, temperature, and so on. Of the four indicators, pH was found to be ideally suited, since a large change was observed near the optimum time to terminate fermentation. A composite graph of the seven profiles of pH versus time (in hours) is shown in Figure 7-2. In this graph, the seven pH-time profiles are superimposed and aligned so that in each case time the value zero on the horizontal axis corresponds to that time when the pH became 4.6, a value previously determined to be approximately optimal for termination of fermentation. As the fermentation proceeds, the pH decreases in a similar manner for this wide range of conditions (see Figure 7-2). (A decrease of one pH unit corresponds to a ten-fold increase in hydrogen ion concentration.) None of the other chemical indicators provided systems of time profiles, when similarly aligned and superimposed, which changed greatly and had such consistent behavior across the entire set of seven runs. The results of this study have been published in the *Journal of Food Science* (Jackels and Jackels 2005).

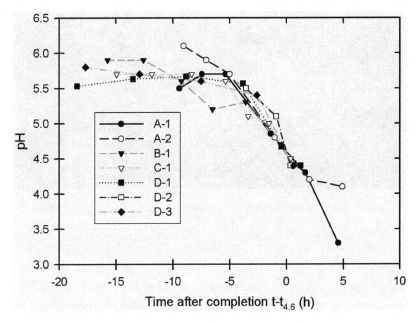

FIGURE 7-2. Time profiles for pH versus time (t = 0 at fermentation completion) for seven fermentation batches studied on four farms.

FIGURE 7-3. Susan Jackels with mobile laboratory on-site in Matagalpa, Nicaragua.

Report to coffee producers and next steps. A report of the field study was prepared, translated, and presented to the coffee producers and the staffs of ADDAC and CRS/Nicaragua. In the ensuing discussion, the coffee producers and ADDAC staff wanted to know if a pH test kit could help them improve quality and consistency of coffee. Subsequent

FIGURE 7-4. Charles Jackels with coffee producers and ADDAC staff, on-site in Matagalpa, Nicaragua.

to the meeting with the farmers, but as another part of the CRS Coffee Quality Improvement project, about thirty farms had their coffee roasted and taste-tested in the 2003/2004 harvest. The results showed that the group was producing average to good coffee, but only a few were close to the desired excellent range. Based on the results of the field study and the interest of the producers, it was proposed that a simple kit be developed for the coffee producers so that they could use pH measurements to monitor and optimize their fermentation. The interest in development and use of such a kit, the need to better understand the coffee fermentation process, and the expressed desire to establish an analytical laboratory at UCA provided motivation for planning an extended involvement with Nicaragua and its coffee farmers. Support for this larger-scale extension of the work came mostly through an NSF Discovery Corps Senior Fellowship awarded to Susan Jackels that provided for student and faculty exchange visits, laboratory equipment deployed in Managua, a training workshop for cooperative technical staff, and more than one hundred kits for use by individual farmers.

Projects with pH field test kit. A prototype pH kit was developed that the farmers could use to optimize and regularize the fermentation of their coffee. The kit needed to be inexpensive, simple to use, and contain necessary equipment to make pH measurements and keep a record of the results. The prototype kit (Figure 7-5) included pH paper, pH color scale, cups, spoons, pictorial step-wise instructions for making measurements (translated into Spanish by CRS/Nicaragua), clip board, data sheets, a watch, a thermometer and a pen. Since it had been noticed that there were few printed materials on the farms, a children's storybook in Spanish was added to each kit (funded by SU students and staff).

In December 2004 ten prototype coffee fermentation kits were distributed to coffee producers. The staff members of ADDAC were trained in the use of the kits at a hands-on workshop held at *la Canavalia*, the association's model farm. The producers were instructed not to modify their normal processing practices, but only to record the measurement of pH at the beginning and end of fermentation. The purposes were to learn if the kits could be successfully used by the

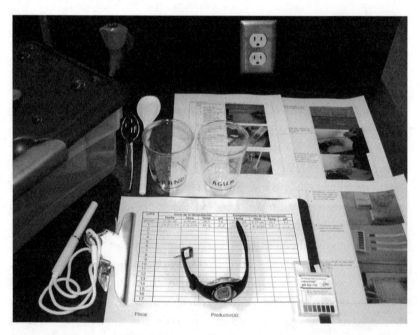

FIGURE 7-5. Prototype pH kit for testing coffee fermentation.

producers and, if so, to characterize the fermentation processes on their farms. Consistent results were obtained in thirty separate coffee fermentation batches monitored by fourteen producers over a five-day period. In twenty-four of the batches, the pH recorded at time of washing was 4.0 or below, and it was apparent that these batches had experienced some degree of over-fermentation, since a pH of 4.6 was considered optimum from our previous studies. It was concluded that the pH measurement with the kit was potentially useful as a test for fermentation by the producer. More research was needed, however, to establish the relationship between the apparent over-fermentation and coffee quality in the cup.

Building upon the previous pilot study, an extensive coffee quality improvement project training staff and deploying pH kits on one hundred of the farms served by CRS/Nicaragua was launched on a trip in December 2005. The purpose was to determine if the coffee farmers could use the kit to *modify* their procedures, reduce over-fermentation, and obtain higher quality coffee. Since most farmers had been over-fermenting their coffee, the desired modification asked of the farmers was to interrupt the fermentation *earlier,* at a higher pH. The evidence from this study was conclusive that the farmers could effectively utilize the kit to increase the pH of fermentation completion and thereby reduce over-fermentation. Figure 7-6 shows a plot of the *change* in fermentation time reported by the farmers versus the *change* in pH at the time of washing. The farmers were trying to achieve *a smaller change* in pH at completion of fermentation by intentional shortening of fermentation time. From this plot it can be seen that most of the points are in the lower right quadrant, indicating a shortening of fermentation time (negative value on vertical axis) was correlated with a higher pH value at the time of washing (positive value on horizontal axis). This inverse correlation, very apparent in Figure 7-6, is statistically significant with less than 0.4 percent probability of occurring simply by chance.

However, there was no statistically significant improvement in coffee quality due to this intervention, as measured by expert cuppers. There were complications due to the study being conducted near the end of the harvest season when the quality diminishes, resulting in the "before" and "after" experiments using coffee of different quality.

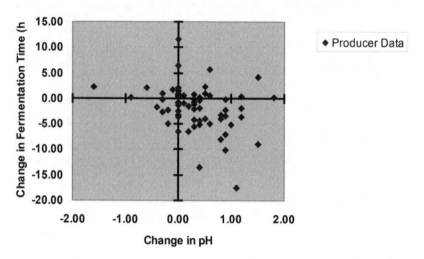

FIGURE 7-6. Correlation of change in fermentation time with change in pH.

However, when the coffee quality data was viewed on the level of the six cooperatives participating in the study, the two cooperatives that were producing the best coffee (scores in the low to mid eighties) did not improve, but the lowest performing cooperatives (initial score in the seventies) improved their average to the low eighties. Clearly, further study was indicated to learn if the effective control of fermentation by the farmers as demonstrated here could result in a measureable quality improvement. A paper describing these coffee project activities was presented to the International Association for Coffee Science and has been published in its proceedings (S. Jackels et al. 2006). Also, a patent application for the coffee fermentation kit was published (Jackels and Jackels 2006).

In fall 2006 Susan visited Nicaragua for approximately two and one-half months to work with coffee farmers and the technical staffs of their cooperatives. The results from the previous harvest season were presented and discussed, and participants were trained in the use of the kit to predict the time of fermentation completion and thereby minimize over-fermentation. Fresh pH strips were supplied to replenish the kits and data sheets supplied to collect and report fermentation pH data for the 2006–2007 harvest season. Workshops were given for technical staff and members of CECOSEMAC and ADDAC (Figure 7-7).

Controlled fermentation experiments. In addition to the pH kit activities conducted directly with the producers, it was clear from the beginning that there was also a need to understand more deeply the fermentation process and its effect on coffee quality. These questions could be addressed with systematic interventions in well-controlled coffee fermentation experiments. Thus, a series of controlled fermentation experiments was conducted at the model farm of ADDAC, *la Canavalia*, in Matagalpa, Nicaragua in collaboration with Professor Vallejos and two students from UCA Managua and SU. These experiments, which systematically investigated the effect of prefermentation washing steps and intentional over-fermentation on the quality of the coffee, were carried out on small batches in specialized fermentation tanks designed for the field laboratory (Figure 7-8). The quality of these batches was assessed by roasting and expert cupping following normal postfermentation selection and drying. The conclusions reached were: There was no evidence that extensive washing of the beans *before* fermentation

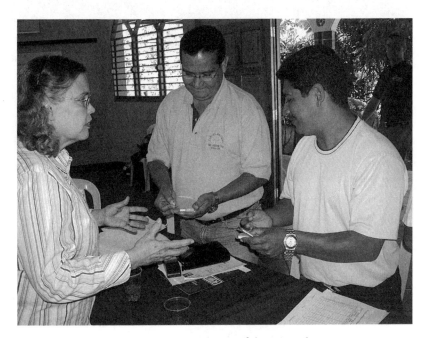

FIGURE 7-7. Susan Jackels instructing in the use of the pH test kit.

FIGURE 7-8. Filling the small fermentation tanks.

resulted in coffee quality improvement, and the evidence from the over-fermented batches indicated that over-fermentation resulted in greater variability in coffee quality and a decrease in quality control.

In December 2005 a larger set of controlled experiments was carried out to further examine the relationship between over-fermentation and coffee quality. Over a three-week period, eleven fermentation batches were studied at *la Canavalia*. Each batch was divided into six small fermentation tanks. In each set the fermentation was stopped at the following pH values: (1) two tanks in pH range 4.5–4.8 (completion); (2) two tanks in the range 4.1–4.4 (approximately 1.5 hours over fermentation); and (3) two in the range 3.6–4.0 (four hours over fermentation). The eleven batches provided thirty-three duplicate pairs of tanks, or sixty-six samples to be taste-tested (cupped) for quality by professional tasters. The results exhibited a decrease in average cupping score from 80.3 for samples in range 1 (pH 4.5–4.8) to 78.8 for those in range 3 (pH 3.6–4.0). Based on pair-wise comparisons of samples within the six-tank batches, this decrease in score was determined to be statistically significant, with less than a 4 percent probability that it would arise purely by chance. A similar analysis for the less severe over-fermentation (range 1 to range 2) showed the mean cupping score also decreased, but by a smaller amount that was not statistically significant (S. Jackels et al. 2006).

These observations gave experimental confirmation and quantification to the "common knowledge" of the coffee farming community, specifically that over-fermentation for several hours, corresponding to a decrease of pH at the time of washing to four or less, has a consequence of several quality points when the coffee is later roasted and taste-tested.

During the next harvest season, in December 2006, two sets of field experiments were conducted in collaboration with four students from UCA Managua. At the suggestion of coffee scientists from Africa (Association for Science and Information on Coffee 2006), we investigated the possible effect of a twenty-four-hour soaking of the coffee beans *after* fermentation was complete and they were completely washed clean, but before they were dried. Some informal results from Africa suggested that such a soaking improved the quality of the coffee beans. A series of ten paired experiments were carried, in which one-half of the coffee beans were fermented, washed, and dried as usual, while the other half of the batch was soaked for twenty-four hours in clean water after fermentation and washing before being dried. After drying, both halves of each batch were selected, roasted, and cupped identically. No statistically significant improvement in coffee quality was observed due to this soaking, and we have not recommended this practice to our partner producers.

Laboratory research. During the 2005–2006 phase of the project, the analytical laboratory at the UCA Managua (Figure 7-9) was established along with its "sister" laboratory at SU. Investigations were initiated in both laboratories on two projects: (1) analysis of *ochratoxin,* a mould-produced toxin that can be found in coffee that is improperly dried, and (2) liquid chromatographic analysis of bio-acids in mucilage from fermenting coffee. These samples had been collected at different fermentation stages in Nicaragua, frozen on-site, and transported to SU for analysis. These studies were initiated by Professor Vallejos and Roberto Rivas, a student from UCA Managua, during a three-month visit to Seattle and were completed by SU undergraduate researchers. Fermentation time-profiles of seven bio-acids and ethanol were determined by liquid chromatography and it was found that both ethanol and lactic acid exhibited very large concentration increases during over-fermentation. These results were presented at the 235th National Meeting of the American Chemical Society in April 2008 (S. Jackels et al. 2008).

FIGURE 7-9. Professors Vallejos and Jackels in the laboratory at UCA Managua.

A project for characterization of coffee aroma profiles by gas chromatography and principal component analysis is continuing in the laboratory at SU. The goal of this research is to determine chemical
"fingerprints" characteristic of different quality coffees and of coffee
that has been over-fermented. Results of this project were presented at
the 239th National Meeting of the American Chemical Society (Ubben,
Jackels, and Jackels 2010).

Beneficio design and construction project. Nicaraguan farmers like our
partners in the Coffee for Justice project generally carry out the depulping, fermentation, washing, and initial drying steps of postharvest processing on their individual farms or at a central site in a small
community of producers. To be done well, processing requires a facility
(*beneficio*) that houses the depulper, the fermentation tanks, and the
washing trough, and provides for responsible disposal of the wastewater. In some of the poorest communities the farmers lack any sort of
proper facility, carrying out the depulping out of doors on a portable,
older machine, carrying out fermentation in sacks rather than in a tank
open to the air, and releasing waste water directly into the surface
water. Generally, the farmers feel that the quality of their coffee is
severely compromised by use of such makeshift facilities.

In 2007 we expressed an interest in a potential *beneficio* design project and were made aware of a community of thirteen small-scale producers who had an older depulper, but no proper facility for mounting
and maintaining it and no facility at all for the fermentation step. In
collaboration with Drs. Michael Marsolek and Jeff Dragovich, professors in the Civil and Environmental Engineering Department at SU and
members of the SU chapter of Engineers without Borders, an exploratory trip was made to the community at La Suana to view and survey
the site in order to determine its suitability for an engineering project
to design and build a coffee beneficio with waste water treatment for
the community. The SU Engineering Project Center secured project
funding from the Seattle branch of Tetra Tech, an international environmental engineering consulting firm, and a student team of four
environmental engineers joined Professors Marsolek and S. Jackels on
this project.

After studying the general problem and becoming familiar with the
wastewater treatment options available in Nicaragua, the team visited
the producer community in December 2007. They surveyed the site,

interviewed the potential users of the *beneficio* had discussions with both their agricultural cooperative, who would act as their agent, and with a contractor who had been selected by the cooperative to build the *beneficio* in their community. The team visited a newly built *beneficio ecológico* or ecological coffee processing mill to see some of the most modern water-handling methods. They observed a *beneficio* in operation at the model farm, *la Canavalia*, making measurements on water consumption and treatment and analyzing wastewater to determine its pollutant loading.

During winter 2008, the team used the data and observations to prepare three design options for the *beneficio* and wastewater treatment facility at La Suana. The design was forwarded to the cooperative, which selected an option and construction began in May 2008 (Figure 7-10). The *beneficio* was completed during fall 2008, ready for operation during the harvest season in December 2008. To complete the project, Professors Marsolek and Jackels visited the site during operation and made follow-up measurements on the wastewater quality to determine

FIGURE 7-10. New coffee processing mill (*beneficio*) for the community at La Suana, Nicaragua.

that the system of settling and infiltration ponds designed for the site was performing satisfactorily (Figure 7-11). See Marsolek et al. (2012) for a detailed report in the engineering service learning literature on the *beneficio* design project.

Conclusion

It was very inspiring to meet and work with Nicaraguan coffee producers who were struggling courageously in the midst of dire economic conditions. These coffee producers are self-educated and highly skilled men and women who have great sense of process and attention to the details of their artisan tradition of coffee production. They also are lifelong learners who are friendly, respectful, and for the most part enthusiastic in embracing and implementing new ideas. We saw that the coffee producers have much to offer us and our students. In particular, they provide our students with very valuable lessons, role models,

FIGURE 7-11. Environmental engineer Dr. Michael Marsolek, Seattle University, with Nicaraguan colleagues at the coffee wastewater processing facility at La Suana, Nicaragua.

and cross-cultural interactions. In this project and partnership, there was a great opportunity to practice applied science in service with, and for, these producers, knowing that they are capable of using the results and that the cause of economic justice will be served. Nongovernmental organizations like CRS/Nicaragua and farm-based cooperative organizations like ADDAC and CECOSEMAC provided a network for delivering technical support to their farming communities and for developing good agricultural practices, including organic and Fair Trade farming. This network provided our project with an essential mechanism to disseminate and implement the methods developed for coffee quality improvement and to provide the necessary follow-up.

Thus, Coffee for Justice will be an ongoing project for sustainability and solidarity, hopefully developing a model for what can be accomplished through the collaboration between people in developed and developing countries, including university professors, students, development/relief agency staff, agricultural nongovernmental organization staff, and coffee producers and their families. In the future, it is hoped that the partnership will take steps toward further development and dissemination of the pH fermentation control kit that can help coffee producers make the best coffee possible within the capability of their farms. In Nicaragua alone, up to 20,000 farms could ultimately benefit. It is clear, also, that in the future the partnership can assist CRS/Nicaragua in its marketing role by advocating for the coffee farmers to US specialty coffee buyers and to the socially conscious American public, promoting a just response to the Coffee Crisis (CRS 2006).

This general theme (and title) of this monograph is "transformation," and the conclusion of Pedro Otriz's story, introduced in the beginning of this chapter, is a clear example of transformation in the world. In February 2006 a group of buyers from the CRS Fair Trade Network visited the farm of Pedro Ortiz and other farmers in six cooperatives supported by Caritas Matagalpa and Catholic Relief Services. The buyers made relationships with the farmers and their families, tasted their coffee, and purchased about 30,000 pounds of newly certified Fair Trade coffee to roast and sell in the United States through the CRS Fair Trade Network. As a result, Pedro Ortiz received a loan from his cooperative and made the improvements on his farm that ultimately translated into a slightly better quality of life for his family. To the extent that the Coffee for Justice project may have played a small role

FIGURE 7-12. SU student Stephanie Kleven and UCA Managua student Roberto Rivas washing fermented coffee at the field laboratory in Nicaragua.

in the good fortune of Pedro and his family it has been an instrument of transformation and justice.

Transformation has also been experienced by the students and faculty, both Nicaraguan and North American, who have been involved in the Coffee for Justice project. Through this engaged scholarship and service learning they have been empowered by the realization that their own scientific efforts, as modest as they may be, can be effective in addressing some of the most serious problems of a developing society. As just one example of transformation of a student team member, Ms. Stephanie Kleven, who participated in the Coffee for Justice field study as an undergraduate in 2005/2006 (Figure 7-12), became sufficiently interested in serving the people of Nicaragua that she returned to Nicaragua after graduation as a Fulbright Scholar during 2007/2008 to work with rural community health care volunteers in Matagalpa. She is now a clinical nurse at the Hospital of the University of Pennsylvania. Transformation occurred in the Nicaraguan team members most frequently in the form of opportunities. For example, Roberto Rivas, a student at the UCA Managua (Figure 7-12), has gone on to pursue an MA degree in Environmental Studies in Hamburg, Germany. UCA Managua Prof. Carlos Vallejos began graduate studies in analytical chemistry at the Institut Quimic de Sarria in Barcelona, Spain. Thus, the educated base of individuals in Nicaragua possibly will be expanded through these opportunities with associated future improvements and transformations for Nicaragua. Finally, we as professors in the United States have been transformed. We have come to believe that our scientific efforts, both applied and basic, can make a difference for people in a developing society (Jackels et al. 2010). Further, the experience of undertaking the projects has been far richer than we imagined and has been transformative for all involved. The most gratifying evidence is that we now buy coffee of origin from companies in the United States that was grown on the very farms on which we worked. We know that our research activities and eventually our future results will cycle back to the farms of Nicaragua and continue to improve lives and families.[2]

8 Personal Transformation and Curricula Change

SUZANNE HETZEL CAMPBELL, PHILIP GREINER,
SHEILA GROSSMAN, ALISON KRIS, LAURENCE
MINERS, AND JOYCE SHEA

Kolvenbach (2004, 59) describes the service of faith and the promotion of justice in American Jesuit Higher Education stating: "The real measure of our Jesuit universities lies in whom our students become." He feels strongly that it is only through contact with the poor and marginalized that "whole persons" of tomorrow can truly be educated in solidarity (60). This chapter outlines the journey of faculty and staff at a School of Nursing through a yearlong faculty and professional learning community (FPLC) and share examples of curricular revisions, pedagogical strategies, and service learning opportunities that promote transformation in both the approach to teaching and learning and in students' perceptions of the world that address Kolvenbach's ideas. The chapter also provides an analysis of lessons learned from this experience regarding how community members, faculty, and students responded to these changes. While the focus and the specific examples of curricula changes given relate to the School of Nursing, the learning community approach is applicable to any school or department.

The FPLC Model

In fall 2007 Fairfield University began a faculty learning community program as an approach to implementing its new university-wide strategic plan. The strategic plan has three main pieces and the learning communities address the integration of learning—integration across core courses, within majors, and among core and major classes. Like most Jesuit schools, the undergraduate core curriculum at Fairfield is large and encompasses about half of a student's credits needed for graduation.

Faculty and Professional Learning Communities (FPLCs) are small groups of faculty and professional staff (six to ten individuals per group) who "engage in an active, collaborative, yearlong program with a curriculum about enhancing teaching and learning" (Cox 2004, 8). Dr. Milton Cox at the Center for the Enhancement of Teaching and Learning at Miami University began using FPLCs about thirty years ago. They have since spread to many colleges and universities. The initiative began first with faculty members, but over time expanded to include members of the professional staff. Learning communities can be either theme-based or cohort-based. As examples, theme-based learning communities could focus on a variety of teaching ideas such as technology, global citizenship, or the environment. Cohort-based learning communities could include junior faculty, mid-career faculty, or department chairs. Participants apply to participate in the program and identify a teaching and learning project that becomes each team member's work. Groups meet for two hours, twice a month, for an academic year— approximately seven meetings each semester. Every learning community has a facilitator who helps guide the group through a mutually agreed-upon set of topics. FPLC group facilitators at Fairfield University traveled to national conferences on learning communities and spent a year developing the FPLC program. A unique feature of Fairfield's FPLC program is that each learning community strives to increase the integration of teaching and learning. Each year, for the past three years, the university has sponsored five different learning communities.

While each learning community is given wide latitude as to how it conducts its meetings, there is a general model, which we developed, that we encourage all the FPLCs to follow. From the outset, we make a distinction between serving on a faculty *committee* and belonging to a learning *community*. Committees have a chairperson that is responsible for setting agendas and shepherding work through the committee. Sometimes there are subcommittees that work on specific tasks, and there may be a great amount or little work to do between committee meetings. Some committee members shoulder a lot of responsibility while others shirk. Learning communities, on the other hand, are about shared responsibility and mutual learning. Participating in a learning community is a new experience for most faculty members and the facilitator needs to model transparency of both purpose and goals and encourage participation by all members. Some faculty members have remarked that the way of proceeding in the learning community establishes a method for their own teaching. This is not unintended.

The format for a typical meeting, arrived at mutually in the initial meeting, is as follows: There is a brief check-in period for participants to catch up with one another and get ready for work. While this may appear like wasted or unproductive time, the check-in helps engender an atmosphere of community, rather than committee, for the group. An agenda is set at the previous meeting, and if there are several topics to discuss the group may agree upon approximate time allocations for each topic. At the end of the meeting community members spend a few minutes writing about what transpired during the meeting. This writing is more about reactions to what took place rather than descriptions of content. Participants share as much, or as little, as they want from their writing. The ensuing conversations are both sincere and personal. Colleagues offer insightful, affirming, and revealing comments about what they are taking away from the meeting.

Problems and items of concern are dealt with as they arise. Decisions are usually made by consensus, rather than vote, and anyone can block a proposed decision if they are strongly opposed to it. Conversation continues until consensus is reached. The road-blocking power of a dissenting voice was recognized by all; as a result the FPLCs strove hard to work together.

The School of Nursing FPLC was unique in that it included attributes of both a cohort-based and theme-based FPLC and faculty were sponsored by the School of Nursing advisory board. All the participants, except the facilitator, were from the School of Nursing, and the group included faculty members from all academic ranks (one of whom was also serving as associate dean), and the director of the School of Nursing's Robin Kanarek Learning Resource Center, a member of the professional staff. The participants' projects included the exploration of innovative teaching and learning techniques applied to specific courses and to simulated learning in core and specialty nursing courses. The faculty wanted to construct a more integrated and cohesive curriculum.

The FPLC allowed a deeper exploration of and reflection on new approaches to pedagogy as well as an opportunity to incorporate some of these approaches into course teaching. The School of Nursing is not large, but prior to participating in the community, faculty members did not have a full understanding of the pedagogical techniques employed by their colleagues. One member shared the following reflection:

> It is being open to the learning process with students, incorporating themes of social justice, and taking concrete clinical experiences to reinforce their learning which was one of the greatest outcomes of the FPLC for me. The FPLC gave me time to "digest" all I was doing, bounce ideas off understanding colleagues, get a sense for when I was on the right or wrong track. It provided time for self-reflection, tweaking of techniques, and assessment of outcomes that are not always available in the day-to-day rush of nursing faculty's lives. It also gave me courage to incorporate the social justice issues and continue to reinforce care of the whole person, mind, body, and spirit.

Through studying the Ignatian paradigm of context, experience, reflection, action, and evaluation, they developed a more unified approach to student learning (Figure 8-1). The sense of camaraderie developed by

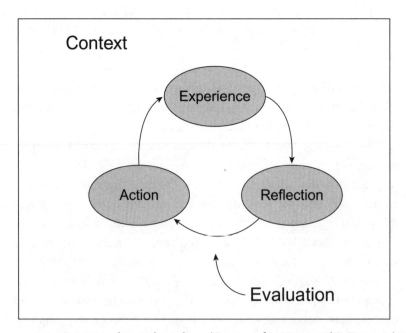

FIGURE 8-1. Ignatian pedagogical paradigm. (Courtesy of L. Miners and R. Torosyan.)

sharing best practices, as well as admitting to challenges and frustrations, led to growth for all involved in the process. The seven FPLC members left with a deeper appreciation of what their colleagues were doing in the classroom and identified ways to build bridges between courses. Another colleague wrote: "For me what worked was when we read the same excerpts, articles or book chapters and then shared our perspective on these and applied them to our own work. I enjoyed hearing how each of the members applied the new information. We did share our thoughts at each meeting but I thought the meetings where we had tangible readings were the best."

The world of baccalaureate and higher degree nursing education includes national accreditation through the Commission on Collegiate Nursing Education (CCNE) and guidance on program content through the American Association of Colleges of Nursing (AACN). As a result, the program content, course descriptions, general content in courses, and outcomes of programs appear rather homogenized, at least on paper. However, our journey as a university faculty and our desire to participate in an FPLC to form community with our colleagues was transformative. Our pedagogy became more focused on the whole student and the student's role in the world around them.

Curriculum Changes

Faculty members participating in the FPLC developed ideas for improving the social justice strand in both the graduate and undergraduate programs. These ideas emerged as a thread in the readings that participants were doing as part of the FPLC. The school does not differentiate faculty assignments as graduate or undergraduate, so all FPLC participants were involved in course development for all the courses throughout both programs. Examples of course changes help to illustrate the inclusion of innovative teaching methods to enhance the social justice content.

Graduate Program Examples

One of the first core courses in the MA program presents theory regarding basic epidemiology, biostatistics, and the promotion of health at the individual, family, group, and population levels. The Epidemiology and Health Promotion course became the first graduate-level course at the university designated as a service learning course as a result of the School of Nursing FPLC. This course includes content on program and grant development specifically to promote individual and population health. Students work in small groups to develop, deliver, evaluate, and report on a health promotion project. Each group selects a community organization with which to work and meets with the organization's administrator and those served by the organization to determine program parameters as well as topical areas the students might address in their course project. Guidance in selecting the community organization is provided by the course faculty member, who has a background in community and public health nursing and a twelve-year history of community engagement in the Bridgeport, Connecticut, region. The primary criterion for selection of the community organization is that the students are able to gain access to a population of individuals that would benefit from a structured educational presentation on a topic with which the students are unfamiliar. Students must meet with the organization's leadership, with the clients served by that agency, and with the course faculty member to determine a topic for presentation to the clients. Students then develop a proposal based on evidence of successful programs for similar clients on the selected topic. For example, last semester a student group selected to work with older adults attending a senior center. The identified topic was improving nutrition for older adults during the winter when fresh foods were in short supply. Students met with a group of older women to ask what they knew about their nutritional needs and what foods they preferred to eat in the winter. From these interviews and a review of the literature, the students developed a list of nutrients to emphasize. The student group then tried to identify foods that would provide most of the missing nutrients. Through their discussion and reflection on the clients' preferences, they realized that soups were a flexible and affordable way to incorporate the nutritional goals and client preferences. The students created a two-phase program where they introduced the nutritional goals and tasted several soups in phase one and then invited the women to bring in recipes and share several different soups in phase two. The clients had to teach back about why a given soup was good for them nutritionally, providing an excellent method of evaluating the effectiveness of the teaching done in phase one.

Through this project process, students engage a community organization and the people served by that organization in ways that are quite different from the student's "clinical" lives. They frequently comment on the transformational nature of the project on their perceptions of the population served and of their roles as nurses. The project also forces students to better understand the lived experience of the people served by that community organization. In this way, students can successfully deliver the project content while developing cultural humility (Tervalon and Murray-García 1998). It is through this exchange that students begin to understand the impact of the social determinants of health, the role that social ecology plays in health behaviors at the community level, and the barriers that are created for individual improvement of health. These experiences prompt discussions of social justice concerns and the roles that nursing students prepared at the graduate level can fill to address those concerns.

Another master's core course, Advanced Nursing Roles and Reflective Practice, added components of reflective practice and cultural awareness. Panels of psychiatric mental health and family practice nurse practitioners, clinical nurse leaders, clinical nurse specialists, and health care managers were invited to class to present their roles, with a specific focus on the character of social justice in their practice and how they evaluate their performance. Using these presentations as a model, students wrote reflective logs after each of their own clinical experience addressing their communication, self-awareness, and partnerships with individuals and groups who are culturally different from those with whom they more frequently collaborate. Ethical leadership content was also incorporated into this Advanced Nursing Roles and Reflective Practice course.

Undergraduate Program Examples

The first clinical course, Geriatric Nursing, offered in the sophomore or second year, was modified to provide students with opportunities to reflect on their clinical experiences. Reflection was selected as a method of enhancing student observation skills and teaching beginning reflective practice skills. This is the only nursing course approved as part of the sophomore year Ignatian Residential College (IRC) living-learning community, therefore the use of reflection was an excellent fit with the Ignatian pedagogy employed by faculty members who teach in the IRC community. (The IRC includes sophomore students from all of the university's colleges and schools. During the year students consider three big questions: Who am I? Whose am I? Who am I called to be?) Examples of statements provided for reflection included: "What ethical dilemmas have you witnessed?" "What constitutes an ideal death?" and "Who are you called to be (as a nurse)?" While students were not specifically asked to comment on social justice themes, social justice resonated throughout their reflections. The techniques learned in the FPLC encouraged a dialogical approach to student learning. Therefore, when several students commented on the lack of resident autonomy and independence they observed in the nursing homes, a deeper discussion of the ethics of resident autonomy emerged. Students shared that the thought of being told when you will get up, when you will eat, and at what time and on which day you will shower was unpleasant to a newly independent college student. This student comment illustrates the recognition of the social justice theme of autonomy: "I remember on my first day overhearing a resident on the phone with what I assumed to be a family member yelling about how hard it was to be stuck in a nursing home. I thought to myself how painful that must be."

Discussions about classroom pedagogy within the FPLC often centered on drawing out the wealth of experience the students bring to the classroom and encouraging them to reflect on that experience in novel and meaningful ways. A new, optional, exercise was added to the geriatric nursing course which asked students to wear an "adult diaper" for twenty-four hours and reflect on the experience. One student noted: "Although I am used to going through the motions with my morning routine, I still stop and think about how a grown man must feel, having a young woman have to change him because he is incapable of changing himself." Another student commented, "I could not even imagine having a friend or, even worse, a stranger changing my diaper for me."

We spoke often about working with adult learners (especially the second degree students and the graduate students), and about strategies to make their learning experiences more meaningful and, therefore, more lasting in terms of effects. We read excerpts from Fink's *Creating Significant Learning Experiences* (2003) and spoke about our own efforts to be reflective after reading chapters from Brookfield's *Becoming a Critically Reflective Teacher* (1995). A couple members of the learning community developed reflective writing assignments based on Brookfield's Critical Incident Questionnaire (1995, 114). These conversations on pedagogy led to a review of specific strategies for engaging students (Bean 1996) and evaluating whether the course assignments were effective at meeting the objective of engaging students (Angelo and Cross 1993). As a group, we encouraged each other to develop more in-class exercises and course assignments that incorporated reflection and tied to students' past experiences and current feelings. These conversations helped one FPLC participant to think about activities that would stimulate self-awareness in students in her Mental Health Nursing class.

Therefore, when students commented on the importance of maintaining patient dignity and on the patients' rights to receive basic nursing care, there was a new opportunity to reframe these ethical principles as social justice issues. Students were asked to answer the Ignatian question of "Who am I called to be? (as a nurse)" One student responded:

> Today was meaningful to me in that I had a chance to see that hard days can happen in nursing and because of this I was able to evaluate why I am called to be a nurse. As a nurse I am called to do the very best for my patients. I am called to be a person that my patients can feel safe with. Even though Mr. S was upset today, it is my job to make him feel comfortable and dignified. As a nurse, I am called to be an advocate for my patients and strongly feel that I must be their voice when they cannot speak for themselves.

These examples demonstrate Kolvenbach's (2004) concept of experiencing solidarity with the marginalized, in this case with their older adult patients, by being in direct contact and sensing their fear, isolation, and pain.

The Mental Health Nursing course in the junior or third year was enhanced with several significant changes. First, current and former patients agreed to come to selected class sessions to talk about their personal experiences with mental health issues and treatment. The inclusion of these individuals helped to move the discussion from content in a book to the lived experience of actual patients. From these presentations, discussions addressed the stigma associated with mental health issues, the problems patients experience gaining access to care, and the difficulties that family, patients, and advocates face in the quest to improve care options and social integration of these vulnerable people.

Second, the selection of movies for the course was modified to incorporate issues related to social justice. While movies have been used in the course to depict various mental health problems, the process used to select movies became more intentional to include movies that also addressed social justice issues. The use of current and former patients and movies more attuned to social justice issues has created a classroom environment that fosters discussion about social justice at the personal, family, group, and societal levels. One new video, "In Our Own Voice," centered on former consumers of mental health services telling their stories of illness and recovery. Other movies and documentaries were followed with reflective assignments. "Homeless in Paradise" followed four individuals with mental illness through a period of time in their lives in Santa Monica, California. These additions prompted students to reveal thoughts that had never been shared before in course evaluations.

The Nursing Care of Women and the Childbearing Family course is to completed second semester junior year or first semester senior year. This course reinforces the global need to value women's lives and issues specific to women's health. It picks up on other course content to look at making health systems work for women by providing equal access to information and care. Recognition of the need for gender policies to prioritize women and girls and comparison of reproductive health rights in the United States and globally are part of the course goals. Outside classroom experiences, documentary films such as "The Business of Being Born," and simulated experiences with robotic mannequins in emergency deliveries are some of the innovative teaching methodologies incorporated as a result of this FPLC. These experiences helped students as they struggle with the many ethical issues inherent in the course content, specifically related to social justice themes of access to care, confronting personal biases, recognizing the potential impact of stigma on patient's care and respect for human life. Their struggle and learning was documented in classroom discussion and end-of-course reflection papers.

One member of the learning community, based on her work in the FPLC and her personal journey with the Ignatian Spiritual Exercises, designed a unique classroom activity. As a "gift" to students on the last day of class prior to Thanksgiving break, she led them through a guided reflection doing a "mini-examen" similar to the Spiritual Exercises. Watching their faces change from stressed, to calmed, to tranquil or disinterested, to engaged was her reward. A student's e-mail comment after the experience was telling: "This was the first time in my four years that a faculty member here has acknowledged the Catholic tradition of the university and brought it concretely to class . . . thank you."

Many of our discussions centered on how students learn—both the biological basis of learning as well as the experiences students can have that create a lasting and meaningful transformation. We began to understand that creating significant learning experiences involved building on strengths and experiences students were bringing to the classroom as well as creating meaningful experiences for them. For example, readings on emotional intelligence and mindful awareness (cf. Siegel 2007) led us to discussions on how to facilitate the transformation of students into nurses. This discussion was preceded by conversations about critical thinking, clinical reasoning, and "thinking like a nurse." This, in turn, led to discussions about the biology of learning and the integration of right and left brain functions and the role of this integration in producing effective and excellent nurses. To enhance our understanding of this area, we read James Zull's *The Art of Changing the Brain* (2002). These readings and subsequent discussions brought us back to how we might actually accomplish this with our students. We knew that the students ultimately had to incorporate much of what we identified as important in nursing into their professional identities (such as sensitivity toward social justice issues); this incorporation couldn't be "taught" by the usual methods. It had to be experienced, felt, digested, and made a part of the person. In one faculty member's class, this led to decisions about the incorporation of personal stories and up-close encounters to facilitate awareness of personal biases and appreciation for social justice issues in people with severe mental illnesses. It is unlikely that we would have read, or had the opportunity to discuss, these kinds of books without the support of the learning community.

Siegel's (2007) discussion of the development of the "prefrontal cortex" in the brain was especially exciting as well as his explanation of the differences between right and left brain processes. Concretely, this book provided us with ideas for reinforcing teaching styles that help students to make connections, such as: personalizing experiences, incorporating service learning or getting them to examine with reflective journaling specific incidents from clinical. For example, a student in the maternity rotation made assumptions about a lesbian couple she would be caring for that day. After working alongside an expert nurse, getting to know the parents, and watching them with their newborn those assumptions were replaced with facts and concrete evidence that despite personal differences, individuals can share development experiences in a similar fashion. The student recognized his/her ethical responsibility to provide nonjudgmental, supportive care to this new family, yet struggled with personal biases and stigma that were part of his/her worldview and culture.

In addition, service learning opportunities such as these that have been provided in the public health and graduate epidemiology courses bring students into communities with great need. Students must work with past experiences and biases to truly meet the needs of the community. In the FPLC we also examined students' way of learning, how this has morphed over time with the millennial generation to include: multitasking; online searching; information over-load and so on. We recalled teaching experiences that were perceived by us as really good and really bad, which was a humbling and exciting exercise and enhanced the trust and respect among group members. This sharing of personal teaching experiences was particularly helpful for younger faculty and staff.

Community Reaction

One of the early goals of the nursing FPLC was to implement strategies throughout the nursing curriculum that would enhance the cognitive (i.e., critical thinking) and metacognitive (i.e., reflective thinking) skills of nursing students. Strategies to reaching this goal were identified by the group as increasing interactive, learner-focused activities and assignments that reflect real-life situations (i.e., integrating a simulation-based pedagogy) and promoting self-reflection (i.e., journaling and portfolio development). Specific outcomes for this goal included that School of Nursing students would demonstrate increased reflective thinking, improved critical thinking, and improved clinical reasoning skills. Potential methods of assessment included the presence of reflective writing assignments in individual student portfolios from each year of the program and individual and aggregate performance on Critical Thinking measurement tools, such as the California CT Skills Test (CCTST) or the California CT Dispositions Inventory (CCTDI) (Facione and Facione 1992, P. Facione 1992).

A second goal was to develop a plan to assess the impact of integrating a simulation-based pedagogy across the School of Nursing curriculum. A strategy to reaching this goal was to assess students prior to initiating this new pedagogy, then annually at the end of their second, third, and fourth year coursework. Outcomes included students' demonstrations of improved mastery of competencies, increased self-confidence, and development of professional identity. Methods of assessment of this second goal included logs of individual student performance in scenarios, videotaped demonstrations and self-critiques, as well as evidence from annual reflective writing assignments, and successful meeting of the Professional Accountability Objective in all clinical courses.

A third goal was to promote the involvement of all School of Nursing faculty members in further developing an integrative and interactive curriculum. Strategies to reach this goal included the sharing of results of the School of Nursing FPLC work and individual member projects with the entire School of Nursing faculty, providing opportunity for one-to-one mentoring of non-FPLC members and developing a repository of suggestions for classroom activities that promote a simulation-based pedagogy and an interactive, social justice–oriented curriculum. Desirable outcomes for this goal included the entire School of Nursing faculty becoming more confident with a simulation-based pedagogy and in the use of technology in the classroom, implementing technology throughout the nursing curriculum, and using more interactive and integrative course assignments that build on content between courses.

Methods of assessment of this third goal included use of a faculty survey on attitudes toward information technology and the stages of adoption of technology (faculty self-rating of perceived stage of adoption), a review of School of Nursing course syllabi to identify course descriptions and objectives that reflect the new pedagogical approach, and the involvement of other School of Nursing faculty in future FPLCs.

These goals represent a technology-focused start of the FPLC toward encouraging faculty and students to enjoy the benefits and challenges of innovative teaching methods. Interestingly enough, this faculty accomplished many of its goals, but the focus on technology transitioned to a quest for more interactive learning styles, matching teaching in an active sense with millennials, Generation X, and adult learners' specific needs.

Faculty in the Nursing FPLC completed an end-of-year presentation at the end of the academic year university-wide FPLC group meeting and with the School of Nursing faculty (see third goal above). This presentation served as an excellent method of tabulating the accomplishments of the School of Nursing FPLC.

The overarching accomplishments the Nursing FPLC identified included both tangible and intangible rewards. The intangible rewards included a sense of community, common goals, cohesiveness, and an appreciation for electronic approaches to enhance teaching and assessment. The tangible rewards included grant funding ($99,999 for the Women's Health Expansion Project), conference presentations (posters, papers), individual course projects (every participant made course changes as a result of participation in the FPLC and reported the findings), and a book project (Campbell and Daley 2009) to which all but one of the FPLC participants contributed a chapter. The book captured a unique assortment of case scenarios that could be used in simulation; each of them included specific suggestions for questions to use that would guide the students through reflections on the case (particularly difficult aspects of the cases or those that raised thorny ethical issues).

As a result of her work in the FPLC, one faculty member was able to introduce several additional learning experiences into her Mental

Health Nursing class that stimulated some serious soul-searching and personal transformations among the students. Students spoke on their evaluations about having had their stereotypical views challenged and seeing people with severe mental illness as "just like you and me." Additional reactions offered by the students in this course included:

> I learned that a mental disorder can happen to the most regular, normal looking people;

> I feel able to rid my mind of the stereotypical thoughts that I had about psychiatric patients;

> I have an understanding of people with mental illness and being able to see the person beyond the illness; My own perspective of mental illness has changed, as a result of the conference, from doubt to the hope of recovery and readjustment; and

> The presentation . . . was more than just an informative lecture, it was a moving experience. . . . People with a mental disorder are viewed as unequal to others on nearly all levels. The presentation proved this stereotype to be entirely wrong.

Another student also wrote a thoughtful reaction to a documentary on homelessness among the mentally ill in California:

> I think the number one issue with the homeless (mentally ill or not) is the attitude of the healthcare provider towards them. . . . It's important to treat them the same as other patients, and try to give them as much dignity as possible. . . . I think it is especially important for the homeless that are mentally ill that we do not force them into mental facilities, they do have a right to make decisions and if they are not harming anyone, they should have at least the power to dictate their lives.

Collectively, these comments represent an emerging awareness on the part of the students for issues of social justice such as human dignity, respect, stigma, prejudice, freedom, choice, and control over one's life. They also capture the development of the students' personal sense of professional responsibility. Participation in the FPLC heightened this faculty member's awareness of these issues and encouraged her to incorporate reflective practice more fully into her pedagogy.

As a result of their FPLC experience, faculty members promoted reflection on teaching practices, focused on case study writing and reflective learning methods, examined various curricula with a goal of improving the students' critical thinking skills, encouraged the use of novel classroom techniques (reflection, sections of movies, YouTube clips, web links), and infused the work of the FPLC into a new simulation-based pedagogy. As an example of one new practice, students in a junior/senior year women's health class were asked to identify instances when patients may be experiencing "spiritual distress" (e.g., fear of death—this could be during labor, with diagnosis of cancer, or related to domestic violence). Students were then guided to consider how the patient's past experiences may influence their approach to present experiences. One student gave the example of a Spanish speaking Central American immigrant who acknowledged to a bilingual student that she was sure she was dying during labor. When the student asked her why she felt this way, the patient said that she had watched her mother and sister die during childbirth. Initially the student diagnosed the patient with "Anxiety, related to lack of knowledge of the normal processes of labor." Her plan was to educate the patient about the process of labor, the normalcy of what she was experiencing, and how the practitioners were there to assure the safety of both mother and baby. It is not surprising that the patient found little comfort in this approach! However, when the student re-examined her assumptions and acknowledged that the diagnosis was actually "spiritual distress related to fear of death in childbirth," she was then able to work with the patient on a way to cope. The patient had a very close relationship with the Virgin Mary and the student helped her to refocus on that relationship, pray for strength, and relax in the knowledge of her loving care. This refocusing, in combination with the student's empathetic behavior and bilingual capabilities, led to the safe delivery of a healthy baby.

The work of the FPLC has been diffused throughout the School of Nursing and the curriculum. In the past year, the School of Nursing embarked on an integration of the new Essentials of Baccalaureate Education for Professional Nursing Practice program and the creation of a new Doctor of Nursing Practice (DNP) program that represents the first practice doctorate at the university. The work of this FPLC group informed the discussion around the DNP, especially with relationship to reflective practice and social justice themes. The grant received for the Women's Health Expansion Project led to the creation of a total of ten scenarios for the Nursing Care of Women and the Childbearing Family course. Finally, the school's study-abroad options were broadened to include several one-week immersion experiences in Managua, Nicaragua.

The one-week immersion experiences in Nicaragua provide an opportunity for traditional and second-degree undergraduate students to participate in a community-based participatory research project. Our nursing students and faculty partner with a local university, their social work department faculty and students, and a community organization, which provides a unique social justice experience. On a recent trip, the partners were collecting information in the community using door-to-door interviews when they came upon a family being evicted from their home. The community partners explained that the family had squatted on space that was reserved for community development and someone complained, so the city government was relocating them (house and all) to another squatter community. Students commented that the eviction process was similar to what they see in the United States and the various partners began to explore the personal impact of the eviction process, the various reactions of community members to the eviction, the lack of affordable housing, and the inability of people to afford land and own homes. It led to a truly cross-cultural discussion of social justice!

Lessons Learned

There are several features of the FPLC model that were appealing to faculty members:

Concentrated/devoted time every other week
Group committed to preparing for their work together
Open/honest communication with no fear of punitive action
Openness to trying new techniques

There are several suggestions for those who may consider replicating this experience.

> Be more transparent with your students about how your FPLC work relates to what your students are doing.
>
> Sometimes while in process, it is hard to see the connections that are being made—become more mindful!
>
> Do scheduling up front and early—time together is "sacred."
>
> Establish fair methods for coming to consensus (thumbs up, thumbs down worked for us).
>
> Allow for the process to unfold—having a timekeeper, a record keeper, setting an agenda, and deciding on readings as a group worked well.

It is perhaps notable that our FPLC was not initially centered on social justice, or on incorporating themes of social justice into the curricula. Our intention was, at its core, to improve our pedagogy. However, because social justice themes are so inherently central to the practice of nursing, improving our pedagogy almost unavoidably involved allowing these themes of social justice to more fully emerge in the classroom. While this lack of intentionality did not hamper the movement toward incorporation social justice issues into our curriculum, a more focused, goal-oriented approach would likely be advisable for others considering this change.

Conclusion

The faculty group found the FPLC model facilitated the following changes:

> Individual courses were enhanced to include reflective components and assisted students to recognize issues of social justice.
>
> Inclusion of social justice themes became intentional and was diffused across the undergraduate and graduate curricula.
>
> The undergraduate and new DNP curricula were substantively improved using information and methods gained as part of the FPLC process.

The involvement of a faculty member external to the School of Nursing allowed the FPLC group to broaden its scope initially and then narrow its focus as the year progressed, adding new dimensions that the group of professors of nursing may have missed.

Over the next academic year the changes described above will become finalized and incorporated into course descriptions, course objectives, program outcomes, and course catalog descriptions that will better reflect the integration of social justice. However, the changes that took place in the lives of individual faculty, the impact of the changes these faculty members made in their individual courses with students, and the role of the FPLC in laying the groundwork for curricular change will have a lasting impact on all involved in this process.

9 Doing Well by Doing Good

The Application of Ignatian Principles to Legal Education

DAVID C. KOELSCH

Before delving into the use of reflective practices—such as the Spiritual Exercises developed by Ignatius of Loyola—by law schools and their students, it is helpful to examine the goal of their use. Simply put, the goal is justice. Seeking justice is a good fit for law schools and law students. Perhaps no other field of academic endeavor is as closely intertwined with justice as legal education. Legal education, at a minimum, instructs students in legal and ethical duties to their clients, the judicial system, and the public. It is a rare law school that does not profess to promote justice and all law schools—secular and faith-based—offer courses that examine principles of justice across a variety of legal fields and disciplines, such as human rights and economics. While reasonable minds can disagree about the justice of various social and legal causes, one principle espoused by Ignacio Ellacuria, SJ (2004), is that "justice . . . involves giving to the people what belongs to the people and struggling to uproot injustice and exploitation, and to establish a new earth, wherein the life of the new human may be possible."

As conceived of in this article, justice is not affiliated with any specific campaign for rights and is a much broader concept than legal ethics or even morality. This idea of justice, rather, is less concerned with the day-to-day conduct of lawyers and whether they are ethical than it is with whether lawyers, through their work, bring peace to clients and resolve contentious issues in a manner that respects the integrity and needs of all. A just result in a legal dispute may be one in which the exploitation of one person by another may be ended or averted but it is also the manner in which the legal dispute was resolved: at the end of the process, do the putative exploiter and exploitee believe that they were respected in the process and, to the extent possible, their needs fulfilled? This result brings about mutual understanding and harmony and, more importantly, promotes a lasting peace where one side or the other is not chafing at a result they believe fails to respect their integrity. This concept of justice is not taught in most law school classrooms. This article charts one path by which reflective practices aimed at promoting justice can be integrated into the law school experience and carried into the legal profession.

The Relevance of Ignatius to Law Students

This article is not intended to be an exhaustive treatise on the Spiritual Exercises; instead, it offers selections from the Spiritual Exercises that may be most vital for law students. Others have commented with great depth and accuracy regarding the writings and teachings of St. Ignatius. What is striking about the Spiritual Exercises is how, across the centuries, they seem to be directed at law students. In Spiritual Exercise 176, Ignatius could have been describing the quintessential law school experience as "a time of alternating certainties and doubts, of exhilarating strength and debilitating weakness, of consolation and of desolation." Ignatius teaches law students to embrace their fears: "As a matter of fact, this time is very privileged, because the discernment of spirits which is called for is an entrance into understanding a language of God spoken within our very being . . . [w]e can gain much light and understanding from the experience of consolation and desolation, and so this time, too, is very special for decision making." Rather than instilling a sense of shame or reproach in law students who may find themselves spiritually desolate, Ignatius encourages them to pause to reflect deeply on how they feel when they are spiritually desolate and, in particular, to contrast those feelings with how they feel when they experience consolation. Spiritual Exercise 317 recognizes that, without experiencing desolation, there can be no consolation: "the thoughts of rebelliousness, despair, or selfishness which arise at the time of desolation are in absolute contrast with the thoughts of the praise and service of God which flow during the time of consolation." Law students could recognize that, to borrow from Dante, embracing and reflecting upon their own "dark night of the soul" using the Spiritual Exercises can lead to a brighter future (Gilmore 2009, 357).

One other application of the Spiritual Exercises to law students lies in their capacity to remind law students of the gifts they bring to the world and to foster a worldview centered on gratitude, trust, and stewardship. With rare exceptions, law students are smart, attentive, Type A overachievers. They have excelled academically and often in other ways and risen to the top of their peers. They often believe that their success is solely attributed to their drive and natural abilities. A tendency among law students is to reject their sense of giftedness and to lose touch with how special they are. In a sense, law students become ungrateful for the gifts with which they are blessed and either denigrate those gifts by failing to recognize them or fail to use them to their full potential. In a letter to Fr. Simon Rodrigues, Ignatius wrote that, "ingratitude is the most abominable of sins" (Young, 55). If law students had a better sense that their gifts came from God and were shaped and molded by their hard work and perseverance, law students might be more grateful for those gifts and embrace more fully the call to serve God in their daily lives as attorneys.

Finally, in a passage that could be quoted by career services personnel at law schools, Spiritual Exercise 16 addresses the internal division facing law students between material gain and service to others head-on:

> If we feel a disorder in our attachment to a person, to a job or position, to a certain dwelling place, a certain city, country, and so on, we should take it to the Lord and pray insistently to be given the grace to free ourselves from such disorder. What we want above all is the ability to respond freely to God, and all other loves for people, places, and things are held in proper perspective by the light and strength of God's grace.

So, too, can law students use the Spiritual Exercises to take their disordered and mixed attachments to God in a search for grace and perspective. The Spiritual Exercises can help law students turn away from a self-centered life and recognize that, as noted in Spiritual Exercise 314, "when we are caught up in a life of sin or perhaps even if we are closed off from God in only one area of our life, the evil spirit is ordinarily accustomed to propose a slothful complacency in the status quo or to entice to a future of ever greater pleasures still to be grasped." If law students are afforded the grace, through the Spiritual Exercises, to gain a more long-range view of their lives, their choices could improve, as is hoped for in Spiritual Exercise 21, which exhorts us to "grow into this freedom by gradually bringing an order of values into our lives so that we find that at the moment of choice of decision we are not swayed by any disordered love".

Law School as a Transformative Experience

While often derided as a breeding ground for lawyers who will live out all of the worst stereotypes associated with attorneys—including greed, trickery, dishonesty, and avarice—law school can also be a transformative moment for law students and one that may determine their ability to practice law ethically and to serve justice. As Fr. Peter-Hans Kolvenbach, SJ (2000), noted in his address at Santa Clara University, the educational goal of all Jesuit universities—including law schools—should be to "educate the whole person of solidarity for the real world." Without mentioning law school clinics by name, Father Kolvenbach certainly tapped their ethos when he declared that "solidarity is learned through 'contact' rather than through 'concepts.'" Indeed, because legal education is intrinsically tied to an examination of rights, law students enrolled in Jesuit law schools have many avenues in which they can express "a willingness not only to recognize and respect the rights of all, especially the poor and the powerless, but also to work actively to secure those rights" (ibid.). Law schools are tightly regulated by the American Bar Association (ABA) in terms of credits, curriculum, required classes, prerequisites, hiring and promotion practices, building size and standards, and a host of other factors. Beyond the requirements imposed by the ABA, Jesuit law schools have the opportunity—and the duty—to rise above the norm and provide their law students with a transformative educational experience through courses, clinics, and other programs in which students directly serve others and, in doing so, expand their substantive legal knowledge and embrace lifelong skills needed to retain their professional and personal integrity. Of course, the concern with creating a transformative experience for law students is not confined to Jesuit or religiously affiliated law schools.

Secular law schools also struggle to help students maintain a personal and professional balance in the face of an academy still somewhat geared toward educating law students primarily in the theory of law with little regard for its practical application or the ability of law students to serve others.

Law school is many things: it is a professional school, it is a winnowing process, and it is a test of survival. After completing the first year of law school, which is focused on the bedrock courses of Property, Torts, Contracts, Civil Procedure, Constitutional Law, and Criminal Law, law students are free to explore courses in their areas of interest, such as Family Law, Criminal Law, Immigration Law, Corporate Law, and on and on. Law students may also enroll in narrowly focused upper-level seminars, moot court to hone oral advocacy skills, legal clinics, which offer direct client contact, and externships in government, non-profit, and private offices. The hierarchical nature of first-year required courses and upper-level electives is nearly universal among law schools in the United States and Canada and, while course offerings vary considerably, the same structure persists in all law schools.

Addressing the Negative Aspects of Legal Education

Law school is not easy, and the pressures of law school exact a high price. The attendant pressure for top grades, securing summer and postgraduation employment, worrying about passing the bar exam, and paying off student loans are universal to law students (Glesner 1991, 668). Compared to their peers, law students are disproportionately neurotic and prone to a variety of dangerous behaviors and addictions (Pang 1999, 241). The pressures of law school do not ease when students enter the practice of law: lawyers have a rate of alcohol and drug abuse greater than one and a half times the national average (Rothstein 2008, 531). In fact, a recent study concluded that 20 percent of female attorneys and 13 percent of male attorneys reported consuming six or more alcoholic drinks per day (Krieger 2002, 212). Attorneys also suffer depression at a rate three times the national average, and male attorneys are twice as likely to commit suicide as their nonattorney peers (ibid.).

In the midst of this depressing data, two questions are highly relevant. First, how can law school faculty and administrators foster a desire among students to serve others—to transform the world—within the narrow confines of legal education and the pressure cooker atmosphere of law school? Second, how can a concentration on serving others make law school less of a traumatizing event and more of a transformative event for law students while also providing law students with the intellectual tools and practical skills they need to navigate a treacherous profession? The answer to both questions is surprisingly simple: law students should be required to enroll in at least one legal clinic as a prerequisite to graduation and law students enrolled in legal clinics should be provided ample instruction in and opportunities for Jesuit-based reflection. A legal education steeped in Jesuit spirituality has the ability to promote justice, in the broad sense outlined above, by giving law students the freedom to reflect on how their actions affect their clients' lives beyond the narrow facts of a legal matter and either advance or detract from the promotion of peaceful and respectful relations. In a more immediate sense, embracing Jesuit spirituality can also transform the legal services industry, ensure the professional competence of generations of attorneys, and save the lives of countless law students and lawyers from a culture of negativity, despair, and the associated vagaries of depression, substance abuse, and suicide.

Ignatian spirituality can be integral to the life of a successful and well-balanced attorney. Gregory Kalscheur, SJ (2000), provides a stirring account of the need for attorneys to embrace Ignatian spirituality both as a means of better serving their clients and preserving their own integrity. In doing so, Professor Kalscheur shares his own journey from lawyer to Jesuit and calls on law students and attorneys to "discern how God is calling us to lives of freedom and wholeness and integrity if we pay attention to the feelings moving in our hearts as we reflect on our own life experiences" (46). Merely by using the Spiritual Exercises to attune themselves to the needs of their clients and their own needs, law students and attorneys can gain a "deeper experience of how God is active in their lives" (46). Once turned on to the benefits of a strong spiritual foundation, attorneys often find greater energy and devotion to their clients (Kronman 2005, 439).

Simply put, Ignatian-based legal education, or some other form of legal education with a serious commitment to reflective practices, can be the difference between death and life for law students and their clients and also advance the cause of justice in the wider community. This is an uphill battle: platitudes regarding the desire to serve others which so often grace the pages of prospective law students' admission applications rarely last beyond the second week of first-year classes. Inspiring law students and changing the culture of educational institutions and a profession is not easy. Law students are nothing if not unduly cynical, and an overt focus by a law school on service to others without meaningful opportunities to actually engage in such service will likely foster yawns and feigned interest.

There needs to be some hook to entice law students and the administration of law schools to shift their focus from learning laws and rules to appreciating the bigger picture of how that knowledge will be used. A justice-based legal education works best when law students are able to recognize a clear benefit to their career paths and earning potential. For that reason alone, the case needs to be made to law students that they will be more marketable to potential employers with a skills-based course in a legal clinic. An implicit goal that may appeal to certain law students is that, by enrolling in a clinic that practices the Spiritual Exercises, they will be less likely to fall victim to the sense of despair that pervades the legal profession. The time for law schools to reexamine their practices is opportune: a sea change is taking place in many law schools—religious and secular—to focus on the need to better prepare law students to practice law, while at the same time serving justice and retaining their integrity (Welch and Wegner 2009, 867; Krannich, Holbrook, and McAdams 2009, 381).

The Connection between Faith and the Promotion of Justice

There is no shortage of ostensibly justice-based programs in law schools. There is, however, a shortage of programs and courses offered by law schools that deeply examine the ways in which justice is achieved and the role of attorneys in furthering justice (Aiken 1997,

212; Shaffer 1996, 195). Other observers have forcefully argued that Catholic and, in particular, Jesuit law schools have lost their way and, while Jesuit law schools "uniformly provide their students with a high level of legal instruction, nothing in the academic life of these institutions sets them apart from schools that do not identify themselves as either Catholic or Jesuit" (Breen 2007, 41; Brown 2009, 293). Of course, Catholic and Jesuit law schools are not alone in this criticism; many religiously affiliated law schools are justly accused of laying aside religious conviction in favor of a secular approach to teaching law to a religiously diverse student body. With their focus on providing a high-caliber education, Jesuit law schools may have let slip some of their spiritual zeal. Indeed, Edgar Alan Poe was said to "have liked the Jesuits . . . because they were highly cultivated gentlemen and scholars, they smoked and they drank, and played cards, and never said a word about religion" (Schroth 2002, 24).

This commentary echoes in modern Jesuit law schools: apart from the presence of crucifixes on the walls of classrooms, in many Jesuit law schools there is little tangible or visible measure of a spiritual mission (Nussbaum 2008, 631). Yet, Jesuit law schools can—and do—play a critical role in that deep examination of justice so that justice is not solely pursued to enhance the reputation of the law school but, instead, is targeted to those persons and communities most in need of justice and includes a reflective element to encourage students to examine their own pursuit of justice (Moore 2007, 459). As Professor Breen (2007, 41) argued, Catholic identity should not be seen as the icing on a cake but, rather, as the air in a balloon is "integral and essential, as something which inspires and gives purpose to the institution." Other non-Catholic law schools also derive a sense of mission from religious affiliation. Dean Bradley Toben (2009, 161) of Baylor University School of Law, a Baptist-affiliated law school, argues that faith-based law schools "need to act with intentionality to preserve their identity in the face of a pervasively secular culture. . . . In other words, the faculty of a [law] school with a faith mission must embrace and actively advance that school's mission for it to endure and color the experiences of those within that community."

It is clear that the Jesuit hierarchy supports justice-oriented service in all Jesuit ministries. Decree 3 of the 34th General Congregation issued a directive for "social centers," which could include clinics operated by Jesuit-affiliated law schools, to place faith more explicitly in their work: "Social centers for and direct social action for and with the poor will be more effective in promoting justice to the extent that they integrate faith into all dimensions of their work. Thus each Jesuit ministry should work to deepen its particular implementation of our full mission of faith and justice, which cannot but be enriched by efforts toward a more effective dialogue and enculturation."

Legal Clinics as a Means to Serve Justice

Most law schools operate legal clinics that serve justice one person at a time, such as clinics serving veterans, low-income immigrants, and the elderly, or on a national or even global scale by addressing human rights abuses or environmental policies. Yet only a handful of law schools require students to enroll in a legal clinic to graduate. The operation of legal clinics is an expensive proposition for law schools (Chemerinsky 2008, 596). Most clinics do not exceed a 1:10 faculty and the same tuition is charged per credit hour for clinics as for all other courses. Legal clinics operate as small law offices, complete with the attendant overhead, including rent, utilities, administrative staff, and filing fees. As a result, it is far more lucrative for law schools to hire professors to teach larger classes or even seminars than it is to maintain legal clinics and, as a corollary, it is expensive for law schools to add sufficient legal clinics to meet demand generated if enrollment in a legal clinic is required to graduate.

For most Jesuit-affiliated law schools, legal clinics are their most visible ministry (Scholla 2004, 1232). Legal clinics play a logical and consistent role in Jesuit law schools as the seekers and defenders of justice. Yet, while providing legal clinics is a step toward promoting service to others, it is not enough if justice is pursued by students enrolled in legal clinics without the integration of faith or any space for reflection on the meaning of service; merely serving the needs of the poor and afflicted does not allow legal clinics at Jesuit law schools to live up to their full potential. If, however, legal clinics create room for law students to examine and share their views regarding justice and how their work in the legal clinic serves justice, law students will come away from the experience committed to serving justice and preserving their personal integrity (McCaffrey 2003, 95). Legal clinics are the ideal laboratory for exploring and doing justice: they are limited in size, they typically represent persons who are victimized and treated unjustly, the faculty-student interaction is very close, and law students can be encouraged—or even required—to reflect upon their work in the clinics and how it may or may not serve justice (Perry 2009, 167).

In addition to general reflections on the meaning of their work on behalf of their clients, students enrolled in legal clinics can use certain intrinsically Jesuit teachings and practices to enhance their ability to seek and do justice and to maintain their bearings in the face of personal and professional challenges. For example, law students enrolled in the Immigration Law Clinic at the University of Detroit Mercy prepare for each class and client interaction with instruction centered on the Spiritual Exercises of St. Ignatius of Loyola. In the first classes of each academic term, students are instructed in the law and procedure most relevant to their work for a particular client and, at the same time, are provided core readings examining the life and work of St. Ignatius as well as the Spiritual Exercises (Fleming 2008).

How the Spiritual Exercises Fit with Legal Education

According to Gerald Fagin, SJ, one of the leading modern interpreters of the Spiritual Exercises, the Spiritual Exercises have a two-fold purpose. First, the Exercises were designed by Ignatius to help a person "to overcome oneself, to order one's life, so one could reach an ordered decision in one's life" (Fagin 2005, 59). A second purpose developed later, as people began to use the Exercises to enrich their spiritual life and to learn how to live out the Gospel more fully in their lives (ibid.) For Father Fagin, the Exercises free up a mind to make a decision without interference from feelings regarding pleasure, power or prestige and, in doing so, that decision will be both authentic to the person but also more in keeping with the Gospel. In many ways, the Spiritual Exercises are uniquely compatible with a legally trained mind. Ignatius was nothing if not a bottom-line thinker and doer just as law students and lawyers are trained to be. For Ignatius, the Spiritual Exercises were a means to an end. The end—the purpose and goal of life—is to praise, reverence, and serve God and to come to eternal life (ibid.). In the face of great and systemic injustices in the world, it may seem somewhat heretical and self-absorbed to suggest that the prime beneficiaries of law students pursuing justice in an Ignatian key are not those served by law students but, instead, are the law students themselves. In defense of such apparent narcissism, Decree 4 of the 32nd General Congregation is helpful: "People today are somehow aware that their problems are not just social and technological, but personal and spiritual. They have a feeling that what is at stake here is the very meaning of man: his destiny, his future. Men are hungry: but hungry not just for bread, but for the Word of God." Contrary to popular belief, law students are humans and they thirst for meaning to sustain them in their careers and their lives. Serving justice and having the space to reflect upon that service enables law students to recognize and embrace that they and their work have meaning.

Decree 4 is a rich vein for justice-minded law faculty and administrators to probe. Justice as its own reward allows law students and attorneys to escape the "cult of money, prestige, and power [which] has as its fruit the sin of institutionalized aggression . . ., and it ends in the enslavement not only of the oppressed but of the oppressor." Unless they come to grips with their part in combating injustice, law students and attorneys drift into the cult of money. The mission of a legal educator is to teach students legal structure, principles, and doctrines and, with respect to legal clinics, to nurture advocacy and client relation skills. No less important to a legal educator is the mission to preserve the integrity and longevity of law students as future attorneys. Substantive knowledge and legal acumen will do little to guard law students against the insidious pressures and alluring prizes they will face as attorneys.

For example, professors can work hard to ensure law students thoroughly understand the basis for successful legal action. Yet, unless professors step up their efforts and expand their instruction beyond the narrow confines of the subject at hand, they cannot prevent their law students from overbilling a client, raiding a client's trust fund, or failing to fulfill their ethical duty to perform pro bono service. Only by including instruction on the reasons why lawyers do what they do and exhorting law students to reflect on their role in doing justice can professors preserve and protect law students (Marlow 2008, 489). Indeed, others argue that "religion should permeate the program of the Jesuit law school. . . . It is a faith that the God of Israel lives and works in the world and calls believers to articulate, evaluate, critique, and act upon their assumptions and values" (Barkan 1993, 6). When they are practicing attorneys, our former students who benefited from a justice-based Jesuit legal education will know the needs of the poor and suffering, use their gifts to serve those needs, and love those they serve and themselves. In so doing, they will gain a mission for their professional and personal lives and be less likely to fall into the dead-end trap of a life lived solely for fleeting and elusive material pleasures.

One important outward difference between the use of the Spiritual Exercises and legal knowledge is that the ends desired by the Exercises are both in the here and now and in the eternal while the ends for law students in legal clinics and attorneys in practice constantly change with the demands and needs of the clients they serve. This dichotomy renders the Exercises particularly useful for law students and lawyers because, as noted above, they are prone to careen from highs to lows in their daily work for clients and are always seeking out the next client, the next strategy, and the next win. The Spiritual Exercises can help lawyers become more aware of their work and how it serves more than material ends and nourishes their souls. Professor Kalscheur (2009, 2) noted that "the commitment to promotion of justice should be manifest . . . in the opportunities for action that are part of the life of the law school." Morissey (2004, 584), among others, has noted the central role of legal clinics in promoting the distinct values of a Jesuit law school:

> The Ignatian spirit of discernment can still be present at the schools where even busy law students should be encouraged to find time for such reflection. . . . In addition, life-long habits of such a commitment should be fostered by work in clinical programs that actively advocate the causes of the poor and by requiring that students perform some pro bono work even while in law school.

Legal clinics, coupled with Ignatian-focused reflection, are a means by which religion—not in a doctrinal sense, but in a practical and justice-based orientation—can be instilled in legal education. Legal clinics, founded on a mission of service and embracing Jesuit principles and precepts, serve that purpose and ensure that graduates of Jesuit-affiliated law schools are not merely technically skilled attorneys but also responsible leaders who will not lose touch with the sense of mission and Jesuit transformation they experienced as law students enrolled in a legal clinic. Professor Rose (2001, 53) noted that "one of the best ways to impart a justice ethic to law students is to allow them, as students, to provide direct legal representation to the poor and other victims of injustice."

An Example of the Use of the Spiritual Exercises

Using the Spiritual Exercises as a guide, prior to each and every client encounter, law students enrolled in the Immigration Law Clinic reflect on the Contemplation to Attain Love of God (*Contemplatio Ad Amorem*). First, law students are taught to regard everything as a gift: their skills, their training, their energy, their client, and even their client's problems are all gifts which allow this encounter to even happen. Second, students are encouraged to recognize that God dwells in all creation and especially that they and their clients are instruments of God for a higher purpose. Third, students contemplate that God is at work in all creation, including the adverse situation facing their client. Fourth, students acknowledge that everything comes from God or, in more concrete terms, that they worked hard and sacrificed to get to where they are but God enabled them to get that far.

One of the more engaging and relevant practices advocated by Ignatius is the Examination of Conscience or *Examen*. Law students use the Examination of Conscience to orient themselves and their work in the clinic. As Fr. George Aschenbrenner, SJ (1972, 21), noted: "Too much attention to our own victories and failures can make us self-absorbed and confirm in us the illusion that we manage our own lives. Examination is rather a question of asking how I respond to God's loving action in my life"

As a final step before any client encounter or beginning any task or project, law students engage in the following brief Examination of Conscience. First, attention is focused on the task at hand and any extraneous concerns of the law students are mentally pushed to the side in order to be fully engaged in the client interview, hearing, or oral argument. Second, students are called on to regard their work with reverence in light of its significance for others; lawyers are charged with safeguarding fame, fortunes, and family, and law students should respect their ability to dramatically alter a client's life for better or worse. Finally, law students remind themselves that they are devoted to the service of God through their service to their clients.

By the end of each academic term, law students instructed in this manner engage in the Contemplation to Attain Love of God and the Examination of Conscience reflexively prior to every client encounter or significant task. Law students report that the use of each Exercise orients them better to the needs of their clients and helps them to appreciate their role in the legal process. In experiencing the Spiritual Exercises, at least on a small scale, law students often reflect that the Spiritual Exercises helped to calm them during the often tumultuous transition from the study of law to the practice of law. In short, to maximize the chance that law students will experience a transformation in how they will practice law, it is not enough for Jesuit legal clinics to be just bricks and mortar and paper and computers. Legal clinics should be required for graduation from a Jesuit law school and legal clinics should embrace Ignatian spiritual precepts and practices in order to serve better justice and the interests of law students (Bryce 2008, 577).

Beyond using the Spiritual Exercises to better attune law students to the needs of their clients, the Spiritual Exercises can also bring law students to a heightened state of indifference needed to make effective decisions. Indifference is a critical construct of the Spiritual Exercises, as it is in the work of successful lawyers. As Father Fagin (2007, 26–27) noted:

> In everyday life, we should keep ourselves indifferent or undecided in the face of all the created gifts when we have an option and we do not have the clarity of what would be the better choice. We ought not to be led on by our natural likes and dislikes even in matters such as health or sickness, wealth or poverty, between living in the east or the west, becoming an accountant or a lawyer. Rather, our

only desire and our one choice should be that option which better leads us to the goal for which God created us.

Law students enrolled in legal clinics need to avoid impulsive decisions on behalf of clients. First-year law students quickly learn that navigating the legal system is a matter of eternal choices: which venue, which jurisdiction, which judge, which law or regulation to cite, which case to emphasize, which witness to call first, which juror to excuse are examples of choices lawyers face every day. Studied indifference to wealth and power and avoiding the temptation to simply make a choice when one does not yet see a clear path, are useful skills for law students. Of course, the indifference sought by Ignatius through the Exercises is different from the colloquial, negative connotation of indifference. Indifference, for Ignatius, does not mean "I don't care." Ignatius meant that "you are so passionately committed to God and to following God and God's plan that everything else is relativized, everything else is secondary to that one goal and one purpose" (Fagin 2007, 28) A lawyer's indifference born out of a genuine appreciation for the complexity of the varied choices under the law and reverence for the consequences of each choice is healthy—as is examining the arrayed choices with respect to how each serves God. The needs of the client and, if Ignatian philosophy is embraced by the law student, the desire to serve God come first over any other consideration.

One note of caution observed in the Immigration Law Clinic with respect to the use of a spiritual- or religion-based approach to the practice of law: most clients will have little patience for an attorney who wishes to overtly engage them in a discussion of their religious beliefs, faith, or spirituality. As noted by Professor Toben (2009, 163), "the daily life of a lawyer does not generally provide fertile ground for open religious expression. . . . The client wants preparation, not prayer. Opposing counsel wants cooperation and even concessions—not witnessing. Christian piety can never be a substitute for professional competence." Jesuit introspection is best confined to the private interactions of law professors and students as they prepare to meet with clients and engage the legal process.

Other Examples of a Faith-based Approach to Legal Education

Other methods of promoting faith and justice in law schools can complement the use of the Spiritual Exercises in legal clinics. Professor Amelia Uelmen (2004, 921) convincingly argues for a realignment of curriculum at Catholic law schools to better serve justice. Professor Uelmen calls for law schools to be inclusive and seek out dialogue with practitioners of other faiths, to present witnesses on the faculty or among practicing attorneys who do connect faith and justice, and to promote religious reflection in addition to concrete acts of social justice. Professor Lucia Ann Silecchia (2000, 182), in a seminal article on this topic, also brought the message that spirituality should be incubated and not left to wither during the law school rite of passage. These steps are all in the same direction as the use of the Spiritual Exercises although it can be argued that the Spiritual Exercises are particularly well-suited for adoption by law schools: the Spiritual Exercises follow set patterns and proceed in a logical fashion. This structure appeals to law students steeped in the building blocks of legal theory.

While legal clinics are central to the identity and mission of Jesuit law schools, there is no reason that efforts to foster a greater sense of justice should be confined to the work of the clinics. Jeffrey Brand (2001), dean of the University of San Francisco School of Law, noted several actions that law schools could take beyond legal clinics to serve justice, including ethical training, street law programs to educate high school students, and community service opportunities. Additional activities could include fundraisers dedicated to providing fellowships to law students externing at nonprofit organizations. The need for Jesuit universities and their law schools to promote this transformative experience has been recognized before. Henry Rose (2001, 53), a law professor at Loyola University Chicago, called on Jesuit law schools to "decide whether they should be countercultural institutions, resisting the trends in legal practice that undercut the public service responsibility of the profession." Too often, studies of practicing attorneys reveal dissatisfaction with their choice of career, high rates of attrition, and regrets regarding the decision to attend law school (Dinovitzer and Garth 2009). Justice-based legal education counteracts the corrosive nature of law practice.

Conclusion

Law school holds a special fascination in the American psyche. Iconic images of law school are formed by *The Paper Chase, One L, Legally Blond*, and the collective lore of stressed-out law students and ritualistic rites of passage, such as bareknuckle competition for class rank, moot court, and law review. Lawyers also engender a special fascination—some would argue revulsion—in the American psyche. As with most collective images, the reality does not match the perception. There is no doubt that law school has an innate tendency to bring out the worst in law students. Competing to get into law school, scrambling for top grades, coveting plum jobs and law school positions, and, as a capstone to law school, cramming for the bar exam would likely make most people somewhat neurotic. While there is no practical way to change many of the inherent stressors of law school or the practice of law, Jesuit law schools have a unique ability to help law students constructively cope with stress while also serving the justice mission of the law school and the broader university.

Legal clinics integrate all aspects of Jesuit legal education: they serve as laboratories for law students to practice their legal knowledge and interact with clients in need, they can offer a backdrop for Ignatian-centered reflection, and they create the conditions necessary for law students to transform into mission-oriented, justice-seeking, and well-balanced attorneys. Not all legal clinics are created equal. In order for legal clinics to maximize their potential, legal clinics should be required for graduation from law school and should provide instruction in the Spiritual Exercises or some other structured format for the reflective practice of law. Legal clinics should stress the need for service to others and, at the same time, provide time and space for inward reflection.

Law students, regardless of their faith, can grow to become "men and women for others" and, in doing so, rise above the pressures of law school and starting a legal career. As Father Kolvenbach (2000) noted, "when the heart is touched by direct experience, the mind may be challenged to change. . . . Personal involvement with innocent suffering, with the injustice others suffer, is the catalyst for solidarity which then gives rise to intellectual inquiry and moral reflection." This is the goal of Jesuit higher education and legal clinics rise each day to meet that challenge.

10 Promoting Social Justice
Closing the Gap Between Rhetoric and Reality

MOLLY B. PEPPER, RAYMOND F. REYES, AND
LINDA TREDENNICK

The mission statement and strategic plan of our university contain strongly worded declarations that valuing human differences and
increasing diversity are part and parcel of our Jesuit mission. Our declarations about diversity are an affirmation of our faith-inspired commitment to an inclusive community where human differences thrive in a
working and learning environment characterized by mutual respect and
the pursuit of social justice. Our differences enrich us individually as
human beings and collectively as a community striving to more completely actualize our university mission. As stated by Fr. Paul Locatelli,
SJ (2009), former president of Santa Clara University, in reflecting on
his experience as a delegate at the 35th General Congregation, "our
mission is one of reconciliation—building bridges—with God, with
other people while also respecting their cultures and faiths, and with
creation" (Locatelli 2009).

If we are to truly build such bridges as an act of justice on our
campus, then it is essential, if not compulsory, that we evaluate our
campus climate for diversity. We see doing so as an opportunity to
cultivate a culture of ongoing dialogue and conversation between faith,
diversity, and justice. Using a survey method, we assessed our campus
climate for diversity. We discovered that there is a gap between rhetoric
and reality on our campus. We talk of valuing diversity, but we have
not yet created an atmosphere where all members of the community
are equally safe and feel equally valued. We anticipated these results
based on anecdotal evidence of the struggles of our campus. However,
these struggles are rarely publicized or talked about among the majority
on campus. Conducting a survey that revealed that white, male hetero-
sexuals feel more accepted on campus than women, AHANA[1] students,
and LGBT[2] students told us that many of the stories we heard were

true. In fact, the survey allowed us to write a more truthful story about our campus.

At our university, we also strive to continuously develop an open awareness of ourselves, our decisions, and our immediate environment necessary for deep moral judgment. Living with discernment, honesty, and justice is never easy. Our university is no different from any other college campus: Things happen on our campus that threaten the dignity, rights, and safety of its members. We are strongly committed to the truth that the only moral response to these incidents is to honestly acknowledge their existence so that all members of the community can understand the causes, reflect on the implications, and strive to limit these unacceptable incidents and turn those that do occur into opportunities for learning and growth for us all.

The service of faith and promotion of social justice begins at home; in this case, we are beginning on our home campus. The end goal of all of our research is to identify the unintentional systemic injustices on our campus and work to change them. This research presents a discussion of our journey toward this goal, as well as a description of the strategies and methods we employed along the way. In writing this, we hope to both live our commitment to transparency as a necessary component to building a truly safe, trusting, and diverse community. We also hope to invite and inspire others to embark on a similar journey.

Emotional Intelligence and the Johari Window

Emotional intelligence is a theory that describes differences in how individuals discern and understand emotional information. Individuals with high emotional intelligence are able to sense and regulate their own emotions while sensing and regulating others' emotions (Matthews, Roberts, and Zeidner 2004). The emotionally intelligent individual is self-aware and empathetic. Likewise, the emotionally intelligent organization is one that is open, transparent and aware of its own workings (Book 2000). The emotionally intelligent organization encourages dialogue between stakeholders and even supports constructive disagreement. To raise the emotional intelligence of an organization, stakeholders need to communicate openly and learn both the formal and informal structures of the organization. In short, the stakeholders need awareness of the story of the organization and the role each individual plays within it.

One model for constructing the awareness of interpersonal relationships, a necessary part of building our understanding of who we are as a complex community, is the Johari Awareness Model (Figure 10-1). The model's name is a combination of its developers' first names, Joesph Luft and Harry Ingham. Commonly referred to as the Johari Window (Luft 1969), the model is a way of thinking about interpersonal functioning. It provides a visual representation of the individual or group's current level of self-awareness and potential for increasing self-awareness. The underlying concept of the Johari Window, like that of emotional intelligence, is that increased self-awareness creates open, authentic communication that improves interpersonal and organizational effectiveness. While often used at the individual level, the model also has been applied at the group and organization level in studies of ethical decision making (Dumville 1995), corporate governance (Mueller 1981), technology information needs (Shenton 2007), sport management (Horine 1990), and mentoring (Whittaker and Cartwright 2000). For example, in research on sport managers and coaches, the Johari Window has been used to describe how teams can reach their highest potential by enhancing their climate for communication and awareness.

	Known to Self	Unknown to Self
Known to Others	Arena	Blind Spot
Unknown to Others	Façade	Unknown

FIGURE 10-1. The Johari Window.

The panes in the Johari Window are as follows:

1. The Arena provides information known to oneself and others.
2. The Blind Spot provides information known to others but hidden from oneself.
3. The Façade provides information known to oneself but hidden from others.
4. The Unknown provides information unknown both to oneself and others.

Increasing the size of the Arena and decreasing the size of the other three panes in the Johari Window increases interpersonal and group effectiveness. Interpersonal relationships are the primary point of intervention for improving organizational effectiveness (Hill and Baron 1976). The larger the Arena, the more effective the relationships. The smaller the Arena, the more there is concealment, denial, deceit, or defensiveness to hurt relationships (ibid.). Luft (1969) proposed that individuals with a large Arena in their interpersonal relationships are less preoccupied with defensiveness and distortion in their attempts to ignore their Blind Spot and protect their Façade. Likewise, organizations that are characterized by open communication through self-disclosure and feedback are more effective than organizations in which communication is limited (Hill and Baron 1976). The interpersonal relationships of individuals with large Arenas are characterized by openness and trust.

There are at least two methods for increasing the size of the Arena. The first is to get feedback from others to decrease the Blind Spot (Figure 10-2). The second is to disclose information to others as a way to decrease the Façade (Figure 10-3). To be able to do either, there must be a climate of perceived psychological safety in which individuals are open to feedback and disclosure (Schein and Bennis 1965). When feedback and self-disclosure exist in a group or organization, trust and awareness are increased (Dumville 1995).

A campus climate survey is a way of increasing the size of the Arena by decreasing the Blind Spot. Our survey questions asked students to confidentially report to what extent our campus climate is infused with the values of respect, inclusion, and compassion that our mission statement and strategic plan say we hold so dear. We counted on their honest answers to make us more known to ourselves.

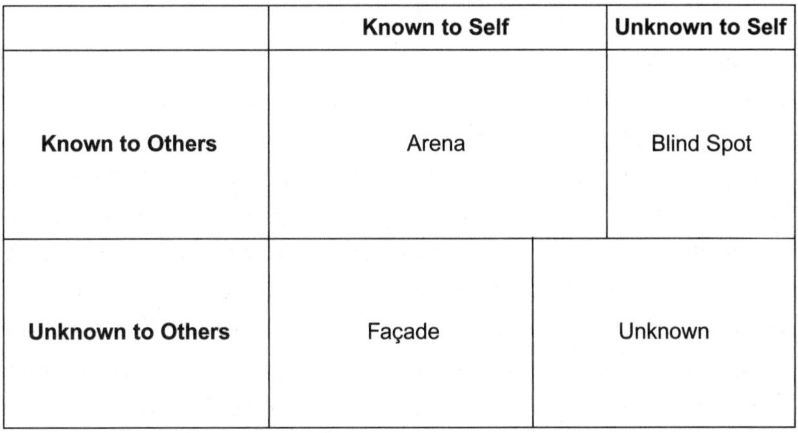

	Known to Self	Unknown to Self
Known to Others	Arena	Blind Spot
Unknown to Others	Façade	Unknown

FIGURE 10-2. Decreasing the Blind Spot in the Johari Window.

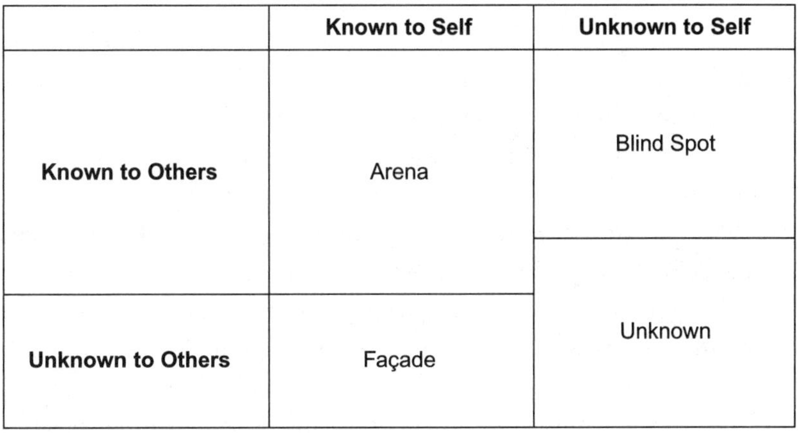

	Known to Self	Unknown to Self
Known to Others	Arena	Blind Spot
Unknown to Others	Façade	Unknown

FIGURE 10-3. Decreasing the Façade in the Johari Window.

The follow-up to the campus climate survey is a way of increasing the size of the Arena by decreasing the Façade. We counted on the empirical data provided by the survey being used by policy makers and program directors to make more information-based decisions addressing academic and student life and mission-driven services to students and thus making the university more known to others.

While the Johari Window specifically addresses interpersonal functioning rather than large group dynamics, we adopted it as our model for understanding campus climate for several reasons. First, we felt it represented the process in which we were attempting to engage. The committee began this project as a way to illuminate our Blind Spot and then authentically decrease our Façade. Second, it is a visual model that is easy to understand and to present to groups. It has the advantage of appealing to all our constituencies—faculty, staff, students, and community—by being meaningful enough to satisfy the lay person and academically rigorous enough to satisfy faculty. Third, although developed at the interpersonal level, the Johari Window nonetheless can describe changing norms at an institutional level. By beginning to be transparent about our climate in small ways, we build a pattern of transparency that allows us to address bigger and bigger issues (Dumville 1995). This moves the entire organization to a new place of greater disclosure and awareness.

Decreasing the Blind Spot

Though there is little formal reporting of bias incidents on American college campuses, the US Department of Justice's informal data collection reveals that American college students frequently hear from their fellow students degrading language directed toward people of color, women, homosexuals, and other groups who have traditionally been targeted for bias and violence (Wessler and Moss 2001). Though we would like to think that our campus is different, our own informal data gathering (i.e., conversations with students) lead us to believe that our problems are similar to other campuses. While we had much anecdotal evidence of problems faced by our students, we recognized that this evidence is biased and incomplete. To truly reveal our Blind Spot, we sought empirical data from a large group of students through a survey methodology. The idea to conduct a survey as a systematic method of gathering information from a large number of students to create a "snapshot" of our campus climate came from a meeting of the university's "think tank" of top administrators. At the meeting, the chief diversity officer asked the group to consider how the university could know "to what extent the campus climate was infused with the experience of respect, inclusion, and compassion." The think tank's answer was to ask the chief diversity officer to convene a committee of staff, faculty, and students to collect empirical data to help answer the question. The committee's first task was to define the variable "campus climate." Based on the definitions outlined in five scholarly articles,[3] the committee developed this definition: "We at Gonzaga University, use the term 'campus climate' to describe the cumulative and continuing perception of the extent to which students, faculty, and staff feel safe and valued. It includes attitudes, experiences, and behaviors, which affect the personal development of the campus community."

In hopes of opening our Johari Window, our study examined these "attitudes, experiences, and behaviors" of our campus climate. Because our study was exploratory, we chose to state our hypotheses in the null form rather than make specific predictions. Again, based on our informal data gathering, we found three areas for study—race/ethnicity, gender, and sexual orientation—and formed the following three null hypotheses:

H_{O1}: Attitudes about the importance of diversity will be equal for all students, despite race/ethnicity, gender, or sexual orientation.

H_{O2}: Experiences on diversity topics will be equal for all students, despite race/ethnicity, gender, or sexual orientation.

H_{O3}: Behaviors in regard to diversity issues will be the same for all students, despite race/ethnicity, gender, or sexual orientation.

Method

The next task for the committee was to create a survey for the students that would capture the "attitudes, experiences, and behaviors" described in the definition. The survey creation process contained three steps: First, the committee compiled more than five hundred survey questions from scholarly articles, a climate survey generously shared by Doane College, recommendations of our assessment coordinating organization (Student Voice), and questions written by the committee. Second, once all the questions were compiled, a subcommittee examined all the questions for face validity. Face validity measures whether questions "appear" to measure the dimension of interest. The subcommittee took out questions that did not appear to measure the variables of interest. Third, the committee reduced the questions that were repetitious or measuring variables beyond the scope of the study (such as campus safety). The remaining questions were grouped into topic areas under attitudes, experiences, and behaviors.[4] As indicated, some questions were asked on Likert-type scales (i.e., strongly agree to strongly disagree), others were yes/no questions, and still others were open-ended. The survey was pilot tested on a group of fifteen students.

In the data analysis stage, the scales were examined for internal reliability. Exploratory factor analysis (principal components analysis with varimax rotation) was used to investigate the initial internal reliability of the questions. The number of factors in such a set of questions was determined by examining eigenvalues (greater than 1) and scree plots. Questions with loadings greater than .33 were accepted. Questions that did not load strongly on factors were dropped. Alpha (reliability) for all the scales reached the acceptable level of .70 or higher.

Measures

Attitudes. Four scales on the survey measured the individual's attitudes about diversity and the campus climate for it. Specifically, the four scales measuring attitudes were:

Perceived importance of diversity. A four item measure assessed respondents' perceptions of the importance of diversity. These items were grouped together to try to answer the question, "Do students perceive that learning about people who are different from them is valuable?" The items were measured on a 4-point scale where 1 = strongly disagree and 4 = strongly agree. A sample item is "I believe that being part of a diverse campus will prepare me for the 'real' world." Cronbach's alpha was .75.

Perceived campus supportiveness for diversity. A three item measure assessed respondents' perceptions of how fairly individuals are treated on campus according to specific diverse dimensions. These items were grouped together to try to answer the question, "Do students perceive that everyone is treated equally on campus regardless of their race, ethnicity, gender, sexual orientation, and/or religion?" The same 4-point scale as above was used. A sample item is "At Gonzaga University, people are treated fairly regardless of their race/ethnicity." Cronbach's alpha was .80.

Perceived importance of celebrating diversity and actual perceived celebration of diversity on campus. On a scale of 1 to 4 (1 = not at all important and 4 = very important), students were asked to indicate *how important* it is to celebrate diversity on campus through fourteen different activities, events and publications such as festivals, theatre, campus magazines, and guest speakers. Likewise, students were asked about *actual perceived celebration of diversity* on campus using the same fourteen items. Students were asked on a scale of 1 to 4 (1 = strongly disagree and 4 = strongly agree), if they believed diversity is continually celebrated on campus through the fourteen items. Exploratory factor analysis was used to identify patterns in the events on the list. Two factors were identified. The first represented special activities on campus (events, programs, workshops, student clubs, magazines/newspapers, guest speakers, campus fliers/posters, dining hall food options) and the second represented daily life (faculty actions, staff actions, student actions, support services, acknowledgement of holidays and campus places). For both scales (importance of celebrating diversity and actual celebration of diversity), the two factors were highly correlated and were combined to create one scale. The alpha for perceived importance of celebrating diversity was .93 and the alpha for actual perceived celebration of diversity was .94.

Experiences. Students were given the opportunity to report if they had ever had any of seven negative experiences based on three diverse dimensions. The seven negative experiences were offensive language or humor, not being taken seriously, discouragement in pursuing career goals, negative or insulting comments, discrimination, harassment, and feeling isolated or unwelcomed. Students could respond yes or no to having each of these experiences on three diverse dimensions: race/ethnicity, gender, and sexual orientation. This scale is the sum of all the times they answered yes to those questions. The highest possible score on the scale was 21 and lowest was 0.

Behaviors. To measure behaviors with diverse others, we used a six item scale shared with us from Doane College. The scale asked students about their interactions with people who are different from them on campus. The items asked students about how frequently they socialized with someone of a different race, ethnicity, or sexual orientation, and how often they held discussions about race, sexism, and sexual orientation with people different from them. Cronbach's Alpha = .77. Despite the many behaviors described here, exploratory factor analysis found the scale to be measuring one factor.

Open-ended questions. Students were given two opportunities to provide more details on their experiences. The first open-ended question asked, "Please describe an incident or incidents that illustrate your experience." The second comment section was the last question of the survey and asked, "Please share any general comments you have about the campus climate community."

Subjects

Subjects in the study were all undergraduate students at Gonzaga University. Of approximately 4,500 undergraduates, 1,554 responded to the survey for a 34 percent response rate. Students received a request to complete the survey from the school's vice president for Student Life via their school e-mail accounts. An enticement of several possible raffle prizes was offered. A reminder e-mail was sent a week later; the survey closed after two weeks and raffle prizes were rewarded. The survey was executed by Student Voice, a professional assessment organization that hosted the survey on its website and provided data collection services. Student Voice facilitates assessment at more than 350 higher education institutions in the United States and Canada. Respondents represented a variety of majors and were evenly divided by year in school.

Results

The demographics of students who responded to the survey are similar to the overall population at Gonzaga. On the survey, there were 634 males and 920 female; 1,219 white students and 183 AHANA students. The university does not collect information on sexual orientation. On this survey, 42 students indicated they were LGBT and 1,333 students indicated they were heterosexual. Means, standard deviations, and correlations among the independent and dependent measures are reported in Table 10-1. To examine the attitudes, experiences and behaviors of students, we conducted one-way ANOVAs comparing student responses

Table 10-1. Means, Standard Deviations, and Correlations

	Mean	Std	N	1	2	3	4	5	6	7	8
1 Race	1.13	0.34	1402								
2 Gender	1.59	0.49	1554	0.89**							
3 Sexual orientation	1.03	0.17	1375	0.04	0.01						
4 Personal perceived important of diversity	3.46	0.47	1344	0.06*	0.16**	0.03					
5 Perceived fair treatment for all	3.04	0.65	1485	−0.11**	−0.08**	−0.17**	0.02				
6 Perceived importance of celebrating diversity	3.22	0.55	1353	0.09**	0.31**	0.08**	0.51**	−0.07*			
7 Perception of continuous diversity celebration	2.76	0.53	1189	−0.08**	−0.05	−0.15**	−0.04	0.43**	0.04		
8 Negative experiences	2.17	2.98	1247	0.17**	0.15**	0.26**	0.04	−0.35**	0.02	−0.22**	
9 Behaviors with diverse others	2.62	0.67	1228	0.08**	0.01	0.14**	0.20**	−0.10**	0.20**	0.15**	0.20**

Race: 1 = White, 2 = AHANA. Gender: 1 = Male, 2 = Female. Sexual Orientation: 1 = Heterosexual, 2 = LGBT
$* p < .05; ** p < .01$

based on race/ethnicity, gender, and sexual orientation. Results are reported in Tables 10-2 through 10-4.

As shown in Table 10-2, null hypothesis 1—that attitudes about the importance of diversity will be equal for all students, despite race/ethnicity, gender, or sexual orientation—was not supported. On the attitude scales, white students rated the importance of diversity and of celebrating diversity lower than did AHANA students. Likewise, male students rated these two variables lower than did female students. There was no difference between heterosexual and LGBT students on the importance of diversity, but LGBT students did rate the importance of celebrating diversity higher than heterosexual students. AHANA students rated the perceived campus supportiveness for diversity and the perceived celebration of diversity on campus lower than white students. Similarly, female students rated both variables lower than did male students and LGBT students rated both variables lower than did heterosexual students.

As shown in Table 10-3, null hypotheses 2—that experiences on diversity topics will be equal for all students, despite race/ethnicity, gender, or sexual orientation—was not supported. On the experiences measure, AHANA students reported having more negative experiences related to diversity than did white students; female students reported having more negative experiences related to diversity than did male students; and LGBT students reported having more negative experiences related to diversity than did heterosexual students. Out of the potential twenty-one negative experiences, the mean score for all students was 2.17 and the median was 1. For AHANA students, the mean score was 3.41 and the median was 2. For female students, the mean score was 2.53 and the median was 2. For LGBT students, the mean score was 6.05 and the median was 5. For white, male, heterosexual students, the mean score was 1.26 and the median was 0.

As illustrated in Table 4, null hypotheses 3—that behaviors in regard to diversity issues will be the same for all students, despite race/ethnicity, gender, or sexual orientation—was not supported. On the behaviors measure of student interactions and activities with people who are different from them on campus, AHANA students reported having more behaviors associated with diversity others than did white students; and

Table 10-2. Individual Analysis of Variance on Attitudes

Source	White		AHANA		df	F
	M	SD	M	SD		
Perceived importance of diversity	3.4	60.47	3.55	0.45	1	5.01*
Perceived campus supportiveness for diversity	3.08	0.64	2.87	0.69	1	15.79**
Perceived importance of celebrating diversity	3.21	0.55	3.35	0.48	1	9.30**
Perceived celebration of diversity on campus	2.78	0.51	2.65	0.60	1	7.57**

Source	Male		Female		df	F
	M	SD	M	SD		
Perceived importance of diversity	3.36	0.52	3.52	0.43	1	36.026**
Perceived campus supportiveness for diversity	3.11	0.65	3.01	0.65	1	8.495**
Perceived importance of celebrating diversity	3.01	0.61	3.36	0.46	1	141.063**
Perceived celebration of diversity on campus	2.80	0.52	2.74	0.53	1	3.429***

Source	Heterosexual		LGBT		df	F
	M	SD	M	SD		
Perceived importance of diversity	3.47	0.47	3.55	0.39	1	1.149
Perceived campus supportiveness for diversity	3.07	0.64	2.44	0.64	1	38.088**
Perceived importance of celebrating diversity	3.22	0.55	3.44	0.43	1	6.839**
Perceived celebration of diversity on campus	2.77	0.52	2.35	0.50	1	23.492**

$* p < .05; ** p < .01; *** p < .10$

Table 10-3. Individual Analysis of Variance on Experiences

	White		AHANA			
	M	SD	M	SD	*df*	F
Negative experiences	1.92	2.74	3.41	3.84	1	33.67**

	Male		Female			
	M	SD	M	SD	*df*	F
Negative experiences	1.62	2.98	2.53	2.93	1	28.408**

	Heterosexual		LGBT			
	M	SD	M	SD	*df*	F
Negative experiences	1.99	2.72	6.05	4.61	1	79.286**

* $p < .05$; ** $p < .01$

Table 10-4. Individual Analysis of Variance on Behaviors

	White		AHANA			
Source	M	SD	M	SD	*df*	F
Behaviors with diverse others	2.60	0.65	2.75	0.69	1	6.66*

	Male		Female			
	M	SD	M	SD	*df*	F
Behaviors with diverse others	2.61	0.64	2.63	0.68	1	0.085

	Heterosexual		LGBT			
	M	SD	M	SD	*df*	F
Behaviors with diverse others	2.61	0.66	3.13	0.54	1	23.179**

* $p < .05$; ** $p < .01$

LGBT students reported having more behaviors with diverse others than did heterosexual students.

Based on the pattern of these findings, we created a new demographic variable to compare the white, male, heterosexual students to all other students. Results of our analysis using that variable are in Table 10-5. The results of these tests indicate that white, male, heterosexual students rate the importance of diversity and the importance of celebrating diversity lower than did other students. They also rated the perceived campus supportiveness for diversity and the perceived celebration of diversity on campus higher than did other students. White, male, heterosexual students reported having fewer negative experiences around diversity than others but there was no difference in behaviors with diverse others between groups.

Open-ended questions asking students to comment on specific behaviors they had experienced were read and content coded by two coders who worked independently from each other and later compared their answers to resolve any discrepancies. The comments were first divided into three categories: positive, negative, or neutral themes on

Table 10-5. Individual Analysis of Variance for White, Male Heterosexual Students and Other Students

| Source | White, Male, Heterosexual | | Other | | df | F |
	M	SD	M	SD		
Perceived importance of diversity	3.37	0.50	3.53	0.43	1	29.39**
Perceived campus supportiveness for diversity	3.14	0.63	3.00	0.65	1	14.84**
Perceived importance of celebrating diversity	3.00	0.60	3.36	0.46	1	133.79**
Perceived celebration of diversity on campus	2.81	0.49	2.74	0.54	1	4.81*
Negative experiences	1.27	2.67	2.55	2.95	1	49.81**
Behaviors with diverse others	2.60	0.64	2.64	0.67	1	0.94

* $p < .05$; ** $p < .01$

campus climate. Of the 791 comments received from undergraduate students, 592 contained negative feedback or a description of a negative incident. The negative comments were further coded for topic areas and nine areas of comments emerged: socio-economics (152 comments), school support for diversity (85), religion (57), race (62), sexual orientation (46), gender (33), disability (6), ageism (5), and parental status, having children (3). The intraclass correlation of the coders' evaluations of the comment was 0.78.

Discussion on Decreasing the Blind Spot

The results of our survey revealed much to us about our Blind Spot. In a sense, the survey data served as a mirror reflecting back an image of the likeness of how some of our students have experienced the learning, living, and working environments on campus. We discovered that our campus climate is most comfortable for white, heterosexual males and that the university is not serving other students as well. Also, there is a gap between our students' own perceived importance of the celebration of diversity and their perception of the university's celebration of diversity. Other results include:

Female, AHANA, and LGBT students rate their own perceived importance of diversity *higher* than do male, white, and heterosexual students and rate their perceptions of whether the campus environment is inclusive and supportive of them *lower* than do male, white, and heterosexual students.

Overall, students' perceptions of how the campus environment supports diversity are lower than their perceptions of the importance of diversity. In other words, our students do value diversity. However, they do not see the university as being supportive of diverse students and ideas. Also, students' perceptions that the campus environment continuously celebrates diversity are lower than their perceptions of the importance of celebrating diversity.

The tabulation of yes/no answers asking students whether they had negative experiences based on race/ethnicity, gender, and sexual orientation indicate that our LGBT students are having significantly more negative experiences on diversity dimensions than other students.

The content of the responses to open-ended questions found that socio-economic status was mentioned more than any other diversity dimension in the comments. Students have negative experiences around their socio-economic status whether it is high or low. Also students indicated having many negative incidents around their religion, whether they are Catholic or not.

The content of the responses also indicates that the Catholic, faith-based identity of the university is important to many students.

On their own, these findings certainly reveal that we have not yet met our ideal of creating a campus climate in which all lives—student, faculty, staff, and community—can be transformed. However, we also believe that it is important to keep in mind that our survey is, to the best of our knowledge, unique. This means that we have no parallel statistics with which to compare our community with the surrounding environment, with our peer Jesuit institutions, or with other university communities. We are not trying to describe our campus as particularly problematic. We can point to an impressive list of initiatives, programs, and actions by individuals throughout our campus all working to achieve our ideal campus. However, it is the nature of an ideal to always remain ahead and above us. There is always more work to be done, and our findings help us pinpoint the nature of that work.

Decreasing the Façade

While the survey results revealed much of our Blind Spot by making us more aware of the gap between rhetoric and reality, this is only part of the equation to increase the Arena. The next part is to share the information with others as a way to decrease the Façade. The interdisciplinary nature of our committee gave us many opportunities to tell the story to different constituencies. For example, one of the staff members on the committee is the director for Residence Life and was able to give the committee access to the meetings of the residence directors and students in the residence halls. Another member of the committee is an administrator and was able to give us access to the board of regents and other administrators on campus. The faculty members on the committee gave us access to faculty meetings by department and as a whole. Sharing our findings became an invitation to the larger community of the university to reflect on its collective identity. In short, it became an opportunity for our organization to both write and revise the story of who we are and who we aspire to be. Such storytelling can provide meaning and belonging in our lives (Witherell and Noddings 1991). In an organizational context, community storytelling can become a strategic mechanism for the work of mission and identity.

Our storytelling about the survey has involved presentations to small and large groups. The largest presentation was to the faculty of the university at our annual faculty meeting. The presentation was well received, with faculty expressing little surprise around the results about race and gender, but some shock about the results on LGBT and socioeconomic issues. After presenting the results to the faculty, we engaged them in a brainstorming activity. This activity further opened our Johari Window by giving faculty the opportunity to write down what we already do to improve campus climate (decreasing the Façade) and to list what we *could* be doing to improve campus climate. The result was 679 current practices done around campus to improve climate and promote understanding of diverse others, including things like sacred dance classes, independent studies on diversity topics, training for faculty on how to help LGBT students, and service-learning opportunities. The exercise also gave us 320 ideas for new practices such as more collaboration with the campus ministry, creating a social justice concentration, ideas for alternative spring breaks, and topics for guest speakers.

Other consultative presentations included the board of regents, Student Life officials, Academic Counseling officials, Residence Life directors and assistants, and the assistant academic vice president. These presentations stimulated a reflective dialogue and encouraged an interpretative response to the survey findings. Overall, the result of these presentations has been both a communication of what we learned and a deeper understanding of how these issues operate in the various arenas on campus. Each group provided us with new ideas for improving campus climate. For example, the residence hall directors suggested posting informational fliers, holding focus groups, and having faculty visit residence halls to see how students live and increase understanding. While most groups reacted similarly to the faculty in being surprised by the results on LGBT and socio-economic issues, the groups comprised of students expressed little surprise on any of the results presented. Overall, the students seemed to feel that the results did a good job of capturing the climate for diversity on campus.

To make the information available to everyone, whether they could attend our presentations or not, we put the survey report on our university website with a request for feedback from the community. Making the results publicly available to the university community and anyone with Internet access was another step toward decreasing our Façade.

Beyond simply presenting the data, we also have tackled some of the specific problem areas revealed to us through the data and open-ended comments. For faculty, we held a workshop on managing productive discomfort in the classroom. This workshop included a panel of students who had experienced offensive remarks in the classroom from professors and fellow students. The faculty participants in the workshop examined how to avoid such comments and how to care for students when such comments are made. They also counseled the students on where to go to report such offensive incidents if the faculty member in the classroom does not do so. The cochairs of the committee have held separate focus groups in residence halls to discuss how issues around diversity play out in the students' living spaces. These group sessions began with a presentation of the data and gave students the opportunity to expand on what they had experienced and discuss what kind of safe living environment they would like to create.

Conclusion

As stated before, the end goal of our research is to identify the unintentional systemic injustices on our campus and work to change them. To become a university known for justice, we have worked to shrink the university's Blind Spot through data gathering about how students perceive the university and then shrink the university's Façade by being honest and open about how the university responds to its new knowledge. According to research on emotionally intelligent organizations and the Johari Awareness Model, this process should allow relationships at the university to be more effective. More important, however, this process allows our university to become closer to its Jesuit ideal.

In his keynote address entitled "Companions in Mission: Pluralism in Action" at Loyola Marymount University on February 2, 2009, the Very Reverend Adolfo Nicolas, SJ, Superior General of the Society of Jesus, suggests a way of proceeding with this question by reflecting on strategic insights inspired by the 35th General Congregation. Father Nicolas reminds us that a critical element of formation for mission in a Jesuit context is discernment and he admits this may seem like an esoteric term. Despite this admitted guilt by abstract association, he affirms that:

> Discernment enables us to engage the world through a careful analysis of context, in dialogue with experience, involving evaluation through reflection, for the sake of action and with openness, always, to further evaluation. Formation in discernment and mission stems principally from serious conversation, where we pay attention to experience, reflect on that experience and then make good decisions, together, based on what is learned through the process. It always involves sharing our own stories. Common mission becomes real through genuine relationships of trust and through shared actions and practices. Joint action can encourage them [colleagues, coworkers, or community members] to live more consequentially as contemplatives in action and authentic companions.

Our first step on this organizational journey was to confirm the gap between the rhetoric of our mission statement and the reality of lived experience within our university community. Our second step was to share the story of the gap and engage in dialogue as a community. John B. Breslin, SJ (1999), discusses bringing faith and culture into dialogue as a hallmark of the decrees of the 34th General Congregation. Father Breslin (1999) reminds us that Jesuit colleges and universities have a rich heritage to draw on for this conversation between what we profess (our rhetoric) in our faith and what is experienced in our intercultural relationships (our culture) in the promotion of justice. This rich heritage is based on both the writings of Saint Ignatius and the 470-year history of the Society of Jesus. Surveying our students about how they experience their living and learning environment allowed us to articulate our narrative structure, give voice to our institutional story, and inspire a serious conversation between faith, justice, and culture. It has, we believe, taken us closer to our Ignatian ideal.

Part III: Our Way of Proceeding

Introduction

REV. STEPHEN A. PRIVETT, SJ

The five articles in this section share a common concern: the Jesuit university's responsibility to educate for justice. They propose opportunities, underscore challenges and hint at the risks involved in educating for a faith that does justice. The authors assume the "higher standard" that Dean Brackley, SJ, first proposed for Jesuit colleges and universities in a 2005 address at Loyola Marymount University, "The Jesuit University in a Broken World," and to which I believe Jesuit higher education should hold itself accountable when assessing overall educational quality. The authors remind us—in their own way—that "academic excellence" by itself falls short as an adequate shorthand summary of what Jesuit universities are ultimately and finally about. Given that no university anywhere would ever lay claim to "academic mediocrity," Jesuit universities must move beyond the ubiquitous banal slogan "seek academic excellence" in distinguishing themselves from other universities. Jesuit universities must not allow themselves to be seduced into substituting rankings from the likes of *US News and World Report* for, as Rev. Jeffrey von Arx states, "the real measure of our Jesuit universities is . . . who our students become . . . and the adult Christian responsibility they will exercise in the future towards their neighbor and the world." For Jesuit universities, "status" does not equal "quality" in the Jesuit tradition. We have a richer understanding of education that dictates a more comprehensive and fulsome set of standards for excellence than those of the popular media.

The overarching criteria against which Jesuit universities measure their success has remained constant since 1548 when the first Jesuit school was established in Messina, Italy. Then and now, the Jesuit tradition is one of humanistic or humanizing education; the intended outcome of such an education is a fully human being. We gauge the success of Jesuit education by who our students become and how they choose to be in the world, not simply by what they bring to us in terms of class rankings, GPAs, standardized testing scores, and acceptance rates into elite graduate programs, and how steep their ascent up the ladder of success. The goal of Jesuit education is success both as human beings and in a chosen career, certainly not professional success at the expense of one's humanity. Such a perspective has solid Gospel roots: "What good is it for a person to gain the whole world and lose her soul" (Mark 8:36).

It is important to underscore the obvious: "human being" does more than name an individual person, it further denotes a way of being in the world that is distinctive of us humans. Clearly, there are human ways of being in the world, less human ways, and even inhuman ways of being in the world as it is. Jesuit education challenges students to "be humanly" in a rather inhumane world, where some 30,000 people die every day from hunger or hunger-related diseases; where two billion people whose daily struggle to simply survive on the two dollars that we might pay for a bottle of designer water; where, as Jennifer Tilghman-Havens points out, 99 percent of the victims of climate change live in the developing world. Anna Brown cuts to the heart of the challenge for Jesuit education when she cites Fr. Pedro Arrupe's observation on how difficult it is to be good in an evil world. Preparing students to be humanly in this inhumane world is a daunting task. The authors of these five essays do a masterful job of exposing us to the realities of the world as it is for the majority of its inhabitants: massive global poverty, increasing environmental degradation and ravaged by war and violence. They suggest the kind of teaching and learning demanded of so that, in the words of Fr. Adolfo Nicolas, the Superior General of the Jesuits, people do not "lose the ability to engage with reality" and succumb to "a process of dehumanization that may be gradual and silent, but very real" ("Challenges of Higher Education Today," April 23, 2010, Mexico City).

It would be salutary for us to step back at this point and remind ourselves that the Jesuit tradition of education traces its origins to the reforms of the renaissance and its focus on the texts of classical antiquity rather than a narrowly moralistic focus on exclusively "Christian" sources. Jesuits embraced those classic texts—Cicero, Virgil, Terence— that others considered "pagan." Jesuits saw in these writings some of the finest expressions of the human spirit. Their thinking was that the humanity of those authors was transferable to students through careful study. The renaissance reformers enthusiastically embraced the Roman playwright Terrence's axiom "nothing human is foreign to me [*nil humanum alienum est a me*]."

The Jesuit and Catholic tradition of educating persons to their full humanity when coupled with the patristic insight that God's glory is the human person fully alive—*Gloria Dei homo vivens* is the theological axiom—endows education with a profoundly religious significance insofar as education accepts the awesome responsibility of leading persons to the fullness of their humanity, thereby realizing the glory of God. Conversely the extent to which people do not reach their full human potential is the extent to which the world, in Gerard Manley Hopkins words is "seared . . . bleared . . . smeared . . . and wears man's smudge and shares man's smell" ("God's Grandeur" in *Poems* [London: Humphrey Milford, 1918]).

In the story of the Good Samaritan the Bible shows us a person who at the same time exemplifies the best of humanity and of religion in his reaching out to the abused person left to die in a ditch at the side of the highway. The martyred Archbishop Romero used to ask, how do we deal with a world where 75 percent of the people are abandoned in a ditch off the main road and out of our ordinary sight line? I argue that the least human way of being in the world is to prosper at the expense of others or to live as though we are not all brothers and sisters, members of the one human family of God. Who of us is not left uneasy by the realization that the quality of our education will ultimately be gauged by how we respond to the needs of the least of our brothers and sisters, those whom Franz Fanon named, "the wretched of the earth."

Sister Peggy O'Neil, a veteran El Salvador church worker, tells the story of a boy and a goat. One day, during the savage civil war in El Salvador when food was very scarce, a single banana fell from an overloaded truck onto the road. An emaciated young boy and a goat both raced for the fruit. Peggy prayed that the boy would get there first, and he did. He successfully fended off the goat and began to peel the banana. A relieved Peggy watched as the famished boy stopped, turned and handed the meat of the banana to an old man huddled at the side of the road whom Peggy had not even noticed. The boy continued on his way eating the skin of the banana. Peggy ran up to the boy, hoping, as she put it, "to see the face of God." She asked why he gave away the banana. "Because the old man was hungrier than me," the boy told her.

It is axiomatic that where we stand determines what we see, and whom we talk to determines what we hear. The squalid favelas of Rio de Janeiro look very different to sun worshippers on the beaches of Ipanema than they do to the desperately poor slum dwellers who populate them. A University of San Francisco (USF) student who took a course on the border in Tijuana, Mexico, wrote, "it is not until we spend part of the day talking with the managers of a factory and the rest of the day talking with the women who work there that we truly get a taste for the contradictions and complexities. This class has truly changed my perspective." Another student referred to her experience in Central America as a pushing away from her comfort zone and daring to understand the world from the perspective of a poor peasant woman. She labeled her experience "mind blowing." A USF nursing student wrote of his time in rural Guatemala, "I lived for two weeks with people who had nothing, but offered us everything they had. They always welcomed me, a complete stranger, like a long-lost relative from California. I have completely changed my priorities." Our perspectives and priorities can change when we stand with and listen to the people who don't keep their food in a fridge or their clothes in a closet.

Dean Brackley talks about the impact on students of a one-semester-long immersion program in El Salvador, called Casa de la Solidaridad. "To their surprise they spend much of their time in El Salvador wondering why these poor people are smiling and why they insist on sharing their tortillas with strangers like them. But as the humanity and dignity of the poor crashes through their defenses, the people break their hearts. They fell disoriented, as people do when they fall in love. . . . As the poor emerge from their two dimensional anonymity, student's horizons open. Their world shakes and eventually gets reconfigured. Some things move from the margin to the center and others from the center to the edge." Where we stand determines what we see, and our perspectives and priorities can change.

In his Mexico City address, Father Nicolas asked Jesuit educators, "How many of those who leave our institutions do so with both professional competence and the experience of having . . . a depth of engagement with reality that transforms them at their deepest core? What more do we need to do to ensure that we are not simply populating the world with bright and skilled superficialities?" He was not posing rhetorical questions but asking for serious programmatic efforts from those of us who educate in the Jesuit Catholic tradition.

In our global context, those of us in Catholic higher education work with a privileged elite—one person in the mythical village of a hundred persons has a college education. The ethical question for higher education generally—and even more so for Catholic higher education—is as much about the ninety-nine people in the village who will never go to college, as it is about the one person who is currently studying at a university. Does what our education is doing with our students offer any hope to the ninety-nine? Can we educate people to be humanly in the world without attending to the two thirds of the population whose lives are marked by grinding poverty and quiet despair—the three billion people who live on less than the two dollars that some Americans pay for a bottle of designer water? To cite Father Nicolas again, "we need to ask, 'who benefits from the knowledge produced in our institutions and who does not? Who needs the knowledge we can share, and how can we share it more effectively with those for whom it would truly make a difference, especially the poor and excluded?'" It is said that on the eve of India's independence and in the face of nearly insurmountable challenges, when Gandhi was asked what he feared most, he replied, "hardness of heart in the educated." It seems that Gandhi's fear was well placed and should resonate with all of us involved with higher education in this country.

When John Donne wrote, "No man is an island entire of itself; every man is a piece of the Continent, a part of the main. . . . Any man's death diminishes me because I am involved in Mankind," he was underscoring the truth that we are inextricably joined to one another and that we cannot achieve the fullness of our humanity in isolation from one another, much less at the expense of others. Fr. Peter-Hans Kolvenbach, the previous superior of the Jesuit order, expressed the same truth somewhat less poetically, when he publicly challenged Jesuit schools to "educate the whole person of solidarity for the real world" in his June 6, 2000, address at Santa Clara University. He further noted that such solidarity is the product of contact not concepts, and that "personal involvement with innocent suffering, with the injustice others suffer, is the catalyst for solidarity, which then gives rise to intellectual inquiry and moral reflection." Notice that the hoped-for outcome of such solidarity is rigorous inquiry and serious moral reflection. Such solidarity is a stimulus, not a threat, to increased academic rigor and intellectual authenticity.

NOT AN Either or

It is a fundamental conviction of contemporary Jesuit education that to be humanly in today's world one must be fully cognizant that our world is not the real world for the majority of people in our global village. The suffering of others touches us—diminishes us—and the more directly we experience those sufferings, the more keenly the pain will be felt. Stepping out of one's "comfort zone," as previously noted, is a recurring theme among students who leave the "bubble" of campus life to interact directly with poor and marginalized persons at home or abroad. Being uncomfortable with the glaring inequities and rampant injustices of our world is a sign of moral health and an indication that a person is plumbing the depth of her humanity.

A former student told me that his volunteer experience in Guatemala taught him that if all the people in the world were stretched out in a single file line, he would be up toward the very front of the line. He decided that rather than spend the rest of his life pushing to be first in line, he would try to look back at the billions of people behind him. That decision, he said, has made all the difference. Another student reflected on her experience in a rural Mexican village, "knowing that 'fresh water' was yellow and came from a well of flies and tires, knowing that homes were lucky if they had four walls or sides, and knowing that families were struggling to have enough food to provide for everyone, I lost and gained a little of my humanity." Two summers ago while in South Africa with USF students, I visited a Black African shantytown that sprang up on the side of a hill that sloped down into a large refuse dump. These desperate families—mostly women and children—literally lived in and on garbage. A woman led me by the hand to her mother's shack—twelve by fifteen feet, card board sides, tin roof, dirt floor no electricity or water, a single shelf that served as table, bed, and work counter. There sat an ancient woman with dark leathery skin staring vacantly into space—"cataracts," her daughter told me. As I squinted in the sunlight, the woman angrily asked me how I could smile knowing that people were living in such squalor. I was not smiling, but that question remains with me today.

Jesuit Humanistic education in the twenty-first century must challenge students and faculty to step out of their comfort zones to directly encounter innocent suffering and wrestle with what sociologist Robert Bellah called "the practical syllogism":

> If the major premise is that basic human rights are to be met and the minor premise is that in some situations basic humans rights are not met, then the logical conclusion is not just about knowledge but about action. What is the just thing to do about it? The practical syllogism does not tell us what to do. For that we need all the wisdom and knowledge and all the judgment we can bring to bear on it. But the practical syllogism tells us that we can't just stand idly by. Often the reality is, we can't do much; but the obligation to what we can do remains. (Robert Bellah, "Educating for Justice and the Common Good." *Conversations* [Spring 2004]: 35)

Jesuit higher education's challenge is to nurture that sense of obligation that calls us to a humane way of being in a most inhumane world, while offering the knowledge, wisdom, passion, imagination, and judgment that enable us to leverage society effectively for good. Father Nicolas has asked and clearly answered his own direct question about the challenges of Jesuit higher education today. "The only answer is: the challenges of the world. There are no other challenges. The challenge is looking for meaning: Is life worth living: And the challenges of poverty, death, suffering, violence and war. These are our challenges."

Father Nicolas proposed that his Mexico City audience engage in an imaginative exercise. He invited us participants to imagine ourselves, not as the university faculty or staff that we are, but as the cofounders of a new religious order trying to discern the most effective way to realize God's hopes for the world. "In this globalized world, with all its lights and shadows, would—or how would—running all these universities still be the best way we can respond to the mission of the church and the needs of the world." That is the overarching question that should engage all of us who are involved with Jesuit higher education. If we cannot answer in the affirmative, then we would do well to focus our minds and hearts toward making the changes that would allow for an enthusiastic "yes" this is the best way for us to respond to the needs of our world.

Opening Remarks to the Jesuit
Justice Conference, June 18, 2009

REV. JEFFREY VON ARX, SJ

Twenty-five years ago, the Society of Jesus committed itself to
the promotion of the justice that is an imperative of Christian Faith.
Faith and justice were to inform its entire apostolic works. In response
to this call, leaders of the Jesuit universities in the United States
planned and implemented three regional conferences in 1999 and con-
vened a national justice conference at Santa Clara University in October 2000. The conference process had three objectives: to assess
critically how the commitment to justice has been made on Jesuit campuses and determine what difference it has made; to develop a better
theoretical rationale of social justice as an essential part of higher education, particularly at Jesuit universities; and to articulate concrete
steps for further implementation.¹ Since the first national conference
at Santa Clara in 2000, three additional conferences have been held:
in 2002 at Loyola University Chicago in Chicago, Illinois, in 2005 at
John Carroll University in University Heights, Ohio, and in 2009 at
Fairfield University in Fairfield, Connecticut. Rev. Jeffrey von Arx, SJ,
president of Fairfield University, opened the 2009 Commitment to Justice conference with the following welcome address.

_____

As president of Fairfield University it is my pleasure to welcome you
all here for this conference, "Transforming the World and Being Transformed." It is a particular honor to be asked to address you this evening,
and to offer my reflections on our mission as Jesuit and Catholic educators to work in the service of faith "of which the promotion of justice
is an absolute requirement."² This mission was given to us and the
whole society by the 32nd General Congregation of the Society of Jesus,
and has been continually affirmed by subsequent congregations and
meditations on our mission as educators ever since.

This weekend we have a rare opportunity to reflect upon how far we
have come in the service of this mission since the Commitment to

Justice in Jesuit Higher Education Conference at Santa Clara in 2000, when Fr. Peter-Hans Kolvenbach, in his keynote address, issued to all our Jesuit colleges the challenge to grasp the impact of this mission and apply it to every aspect of our institutions. In the years since—and with the additional inspiration and refinements offered by Paul Locatelli and Dean Brackley at the conference at John Carroll University in 2005—all of our institutions have changed, and in varying ways have reinvigorated our obligation to serve the promotion of justice. We have enhanced those programs that expose our students to the "gritty reality,"[3] as Father Kolvenbach put it, of poverty, illiteracy, oppression, hunger, exploitation, and a host of other global issues that we are duty-bound to embrace as our apostolate.

I hope and expect that this conference will serve as further inspiration for us to renew our commitment to this mission with optimism, and as an opportunity to share ideas with one another—what has worked, what hasn't worked, how much deeper can we go—so that we can progress on this path in unity and with a shared sense of purpose.

It has been almost ten years since Father Kolvenbach's address, and what I hope to do this evening—somewhat in the spirit of the Jesuit tradition of the "Examination of Conscience"—is to reflect on what has transpired over the past few years, giving thanks to God for the gifts we have received, and then suggest some challenges we face as we take this transformative mission into a new decade.

You are all aware of the justice-related activities at your universities, and indeed, it is impressive to visit the Justice website maintained by Loyola College in Maryland and to look at what is going on in each of our twenty-eight institutions. Of course I'm most familiar with what we are doing at Fairfield, but a brief tour of the service programs on the site illustrates how central the promotion of justice has become for us.

As Father Kolvenbach put it, "The real measure of our Jesuit universities lies in who our students become . . . and the adult Christian responsibility they will exercise in the future toward their neighbor and the world."[4] I think we have taken that message to heart, and we have much to be thankful for in the degree to which our students, faculty, and staff have thrown themselves into our service-learning, sustainability and community engagement programs.

To draw attention to just a few: At Wheeling Jesuit University, students do service work in Appalachia; Santa Clara maintains a student immersion program in El Salvador; at Rockhurst, students teach computer and literacy skills to Haitian immigrants in Kansas and Burundian refugees in Omaha; students at Marquette are in the midst of their preparations for an immersion trip in January where they will work in the schools of Belize; at Regis University, the "Tinsana" project is engaged in an ongoing commitment to develop libraries for schools in Ghana.

"I want to influence my friends to get involved . . . I came to see the realization that I've lived a sheltered life," said one Creighton student after a service trip in Calhoun City. This is precisely the kind of conversion of heart and intellectual and moral epiphany that we hope for when we ask our students to step outside their comfort zone and engage with the "gritty reality" of the world. As Father Kolvenbach said, as Jesuits we have always sought to educate the "whole person," but the "whole person" of the twenty-first century is not the "whole person" of the Renaissance. In the current global reality, full of possibilities and contradictions, a world that is pluralistic and interrelated to an unprecedented degree, the "whole person" of our age cannot be whole without an educated awareness of the inequities and suffering that are the lot of the majority of our brothers and sisters.

It is our mission as educators to "raise our Jesuit educational standard to 'educate the whole person of solidarity for the real world.' Solidarity is learned by 'contact' rather than 'concepts,'" Father Kolvenbach continued. "When the heart is touched by direct experience, the mind may be challenged to change. Personal involvement with innocent suffering, with the injustice others suffer, is the catalyst for solidarity which then gives rise to intellectual inquiry and moral reflection."[5]

At Fairfield—where I have a more immediate grasp on things—about four hundred of our students participate every year in service learning programs. Meanwhile, our Center for Faith and Public Life focuses faculty research in areas of international justice like the economic exploitation of undocumented populations in this country and around the world. Out of this has sprung the Jesuit Universities Humanitarian Action Network, a project initiated by Fairfield in conjunction with Georgetown and Fordham to prepare our students to respond to humanitarian crises, such as the Asian tsunami, Hurricane Katrina, and so on. It is our hope that this project will serve as a point of coordination on humanitarian action for the twenty-eight colleges and universities in the ACJU.

Many of these programs were in place in some form prior to 2000, but I think it is fair to say that the "promotion of justice" has gathered impetus over the last nine years. The "contact" encounters that convert the hearts of our students happen more often than they ever have, and for that we must be grateful.

So, where do we go from here? Well, I believe that the "seven higher standards for higher education"[6] put forward by Fr. Dean Brackley at the conference in 2005 remain as pertinent today as they did four years ago. He summarized them this way:

> First, a Jesuit university strives to understand *reality*, the real world. Second, since Christian education pursues wisdom, the central focus of study is the drama of *life versus death*, of *good versus evil*, injustice versus liberation. Third, we must pursue a discipline that will *free us from bias*. Fourth, education should help people to discover their *vocation* in life, above all their vocation to love and serve. Fifth, a Jesuit university must be a place where the *Catholic faith* is studied and handed on to those who would embrace it. Sixth, we must reach out to those *who otherwise could not afford to come*. Finally, we must *communicate knowledge* and criticism *beyond the campus*, into the wider society.

I'd like to draw particular attention this evening to just three of these challenges that I believe require deeper reflection

Access to Education

First, I think a matter that must be of grave concern is the rising cost of higher education and the disturbing truth that it is becoming increasingly difficult for talented students from lower income families to attend our universities. This is an injustice that we must make a priority, because our American Jesuit universities were "originally founded to serve the educational and religious needs of poor immigrant populations,"[7] and it is the tradition of the Jesuit mission to bring education to those who might otherwise be deprived of it.

St. Ignatius, after his conversion, dedicated the next stage of his life to seeking the education he needed to realize his vocation. This is why we have put education at the center of our Jesuit way of proceeding— because Ignatius believed that God was, in truth, *The Educator* par excellence and that God was *intentionally educating him* from one moment to the next, developing him into a whole person, prepared for the task God set before him.

We are educators because we believe that through education, men and women are liberated into the fullness of their true human potential, as Ignatius was liberated. What could be more critical then to the "promotion of justice" in our country and in our world than to address the yawning gap between the rich and the poor where access to education is concerned?

Yet the trends even within our own universities are a cause for alarm. The current global economic recession, the implications of increased unemployment, decreasing state and federal aid, smaller endowments, decreasing alumni contributions—the percentage of alumni making contributions has decreased in the AJCU every year since 2003—and other economic pressures on families suggests that at least in the foreseeable years, providing access to those who would otherwise go without higher education may be the most critical justice issue that we face.

Just to give you some perspective, according to the National Center for Public Policy, the cost of higher education has increased by 439 percent since 1982, while the median family income has increased by only 147 percent in that time. It seems clear that the economic trends are making our universities more exclusive—and not more inclusive. By one estimate, a family in the upper income bracket may have to pay up to 9 percent of its income to send a student through a four-year college, while a family in the low-income bracket may have to spend as much as 55 percent of its entire income to do the same. This is obviously more than we can expect lower- and middle-income families to bear.

The result of these trends is predictable enough: According to the Advisory Committee on Student Financial Assistance, between 1.4 and 2.4 million students who were qualified and capable of attending a four-year college over the last ten years did not do so because of the cost. This number will now certainly increase.

Given this, you might expect that universities—most of which have an expressed interest in increasing the diversity of their student populations—would be assigning more of their financial aid to students based on need. But this is not so, and in a number of our Jesuit universities, the trend is in the opposite direction, toward more merit-based financial aid. The majority of university financial aid in this country goes to students with families earning over $100,000 a year.

At Fairfield, we have developed programs like the Bridgeport Tuition Program, which provides free tuition to students in our area whose families earn less than $50,000, and we are increasing our need-based financial aid. Other universities have similar programs.

But justice demands that we do more. Clearly, if we intend to "promote justice" we had better be prepared to do so in our own backyard and put our money where our mouth is. I suspect what this demands is that we should all be prepared to shift more of our financial aid away from "merit-based" financial aid, toward "need-based" financial aid, and I challenge all of our Jesuit colleges and universities to do so. If we want our universities to serve as communities where transformative dialogue can take place between different faiths, cultural backgrounds and socio-economic perspectives, then we need to ensure that students from every background have the opportunity to take part.

This shift will have implications: First, with fewer resources and more student need, we will have to make tough decisions about where our money goes. We need to look at things like big time varsity athletics, elaborate facilities, and boutique programs of various stripes and ask in what way and to what degree do they work in the "service of faith and the promotion of justice."

We may also have to look at our graduate schools and professional programs. In many cases they add to the prestige of our universities and attract gifted faculty, but as our resources contract, we need to question whether they should all be sustained. This is particularly true where our graduate programs are not very highly regarded. As Jesuits with a commitment to academic excellence and the "Magis" asking ourselves whether we should be dedicating resources to programs that are not making serious scholarly contributions in an already glutted graduate school environment is a course we should pursue. Perhaps we should be looking at greater cooperation when it comes to our graduate programs—an idea incidentally, that has been kicked around by American Jesuit colleges and universities in the past but never seems to go anywhere.

As we assess the direction of graduate and professional programs in a time of shrinking resources, we need to ensure that our Jesuit values are integral to the mission of these programs, and not just a "bonus" feature, tacked on as an afterthought.

Should our professional programs—our medical, law, business schools, and so on—be tailored specifically toward the "service of faith and the promotion of justice" as our primary focus, to the exclusion of more secular concerns? Pope John Paul II, writing in the 1987 encyclical *Sollicitudo rei Socialis* on the twentieth anniversary of Paul VI's *Populorum Progressio* wrote that "The motivating concern for the poor—who are in the very meaningful term, 'the Lord's poor'—must be translated at all levels into concrete actions" by Christians until we decisively attain a series of necessary reforms.[8] He goes on to list the reforms that are required to include reform of the international trade system; the reform of the world monetary and financial system; the framework of the international juridical order, and so on. We might add, the reform of systems that allow for the exploitation of migrant workers in this country and around the world; and the inequities in health care between rich and poor.

My question then is this: should our business, law, medical, and other professional schools be explicitly dedicated to educating young men and women who will tackle these problems—men and women who are trained specifically for "contact" as Father Kolvenbach put it? Are we prepared to take such a step with the knowledge that it might mean that some of our schools would slip out of the mainstream or—horror of horrors!—move down in the rankings? Are we prepared to turn off many potential students and faculty in doing so?

I don't propose to answer those questions tonight, but simply to suggest that our obligation to make a Jesuit education accessible will mean making hard decisions about all dimensions of our institutions in the future.

Free Us from Bias

I also want to touch briefly on the question of bias. The purpose of our service learning and immersion programs is precisely to expose our students and faculty to "contact" with other perspectives. But one thing I think we need to maintain in our consciousness as we move forward, particularly in the developing world, is that we fully understand what is meant by a "well-educated solidarity." Specifically, we need to monitor our thinking, and shift our focus from what *our* interests are, to a more "global consciousness" that considers the mutual interests that we share with the "Lord's poor" in the developing world, or the poor within our own borders.

There's no question that we want our students to have "contact" with the "gritty reality" of injustice, but we need to be careful that we don't indulge in some kind of spiritual and moral tourism in the process, where we dip our students and faculty into the "gritty reality" for the purposes of their formation, without really being conscious of what the experience of our presence is like for those who happen to live in that "gritty reality" full-time. What kind of emotional and spiritual footprint do we leave when we engage in these programs?

I'm not suggesting that we would be consciously insensitive. But we do need to ensure that we are really listening to what those who are suffering are asking for, and that we are motivated by a sincere desire to respond empathically to their needs and not by our interests in the formation of our students, or the conduct of our research.

What I'm suggesting is that the center of gravity needs to shift from *us*—the promoter of justice—to a fuller consciousness of the *we*—the full mutuality of relationship that is only possible when we truly open our doors and give all that we have to give and receive what is being offered to us in return.

Catholic "solidarity" is the understanding that each of us is alike in dignity, and is in fact—whether friend or enemy, oppressed or oppressor—made in the image and likeness of God.

As Father Locatelli pointed out in 2005, "solidarity" calls for more from us than merely a passion for justice. It calls on us to understand that our own freedom and full potential is only realized within a community of persons, within a communion that is bigger than mere "interconnection or interdependence."[9]

To grasp this understanding of solidarity then is to grasp that the preferred "point of view" on the world is not ours. It's isn't something that we have some privileged access to as well-educated representatives of American universities. The preferential option for the poor is also a call to adopt the priorities of those whom we are presuming to help.

In practical terms, this may mean that we should be thinking about how to bring more students to our universities from the developing world; that we should be bringing more faculty into our campuses from the developing world; and that we find ways to share the great resources that we have.

One practical idea that was presented to me that I like very much is making our library and research facilities more accessible to our academic colleagues in these countries. For no cost and little effort, our universities could add hundreds of academic colleagues to our personnel databases as "research affiliates," giving them access to more up-to-date information and research in their areas of expertise. By doing so, we could collectively have a significant impact on the educational programs in many nations.

We are fortunate this weekend to be joined by representatives from Nicaragua, India, and Colombia, and I look forward to hearing their thoughts on the question of bias over the next couple of days.

The Catholic Faith

Finally, I want to touch briefly upon our obligation as Catholic and Jesuit educators to teach and encourage the Catholic Faith.

Since the foundations of the Society in 1540, Jesuits have been "officially and solemnly charged with 'the defense and the propagation'" of the faith,[10] although the wording was changed by the 32nd General Congregation to that of the "service of faith." This service of faith cannot be separated from the "promotion of justice." Rather, the promotion of justice is our responsibility because the teaching of our faith and the love of God that is the heart of the Christian experience moves us in compassion and charity toward a love of our fellow men and women. It is because we love, and because our faith demands that we love, that we are moved to transcend our own personal egoism and seek what is good and true, not just for ourselves, but for our neighbors. As Decree 4 of the 32nd General Congregation puts its:

> The Christian message is a call to conversion: conversion to the love of God, which necessarily implies conversion to the love of men, which necessarily includes conversion to the demands of justice. If then, we are to be faithful to our apostolic mission, we must lead men to the fullness of Christian salvation: to the love of the Father in the first instance, and to the love of neighbor as an inseparable consequence of that love.[11]

So the "promotion of justice" is not something that we can split off from our obligation to serve the faith, it is rather something we are called to do as a consequence of our faith. Nor can justice be promoted and pursued as an end in itself, with our duty to be of "service" to the Catholic faith placed in the background as an afterthought. Rather the "promotion of justice" is an extension of our obligation to love our fellow men and women that is itself a naturally flowing extension of God's love for us, and our love of God.

Lest we be in any doubt about what this means for us, Pope Benedict XVI in his meeting with catholic educators at the Catholic University of America last April said that first "and foremost every Catholic educational institution is a place to encounter the living God who in Jesus Christ reveals his transforming love and truth."[12] As Catholic educators, it is our mission to awaken in our students a love for an objective truth that transcends the personal and the subjective, and leads them toward a lived experience of the unity of truth, an experience that liberates our students into a genuine freedom. That freedom finds its ultimate expression in a life of faith.

This is a notion of freedom that is at odds with a secular notion of personal liberty, and it is a notion of freedom that is at odds with the life that many of our students will have been living prior to their arrival on our campuses. This is not the freedom of being able to do whatever you want to do whenever you want to do it, what the pope calls in this document a "distorted" notion of freedom. He continues: "Freedom is not an opting out. It is an opting in—a participation in Being itself. Hence authentic freedom can never be attained by turning away from God. . . . A particular responsibility therefore for each of you and your colleagues," he says, addressing all of us in Catholic higher education, "is to evoke among the young the desire for the act of faith, encouraging them to commit themselves to the ecclesial life that follows from this belief."[13] This raises a number of difficulties: First, as universities with a commitment to academic freedom and cultural pluralism, how do we "evoke among the young the desire for the act of faith" without trampling on our students personal liberty, their freedom to experiment, to embrace other faiths, or to embrace no faith at all?

Second, as academic institutions pursuing work with scholars of all backgrounds in the common pursuit of knowledge, how do we put faith at the center of what we do without being perceived as having a proselytizing agenda that undermines our expressed commitment to open and unbiased scholarship?

These are legitimate dilemmas that Jesuit institutions have been wrestling with—in some degree or other—since the beginning. At this point, I would simply say that we will have to continue to make calibrated adjustments in the ways in which we present and encourage the Catholic faith so that we do so in a way that is measured and appropriate to each circumstance.

However, the "service" and "encouragement" of faith does remain an obligation of Jesuit universities. The reason that we need to "encourage" religious faith in our students, is that if we want them to grow to become men and women for others then we are probably in many cases going to have to teach them how to love along the way.

In his first encyclical, *Deus Caritas Est*, Pope Benedict meditates on the nature of love, and he describes what he calls a "path of ascent"[14] through which our human attraction for one another—*eros*—is brought into a great unity and expression as we grow in love. If love develops within us and grows, then God becomes implicated by necessity, and *eros* becomes a first step toward a bigger and broader capacity for love. Eventually, erotic attraction develops to include a perspective in love that experiences selfless concern for the wellbeing of the other. This love "increasingly seeks the happiness of the other," the encyclical continues, "is concerned more and more with the beloved." Empathy develops, and out of that empathy and genuine love for one person becomes a capacity to care for the well-being of others in general.

So human love, which may begin as erotic attraction can develop and deepen and lead toward the experience of *agape*, of selfless love for our fellow men and women. This then, is what is meant by the path of ascent in love: "True eros," the Pope writes, "tends to rise in ecstasy toward the Divine, to lead us beyond ourselves."[15]

In Catholic terms, the active expression of *agape*—a love that transcends self-interest and is concerned for the wellbeing of others—is *caritas*, or charity. Now charity is a concept that is often placed in contrast with that of the promotion of justice, and the word has taken on a negative connotation for many in the field of Catholic social thought and in the minds of various Catholic activists. For many charity has become synonymous with a kind of passivity, whereby Christians who are involved in charitable activities—dispensing food or money or clothes to the poor, for instance—do so without paying any attention to the unjust social structures that made the poor *the poor* in the first place. In other words, charity, in the eyes of some, preserves the status quo and in fact, can work in the service of injustice by propping up the power structures and putting a band-aid on the suffering those structures generate.

The promotion of justice by contrast, is seen as a deeper and more committed Christian stance. The promotion of justice is a willingness to take direct action to reverse or overturn or confront the social structures that are responsible for creating poverty and oppression, leading to long-term solutions.

But I think Pope Benedict's point about charity in the encyclical and elsewhere is that it is the duty of all Christians to seek justice and it is *specifically the duty of lay Catholics* to seek the "just ordering of society"[16] through political means. Indeed, the Pope writes that "the Church wishes to help form consciences in political life and to stimulate greater insight into the authentic requirements of justice as well as greater readiness to act accordingly."[17] But he goes on to clarify that the specific duty of the Church as Church is to be a body of faith, and it is through that faith that we come to a love of God, that leads to a charitable orientation of heart that directs us toward what is just.

So, charity is the practice of the Church as a community of love. It is not "a kind of welfare activity which could equally well be left to others, but is part of her nature, an indispensable expression of her very being."[18] It is out of Christian charity then that our desire for true justice springs.

We are left, then, with the responsibility that as Jesuit educators, concerned with the promotion of justice, one of the things that we need to do is to encourage our students in the faith. More specifically, we need to encourage our students along the "path of ascent" of love, because we can't presuppose that our students come to us with a developed capacity to love or that the "path of ascent" is all that clear to them. Many will come to us from difficult family circumstances that have hurt them; they come to us exploited by a culture that relentlessly preys on their insecurities and anxieties, that tells them explicitly that "hooking up," for instance, is a harmless, casual activity and that appearing on a television reality show is a reasonable way to go about seeking "love"; they come to us saturated by the narratives of material success and sensual gratification that are predominant in our culture and may make generosity seem like a weakness; they may come to us with prejudices that make them unwilling to embrace the welfare of others.

This is why our efforts to create community living situations for our students, and to develop integrated learning and living experiences are so important. The "path of ascent" from desire to *agape* requires a process of developmental maturation, deepening relationships, and time for moral and spiritual reflection. We need to maintain and promote the environmental conditions that make this possible. This is where the Spiritual Exercises and the time-tested methods of Ignatian pedagogy come into play. We do have to create a learning environment that will free our students to explore their capacity to love, so that out of that love will come a charitable heart that will be drawn to work for the promotion of justice.

Conclusion

Our mission in the service of faith and the promotion of justice, as Father Kolvenbach noted when he launched us firmly on this path nine years ago, is "not something that a Jesuit University accomplishes once and for all. It is rather an ideal to keep taking up and working at, a cluster of characteristics to keep exploring and implementing, a conversion to keep praying for."[19]

As we push deeper into this mission, and more fully appreciate the "gritty realities" that we are called upon to make the focus of our efforts, I am suggesting that we also need to be more willing to confront the "gritty realities" of our institutional blind spots and limitations.

As we gather this weekend to talk about the things that we would like *to do* to transform the world, it is my hope that we will also be prepared to talk seriously about what we are prepared to *do without* as we transform ourselves.

There is no question that opening our doors to more talented students is our number one obligation in the service of justice. That means that we are going to have to find, or more probably, reallocate, the money to make this happen. I suspect it means that we are going to have to give up some of what we are currently holding onto—programs that serve our institutional pride as opposed to our fellow men and women. Most specifically, we need to challenge our institutions to shift from a "merit-based" to a "need-based" financial aid model. There's no point in talking about promoting justice around the world if we aren't going to promote it in our own institutions.

Second, as we embrace more fully a global consciousness, we have to deepen our understanding of what is meant by a "well-educated solidarity." What stands in the way of our shifting our consciousness from *us* to *we*? Are we aware of what it is like to be on the receiving end of our justice and service initiatives? Do we ask?

We know from experience that our students return from their service learning experiences with a jolt to their perspectives and often, with an experience of conversion of heart and a desire to do more. But then what? Do we have a "next step" in place so that this temporary conversion can be nurtured into a more permanent revolution of consciousness? Are we making the resources of our institutions available to the global community, bringing scholars from the developing world to our campuses in significant numbers? Are we doing all we can to make our facilities available? Are we listening to what those in need are asking for, or are we—perhaps unconsciously—exploiting those we purport to serve for the purposes of the formation of our students?

I would suggest that this exploration of our own cultural bias requires a ceaseless process of self-examination, one that calls on us to do less talking and more listening.

Finally, and perhaps most fundamentally, we have to bear in mind that "the way to faith and the way to justice are inseparable ways,"[20] and that the promotion of justice cannot and should not be undertaken in isolation from our duty to encourage the faith. This is not simply a matter of having Catholic Studies programs and making religious studies part of our core curricula—though it does mean that. What it truly means is that we need to become communities bound together by love, and infused therefore with the virtue of charity, which is the love of God as it is expressed in the love we have for one another. I would suggest that charitable love is the wellspring of the love of justice, and that a pursuit of justice that is not fundamentally an expression of charity is not in keeping with our mission, or with our fundamental identity.

We are being asked by the Church as Jesuit and Catholic Universities to embrace more deeply an understanding of charity and to make our institutions places where the faith is encouraged and developed, and so we must do this.

To say that our universities and colleges are fundamentally about teaching people how to love is a pretty big step. To say so, may even expose us to ridicule in some quarters. But it would seem to me that teaching people how to love is precisely the mission of the Society of Jesus—it always has been.

The service of faith and the promotion of justice is the road that we are called to follow as Jesuit institutions—this "undivided road, this steep road, that the pilgrim Church must travel and toil,"[21] in the words of the 32nd General Council. As we meet together in fellowship this weekend, let us ask for God's guidance and inspiration as we take another step along this road together.

12 Transforming Ourselves in Order to Transform the World

KENT KOTH, LÊ XUÂN HY, AND T. DAVID HENRY

The focus on justice in Jesuit higher education frequently inspires faculty and staff at Jesuit colleges and universities to want to contribute their expertise in the wider community. Their enthusiasm presents an opportunity for engagement, but several challenges exist. Frequently, because of their busy schedules faculty and staff rush into providing a "service" that is only in one direction and does not respect and take into consideration the overall context of the situation. In addition, because of their significant academic training, faculty and staff often approach community engagement with the perspective of the "expert" coming to serve those in "need." These common pitfalls can sometimes lead faculty and staff to enhance negative stereotypes such as "the poor are lazy and uncooperative." It also can lead the community to view faculty and staff with suspicion and distrust. So what approaches to engaging faculty and staff in the community offer possibilities of overcoming these challenges? Moreover, what types of community engagement experiences might lead faculty and staff toward personal and professional transformation?

In this chapter, we describe how Seattle University has explored these questions by creating a series of local immersion experiences for faculty and staff. In addition, we draw upon multiple assessment measures to present the results and lessons learned from our design and implementation process. We conclude by commenting on the significance of these types of faculty and staff development activities for Jesuit higher education.

The Idea

Recognizing that faculty and staff might benefit from participating in an immersion experience, the Seattle University Office of Mission and

Identity offers an annual ten-day international immersion for approximately fifteen faculty and staff. Seattle University is not alone in offering such experiences. In recent years, several other colleges and universities, particularly Jesuit institutions, have sponsored similar international opportunities for faculty and staff. In a recent editorial in the *Chronicle of Higher Education*, University of San Francisco President Steven Privett, SJ (2009), described his institution's commitment to taking upper-level administrators to Latin America as "a process of developing a deepening and profound personal awareness of our world, and of our consequent responsibility and capability to change it for the better."

Participants in the Seattle University Nicaragua immersion have incorporated their experiences into their work back on campus. For example, one former participant, a chemistry professor, has reoriented her research to help Nicaraguan coffee growers improve their crops. Another former participant, the bookstore manager, has begun to sell Nicaraguan crafts purchased directly from artisans. After participating in the immersion, the director of the University's Center for Service and Community Engagement (CSCE) began to explore whether a local immersion program for faculty and staff could complement this kind of global experience.

A local program could be beneficial in numerous ways. First and probably foremost, a local immersion would enable the university to learn more about its immediate neighbors, in an effort to become a more respectful member of the community. Second, it would require far fewer resources than an international trip, and thus could engage more people in a process that is less taxing on the environment and potentially more sustainable. Third, compared with international experiences, local immersion experiences might be less likely to promote a "tourist curriculum" (Derman-Sparks 1989) because it is easier to develop long-term relationships between campus and community and the local experiences are not totally separate from the participants' daily lives. Finally, local immersion would provide participants with a hands-on opportunity to better understand the Jesuit principle of a "faith that does justice."

And so, with these considerations in mind, the CSCE Director, in partnership with a member of the faculty, began to examine the feasibility of drawing upon the model of the Nicaragua immersion to offer local immersion experiences for faculty and staff.

Implementation

Over the course of an eighteen-month period, fifty-one faculty and staff participated in five immersions. Twenty-six of the participants were faculty representing seventeen disciplines. Eighteen of the participants were staff from ten offices. The remaining seven participants were members of the university executive team including the president, provost, and executive vice president.

All of the immersions occurred in the Bailey Gatzert/Yesler Terrace neighborhood of Seattle, Washington, which is just south of the Seattle University campus. Approximately 20,000 people live in the two square mile neighborhood (Rucker 2010). Forty-five percent of these residents are white, 21 percent are African or African American, and 21 percent Asian or Asian Americans (American Community Survey 2007). Approximately 36 percent of the residents live at or below the federal poverty level (ibid.). The rate of poverty among children is even higher as demonstrated by the fact that 93 percent of children attending the local elementary school are on free and reduced lunch (Seattle Public Schools 2009). The neighborhood has experienced significant challenges with crime including having the highest level of gang-related gun violence (Seattle Youth Violence Prevention Initiative 2008). The neighborhood also has many assets including dozens of engaged resident leaders and many physical resources including sixteen parks, three community centers, two libraries, and seven food banks (Rucker 2010).

While the themes and activities of the immersions varied widely, each of these experiences had a similar set of goals for participants that included:

Deepening the experience of and commitment to the university's mission.

Learning more about the assets and needs of the Bailey-Gatzert/
Yesler Terrace neighborhood in order to develop ethical and
respectful long-term community partnerships.

Developing new ideas for service learning courses, community-based
research and other activities, as well as expanding upon existing
initiatives.

The strategy for pursuing these goals focused on a process of *disorientation*—placing participants in contexts that would significantly stretch
their comfort zones, engage all their senses, and challenge them to see
and understand other perspectives. We pursued this process through
intensive activities that engaged participants in the lived experience of
the diverse communities within walking distance of campus. For example, during one immersion, participants ate a silent meal with monks at
a Vietnamese Buddhist temple; during another experience, participants
listened to a presentation on Somali culture and the Islamic faith by a
group of immigrant youth; and during yet another immersion, participants visited the county Juvenile Detention Center, located a few blocks
from campus, where they listened to poetry written and read by two
young, incarcerated men.

As with any immersion experience, stepping outside one's comfort
zone and embracing the accompanying sense of disorientation and vulnerability allows for the possibility of new insights and inspirations.
One participant described this phenomenon, based on his immersion
experience, as follows:

> In talking with my wife after Friday, I said, "This immersion was
> dipping me into vats, like a piece of metal. Acid baths to prepare the
> surface, others [vats] to prepare the foundation for positive layers.
> Then the good stuff, like paint, to add color and substance." So the
> visits—combined with reflection—and the faces and eyes of the
> youth, all worked. Some stripped me bare, others added protection,
> while some added hope.

The CSCE staff provided key leadership in developing and implementing the immersions. In recruiting faculty and staff to participate,
the CSCE staff strategically invited individuals who were already familiar with the concept and practice of community engagement, as well as

upper-level university administrators who had shown a prior interest in learning more about the community. Center staff also attempted to recruit a diverse group of participants representing all schools, divisions, and multiple departments. The center staff also asked deans to send invitations to all of their faculty and staff in their respective colleges. Through this highly focused approach to recruiting participants, we hoped that the immersions would not only impact faculty and staff on an individual level but that the diversity and positional influence of the participants would have a ripple effect on many academic programs and high profile offices, thereby impacting the overall vision and mission of the university.

The CSCE staff also coordinated each immersion and drew upon the expertise and social networks of several community leaders to develop the immersion activities and schedules. By asking community leaders to assist us, we hoped to avoid the pitfalls of tokenizing or trivializing the diverse communities we encountered enabling us to move deeper into the realities of the wider community. Recognizing the importance of providing space and time to make sense of experiences, CSCE staff facilitated reflection discussions during the immersions and invited participants to attend a follow-up lunch several weeks after each experience. The university's Mission Fund provided basic funding for expenses such as transportation, meals, and stipends for community leaders who assisted with coordination of activities. These stipends, while modest in amount, further demonstrated our recognition that the community had much to teach us through these experiences. Participants did not have to pay for their experience nor were they paid to attend.

Drawing upon the goals and strategies described above, the first local immersion experience engaged eleven faculty and staff in a three-day exploration of the Little Saigon neighborhood. Just a short walk from the Seattle University campus, the neighborhood has served as the economic and cultural hub for a community of over sixty thousand Vietnamese and Vietnamese-Americans in the Seattle area for three decades. Participants in this three-day immersion explored issues faced by Seattle's Vietnamese and Vietnamese-American population by conversing with monks at several Vietnamese Buddhist temples, attending mass at a Vietnamese Catholic church, visiting several nonprofit organizations and businesses in the Little Saigon neighborhood, and meeting with Vietnamese-American Jesuits whose families immigrated to Seattle. The immersion ended with a celebration at a farm owned and operated by a Vietnamese-American family.

Participants in this initial group represented several key university offices and positions. We invited the director of the Office of Jesuit Mission and Identity, who leads the Nicaragua immersion program, because we wanted to learn from his experience of leading the Nicaragua program and we wanted to be sure that the local immersion complemented the international program. We invited the director of the Academic Service Learning Faculty Fellows Program, hoping that his participation would lead to the participation of additional faculty practitioners of service learning in future immersions. Finally, we invited the director of the Center for the Excellence in Teaching and Learning, hoping that she might provide feedback and advice on how the experience could best be structured to connect to coursework and instruction, since her program is the main resource for faculty to improve their teaching.

A key component in the success of this initial immersion was the role played by a Vietnamese-American psychology professor. Through his position as the Pigott-McCone Chair in the College of Arts and Sciences, he provided leadership in conceptualizing the overall idea and purpose for the immersion as well as connecting with community organizations, assisting with interpretation during community visits, and bridging the cultural divisions between participants and the community. In addition, in holding an endowed chair position, he provided academic credibility to the immersion concept and assisted with a rigorous assessment of the experience. Finally, as a means of preparing for the cultural, language, and historical contexts of the local experience he accompanied the CSCE director on a trip to Vietnam prior to the immersion.

Drawing upon the success of this initial experience, we engaged forty additional faculty and staff in four other immersions in the neighborhoods adjacent to the university. We offered two of these immersions during the summer months and two during the academic year. Like the initial immersion, each of these subsequent experiences focused on a specific topic including:

Little Saigon. An additional three-day experience modeled after the initial pilot project described above.

Yesler Terrace. With a current population of 1,500 residents, Yesler Terrace is the oldest public housing community in Seattle and was the first racially integrated housing project in the nation. Participants in this three-day immersion visited with Yesler Terrace residents, spoke with Seattle Housing Authority staff members who worked at Yesler Terrace, and participated in several activities at social service programs that supported the residents. Participants conversed with leaders of the various faith traditions of the residents, shared meals with residents and community partners, and visited local businesses that serve the Yesler Terrace community.

Voices of Youth. The neighborhoods adjacent to the Seattle University campus have some of the highest rates of children living in poverty in the Seattle metro area. Participants in this two-day immersion visited several agencies and schools that strive to meet the needs of these youth. Participants also met with several groups of local young people during visits to the county juvenile detention facility, a Boys and Girls Club, the Vietnamese Catholic Church, and a Somali youth organization. In addition, participants conversed with Seattle University students who have served at various community organizations that work with local youth.

Faith Seeking Justice. A key principle of the Society of Jesus is, "a faith that does justice." Participants in this three-day immersion investigated how different religious traditions seek to address the common needs of humanity by exploring the relationship between justice and faith. Participants visited faith-based organizations that operate food banks and other social service programs. Participants also attended a Catholic mass, visited a Buddhist temple and met with a Muslim youth group.

Five methods were used to assess the outcomes of the immersions, including: (1) qualitatative and quantitive surveys completed by participants at the end of the program, (2) participant focus groups held several weeks after the program, (3) qualitative and quantitative surveys completed by community partners, (4) observational notes on the follow-up activities between immersion participants and the community partners they met during the program, and (5) lengthy postimmersion debrief meetings between the immersion organizers. These assessment measures revealed several noteworthy results as well as some significant lessons learned.

Findings

While our assessment process focused mostly on formative methods to help us improve future faculty and staff immersion experiences, the data we collected did lead to several noteworthy results.

Recognizing and preparing for the ethical and cultural dilemmas. As described previously, many of the immersion experiences focused on diverse ethnic, racial and cultural communities near the university including the Somali, Eritrean, Ethiopian, Vietnamese, Vietnamese-American and African-American communities.

Participants expected a rigorous and well-organized program, and they experienced how such a program may fall apart in a cross-cultural situation. For example, during the first morning of the initial Little Saigon immersion we planned short visits to four Vietnamese Buddhist temples. At the first temple, scheduled for mid-morning the abbess surprised us with a full lunch prepared for our group. Our initial reaction was to decline the lunch to keep the schedule with other temples. Then we realized that we were valuing our schedule more than the hospitality of the abbess. From this experience we learned about both others and ourselves. We were overwhelmed by the abbess's surprising and inconvenient generosity. We also realized that the temples are much more flexible with time than we were.

Several immersion experiences have included a visit with Somali youth and their parents who live in subsidized housing just a few blocks from campus. During these visits, the parents have expressed an interest in getting support for their children to pursue higher education. In deciding how to ethically and effectively respond, we recognized that our actions would directly influence future relationships with both this group and the local East African community as a whole. In short, we faced an ethical question of how to appropriately follow-up or face the critique often made of such programs—namely, that they are little more than exercises in "cultural and poverty tourism." As a direct response to the parents' requests, the university has significantly expanded its commitment to supporting youth and children in our immediate neighborhood.

Navigating cultural differences that arise poses another dilemma. For example, on several occasions immersion participants have eaten lunch at a local Vietnamese Buddhist temple. Wanting to express gratitude, we wished to offer a payment to the temple. In the Vietnamese culture, it would be more natural to eat the free temple food and to make a free-will donation. However, the university operates in a culture of contract making, not donating to other nonprofit organizations. For this reason, we carefully explained the situation to the university controller in order to obtain a check without the formality of a contract.

In encountering these and other dilemmas, we realized that we had an obligation to pursue community partnerships based on reciprocity. We also recognized that in connecting with the community, participants often faced a significant temptation for their "heart to write checks that the body cannot cash." For this reason, we encouraged participants to remain aware of their capabilities, skills, and ability to follow up. Balancing these various tensions proves challenging but is essential to using the local immersions as a springboard for additional community engagement activities.

Many participants commented on the valuable perspective this provided. One faculty member reflected: "I have taught ethnic and cultural sensitivity issues in my classes for many years. I have new material to add as a result of this immersion." An upper-level administrator summarized the sentiment of several participants as he reflected, "I can see better how our education could be made more real through concrete experiences like this linked to educational programs. This is just an introduction. Shows me that we have to do a much better job at Seattle University teaching students how cultures work."

Connecting local and global thoughts and actions. Local immersion may appear to compete with international programs, but they can be connected. For example, the immersion experiences that focused on the local Vietnamese community have led several participants to develop curricular initiatives for students to learn about Vietnamese culture, history, and language in the local neighborhood as well as in Vietnam.

Participants in the local program have been organizing trips to Vietnam for themselves as well as others. The familiarity with the Vietnamese community of Seattle helps them enjoy Vietnam more, and their familiarity with Vietnam helps them win confidence with local Vietnamese.

Developing long-term service learning and other campus-community activities. As stated previously, a key immersion goal focused on strengthening connections with the community to expand and deepen the use of service learning. To a certain extent the immersions appear to have accomplished this goal. For example, three faculty who had not previously shown an interest in service learning developed plans to offer a service component in one of their courses. In several other cases, participants reported making new connections with community organizations and expanding their use of service learning. This is evidenced by a law school staff person's statement that "there are specific legal issues that were identified by community members and service providers that I can connect students with."

One advantage of local engagement is the ease of continued engagement. Once our participants made connections with the local organizations, services opportunities presented themselves. In this way, we learn to respond to community leadership, instead of imposing our expertise on them. For example, one agency needed posters for their events; our photography professor sent several of her students to the agency for the whole quarter to learn about the agency and create posters that the agency considered their very best in decades of service. One temple had difficulty with zoning issues, and one law professor provided a referral. Another law professor responded to questions from several senior citizens on social security benefits. One professor went to an individual's residence to fix his computer. Another group of professors attended the fund-raising dinner for an agency they had visited during an immersion.

Understanding the complexity of community issues. Many participants commented that the experience significantly altered their perceptions of the local community and led to a more nuanced and complex understanding of community issues as well as strengths. One participant summarized this sentiment, expressing that, "this immersion deepened my understanding of the community around us in a way I have never experienced before." In addition, several participants recognized the need to continue to learn about the community in order to further connect their teaching, research, and other community engagement activities to issues that matter. While these results are quite positive, many participants also noted that the immersion experience is just one step in a much longer process of learning about the wider community and pursuing authentic community partnerships.

Exploring and understanding of the university mission. An encouraging result of the immersion experiences was the connection between the program and the university's Jesuit Catholic mission. Numerous participants commented on this link as evidenced by one participant's statement: "This was absolutely a valuable experience for me. I was very moved by the stories of our neighbors and inspired by the work that is being done in the community. Helps me to understand and live our mission in a more meaningful way. It has been very transformational for me personally." While the immersions seemed to provide participants with a better understanding of the university mission, participants also frequently commented that the experiences led them to become stronger advocates of how the university could further embody its mission.

Developing a shared vision for community engagement. One of the major obstacles that prevent universities from effectively engaging in the community is the fragmentation created by the divisions between disciplines, departments, and offices. All too often, faculty and staff from different programs do not communicate about their work in the community, which limits the institutions' ability to effect comprehensive change in the wider community and offer a coherent community engagement program for students. By bringing together individuals from many parts of the university, the immersions created a space for dialogue to occur, friendships to develop, and collaborations to begin. The sense of unity that arose among participants increases the university's potential to develop a cross-disciplinary and shared vision for community engagement.

In light of the above themes, it seems clear that the faculty and staff immersions led to several successes. Through the experience, participants appear to have deepened their understanding of and commitment to the wider community, strengthened their commitment to the university mission, and expanded their ability to collaborate with like-minded

colleagues from the campus and the community. While these prelimi-
nary findings are noteworthy, to make definitive conclusion on the
efficacy of local immersion experiences requires a more comprehensive
study.

Lessons Learned

The experimental process of developing and implementing a series of
local immersions for university faculty and staff also provided many
lessons in effective practice. With no blueprint guiding us through the
process, we experienced several challenging moments and distinct
learning opportunities, particularly during the first several immersion
experiences. Our process of assessment and program improvement
forced us to consistently clarify the strategies we were pursuing to
attain our goals. Drawing upon the collective wisdom garnered from
our assessment process, we offer the following lessons learned.

Lesson 1: Be strategic in recruiting participants. As noted earlier, one
of our underlying assumptions in creating the local immersions was
that by engaging a diverse and influential group of faculty and staff in
these experiences, we might influence the overall ethos and direction
of the institution with regards to community engagement. With this in
mind, we viewed the recruitment of participants as an extremely important aspect of the organizing process. Months prior to each immersion
we developed a priority list of the people we wanted to invite to participate. For example, we hoped to engage the university president, vice
presidents, and deans in an immersion. We also hoped to engage other
highly regarded faculty and administrators. Once we finished prioritizing our list we sent personalized e-mail invitations to each individual.
On several occasions we set up meetings with potential participants to
explain the idea and offer an invitation. Many of the individuals we
invited had participated in the university's Nicaragua immersion, which
made "selling" the local immersion idea much easier. In addition, the
university president participated in the second immersion, which significantly enhanced the visibility and credibility of the immersions, further enhancing our ability to recruit. If an individual declined our
invitation to participate in one immersion we asked if they wanted to

participate in a future experience. Most did, and so over time we were able to engage almost all of the individuals on our prioritized list.

One limitation to our recruitment process is that it could lead to perception of elitism. Yet, we viewed our "invitation only" approach as a part of a larger organizing strategy that would move the university further into partnership with the wider community. Essentially, we hoped that by engaging influential campus leaders in a local immersion they would return to campus and advocate for additional community engagement activities, which would lead to many more opportunities for involvement from all faculty and staff.

Lesson 2: Develop an organizing theme. The idea of providing faculty and staff an opportunity for more meaningful engagement with our local community is a good one, yet how exactly does this happen and how do we, for lack of a better word, "sell" the idea? Why would busy people choose to commit a significant amount of their time to such an experience? In response to these issues, we chose to base each immersion on an organizing theme.

The initial two immersions focused on the Vietnamese-American population living and working in the Little Saigon neighborhood of Seattle. The focus on this specific geographic area and distinct ethnic and cultural subset of Seattle appealed to many participants. Concentrating on a smaller segment of the metro area also created an opportunity to go deeper and discover intersections between different aspects of the community such as faith, work, recreation, family, and health. In addition, the focus on a particular neighborhood made it possible for participants to learn more by walking from appointment to appointment. Finally, since most of the immersion participants were not Vietnamese American, the cultural and language barriers the group encountered created an appropriately disorienting context for the experience.

After focusing two immersions on the Little Saigon neighborhood, we developed additional themes for subsequent immersions. We pursued this strategy in order to avoid burdening the community partners, faith communities and residents whom we depended upon to host and teach us. Furthermore, by diversifying our orienting themes we piqued the interest of a wider range of faculty and staff. These specific themes also created natural criteria for choosing activities and organizations, as well as designing a cohesive set of learning goals.

A risk of having organizing themes that focus on ethnic, cultural, and religious distinctions is that it could lead participants to trivialize or tokenize the individuals and communities they encountered during the immersion. To try to avoid this phenomenon we recruited participants who already possessed high levels of cultural competency and religious literacy. We also intentionally referenced this issue in our participant orientation. Finally, we encouraged participants to view their immersion experiences as one experience in a long-term process of exploring local issues of race, culture, and religion.

Lesson 3: Be intentional in creating a daily schedule. A key consideration in designing a schedule includes whether to offer an overnight or daytime-only experience. The initial Little Saigon immersion included an option for participants to spend the night at a Buddhist temple but few participants expressed an interest. Participant feedback led us to conclude that it is unrealistic to expect many faculty and staff to participate in a multiday overnight local immersion, particularly during the academic year. For this reason, we have limited the schedules to a three-day experience, generally between the hours of 9:00 a.m. and 7:00 p.m.

Taking time to build trust within the group greatly enhances the participants' comfort level with one another and hence their potential to engage in deep dialogue. With this in mind, on the morning of the first day, we gather participants for introductions and an overview of the upcoming immersion. We address logistics and offer orienting principles such as the importance of listening and learning versus trying to "fix" the community. During this initial orientation we also ask each participant to share why they chose to join the particular immersion.

We begin each subsequent day of the immersion with a preview of what to expect and a contextualization of the upcoming experiences. We typically visit two sites or community groups in the morning, with a break in between for informal processing of the experience and decompression. Since sharing food provides a good way to experience another culture and build relationships, we have usually scheduled a lunchtime panel discussion with local community members. The afternoon includes one or two additional visits with a community partner or group, followed by a closing reflection.

During the initial immersions we packed the schedule with too many activities and did not allow enough time for participants to make sense of each experience. Without sufficient time to reflect, the emotional and mental intensity among participants grew hour by hour. When finally given a chance to reflect, the discussions went in multiple directions with little coherency and connection. What we learned from our analysis of this experience was that perhaps the most important component of the daily schedule is the time when the group reflects on their experiences. As a result we have added more reflection time to each immersion and cut back on other activities.

Frequently the reflections have included individual writing, sharing with a partner, and discussion with the entire group. Having a Jesuit, who happened to be the primary coordinator of these immersions, on staff greatly enhanced the quality and variety of these reflection activities. Guiding participants in the Daily Examen prayer of St. Ignatius became an important component of the reflection process. It provides a unique opportunity for the group to experience Jesuit spirituality while engaging in a meaningful reflection activity directly related to the immersion experiences.

Lesson 4: Incorporate student voices. Incorporating the perspectives of current Seattle University students has become an integral component of the local immersions. We stumbled upon this insight by happenstance. One immersion focused on the theme "Voices of Youth." During the planning stages, we realized our students were in fact "voices of youth," so we invited them to lead a panel discussion about their experiences serving and learning in the local community. These student-led sessions—whether via a well-structured panel or more informal conversations at a local coffee shop—energized participants and consistently received strong reviews on evaluations. One faculty member offered the following comment on the importance of incorporating student voices: "I find great value in this experience for faculty and staff at Seattle University. Faculty and staff can have a clearer understanding of what our students experience when they are doing service learning or participating in local immersions. Having this understanding will further help us in guiding our students through such experiences."

In their presentations to the faculty and staff, several students commented on the relationship between their perception of whether or not a professor "walks the talk" of community engagement and his or her ability to effectively teach a service learning course. The students commented that when faculty have visited community sites and know community leaders they are much more effective instructors.

Lesson 5: Invite community partners to play a role in developing the immersion. One of the underlying reasons for offering a local immersion is to recognize that the community has something to teach the campus. Through the immersion, participants seek to learn from community leaders in order to become stronger educators of their students. With this consideration in mind, we have asked community leaders to help us develop and implement the immersions. Community leaders have played a particularly important role in advising us about the political, ethical and cultural dynamics of the community. For example, leaders of a local nonprofit focusing on the needs of the Vietnamese community helped schedule meetings with various community leaders during the Little Saigon immersions. They provided particularly helpful guidance in approaching individuals and groups with opposing viewpoints. In addition, an Ethiopian-American leader of a local nonprofit assisted us in making strong connections with the East African community during the Yesler Terrace immersion. In both instances we offered a small honorarium to the community leaders as a token of our gratitude for assisting us.

While the principle of engaging the community as a partner in developing the immersions is essential, it does bring added complexity to the organizing process. For example, during development of the initial immersion we did not clearly specify the roles of the community leaders and the CSCE staff member, and as a result, tensions arose regarding the overall vision of the immersion. From this challenging experience, we learned the importance of clearly defining the roles of all immersion organizers. The added complexity of role clarification takes more time but the value of engaging community leaders in the creation of the immersions is well worth it.

Lesson 6: Develop a sustainability plan. After offering five local immersions in eighteen months, the two central questions we now face are: How many resources are needed to offer a high quality local immersion experience? And how many immersions to offer in a given year?

Our first immersion was organized with a limited budget and no designated staff. The CSCE director and a faculty member led the effort but worked overtime to fully coordinate all aspects of organizing the immersion. In recognizing the need for an appropriate level of staffing, a Jesuit scholastic took the lead on coordinating subsequent immersions. Working part-time as a member of the CSCE staff, the scholastic took the lead on coordinating all aspects of the immersions, seeking assistance from the CSCE director and a faculty advisor when needed. While requiring additional resources for the scholastic's salary, having a dedicated staff person made a significant difference in our ability to offer so many experiences in such a short period of time.

One limitation in our staffing structure was that the Jesuit scholastic would only be able to work in the position for eighteen months. For this reason, we pursued an ambitious schedule of immersion programs over a relatively short period of time. One clear lesson we learned is that offering immersions during the less hectic summer months was much easier than during the busy academic year. The immersions during the academic year went well but often seemed to contribute to fatigue among participants, resulting in less immediate follow-up in the community. Keeping these considerations in mind, in the future we will likely offer one or two immersions each summer and not offer programs during the academic year. We will also incorporate the coordination of immersions into the job description of a CSCE staff person.

Lesson 7: Pursue solidarity. As noted previously, we believe that local immersion experiences for faculty and staff can be a key strategy to move the university further into solidarity with marginalized people living in our local neighborhood. Recently, this premise has begun to bear significant fruit. Under the auspices of the president and with support of a $250,000 planning grant, the CSCE staff facilitated a planning process for a major university-wide community engagement initiative focused on youth in the Bailey Gatzert/Yesler Terrace neighborhood. The plan lead to significant additional engagement activities across all disciplines and programs and has become a signature university program receiving local and national recognition. Many immersion participants have played a central role in the planning and implementation process. Thanks in part to the relationships that the faculty and staff developed with community members during the local immersions, the launch of this major new initiative has gone smoothly and issues of trust and turf that sometimes occur in such endeavors have been minimal.

Conclusion

The most recent gathering of the highest seat of authority within the Society of Jesus, the General Congregation, affirms the commitment of Jesuit institutions of higher education to pursue justice and solidarity through institutional and personal transformation.

> The complexity of the problems we face and the richness of the opportunities offered demand that we build bridges between rich and poor, establishing advocacy links of mutual support between those who hold political power and those who find it difficult to voice their interests. Our intellectual apostolate provides an inestimable help in constructing these bridges, offering us new ways of understanding in depth the mechanisms and links among our present problems. (Decrees of the 35th General Congregation, 2008, Decree 3, no. 28)

Creating opportunities for university faculty and staff to step off-campus and into the reality of our local communities is one essential strategy to fulfill this commitment. By offering local immersion programs, we encourage faculty and staff to enter the community seeking only to humbly listen and learn, and we sow seeds that may potentially grow into personal relationships of mutuality. When this happens, our faculty and staff become more deeply invested in striving toward the Jesuit's vision of solidarity and justice. In doing so, we move one step closer to transforming ourselves, our institutions and our world.

13 Nonviolently Transforming the Road to Jericho

ANNA J. BROWN

In September 1965, Saint Peter's University[1] awarded Dr. Martin Luther King Jr. an Honorary Degree of Doctor of Laws and Letters. Saint Peter's is the only Jesuit university or college to have awarded him such a degree. In my eighteen years of teaching at the university, I have been inspired and challenged by King's teachings, writings, and actions, particularly those that point to the good works of community service, the prophetic voice of social justice, the deadly scourge of militarism, and the creative power of nonviolence. If Dr. King were to speak in the university's Roy Irving Theater today, as he did forty-five years ago, what would he say to those committed to an "education informed by values" (Saint Peter's University Mission Statement 2013, 1)?

In April 1967, less than two years later, Dr. King gave his "A Time to Break Silence" speech in New York City's Riverside Church. He called for a "true revolution of values" (King 1991, 240), by which he meant prioritizing human life over profit-making. He astutely pointed to the interplay among the "giant triplets of racism, materialism, and militarism"(240). He also referred to the story of the Good Samaritan: "On the one hand, we are called to play the role of the Good Samaritan on life's roadside; but that will be only an initial act. One day we must come to see that the whole Jericho road must be transformed so that men and women will not constantly be beaten and robbed as they make their journey on life's highway" (241). Human life will flourish only when unjust political and economic structures are dismantled, war making ceases, and nonviolence is put into practice.

King decided he had to break the silent acceptance of the Vietnam War by the American people. Eschewing what he called an inappropriate "smooth patriotism," King championed the "mandate of conscience" and a careful "reading of history." He also spoke quite specifically about the human cost of war: "This business of burning human beings with napalm, of filling our nation's homes with orphans and widows, of injecting poisonous drugs of hate into veins of people normally humane, of sending men home from dark and bloody battle-fields physically handicapped and psychologically deranged, cannot be reconciled with wisdom, justice, and love" (241). King closed his talk by extolling the "fierce urgency of the now" (243) and by cautioning against procrastination on the war question. He stated that a critical choice had to be made for either "nonviolent coexistence or violent co-annihilation" (243). He encouraged his listeners to find new ways of speaking and acting for peace and justice lest we become a people "who possess power without compassion, might without morality, and strength without sight" (243). Were King to give this speech at St. Peter's in September 2013, his essential points would be just as vital as they were in 1967.

In this chapter, which seeks to respond to King's points from the perspective of one who teaches at a Jesuit university, I first note the striking prevalence of community service programs over peace and social justice programs in Jesuit colleges and universities (Crews 2009). Does this imbalance inadvertently keep us from moving beyond the "initial act of the Good Samaritan" and from fully entering into the work of "transforming the whole Jericho road?" Are the prophetic claims of peace and justice articulated, heard, and seriously responded to in our Jesuit academic communities? Next, I will consider whether or not an uncritical acceptance of military recruitment, the ROTC, and millions of dollars in grant monies from the Department of Defense helps to perpetuate warfare, "the business of burning human beings with napalm," and moves us away from our Christian vocation as peace-makers and our academic vocation of seeking truth. Finally, I will sug-gest that the promotion of the principles and practices of nonviolence on Jesuit campuses is one way to reconcile the good works of commu-nity service with the prophetic confrontation of a social justice program and to uplift the study and work of peacemaking to its rightful place among the many voices within our Jesuit academic communities. As we wend our way through an era of catastrophic political, economic, and environmental crises, both local and global in scope, will our Jesuit colleges and universities find the will to be leaders in peace making and nonviolence? Can this be one of the values that distinguishes being "Jesuit-educated?" Can we be companions of the nonviolent Jesus in the twenty-first century?

A Prophetic Formulation of Service and Justice

In his opening address to participants in the June 2009 Justice in Jesuit Higher Education Conference, "Transforming the World and Being Transformed," Jeffrey von Arx, SJ, formulated the "good works" versus "prophetic confrontation" debate this way: "Now charity is a concept that is often placed in contrast with that of the promotion of justice, and the word has taken on a negative connotation for many in the field of Catholic social thought and in the minds of various Catholic activists" (von Arx 2009, 23). For the Catholic activist concerned with transforming social structures that have impoverished people, von Arx continues, the corporal works of mercy actually keep people poor because in and of themselves they do not challenge, for example, an unjust political economy (24). Seen in this light, the serving of soup, for example, is a patronizing act.

Von Arx settles the "good works" versus "prophetic confrontation" debate by saying, implicitly, that it's not really a debate at all. Rather, it's a matter of a right ordering. He makes good use of Pope Benedict's encyclical, *Deus Caritas Est*, to show that it is the "duty of all Christians to seek justice and it is specifically [the] *duty of lay Catholics* to seek the 'just ordering of society' through political means" (24). The work of justice, however, flows from a charitable heart, a heart that is turned toward God through faith. "So charity," he concludes, "is the practice of the Church as a community of love. . . . It is out of Christian charity then that our desire for true justice springs" (25).

The preponderance of community service programs at Jesuit colleges and universities well reflects the "community of love" that von Arx speaks of, or, as King would phrase it, the building of the "beloved community." Where we need to do more is in the area of creating a framework and institutional practices that would help to instantiate the "desire for true justice." To help us in this work of justice, we have at our disposal Fr. Pedro Arrupe's address to the 10th International Congress of Jesuit Alumni, "Men [and Women] for Others: Training Agents of Change for the Promotion of Justice"(Arrupe 1980). Like Pope Benedict XVI and Father von Arx, Arrupe grounds his work in a love that springs from the depths of faith. What Arrupe tends to emphasize, however, is a heightened awareness of unjust social structures and the responsibility of the Jesuit educated student to confront and dismantle those structures.

Arrupe begins his talk by recognizing that a Jesuit concern for social justice represented a "new awareness within the Church, [one in which] participation in the promotion of justice and the liberation of the oppressed is a constitutive element of the mission" (124). He concedes, in the early part of his address, that Jesuits have not done enough to educate young people for the work of justice. Upon admitting this inadequacy, he calls upon his audience to help the Jesuits "repair this lack in us [the Jesuits], and above all make sure that in the future the education imparted in Jesuit schools will be equal to the demands of justice in the world" (125).

He defines what he means by the work of justice in institutions of higher education in a section of his address entitled, "Love and Justice Meet." For Arrupe (1980, 130), the practices of charity and of justice are one and the same: "How can you love someone and treat him unjustly?" The "someone" of whom he speaks is not only our neighbor, but also our enemy. He also says "our love issues forth in the works of justice" (130), though this is not to be understood simply as an individual act. Arrupe then defines the work of justice as follows:

First, a basic attitude of respect for all men which forbids us to ever use them as instruments for our own profit.

Second, a firm resolve never to profit from, or allow ourselves to be suborned by, positions of power deriving from privilege, for to do so, even passively, is equivalent to active oppression. To be drugged by the comforts or privilege is to become contributors to injustice as silent beneficiaries of the fruits of injustice

Third, an attitude not simply of refusal but of counterattack against injustice; a decision to work with others towards the dismantling of unjust social structures so that the weak, the oppressed, the marginalized of this world may be set free.

In the next section of his address and building upon his third quali-
fication, Arrupe once again moves the discussion of justice away from
simply a concern for personal transformation—though a necessary element in the work of justice and, for Catholics, for salvation—and
includes social, economic and political institutions and systems. For
Arrupe, if these institutions and systems have "injustice built into them,
[they are] concrete forms in which sin is objectified" (131).

In response to a rhetorically posed question, "What is a man for
others?," Arrupe suggests that three "attitudes must be cultivated"
(136): one must live more simply and against the tide of consumerism;
one must never profit from injustice, with a particular referent to the
very poor; and, one must resist and reform unjust structures within
society. Arrupe ends his address by stating that the development of a
"man [and woman] for others is to be the "paramount objective" of
Jesuit higher education (137). He also reminds his listener that the
whole of the work of justice must be grounded in love: "To be just, it
is not enough to refrain from injustice. One must go further and refuse
to play its game, substituting love for self-interest as the driving force
of society" (136).

There is no direct mention of community service in Arrupe's talk,
though one could make the case that service to others is certainly
implied. What is defined and unpacked in Arrupe's talk, it seems to
me, is more the work of a social justice program. Why, then, is the
language of "men and women for other's" used on Jesuit campuses and
in its literature more often when speaking of community service and
less often when speaking of social justice? Is community service meant
to satisfy the definition of social justice? If so, does this conflation of
community service do justice to the literal text and spirit of Arrupe's
phrase, and to the right order suggested by von Arx and Pope Benedict?
Finally, if we make the moves that I have just described, are we stuck
in the "initial act" of service? Can we do "even more" to help transform
national and global social, political, and economic structures?

Many of our Jesuit colleges and universities commemorated three
anniversaries in the 2009–2010 academic year that presented the
opportunity to rethink how we live community service and social justice, or, in other words, to fulfill the right ordering of Christian charity:
November 16, 2009, was the twentieth anniversary of the killing of the

University of Central America (UCA) Jesuits and their housekeepers; March 24, 2010, was the thirtieth anniversary of the killing of Archbishop Oscar Romero; and, December 2, 2010, was the thirtieth anniversary of the killing of three North American nuns and a laywoman volunteer in El Salvador. These men and women died not simply for their works of service; they died because they confronted unjust political and economic structures, institutions and ideologies (Brackley 2009). They died because they refused to abandon those Salvadorans with whom they worked and lived and who were being tortured, disappeared, and killed on a daily basis. They also challenged the violence employed by the military in order to keep these unjust structures in place. Common to all three sets of deaths was the direct involvement of soldiers trained at the [formerly named] School of the Americas based in Ft. Benning, Georgia (Gill 2007).

Allowing for the fact that twenty and thirty years have passed since the deaths of these men and women, I suppose it's fair to ask—as my students often do—why we need to know about the UCA Jesuits, Archbishop Romero, and the four American churchwomen? How are they relevant to our lives today? What did these men and women have to say about service and social justice? One answer is that the lives and deaths of these men and women help us to see the depth of commitment required if we are to be men and women for others. Through their example, we see that lives rooted in faith, service, and justice tends to bring forth the best in our humanity.

Another answer is given by Fr. Jon Sobrino, SJ, in his recently published book, *No Salvation Outside the Poor: Prophetic and Utopian Essays*. He points out that while the world had indeed moved on chronologically (since the time of these men and women), it has yet to move truthfully with regard to the impoverishment and degradation of so many of its people. He cites a phrase uttered by Fr. Ignacio Ellacuria, SJ, in the last speech he gave before he was murdered: "This civilization is gravely ill—sick unto death" (Sobrino 2008, ix) and then continues by writing:

> Today's world, the official and politically correct world, refuses to listen, and in any case to take the radical action required by the utter

gravity of the problem. An example from our own time: In Nairobi, where the World Social Forum has just ended, 2.6 million people—60 percent of the population—live in appalling shacks. In Kivera alone, eight hundred thousand people live with one sordid latrine for every two hundred people. Some people may say that in the official world we have already come out of the dogmatic sleep from which Kant sought to free us. But we have yet to awaken from the sleep of the cruel inhumanity of which that sixteenth century monk in La Espanola accused the landowners, perpetrators of cruelty and extermination, on the third Sunday of Advent, 1511: "Are these not human beings? Do they not have rational souls? Do you not see this? How can you stay in such a lethargic sleep?"

I am in agreement with Ellacuria's sense of our "civilization" and Sobrino's indictment of the "official and politically correct world"; even a basic introduction to political science class would (or should) verify their empirical claims. More troubling, at least for those committed to "education informed by values," is the refusal of the "official" world to listen to the cries of the poor, the inability to see the oppressed other as a fellow human being, and the hesitance to take radical action—instead of a \$680 billion budget for the US military, for example[2]—will we ask that this almost unimaginable amount of money (or at least some of it!) be allocated to education, housing, jobs, among other needs. For those of us situated in one of the wealthiest nations in the world and in academic institutions with access to a wealth of information, how is it possible to be so deeply asleep on these matters? Perhaps we do not realize how deeply we are asleep, which is what Daniel Berrigan, SJ (1968, 25), suggests:

It occurs to me beyond any doubt that Americans are "prisoners of war," locked in dungeons of illusion, of fear, of hatred and contempt and joylessness; all of us hearing the closure in our faces of the hinge of fate, strangers to our own history, to moral passion, to the neighbor, strangers to the immense and vagrant and splendid mysteries of life itself, the forms of community that await the "trial of peace," men [and women] who advocate formal and legalized murder as a method of social change.

Community Service, Social Justice, and the War Question

Where we are situated as a university matters;[3] if we are unwilling to analyze the political, economic, and social structures that shape the university and our life within it; if we are unwilling to consider the ways in which we support "legalized murder as a method of social change," then we may be among those who "cannot hear, refuse to act and keep themselves locked in prison" while the killing of so many around the world through warfare continues "day after Christian day" (Berrigan 1998, 134). Instead of displacing war, we continue to serve bowls of soup to those displaced by war. Instead of helping the poor, war will continue, in the words of Dr. King (1991, 233), to "draw men and skills and money like some demonic destructive suction tube."

Father Arrupe (1980) gets to the heart of the matter when it comes to community service, social justice, and the war question. In "Men [and Women] for Others," he asks, rhetorically, how it is possible to be loving and just in an egoistic and unjust world. His response is what compels me to think through the relationship between community service and social justice and challenges me to do the work of peace making:

> And yet it [to love and not to hate] lies at the very core of the Christian message; it is the sum and substance of the call of Christ. Saint Paul put it in a single sentence: "Do not allow yourself to be overcome by evil, but rather overcome evil wit good." This teaching, which is identical with the teaching of Christ about love for the enemy, is the touchstone of Christianity. All us would like to he good to others, and most of us would be good in a good world What is difficult is to be good in an evil world, where the egoism of others and the egoism built into the institutions of society attack us and threaten to annihilate us. (135)

Community service programs help us to be good to one another. Peace studies and social justice programs, with their emphasis on analysis and direct action, help us to understand the political, economic, and social instantiation of egoism in the world and make the effort to dismantle such "structural egoism" as well as to rebuild just systems. The study and practice of nonviolence helps us to "be good in an evil world" and to "love our enemies," what Father Arrupe calls the "touchstone of Christianity." We would do well on Jesuit campuses, therefore, to maintain our programs of service but also to build our social justice programs so that they are proportionate to the service programs. In addition, Jesuit schools would do well to launch a major effort in the studies and practices of nonviolence.

A bumper sticker, attached to the front door of the Dr. Martin Luther King Kairos Social Justice House at Saint Peter's University reads, "When Jesus said 'love your enemies' I think He probably meant don't kill them" (Williams n.d.). When we wage wars we do kill our enemies, and, however unintentionally, noncombatants, our friends and our own. In an article that introduces two new books of war photographs, former war correspondent Chris Hedges (2010) writes rather starkly about the nature of this particular kind of killing:

> War begins by calling for the annihilation of the others but ends ultimately in self-annihilation. It corrupts souls and mutilates bodies. It destroys homes and villages and murders children on their way to school. It grinds into dirt all that is tender and beautiful and sacred. It empowers human deformities—warlords, Shiite death squads, Sunni insurgents, the Taliban, al-Qaida and our own killers—who can speak only in the despicable language of force. War is a scourge. It is a plague. It is industrial murder.

When military recruiters visit Jesuit colleges and universities with promises of full tuition payment, there is much talk about military service and valor but little talk about the destruction of war, the reasons for waging war, the damage done to our student soldiers, and so on. Like King did in *A Time to Break the Silence*, we Jesuit school scholars may need to write specifically about the human costs of war in our own time, at the very least to balance the information presented in recruiting literature. We could do so, for example, in the manner of Susan Galleymore (2009), whose son joined the military and is stationed in Iraq, in her book, *Long Time Passing: Mothers Speak About War and Terror*. In an excerpt from one of the book's interviews, she writes of a rather common war experience: "Anwar [an Iraqi mother] described to me how her husband, oldest son, and two other daughters were shot to death by US soldiers" (23). A two-month investigation published in *The Gazette of Colorado Springs* revealed that "[Iraqi] taxi drivers got shot for no reason, and others were dropped off bridges after interrogations" (Philipps 2009). Kenneth Eastridge, an infantryman in Iraq who is now serving a ten-year sentence for being an accessory to murder in the United States, suggests that violence becomes a way of life, both in war and at home: "The Army pounds it into your head until it is instinct: Kill everybody, kill everybody. And you do. They think you can just come home and turn it off" (ibid.). Eastridge's battalion, the 2nd Battalion, 12th Infantry Regiment of the Ft. Carson's (Colorado) 4th Brigade Combat Team referred to itself as the "Lethal Warriors." Eastridge had close to 80 confirmed kills while in Iraq (ibid.). Though not a pacifist, Dr. Gilbert Burnham, a Johns Hopkins researcher and coauthor of the report, "The Human Cost of War in Iraq (2002–2006)" concludes that at least 654,965 Iraqi were killed in the four-year period of their study (Burnham et al. 2006). In an April 2010 interview with *The Guardian*, Mohammad El Baradei, the former Director General of the International Atomic Energy Agency and Nobel peace prize winner, claims that "those who launched the war in Iraq were responsible for killing a million innocent people and could be held accountable under international law" (Martin 2010).

Soldiers also suffer greatly in warfare. As of June 2009, the number of US soldiers killed in the Iraq and Afghanistan wars was 5,000 (Blimes and Stiglitz 2009). Over 300,000 US troops have required medical treatment since returning from Iraq (ibid.). Galleymore (2009, 245) reports that in 2003, "the military-documented suicide rates for soldiers in Iraq were 13.5 per 100,000," a percentage that is greater than that of the general population. Approximately 6,500 veterans (from all wars) take their own lives each year ("Military Suicides" 2008). A recent report out of Walter Reed's Defense and Veteran Brain Injury Center notes that nearly 52 percent (about 10,000) severely injured soldiers from the wars in Iraq and Afghanistan have been diagnosed with a traumatic brain injury (Mainichi Daily News 2009). Soldiers also take the lives of others once they return home. From 2001 through 2006, there was an 89 percent increase (from 184 cases to 349 cases) of homicides committed by active-duty personnel or recent veterans (in at least 75 percent of the cases) of the wars in Iraq and Afghanistan (Galleymore 2009, 243).

Aside from the human cost of the wars in Iraq and Afghanistan, there are also the economic costs. Harvard University economist Joseph Stiglitz, a Nobel Prize winner in economics, and Linda Blimes have estimated that "the US has already spent $1 trillion on operations [in Iraq] and related defense spending, with more to come—and it will cost perhaps $2 trillion more to repay war debt, replenish military equipment, and provide treatment for US veterans back home" (Blimes and Stiglitz 2009) Stiglitz and Bilmes assert that this level of spending on the Iraq war is a "major contributor" to the present financial crisis faced by the American people.

The Iraqi people have fared even worse, at least according to Antonia Juhasz, a Foreign Policy In-Focus scholar. She points out that the economic orders put in place by L. Paul Bremer III, who had been the US administrator of Iraq from 2003 until 2004, "allowed foreign investment in and the privatization of all 192 government-owned industries (excluding oil extraction)" (Juhasz 2005). In 2006, legislation was passed that would be "very promising to the American investors and to American enterprise, certainly to oil companies" (ibid.). As of 2008, 60 to 70 percent of Iraqis were unemployed (Ali and Jahmed 2008c); 70 percent of Iraqis were without safe drinking water (Ali and Jahmed 2008a); and, some cities had electricity for only one to two hours a day, if at all (Ali and Jahmed 2008b). Human Rights First, an international human rights organization, reports that approximately 2.2 million Iraqis have fled the country with another 2 million living as internally displaced refugees within Iraq (all told, about 16 percent of the Iraqi population has been displaced) (Human Rights First 2008) Once we write about those Iraqi and Afghani "men and women who are beaten and robbed as they make their journey on life's highway," we must also think through and take responsibility for the ways, both directly and indirectly, in which we have contributed to this "beating and robbing."

Having observed military recruitment practices on my own campus, read through college catalog and website descriptions about military service, and considered college press releases about Department of Defense grants, I would safely bet that a description of war like that of

Hedges's or a description of the cost of war like that of Juhasz's would not be included. The voice of the "official world," as Father Sobrino writes, is silent on such matters. Jesuit colleges and universities, however, are truth-seeking institutions rooted in a Catholic and Jesuit tradition. How is it possible, then, that the atrocities and costs of war are not accounted for in our college catalogs, websites, literature, and so on?[4] Have there been internal and corporate—for example, within the Association of Jesuit Colleges and Universities—discussions that seriously consider our participation in the process of war making? On what grounds has the decision been made to allow for our active engagement with the military?

Perhaps it is the practical that tends to silence the prophetic voice, the voice of war's victims, and the voice of social justice. By that, I refer to the practical matter of the Solomon Amendment (1995), its revisions (1996 and 1999) and the current Solomon Law (2005) which allows the Secretary of Defense to deny federal funding to those institutions of higher education that restrict access to military recruiters, student directory information to the military, and ROTC programs ("Solomon Amendment" 2000) One notable exception to the law's mandates is reserved for "the institutions of higher education [which] has a long standing policy of pacifism based on religious affiliation" (ibid.). Perhaps it may also be the Just War theory and tradition within Catholic social teaching and the Church that allows for the military on our campuses in ways that, for example, the abortion services of Planned Parenthood would not be allowed.

Transformation through Nonviolence

In an address given on World Peace Day 2006, Pope Benedict XVI stated "the obstacles to peace originate in lying . . . how can we fail to be seriously concerned about lies in our own time, lies which are the scenarios of death in many parts of the world? (para. 5). It seems to me that Benedict's emphasis on the necessity of truth telling opens the door to the work of peace making within Jesuit colleges and universities. The university, by its very nature, is an institution committed to the pursuit of truth; as such, it has a multitude of resources at hand with which to make an important contribution to the "telling of truth" with regard to the waging of war.

Do Jesuit colleges and universities, with their commitments to ROTC programs[5] and their military and Department of Defense grants, have the will to do this kind of truth telling work? The pockets of the Department of Defense run deep whereas those of many of our Jesuit colleges are not; in this time of economic recession and uncertainty, it is understandable that millions of dollars in weapons research funding, for example, is a welcome sight. Still, we must ask, at what cost to academic integrity and conscience do these grants come?

Daniel Berrigan (1982, 1) puts this question more specifically to the Catholic university or college:

> Military presence, military instruction, maneuvers; and then the word of God. In uneasy conjunction? Inducing second thoughts in those responsible? Not at all, in my experience—or hardly ever.
>
> I recall that in the past years, I have been invited to the campuses of at least five religious orders, including my own; Vincentians, Holy Cross, Franciscans, Benedictines, Jesuit. One each campus, theology looms large; on each campus also, ROTC. The Big Buck stalks the Little Book, all but slams it shut. The theologians who consider such matters to be morally grotesque are few and far between. There occurs, so to speak, in contravention of the ancient Easter hymn, no life and death wrestling between the adversaries named Life and Death. Indeed not. The two, reconciled at last, lie in one bed, a discreet bundling board between. Half dead, shall we call them? In any case, only half alive.

Just about a month before the March 2003 start of war in Iraq, the Social Justice Secretariat of the Jesuits sent a letter to each Jesuit province stating that the impending war was unjustifiable. The secretariat found the doctrine of preventive war to be morally indefensible; believed that war would increase hostilities between Middle Eastern Christians and Muslims; thought the war to be primarily economically motivated; stated that a unilaterally led war was an unacceptable action within the context of a global community; and pointed out that the poor will suffer the most because of the war. The secretariat called for prayerful reflection and for collaborative public actions, a call that was heeded by all twenty-eight North American Jesuit colleges and universities.

The secretariat's 2003 call for prayerful reflection and public action stems from its judgment, *jus ad bellum,* that the impending war in Iraq was not justifiable. The secretariat did not, however, call for the removal of ROTC programs, the end of military recruitment, or the rescinding of Department of Defense monies from our Jesuit campuses. Given the exorbitant human, economic, and environmental cost of the war in Iraq—and of war in general—I am wondering, however, if it's not time for Jesuit colleges and universities to do "even more" to prevent the waging of war. If Just War theory provides the opening for military recruitment and the ROTC on our Jesuit campuses, what happens when it can be shown that a particular war is unjustly begun or unjustly waged? Are we then in a position of knowingly supporting and committing acts of injustice? If so, are we reneging on a moral responsibility which may well demand that we cease to cooperate in the harming of other human beings? If our Jesuit colleges and universities believe they are compelled to cooperate with the military because of the Solomon Law, must we also cooperate without question, in the waging of unjust wars? And if we find an increasing dependence upon Department of Defense grants for research purposes, what happens to our academic integrity? Will academic freedom and truth telling be honored or will we find ourselves beholden to the agenda of an institution that can provide millions of dollars in grants? Finally, do we find evidence that our Jesuit campuses also recognize the tradition of nonviolence that has been equally present in Christian thought and practice?

Patrick O'Neill (2001) cites the 1982 US Bishop's Pastoral Letter, "The Challenge of Peace: God's Promise and Our Response," in order to remind us that the "purpose of the moral theory, in the first place, is not to legitimize war but to prevent it . . . the presumption is against the use of force." If we consider the practice of military recruitment on campus, for example, we find that a student is promised the payment of tuition[6] or a job after graduation in exchange for at least eight years in the armed forces (ibid.). The presumption of the military is not against the use of force; the military must be prepared to fight wars. Once a student enlists in the military, it is quite difficult to leave the military. The military, for example, "considers it a crime for [one] to leave [one's] unit or to disobey an order" (ibid.). In our current economy, which is wreaking havoc in our Jesuit schools, particularly the less financially secure ones such as Saint Peter's University and which is not promising for our recent graduates, Just War theory's moral presumption against the use of force will most likely take a back seat to the promise of an education or a job for an organization which does not share this presumption.

If we are to maintain our relationship with the military on the grounds of self-defense, I suggest that Jesuit schools at least provide the following to its academic communities: (1) a solid education in Just War theory, a rigorous critique of Just War theory, and a serious study of nonviolence; (2) a thorough understanding of what happens in war to human beings, to communities, to our soldiers, to the environment, and so on,[7] as well as the domestic costs of diverting monies to maintain the massive military might of the United States;[8] and, (3) training in becoming a conscientious objector should a student soldier find herself in the position of being directed to fight in an unjust war. Much like it does in the matter of abortion, the Jesuit university must act decisively in matters of war; if a war is unjust, then it must say as much and refuse to cooperate in the waging of such a war. Michael Baxter (2004) claims "when just war tradition is faithfully theorized and practiced, it calls for a politically disruptive witness on the part of its practitioners." As far as I can tell, Jesuit colleges and universities did not engage in "politically disruptive" activities during the waging of the Gulf wars, or the "War on Terrorism," which employed, among other questionable [under Just War standards] tactics, the use of torture.

In addition to the "no" of "politically disruptive activities," I suggest also the "yes," that is to say, the development of a culture and practices of peace to be a necessary next step if we wish to do "even more" for the sake of justice and for the sake of peace. The first steps in creating a culture and practices of peace are those of recognizing what has been done and taking responsibility for it. Josh Steiber and Ethan McCord (2010), former US Army specialists,[9] demonstrate how to begin this work. In their open letter, they write:

> We write to you, your family, and your community with an awareness that our words and actions can never restore your losses. . . .

We have been speaking to whoever will listen, telling them what was shown in the Wikileaks video only begins to depict the suffering we have created. From our own experiences, and the experiences of other veterans we have talked to, we know that the acts depicted in this video are everyday occurrences of this war: this is the nature of how US-led wars are carried out in this region. We acknowledge our part in the deaths and injuries of your loved ones as we tell Americans what we were trained to do and carried out in the name of "God and country." The soldier in the video said that your husband shouldn't have brought your children to battle but we are acknowledging our responsibility for bringing the battle to your neighborhood and to your family. . . . Though we have acted with cold hearts far too many times, we have not forgotten our actions toward you. Our hearts still hold hope that we can restore inside our country the acknowledgment of your humanity that we were taught to deny. . . . Our Secretary of Defense may say that the US won't lose its reputation over this, but we stand and say that our reputation's importance pales in comparison to our common humanity.

The truth telling, integrity, and courage of Steiber and McCord must be honored; at the same time, and in their words, "there is no bringing back all that was lost." Is it possible to find a way for such grievous losses not to happen in the first place? One way is to lessen our dependence upon grant monies that would have our students research and design the weapons that are used to kill other human beings; another way is to lessen our students' dependence upon military scholarships so that they can afford to go to school. These suggestions present an obvious question: How do our Jesuit colleges and universities make up for lost monies and scholarships? One answer to this question is to organize and advocate for a shift in how our federal monies are allocated, that is, less for military spending and more for education. The National Priorities Project estimates that US taxpayers have paid $1.4 trillion for total war spending (Iraq and Afghanistan) since FY 2001. If this money had been allocated differently, it could have paid for 174.8 million scholarships for university students for one year (National Priorities Project 2013, 1). More immediately, and more directed toward our ROTC students, would the administrators and faculty of our Jesuit colleges and universities be willing to offer a certain amount of their salaries so that a scholarship fund could be set up for those students whose only means of affording school is to join the military? These suggestions are preliminary at best, and would certainly require deeper conversation and planning, but they would help us to begin the work of creating a culture of peace and nonviolence.

There is, of course, much more that needs to be done. At the 2009 Commitment to Justice in Jesuit Higher Education conference, neither the "war question" nor nonviolence was widely discussed. By my count, there were only three panels in which nonviolence was mentioned; two panels in which war was mentioned (and one of these panels overlapped with a panel discussion of nonviolence); and, one panel on peace and justice studies programs at Jesuit colleges and universities. Further, the life and thought of Daniel Berrigan, certainly a major Catholic thinker and activist in peace making and nonviolence has never, to my knowledge, been seriously discussed at any of the Commitment to Justice in Jesuit Higher Education conferences. Given the agenda-setting nature of these conferences for our Jesuit justice programs, we may well consider the question of war, peace making, nonviolence, as well as Berrigan's influential contributions to these subjects a priority for our next national conference.

To my mind, there are few things more compelling than to deepen our thought and work in nonviolence on our Jesuit campuses. Given the complexity of the war question, the practice of nonviolent conversation circles on each of our campuses would be a good first step in trying to think through this question, particularly with regard to our relationship with the military and grants monies from the Department of Defense. Thomas Merton (1996, 254) writes about the particular gifts of Christian nonviolence that would be of great benefit to such conversations:

> Instead of trying to use the adversary as leverage for one's own effort to realize an ideal, nonviolence seeks only to enter into dialogue with him in order to attain, together with him, the common good of man [sic]. Nonviolence must be realistic and concrete. Like ordinary political action, it is no more than the "art of the possible." But precisely the advantage of nonviolence is that it has a *more Christian and more humane notion of what is possible.* Where the powerful

believe that only power if efficacious, the nonviolent resister is persuaded of the superior efficacy of love, openness, peaceful negotiation and above all truth. . . . Only love can attain and preserve the good of all.

The practice of nonviolence on our Jesuit campuses could foster a deeper knowledge of Catholic social teaching and of its pacifist tradition, as well as introduce our students to lives and struggles of nonviolence peace activists, a number of whom are Catholic. There is, for example, the witness of Dorothy Day, the cofounder of the Catholic Worker, who devoted her life to the impoverished. She gives an example of courageous and consistent witness to the practice of nonviolence. As we move into an age of social crises and uncertainty, the time is ripe to rediscover the richness of nonviolent theory, practice and examples within the Catholic tradition, as well as in many of our world's faith traditions.

I think also of the example of St. Ignatius of Loyola who in 1522, after a three-day vigil and confession of his sins, lay down his sword and dagger in front of a statue of the Black Madonna at the Benedictine Abbey in Montserrat, Spain. He then took up a pilgrim's staff, donned beggar's clothes and made his way to Jerusalem, now with a different understanding of his own humanity. Is it possible for us to retrieve this moment in Ignatius' life as a moment of the realization of a nonviolent way of life? Can it be the start of a nonviolence practice in our lives on Jesuit campuses? May we imagine and envision a Jesuit education as one that would include academic excellence, a faith that does justice, and the promotion of nonviolence? Can we see our students as future leaders in nonviolence practices toward one another and toward the earth? If so, studies and practices in nonviolence must become a full fledged academic course of study, must be integrated into extracurricular activities, and must be part of the practice of our faith lives on campus.

Conclusion

In *A Time to Break Silence*, Dr. King addresses those who criticized him for speaking out against the waging of the Vietnam war. He responded by saying that the comments of the critics "suggest that they do not know the world in which they live" (King 1990, 232) and that "we are [all] called to speak for the weak, the voiceless, the victims of or nation and for those its calls enemy, for no document from human hands can make these humans any less our brothers" (234). Within our Jesuit and Catholic justice traditions, we have heard a formulation similar to that of King's. Fathers Ignacio Ellacuria and Jon Sobrino have asked that we use our intellectual gifts and studies to understand the reality of the world. The good works of our community service programs well attend to the weak, the voiceless, and the victims of our world, while our social justice programs do well in confronting social structures that have impoverished and crushed our brother and sisters. Fathers Pedro Arrupe and Daniel Berrigan as well as recent papal encyclicals have placed special emphasis upon learning how to love the enemy and practice nonviolence.

Our work is to retrieve and renew the rich strands within these traditions and to integrate them into a course of academic study and communal practices. To my mind, the development of a program of "revolutionary nonviolence"[10] alongside a well-developed community service and social justice program is our best hope for the transformation of our humanity and of our world. This is the work, as Berrigan (2004, 218–19) puts it, of "awakened minds [and] mindful hearts . . . [of] awakening to the hope of Christ."

14　The Ethic of Environmental Concern and the Jesuit Mission

JENNIFER TILGHMAN-HAVENS

We live in a time in history when the global crisis of climate change cannot be ignored. The rising of the oceans, the drying of lands, and the reduction in the biodiversity in our ecological system are realities that face our current generation and that must be at the forefront of the policy plans for future generations to come. Many of the problems facing humankind today—climate change, poverty, species extinction, peak oil—have arisen from a worldview that understands humans, the economy, and the environment as disconnected issues. The solutions to global problems require a shift in perceptions and values that acknowledges all living beings as bound together in a network of interdependencies.

Jesuit Catholic universities must discern whether we are called in an urgent way to embrace an ethic of environmental concern. If we heed Fr. Peter-Hans Kolvenbach's call to bring to life "the service of faith and the promotion of justice" at Jesuit Catholic universities then we must consider the earth as a focus of our educational efforts. This is not a detour from concern for social justice, but an integral part of our commitment to human rights and the common good.

The statistics regarding the impact of global climate change on the poor reveal a host of dire realities that are too little known by those of us who live in the relative comfort of what we call "developed nations." Those who "have" are allowing the by-products of privilege to poison the pot for those who "have not." Ninety-nine percent of those who become casualties of the effects of climate change live in the developing world (Vidal 2008). Further, the least developed nations are not the ones emitting the carbon that is causing this crisis. The fifty poorest nations, in aggregate, contribute a mere 1 percent of the harmful emissions that pollute our air and redden our thermometers.

The ecological crisis has quickly become a humanitarian crisis. For example, as the global climate begins to rise, malaria has begun to reach further into the highlands of Kenya, where historically it has been too cold for the parasite-carrying mosquitoes to survive (Barclay 2008). This population has no developed immunity to the disease, and it is beginning to fuel an epidemic. In Bangladesh, climate change sparks flooding that erodes healthy soils, inflicting unexpected famines. According to Oxfam, approximately 17 million Bangladeshis could find themselves without homes by 2030 due to flooding, cyclones, and tornadoes (Oxfam 2009). The World Development Movement predicts that more than 200 million environmental refugees will be created by 2050, as a direct result of rising sea levels, erosion, and agricultural damage (Oliver 2008).

The Jesuit Catholic Tradition and Sustainability

At the Santa Clara Justice Conference in 2000, Fr. Peter-Hans Kolvenbach, SJ, challenged Jesuit universities to become practical about the promotion of justice. "Since Saint Ignatius wanted love to be expressed not only in words but also in deeds, the Congregation committed the Society to the promotion of justice as a concrete, radical but proportionate response to an unjustly suffering world" (Kolvenbach 2000). Our commitment thus must be to both the earth itself and its people—the two are inextricably joined as one.

As we attempt to address these crises, a holistic, sustainable approach is required. Sustainability is a framework for making decisions that integrates human, environmental, and economic needs as a whole system (Price 2008). In 2006 the Oregon Province of the Society of Jesus took a significant step toward adopting such a framework. In a document entitled "Regional Sustainable Development: A Plan of Action," the province defined how a sustainable decision-making framework provides solutions to global problems:

> Sustainable development is a commitment to respect and care for the community of life. It is economic growth that promotes the values of human rights, care for the natural world, and the striving for the common good of the whole earth community, especially the poor

and most vulnerable. It involves sustaining the present generation without imposing long-term costs or penalties on future generations. It replaces the use of non-renewable resources with renewable ones and reduces the consumption of all resources. It entails reuse, recovery, and recycling wherever possible; and replenishment or restoration of the natural balances affected by our actions. It implies sound life-cycle planning and economics—economics that truly reflect the environmental and human costs of our technologies and decisions. Sustainable development will succeed only if it expands to include a vision of sustainable communities which hold all creation as sacred. (Society of Jesus 2006)

This definition of sustainable development encourages a comprehensive approach to policies and practices that value care for the earth, social equity, and economic development as interrelated issues.

While the adoption of such a definition represents a significant step forward, important debate continues about how sustainability and economic development can find an equilibrium. Some authorities have long argued that in order to sustain the earth and its people, we must reach a point of zero population growth and reverse our rates of consumption, risking potential economic decline (Davis 1973). The Jesuit scholarship on sustainable development adopts a less radical tone, echoing the nuanced approach referenced in the Brundtland Commission report, which called for international cooperation on sustainable development and affirmed the need to reprioritize our development goals along these lines:

Thus the goals of economic and social development must be defined in terms of sustainability in all countries—developed or developing, market-oriented or centrally planned. Interpretations will vary, but must share certain general features and must flow from a consensus on the basic concept of sustainable development and on a broad strategic framework for achieving it. (Brundtland 1987)

Multinational organizations have adopted as axiomatic that economic development can enhance the health and quality of life for the impoverished countries of the world. It is apparent that all nations must adopt efforts toward economic development that prioritize a sustainable approach.

Ignatian Roots

For Jesuit institutions, the Ignatian roots for this commitment to sustainability run deep. The principles that guided St. Ignatius' understanding of God reveal to his reader the importance of care for creation. For Ignatius, God was present in and through creation. It was by the River Cardoner that Ignatius came to a new understanding of God and God's great love (Olin 1992). The natural beauty of the river valley revealed to Ignatius a truth about God that compelled him to live in a new way. For Ignatius, God is not equated with creation, as though God were the plants and animals, lands and waters in our midst, but God is reflected in these elements of our ecological landscape. Ignatius' spiritual lens spurred him to find God in all things, and he found God particularly and viscerally present in creation.

Ignatius invited others into his endeavor when he composed the Spiritual Exercises of St. Ignatius. During the Fourth Week of the Spiritual Exercises, the retreatant is called into action on behalf of love, in what is called the Contemplation ad Amorem, (literally translated "contemplation to gain divine love"). Love is expressed not just in sentiment or words, but in deeds. The directee is meant to contemplate God's divine presence in all that is created. "I will consider how God dwells in creatures; in the elements, giving them existence; in the plants, giving them life; in the animals, giving them sensation" (Ganss 1991). One might consider how our colleges and universities are meant to see ourselves communally as receivers of this spiritual invitation to consider God as intimately present in living things, worthy of our preservation.

Such a reverence for creation continues to be expressed in contemporary Jesuit scholarship. Paul Fitzgerald, SJ (2009), posits that if God is to be found in nature, in creatures, and in the earth herself, then to inflict harm upon this creation can be considered sinful. Intentional disregard for the earth in our decision-making and practices obstructs the fullness of God from being revealed through creation. The God of

Genesis, upon creating all living things, exclaims their intrinsic good-ness. "God saw all that he had made, and it was very good. And there was evening, and there was morning—the sixth day" (Gen. 1). The created world is deeply cherished by the Judeo-Christian God. Reflect-ing upon sustainability from this theocentric point of view, Fitzgerald describes the moral mandate that arises:

> Such a [theocentric] stance would oblige us to close the loop on our production and distribution systems so that the basic needs of all are met before the luxuries of a few are entertained. And it would extend our regard well into the future, leading us to ask and to answer the hard questions about the long-term consequences of our choices, actions and inactions, our since of commission and our sins of omis-sion, against generations unborn.

If our Jesuit Catholic institutions are founded on the Judeo-Christian understanding of God that has been inspired by the mythical stories of Genesis, then this divine awe toward the created world should be reflected in our current way of proceeding.

The Society of Jesus adopted this way forward in General Congrega-tions 34 and 35, which both emphasized care for creation as an apos-tolic priority and urged local provinces to develop actualize-able plans for care of the environment. Decree 20 of General Congregation 34, "We live in a broken world," states:

> We need to learn—both scientifically and theologically—about our entanglement in the processes causing environmental degra-dation. . . . Religions [including our own] have also been responsible for sinful elements of global dimensions: injustice, exploitation and destruction of the environment. . . . We might do something to pro-tect the environment or promote ecology, if we sincerely repent our sins of complicity. (Czerny 1999)

General Congregation 35 continued this emphasis. In Decree 3, "Recon-ciliation with Creation," the connection between social and ecological justice is made explicit:

> The drive to access and exploit sources of energy and other natural resources is very rapidly widening the damage to earth, air, water,

and our whole environment, to the point that the future of our planet is threatened. Poisoned water, polluted air, massive deforestation, deposits of atomic and toxic waste are causing death and untold suffering, particularly to the poor." (Society of Jesus 2008)

According to these decrees, if the earth is truly a place where we can encounter God—where the expression of God's intention finds its place and where God communicates to us through the natural world—then it is worthy of our active commitment to protect and preserve it.

Catholic Social Teaching

The rich and often unmined tradition of Catholic Social Teaching also urges us toward an ethic of sustainability. Roman Catholic leaders in both national and international arenas have described the need for accountability to the earth. The US Conference of Catholic Bishops has given voice to climate crisis for almost twenty years. In the document "Renewing the Earth," the Catholic Bishops write:

> The environmental crisis of our own day constitutes an exceptional call to conversion. As individuals, as institutions, as a people, we need a change of heart to save the planet for our children and generations yet unborn. So vast are the problems, so intertwined with our economy and way of life, that nothing but a wholehearted and ever more profound turning to God, the Maker of Heaven and Earth, will allow us to carry out our responsibilities as faithful stewards of God's creation. (Catholic Bishops 1991)

From the heart of the Roman Catholic Church, Pope John Paul II (1991) wrote in the encyclical *Centesimus Annus*, "Equally worrying is the ecological question which accompanies the problem of consumerism and which is closely connected to it. In his desire to have and to enjoy rather than to be and to grow, man consumes the resources of the earth and his own life in an excessive and disordered way." In our current day, Pope Benedict XVI is furthering this Catholic commitment to sustainability. He has been called the "green Pope" and has not only published Vatican teachings about the integration of faith and ecological commitments, but also has begun to make investments within the facility of the Vatican itself which reflect the Magisterium's teaching and which will lower its emissions. The roof of the papal audience hall now boasts an array of 2,700 solar panels to supply energy to its main auditorium, generating enough power from the sun to heat, cool and light this large building. The Vatican also funds reforestation of lands in Hungary to offset its greenhouse gas emissions. These small examples attempt to illustrate that theological commitments to sustainability find expression in practical application to one's immediate environment.

Our Way of Proceeding as a Jesuit Catholic University

Our universities have a responsibility to respect and further the foundations laid both by St. Ignatius and recent Jesuit scholarship, and by the historical and current Church teaching illustrated in the leadership of Pope Benedict in honoring creation and making practical changes to lessen our impact on the earth. If we reflect in our local practices the ideological commitments expressed through the recent General Congregation documents, then our "way of proceeding" stems from our commitment to justice and our deep concern for creation. A response to Kolvenbach's call in 2000—to act more justly in our "ways of proceeding" as Jesuit universities—includes a care for the earth. Each university must discern a path toward the service of faith and the promotion of justice that attends to environmental and socio-economic concerns simultaneously as interconnected issues. The character of our universities must reflect these commitments in all that we do—in our teaching, research, student development opportunities, and operations. Indeed, if we take seriously the directives of the authorities above, the very integrity of our apostolic work as a Jesuit Catholic institution depends on the extent to which our priorities reflect care for the earth. As scholars and teachers and professionals choosing a "preferential option for the poor," as mandated by Kolvenbach and backed by Jesuit and Catholic teaching, we take responsibility for all aspects of creation that have become impoverished through our consumerism, irresponsible development, and malignant neglect of our natural resources and our human family.

A serious commitment to the Ignatian and Catholic call to honor creation finds its legs in practical, daily decisions affecting the life and operations of a university.

The value commitments made by our Jesuit leadership could easily stand as moral statements that have no place in praxis, especially within the operations of institutions where budget concerns tend to dominate, especially in a stressful economic climate. While the preceding sections of this paper attempted to lay the theological and doctrinal foundations for a critical moral commitment to sustainability, the remaining sections focus on action, in particular the daily practices regarding energy, water, paper, transportation and waste. It is these practices that have direct and immediate impact on our local and global community.

The arguments made here for a culture of sustainability within our Jesuit universities have been built upon theological and ecclesial mandates for sustainability, which intend to motivate from within the tradition of Jesuit and Catholic care for the earth. The evidence of an economic argument for sustainability—one that inspires behavioral change based on profitability and benefit to an institution—is also growing. As Laitner (2009) points out in his economic assessment of energy conservation efforts, improved innovation and energy efficiency, when substituted for the current conventional consumption and production of energy, can contribute to a noticeable difference in economic growth. Although many strategies toward greenhouse gas abatement require economic investment, the macroeconomic benefits are becoming clearer. A recent McKinsey report found that "a concerted nationwide effort to reduce greenhouse gas emissions would most certainly stimulate economic forces and create business opportunities that we cannot foresee today" (Creyts 2009).

At the microeconomic level, the cost-benefit analysis of sustainability is finding traction in the for-profit sector. A review of topical literature finds many titles along the lines of Kevin Wilhelm et al., authors of "Return on Sustainability: How Companies Can Increase Profitability and Address Climate Change in an Uncertain Economy." The benefits of sustainable business practice outweigh the costs, and even improve performance. In a recent interview, Stonyfield CEO Gary Hirshberg notes: "When companies say they don't have the staff or the money to pursue socially responsible projects, our response is they can't afford not to. Reducing packaging, shrinking the waste stream, reducing energy use saves money. And the more money you spend in those areas, the more you'll save if you just examine better strategies in the areas of production, waste management and energy use" (cited in Kenney 2008). Though outside the for-profit sector, a university's multiple bottom lines also benefit from adopting sustainable practices. Further research could be explored regarding how student applications, alumni and donor giving, and faculty and staff workplace satisfaction might all be affected by an intentional culture of sustainability on campus.

Grounded in the Jesuit Catholic mission and sound economics, universities can take concrete steps that will make the brick-and-mortar elements of the institutions more green and cost effective. As universities attempt to initiate plans for moving toward their own greening goals, they should consider the "low-hanging fruit" that requires little outlay of resources and fairly rapid financial reward. There are myriad creative ways to reduce the consumption of energy, water, and resources and to encourage alternative transportation. Depending on an institution's utility costs, installing water- and energy-efficient fixtures offers relatively swift payback. Urinals, toilets, aerators, showerheads, dishwashers, and irrigation equipment that surpass the building code's minimum thresholds for water efficiency greatly reduce an institution's water and sewer bills. Low investment energy conservation methods include highly efficient fluorescent lighting, ventilation, night setback controls which turn off heat and air conditioning when buildings are not occupied, and temperature setbacks to keep buildings slightly cooler in the cold seasons and warmer in the hot seasons.

To encourage alternative transportation to and from campus, it is possible to create incentives for bus ridership, carpooling and biking, especially in an urban environment. An increase in campus parking prices can provide needed revenue for these incentives, while also discouraging single-occupant vehicle commuting.

Waste prevention initiatives can maximize budget dollars and decrease disposal costs. Paper purchasing can be reduced by switching to double-sided printers and setting all computers to default double-sided printing. Beverage discounts for reusable mugs—equal to the cost of the paper cup—reduce the amount of material in the waste stream. A donation option for year-end residence hall moves, to collect students' unwanted clothes, nonperishable food, school supplies, and household goods, fosters community good will while lowering a university's disposal costs. Each of these options requires relatively low-investment and a strong return on investment. As Jesuit universities begin to take seriously the mandate for greener practices, these initial sparks might ignite the effort toward a more holistic approach.

Models for Coordinating Sustainability Efforts

The coordination of sustainability efforts by a central office or individual can catalyze a campus in an integrated, system fashion. The hiring of personnel to champion sustainability efforts is, by and large, a recent phenomenon. A recent study by Association for the Advancement of Sustainability in Higher Education (AASHE) showed that 90 percent of salaried Sustainability Officer positions were created within the past ten years, and 74 percent were created within the past five years (Matson 2008). Thirty-two percent of sustainability officers nationwide are housed within the facilities division, which most often implements the practices that have a physical effect on the campus and where practical decisions are made regarding energy, waste, and building use. A model employed by 11 percent of institutions is to ground sustainability in the academic emphasis of the university, highlighting the integration of sustainability topics into the curriculum (Matson 2008). Thirty-one percent employ a model that has multiple areas of entry through a center or Office of Sustainability, which combines both the practical concerns around facilities as well as the scholarly emphasis on the study of sustainability efforts broadly.

The majority of sustainability officers, while engaged in the overall sustainability coordination for their campus, also manage energy efficiency, recycling and waste reduction, community outreach and work with students, and data collection and reporting. While a handful of universities rely on grants, savings from sustainability initiatives, student fees, donations, or a sustainability endowment to fund their efforts, the vast majority fund sustainability initiatives through their general fund, which provides a consistent and secure source of funding and demonstrates an ongoing commitment by the university. Based upon the variety of contexts and reporting structures at Jesuit colleges and universities, the human capital offered to this crucial role will depend upon the institutional culture and resources available to the task.

Sustainability and the Jesuit University: A Case Study

Seattle University is an example of an institution that recognizes that its Jesuit identity mandates a drive toward sustainability, and thus presents a unique case study. Its urban campus is located in Seattle, Washington. Established in 1891, it has grown to over 30 buildings on 50-plus acres, which are home to 7,500 students and over 1,200 faculty and staff. Seattle University has undertaken several key initiatives as a leader in the sustainability movement and has developed several mission-grounded practices that reflect this commitment.

It should be noted that Seattle University's physical and political context facilitates the availability of specific resources and the achievement of basic standards that may not be common in other parts of the country or the world. The state of Washington, King County, and the city of Seattle have not only set policies that encourage sustainable management of resources, but each level of local and state government has also set an example by taking the lead on "greening" their own standards and practices as political subdivisions. For example, King County has detailed in the King County Climate Change Initiative that 20 percent of its county vehicles will run on biodiesel fuel in the near term. Former mayor of Seattle Greg Nickels launched the US Mayors Climate Protection Agreement in 2005, which has challenged mayors across the country to meet or beat the Kyoto protocol's carbon emissions reduction goals. The Washington State Commute Trip Reduction Law mandates that all companies with at least one hundred employees have to provide incentives for employees to use alternative transportation.

The city of Seattle has a well-deserved reputation as a "green" city. Regarding waste reduction, compost and recycling, Seattle Public Utilities has an infrastructure in place for businesses and residents to recycle and compost utilizing the city's curbside pick-up. Residential and commercial construction waste can also be recycled at local facilities. The Seattle energy code for new buildings also enables green building by mandating basic standards that meet the energy efficiency prerequisites for LEED (Leadership in Energy and Environmental Design), a national, voluntary green building standard set by the US Green Building Council.[1] The context within which Seattle University finds itself serves as a catalyst for its commitment to green building, waste management, and resource conservation, and the regulations and infrastructure of the local and regional governments provide a context that supports Seattle University's efforts toward sustainability.

Within this context, the university has institutionalized its commitment to sustainable practices. In 2005 Seattle University was one of the first colleges or universities to hire a sustainability manager, whose role is to oversee and coordinate all of the efforts toward sustainable practices on campus. As part of the facilities team, the sustainability manager maintains, expands, and develops programs aimed at reducing the environmental impact of Seattle University's operations, projects, and practices. Described below are some of the elements of an overall plan to shift an institution's paradigm from standard operating procedure to intentional planning and implementation around energy use, waste, building design, and soil and air quality. The best practices described in this paper reflect the work of a facilities team that has committed itself to best practices in sustainability.

Waste

A campus-wide effort has been underway since 1988 to reduce the university's contribution to our region's landfills. Through both the recycling and the compost programs, waste has been reduced significantly. The university's sustainability initiatives began when the Environmental Health and Safety Coordinator initiated a metal, paper, and glass recycling program over twenty years ago. The program has expanded to include the recycling of batteries, books, CDs, cell phones, computers, electronics, light bulbs, furniture, pallets, scrap metal, packing material, and toner cartridges. Recycling bins are at every desk, and in the hallways and outside of all campus buildings.

From February to April 2007 a Seattle University student intern conducted a waste audit of the trash and paper recycling bins in a sampling of buildings on campus. The largest portion of the contents in the faculty and staff desk-side containers was coffee cups, followed by paper plates, napkins, and food. These paper products, which can either be composted or recycled, made up between 25 percent to 62 percent of the contents of each person's trash bin. As an incentive to prevent the coffee cups from finding their way to the trash, all new members of the faculty, staff, and student body are now given reusable mugs when they come to campus and receive discounts on beverages. All paper plates, napkins, utensils, and food are now routinely composted. Seattle University's food service vendor, Bon Appetit, converted all petroleum plastic containers and utensils to biodegradable plastic to facilitate the university's composting efforts.

Food waste from the campus kitchens plus coffee grounds, called pre-consumer food waste, has been composted since 1995. In 2002 the university built its own pre-consumer food waste facility to compost the twenty-five tons of annual food waste for fertilizer on the campus grounds, earning the 2007 Sustainability Innovator Award from the Sustainable Endowments Institute. Postconsumer compost is collected in various bins outside of campus buildings and hauled to Cedar Grove Compost, a private company, where it is mixed with food scraps from Seattle city residents and made into sale-able compost for gardens across the area.

Energy

According to the Northwest Energy Coalition,[2] a clean environment begins with energy conservation. Seattle University is committed to the wise use and conservation of all utility resources, including electricity, natural gas, steam, and water. The university began an energy conservation program in 1986 when the Department of Energy and the local utility started offering assistance for conservation projects. In the early 1990s, an Energy Manager was hired to facilitate energy conservation projects, and since then, the university's energy bill has been reduced by over $350,000 annually. The university has committed to directing some of this savings toward the purchase of renewable energy, offsetting 15 percent of the campus's electricity consumption.

A joint effort between mechanical engineering students, facilities services staff and Seattle City Light brought solar power to campus in summer 2005. This solar demonstration project on the Student Center meets part of the building's electricity needs. The students designed the system and installed it with the help of facilities staff, enhancing their education with a hands-on experience of putting green technology to work, and Seattle City Light paid for the equipment.

Buildings

The policy for new building and renovation projects at Seattle University requires that all new construction and major renovations be designed to meet LEED Gold standards. LEED is the nationally accepted benchmark for the design, construction, and operation of high performance green buildings. The Seattle University Student Center, a three-story building that includes offices, meeting space, and a cafeteria, achieved LEED Silver Certification in 2002. Several aspects of the building, including materials, fixtures, and indoor environmental quality and innovative design contributed to its LEED certification. To encourage alternative transportation, the building planners included locker rooms and showers, a bike rack, and preferred parking for car and vanpools. The center's roofing material reflects the heat produced by the sun. Eighty-three percent of the construction waste was recycled or salvaged, and much of the new building materials include recycled-content. All the adhesives, sealants, paints, carpets, and composite wood emit low levels of volatile organic compounds (VOCs)—chemicals that evaporate easily at room temperature. Each of these aspects not only lessens the impact of this building on the environment, but also increases the health and safety of its occupants.

The twenty-year facilities master plan, which guides decisions about building use, landscaping, and traffic flow, includes the goal to incorporate the principles of sustainable design throughout campus, in all aspects of site and building design, construction, maintenance, and operation.

Landscaping and Grounds

A shift to sustainable landscape practices began in 1979 with the adoption of an Integrated Pest Management program that focuses on organic solutions, building healthy soil, and providing habitat for beneficial insects and birds. The Grounds Department has successfully and beautifully maintained the fifty campus acres since 1986 without the use of pesticides and herbicides. The grounds were designated a Backyard Wildlife Sanctuary in 1989 because of the healthy habitat that attracts and sustains wildlife in a dense urban environment. One biology faculty member affirms this intentionality: "The grounds department has made an incredibly impressive commitment to organic treatment and integrated pest management by avoiding chemical fertilizers, herbicides, and pesticides. It is incredible that on an urban campus students can eat what grows here."

Stormwater Management

As one might imagine, the consistently rainy winters in Seattle can cause pipes to back up and the grasses and walkways to flood. When faced with the decision about how to ward off flooding in vulnerable buildings, the university had two cost equivalent options: build a conventional stormwater detention system or build an environmentally conscious rain garden. The rain garden, which is an excavated depression planted to look like a garden, provides a natural stormwater management strategy that mimics nature. Stormwater infiltrates through layers of soil and gravel as plants transpire moisture and help attenuate pollutants. The Seattle University rain garden is ten feet deep, lined with a special fabric and perforated drainage system, and filled with a soil mixture designed to absorb and retain as much water as possible.

Water

Multiple efforts are underway to prevent waste of the increasingly precious resource that is our clean water supply. Waterless urinals, dual-flush toilets, faucet aerators, showerheads, washers and dishwashers, and kitchen spray heads that surpass the building code's minimum thresholds for water efficiency have replaced older lower efficiency models. The university's irrigation system is monitored daily by computer. The irrigation clock schedules are adjusted bi-monthly and are programmed to come on in the evening when applying water is most efficient. Rain sensors were installed at each site to stop irrigation for measurable rain events. For maintenance of the pool at the on-campus fitness center, a Seattle University staff member developed an enclosure system that allows maintenance staff to repair an area of the pool without draining it. This alone saves approximately 189,000 gallons of water every time the pool needs repair.

Green Cleaning

Conventional cleaning products can contain chemicals that can cause cancer, reproductive disorders, respiratory ailments, and eye and skin irritation, putting our students, custodians, and other employees at risk. As they make their way from a sink or toilet through a sewage treatment plant and back into our water supply, these toxins affect drinking water quality, local bodies of water, plants, and animals. Green Seal is a nonprofit organization that tests products to ensure they meet rigorous, science-based environmental standards to ensure that they are nontoxic and nonpollutant. At Seattle University, Green Seal–certified cleaners are the standard for all custodial teams.

Transportation

At many organizations, transportation represents a large portion of the facility's ecological footprint. At Seattle University, that footprint is shrinking as campus-owned vehicles become more efficient and the Seattle University community chooses alternative options for getting to and from campus. Facilities purchased its first electric vehicle in 2001. There are fourteen electric vehicles and one electric-assist bicycle used by staff working the grounds, the building trades, and custodial. Electric vehicles comprise 33 percent of the entire fleet and B50 biodiesel (50 percent biodiesel, 50 percent petroleum diesel) is used for a backhoe, diesel mower, and bobcat at our onsite compost facility. Two Ford Escape Hybrids transport students on the evening shuttle. Public safety officers patrol campus on mountain bikes. For commuters, Seattle University offers discounted bus and train passes, a locker room and showers for walkers and bikers, preferred parking for carpools, a hybrid Zipcar for doctor's appointments and errands, and a guaranteed ride home in case of an emergency for employees who do not take their car to work. For these efforts and others, Seattle University was one of twenty local organizations that received a Diamond Award for commute trip reduction in 2006. One staff member remarked, "I am so grateful to belong to a campus community that walks its talk and lives, breathes and supports environmental sustainability each and everyday. I am reminded of this daily, as I ride the bus to work each morning (made possible by a bus pass that is significantly subsidized by my employer) and when I walk my compostable paper plate (provided by the university's catering service) following an event directly outside of my building to the compost bin. Seattle University makes it easy for me to be green!"

Food Service

Seattle University selected Bon Appetit as its food vendor based on the quality of the food and its commitment to socially responsible practices. Bon Appetit's standards include sourcing 30 percent of all produce from local farms, buying organic produce when possible, and changing the menu based on the seasonality of regional fresh food. It serves fair trade, shade-grown, organic coffee and fair-trade bananas. All eggs are from cage-free chickens, all seafood is caught wild, and all meat comes from hormone-free and range-fed livestock. The milk is from a local dairy and free of antibiotics and artificial bovine growth hormone, and the baked goods use local, sustainably harvested grain. No trans-fats or high fructose corn syrup are used in the cooking on campus. Bon Appetit's low carbon diet program emphasizes foods that require less energy to make, package, and transport.

Greenhouse Gas Emissions

In 2007 Seattle University joined the American College and University Presidents' Climate Commitment as a charter signatory. The commitment is an effort by the nation's higher education institutions to neutralize their greenhouse gas emissions and accelerate educational efforts and research to help restabilize the earth's climate. The university is developing a plan for the achievement of climate neutrality by reducing emissions caused from heating, cooling and lighting buildings, sending waste to the landfill, employee air travel, and employees and students commuting to campus. The plan will also include student education initiatives, both in and out of the classroom.

As illustrated by the specific steps described above, Seattle University has concretized its mission-driven commitment to sustainability in facilities, grounds, and community incentives. This focus on efficiency of resources, healthy grounds and food, and reduction in waste, while not always visible to the eye, quietly affects all decisions regarding the physical movement of people and materials in and around campus. Such initiatives serve the finances of the university and its public image, but more important though is the embodied commitment to the care of creation at the heart of the Ignatian Catholic tradition.

Sustainable Initiatives by Faculty, Staff, and Students

The primary emphasis of this case study has been the practical application of the Jesuit Catholic sustainability commitment as implemented by operations and facilities within Seattle University. Equally deserving of mention are curricular integration, student leadership initiatives, and strategic planning. At Seattle University, faculty members from each of the seven colleges and schools have found creative ways to integrate sustainability into their scholarship and teaching. Courses from Renewable Energy Systems in Engineering to Nature Writing and Environmentalism in the College of Arts and Sciences to Natural Resource and Environmental Economics with the Albers School of Business and Economics have grounded students' understanding of sustainability in research and scholarship. Many of the colleges and schools have internal committees on sustainability to guide curriculum planning and policies.

The president's Committee on Sustainability on campus is an active group of students, faculty, and staff spearheading several initiatives to coordinate efforts toward sustainable practices across the university. In 2008 the committee piloted a sustainability challenge, which organized teams of people to earn incentives for reducing their energy usage, finding alternative transportation, eating less meat, and educating themselves about sustainability. The committee was also instrumental in providing input toward Seattle University's five-year strategic plan, which emphasized sustainability as a strategic priority to be addressed in each of the university's strategic goals.

Students have also been leading the charge as catalysts for change on campus. A group of well-organized student leaders petitioned administrators at the university and within Bon Appetit catering services to end the sale of bottled water on campus. Their "ban the bottle" campaign found broad-reaching support among faculty, staff, and students, and within the next several years, various vendors across campus have committed to significantly reducing and possibly eliminating bottled waters from vending machines and cafeterias, offering instead filtered water to be poured into reusable bottles and cups. Harnessing student enthusiasm about sustainable practices and providing meaningful responses to student efforts in this direction enhances the university's philosophical credibility in the eyes of students, illustrating in real terms that the Jesuit mission strongly influences decisions about the allocation of resources across the institution.

As Seattle University looks toward the future, students remain committed to continually raising the bar. In a 2007 survey students requested a variety of environmentally friendly goals to be met by the university: a community garden at each hall for students to grow food and flowers, more energy conservation, more low-flow water fixtures, more vegetarian options, secure indoor bike racks and bike rentals, and expanded eco-awareness learning communities. Seattle University's senior leadership is poised to respond to this earnest desire. Fr. Stephen Sundborg remarked at a recent university convocation: "We are proud that we win more awards for sustainability than any other university in the state, but we can do more to do our part to face a world-wide critical challenge, we can set the pace for others, and we can make our campus an educational example for our students' future lives and choices. We welcome this challenge and opportunity" (Sundborg 2008).

Conclusion

Jesuit Catholic institutions are defined by their character. Throughout the past five hundred years, Jesuit colleges and universities have been recognized for their academic rigor and excellent pedagogy. These qualities have since been replicated in places of higher learning across the globe, as Ignatius' vision for an organized, rigorous, and increasingly specialized system of learning has become a standard. In the past forty years, one distinct hallmark of Jesuit educational institutions that has set them apart is a commitment not only to academic excellence that prepares excellent scholars and practitioners, but to the formation of the individual student such that she sees herself as a moral agent able to transform our society toward justice. Recent Superiors General Fr. Pedro Arrupe[3] and Fr. Peter Hans-Kolvenbach, inspired by a theology of liberation, reformed and refined the Jesuit emphasis on intellectual development of the student to include a holistic development of not only our students but also our faculty, staff, and wider university community such that the thrust of the entire enterprise might be aimed toward social justice.

In the past decade, this movement toward justice in the official decrees and teachings of the Society of Jesus has been articulated to include not only human beings, but also the earth and all of creation. The integrity of the Jesuit Catholic character of our universities depends upon our willingness to employ financial resources, human capital, curricular efforts, and mission focus as we heed Kolvenbach's call in a holistic way through the service of faith and the promotion of social and ecological justice. Scientific evidence abounds that our ecological systems, exploited to meet the needs of relative few, are signaling their own destruction. A "preferential option" toward our fragile environment is crucial. Individually and collectively, our 28 Jesuit colleges and universities, 3,700 Jesuit schools worldwide, and the millions of students, faculty, and staff therein can be agents of change to stem this tide. Our way of proceeding as Jesuit universities must become practical, through internal policies, educational efforts, allocation of resources, and campus operations that protect the environment, conserve resources, and soften our heavy footprint.

Our mandate as Jesuit universities committed to the service of faith and the promotion of justice demands creativity in our approach to the earth and to its people. May our way of proceeding reflect the centuries-old Jesuit Catholic commitment to reverence for all of creation and revive our collective energies toward ecological justice, for the transformation of the earth and all the creatures who inhabit it.

15 Companions, Prophets, Martyrs

Jesuit Education as Justice Education

JEANNINE HILL FLETCHER

> Each Jesuit university must examine its own social environment, including its own commitment to justice and solidarity. Through community service, service-learning projects, immersion experiences, and faculty–student research projects, more and more Jesuit institutions have provided supervised opportunities for their students to meet and to learn from people from other economic and social groups. By confronting the poverty both in themselves as well as in others, students, faculty, staff, administrators, and board members have come to understand how precious is human dignity and how dependent it is on adequate food, water, housing, health care and education.
>
> —Communal Reflection on Jesuit Mission in Higher Education[1]

The ideal of shaping students for solidarity in a world in need thankfully motivates many within the systems of Jesuit education. Yet while the twenty-eight colleges and universities in our network have centers for service and justice as well as programs of service learning, authentic development of students in a well-educated solidarity requires continual sacrifice and ever-deepening engagement. The promotion of service is not enough. While the recognition of disparity and the "gritty reality" of socio-economic injustices which may come from students' work with communities in need is essential, the placement of students in service is but one component of a Jesuit justice education.[2] Since the majority of students attending a Jesuit college or university represent the minority of the population in terms of economic privilege, and all institutions of higher learning provide privileges that will carry students further away from the realities of poverty, sending students into service can participate in injustice.[3] In Sharon Chubbuck's

(2007, 244) view, "the emphasis on quality of education and formation of character promoted in Ignatian pedagogy without equal attention to critical analysis and reform may result in graduates who, though rich in acts of mercy, may be deficient in the acts of critical analysis, political advocacy and societal reform required to address injustice at its root."

Not only does placement in communities in need have the potential to leave unexamined the root causes of injustice, participation in service can replicate the gap of rich and poor, privileged and dispossessed and reinforce stereotypes long-learned. We therefore need to equip students with the tools to understand systems of structural injustice and their position within them. To do this, we, educators in the Jesuit tradition, must be willing to be companions, prophets, and martyrs.

The Call of "Companion"

Shorthand in the Jesuit tradition for those who walked with Ignatius of Loyola, "companion" recalls companionship with Christ. According to Joseph MacDonnell (1995, ix), Ignatius described his own society with this word because "he did not want his followers to be named *Ignatian* after him, but instead wanted his followers to be called *Companions of Jesus*." In *MacDougall's words*, "Companions work together for a common goal: they do more than collaborate, they are friends inspired by the same person, animated by the same principles and enthused about the same work" (ix). In order for Jesuit education to be justice education, we are called to be companions in a multiplicity of ways.

Becoming Companions in the Community

As students go out into service, they need to be equipped with the resources to become companions in the community. Becoming companions in a community in need requires a vision that transforms the charity model of self-giving by relearning to see whole human beings in the complex reality of our unjust world. Going into communities in need with a culturally conditioned lens that includes negative stereotypes, often students can only see data that confirms stereotypes about "the homeless," "the poor," "people with AIDS," and "immigrants."

Without challenging the assumptions our society provides, our students see teachers who "cannot teach," they see parents who "do not care," they see nonprofit organizations that are "totally disorganized." Through the lens of privilege, students criticize the disempowered and rush to their rescue. Even while making connections with their academic courses, too often students articulate that they will "bring their knowledge" to the "uneducated" to "better their situation." Students engaged in service too often find comfort in the work they do, consoling themselves that "every little bit helps" and "even a smile can change someone's day." They end their service reflections "feeling good I do my part." In the words of one especially honest and self-reflective student:

> I don't see why I was born into the family that I was born into, or why I have the things that I have, when so many people don't even have enough money to eat, let alone eat well. Because this seems unfair to me, I want to do something to balance things out, and this is one of the ways I can do that. By volunteering my time to people less fortunate I can assuage some of that guilt, and enjoy the blessings I have more fully because I feel more justified in having them.

Simply placing students in service does nothing to challenge such self-referential understanding of work in the community. Without the difficult work of critical analysis, service remains self-serving: for students, instructors, and institutions alike. The community remains "them" and "we" are better for having served. Disrupting the cycle of privileged benevolence in charity requires a justice-curriculum that unveils subconscious stereotyping, analyzes the history of systemic structures of oppression, and provides tools for social analysis toward social change. As such, justice learning is *academic* (using scholarly tools to understand and respond to the realities of our world) and it is *civic* (encouraging students to learn from, and about, the community in order to be shaped as citizens in our communities). But it also must be *eudemonic* (focused on students' personal development) such that we are all required to recognize not only the problems "out there" and our vision of a future citizenry, but the necessary *personal* culpability within these realities—our response and responsibility to the world in need.[4]

At the intersection of the personal, academic, and civic, students must learn to recognize their own stereotypes as ones inherited from the wider culture and active in our living histories. Fearful of being labeled racist, sexist, classist, and so on, most of us are reluctant to admit that the stereotypes that float around us in our society actually do shape the way we see things. Recognizing the shade of our lenses is a first step toward looking at reality through different ones. But, recognizing our prejudices is only a first step to the right relation in the community. Students must see their local situation in light of a larger reality of systemic injustice, uncovering privileges embedded in history that impact their own lives. A historical understanding of the structural injustices of racism, sexism, and socio-economic disadvantage enables students to wrestle with the implications of this history as we live within them today. Privilege studies and exercises designed to illuminate privilege must be engaged as part of our service learning practice.

Recognizing stereotyping, privilege and disparity are aspects of a more fundamental set of information to which students must be introduced, that is, students must be given the tools to recognize the systems and structures that are root causes of the injustice they encounter through service. In the words of Chubbuck (2007, 258), "acts of service and volunteerism . . . though much needed in society can mask the need for more controversial critical analysis and activism needed to transform unjust structures and institutions." While the move from charity to justice is embraced by many of the Jesuit programs that place students in the community, what types of resources are allocated to truly understanding the structural realities? Where is the curricular sharing of syllabi, readings, documentaries, and exercises that help illuminate the structural realities that are root causes that perpetuate the need our students encounter in service? How are funds dedicated to speakers, workshops, and instructional teams who can support this critical learning? How are these conversations not the responsibility of a special sector of the university (like multicultural affairs or centers for justice) but shared across the disciplines by administrators, faculty, and staff alike? If we are going to continue to send students into communities in need as part of justice education, we must share the tools across the university for recognizing the deep structural realities which are the root causes of the problems their service work addresses. We must help our students to recognize the structural realities as active decisions that have been made by collective agents in our society in order to work together to identify paths for social change.

Thus, Jesuit education as justice education must include a curriculum of social analysis that can lead to social change, if we are to form our students as companions in the community. This curriculum should include historical and structural analyses of race, gender and class as well as the invitation for self-transformation through the recognition of privilege. This transformative pedagogy provides resources for the tenuous and problematic work our students will engage in the community. Without attention to these systems of injustice and their place within them our students cannot sufficiently recognize the systemic gulf that has been created between "us and "them" in order to begin the work that might precariously bridge it. Programs of justice learning and service learning must provide the tools for students to wrestle with privilege and relinquish their own status in order to stand in that solidarity the Jesuit vision so compellingly asserts.

If the Jesuit vision of education includes shaping students in a well-educated solidarity, the institution will insist on social justice learning across the curriculum as "academic neutrality . . . can support oppression by default" (Applebaum 2009, 384). We must press the question of how all areas of university exploration—economics, theology, anthropology, the sciences, philosophy, business, social work, education, literature, language and more—are all implicated in systems of privilege and structural injustice, and also have unique tools to address root causes. If we recognize injustice in the world and our academic resources do not actively address these structures, leaving them unexamined under the guise of "neutrality," our work in teaching can support the status quo. Faculty forums must be made available for the authentic examination of social justice issues that intersect each discipline and each course of study. Faculty must be empowered to articulate both an institution-wide *and* discipline-based rationale "to support the difficult work of socially just teaching" (Chubbuck 2007, 260). It is far easier to allow the dictates of current practice to maintain the status quo. To be a "companion" in the education of students for justice requires a shift in pedagogy toward a curriculum that consistently raises questions of structural injustice and social analysis for social change. It is unlikely that we can do this without self-interrogation into our own privilege. In this way, we become colearners with our students in justice education.

Companions in the Classroom

The pedagogy of service learning insists upon yet another shift in teaching style toward one that equalizes power within a classroom and invites expertise from within the community (Howard 1998). In courses that employ service as a learning resource alongside the traditional resources of text, lecture, discussion, and so on, students are invited to be active learners in companionship with the professor and in work with the wider community. Both faculty and student are invited to consider the partners in the community as coinstructor, privileging the role of the engaged expert in the work of social justice. This shift in the locus of expertise (from professor to activist in the community) allows students to actively incorporate many different ways of knowing into the exploration and examination of course material. It disrupts the top-down dynamic of education (where the professor has the syllabus, agenda, and answers), and insists on allowing students to pose the live questions that emerge from their work in the community.

The service learning pedagogy, then, is *counter-normative* as it works toward equalizing the relationships *within* the classroom as well as those outside the classroom. As Jeffrey Howard (1998, 27) describes the synergistic classroom of service learning pedagogy:

> Discussion comfortably embraces both the content of academic readings and observations and experiences from the students' community placements. The instructor may be difficult to identify, though she or he might be seen facilitating the conversation to maximize the students' efforts to integrate the community-based and academic learning, contributing her or his own knowledge and relevant experiences to the discussion, or managing the discussion so that there is equal attention paid to the objective and subjective ways that students come to know.

In the service learning classroom, the "text" of experience in the community is engaged alongside the traditional "texts." In Howard's description, the instructor's role continues to be one of facilitating the learning and leading students to help make sense of their experience as it contributes to the investigation of course material. However, learning from the confusing "text" of work in the community is not an easy task. In Howard's words, "Service-learning students must not only master academic material as in traditional courses, but also learn how to learn from unstructured and ill-structured community experiences and merge that learning with the learning from other course resources" (5).

In order for the instructor to facilitate this learning in an authentic way, she or he must have committed some effort to become companion to the community so that she or he understands what it is that is going on in the community. Opening the walls of the classroom to include work with a community partner further equalizes faculty and students as partners in learning. In the service learning classroom, "discussion about theory and discussion about experiences is embraced by all, and efforts to integrate the two are made by all parties. The lines of distinction between the student role and the instructor role become blurred, so that students are teachers and learners, and instructors are learners as well as teachers." (Howard 1998, 27). Key in Howard's description of a "synergistic classroom" is the role of student and instructor as "companions" in learning. The relinquishing of control and a redistribution of the balance of power within the classroom provides the opportunity for Jesuit education to be justice in practice. How does encountering our students as whole persons require that we empower them to be agents in their own active learning, rather than passive recipients of our own findings? The service learning pedagogy as described by Howard encourages a dramatic transformation from traditional "information-dissemination" models of passive learning to active learners in a complex and changing world.

With the shift of agency and decision making from sole prerogative of the professor to a dynamic classroom of exploration, students open up the investigative process by drawing on their work in the community. With this comes one of the most challenging places where being "companion" in the work of justice education will require the transformation of our university practices. For, as students bring in the questions, complications and learning that emerges from service, we as instructors cannot help to harvest the learning unless we know the "text" of service from which our students draw. We cannot help them unpack the experience, if we do not have a sense of the texture of that experience. We cannot join them in the journey of learning from their companions in the community if we ourselves are not on that journey. To truly employ the service learning pedagogy, faculty also must situate themselves as companions in the wider community. In the vision of Jeffrey von Arx (2009), "What I'm suggesting is that the center of gravity needs to shift from 'us'—the promoter of justice—to a fuller consciousness of the 'we'—the full mutuality of relationship that is only possible when we truly open our doors and give all that we have to give and receive what is being offered to us in return." Faculty must be willing to take their teaching into the community and devote some part of faculty activity to the well-being of that community. Identifying paths for social change, we must commit ourselves to following them. And the college or university will need to account for this commitment as "of a piece" of faculty activity.

But the university must also move toward a fuller consciousness of the "we" in its promotion of justice. While placing students in service and being present as faculty in the community may help us move toward the reality of "we," von Arx challenges Jesuit institutions even further in this pursuit. It is not enough to seek justice "out there," but justice must be installed "in here." Here, we might be compelled by von Arx's vision as he calls us to be faithful companions of the Jesuit mission in educating those on the margins, offering an education to those who otherwise would not have one. What this means in a practical sense, von Arx assesses, is the commitment to expanding need-based scholarships instead of merit-based ones. From a structural perspective, merit-based scholarships often reward those who already benefit from systems of inequality and privilege. To truly engage in justice learning, the Jesuit university must extend its justice to the formation of its student body.

As Jesuit colleges and universities continue to pursue justice in the process of acceptance and aid, we not only need to equip our students of privilege to become companions in the community, we need to equip our faculty to create conditions for real companionship in the classroom. What this requires, then, of the teaching faculty, is new teaching techniques as well as new social justice curricula (envisioned above and more). If the effects of injustice are not only "out there" in the world but "in here" within our classrooms, we need to be empowered with tools that enable us not only to teach justice, but to teach justly. With admission and aid policies in place to recreate classrooms with a more just distribution of socio-economic positions and cultural difference among our students, faculty will need to be empowered to teach in such a way that does not place "privilege" once again at the center. In the words of Iris Marion Young, "If group-based positional differences give to some people greater power, material and cultural resources, and authoritative voice, then social norms and discourses which appear impartial are often biased" (Young 2000, 108). Justice education at Jesuit institutions will require not only equipping students for new kinds of learning (attentive to their own privilege in social analysis) but new kinds of teaching (attentive to the ways teaching in institutions of privilege can reinscribe privilege).

In visioning our Jesuit institutions toward a fuller embodiment of justice education, the preceding discussion has held a horizon toward which to extend ourselves in becoming companions to our local communities. Within this visioning, I have also suggested avenues that can be translated into very practical and followable strategies for change. Readers might ask themselves which of the following steps they are committed to taking:

Since community-based learning must be integrated with distinctive disciplines in unique ways, a reader might ask, "Is learning from, with, and for the community in need articulated as part of my department's aims and objectives?" The reader might begin the conversation within his or her department by asking that such a discussion be placed on the agenda of a departmental meeting. The conversation can be framed quite simply around the topic: to what extent do the local realities of injustice inform courses and programs offered within our department; and in what ways is a Jesuit justice curriculum relevant to the aims and objectives of the department?

As faculty members or program administrators, the reader might ask him- or herself, "How does my work introduce students to forms of social analysis that can lead to social change?" Practically, I have suggested three possible starting points for developing a social justice curriculum which includes: (1) unmasking stereotypes about "communities in need," (2) recognizing privilege on the part of members of the university community, and (3) examining the historical and human choices that have created the structures of injustice and privilege that currently shape the relationship between a university or college and local community. To implement this basic curriculum will require that faculty and staff engage in interdisciplinary investigation to understand the realities of the local community and its history. Classes and programs engaging the community will be informed, then, by this locally based, interdisciplinary lens.

To support the development and integration of "justice curricula," I have suggested that university- and college-wide forums be promoted to collaboratively develop such a conversation and share resources on local histories and current realities. Thus, while departmental conversations will pursue the question of how English or Economics (for example) can incorporate community-based and justice-learning as integral to the aims of the discipline, interdepartmental forums can provide opportunities to share community-based information and interdisciplinary teaching strategies. Readers might seek funding for a college-wide seminar for this kind of interdisciplinary work.

In developing locally based justice understanding, members of the local community should be invited to join as experts with faculty and staff. Drawing in the living knowledge of work in the community, partnerships with the local community are essential. Thus, the creation of "justice curricula" to be shared across disciplines should include insights from the local community. Each reader might ask him- or herself, "Who do I know in the local community-in-need with whom I might partner to develop my understanding of the history and reality of this community?" As a very practical way of establishing such relationships, the reader can commit to ongoing work in the community through any one of the many nonprofit, justice-oriented agencies that meet live needs and form the fabric of our local communities.

Partnering with local communities in need should raise an awareness of the opportunities universities and colleges have to offer to those communities in need in the form of scholarship. Members of a university or college who share a commitment to Jesuit education as justice education might ask themselves, "What sorts of opportunities are there to raise my voice within my university or college to influence administrative decisions in these areas?"

As justice education and implementation demands lifelong learning, opportunities for professional development in the area of pedagogy for justice teaching (in classrooms marked by a range of disadvantage and privilege) can be creatively envisioned and developed on an ongoing basis. Efforts like "Undoing Racism" offered through the People's Institute[5] or the SEED (Seeking Educational Equity and Diversity) project[6] should be regularly introduced as opportunities for professional development and implemented on our campuses.

What It Means to Be a "Prophet"

The foregoing argument insists that in order for Jesuit education to be justice education, very different styles and content for education must be put in place. First, the counter-normative pedagogy of service learning will invite students and community members to be active coinstructors with our faculty. Second, faculty across the disciplines must interrogate the systems of privilege, which constitute our world, and form curricula and rationale for employing the tools for social justice which are inherent within their particular discipline. Third, Jesuit institutions must not only place students in service and instruct them in social analysis for social change as a way to bridge the gap between "us" and "them" (privileged and dispossessed); Jesuit institutions must also revise admissions and aid policies to provide increased places for the dispossessed within Jesuit classrooms. Fourth, and this follows immediately upon the third point, if Jesuit institutions truly transform the classroom through practices of justice admissions and aid, we must also learn how to employ teaching strategies that do not reinscribe privilege under the guise of neutrality (or even under the banner of "privilege interrogation"). The pursuit of Jesuit education as justice education is no small task, but it is feasible with the commitment of prophets willing to cry out for justice and pursue it within our institutions.

Abraham Joshua Heschel identifies the prophets as lone voices calling communities to deeper enactment of justice. Fierce in their pronouncements and appearing to be over-the-top, the prophet "exposes scandalous pretensions" in which an unjust status quo is able to appear reasonable (Heschel 1969, 10). In Heschel's description, prophetic speech is empowered by adopting God's own perspective on a world created for justice that nevertheless abounds in injustice. Among the things that the prophet demands, none is more straightforward and challenging than Micah's: "To act justly, love mercy and walk humbly with God" (Micah 6:8).

It is undeniable that there are prophetic voices in the Jesuit tradition calling society to God's justice. Von Arx (2009) cites the 32nd General Congregation in which the Jesuit vision is one "of which the promotion of justice is an absolute requirement." The radical call of "absolute" is a prophetic call to Jesuit universities and colleges to infuse all areas of university life with this justice value. Indeed, many individuals within the Jesuit traditions of education have been leaders in this prophetic movement. Members of the university can stand as prophetic voices, calling the university to its task of justice; but can the university itself speak as prophet?

The life's work of Ignacio Ellacuria suggests that the university can stand in this role, as his own institution (Universidad Centroamericana, UCA) was one that was attuned to a society in need and committed to its future. In 1985, when the UCA awarded Archbishop Oscar Romero an honorary doctorate posthumously, Ignacio Ellacuria recommitted his university to carrying on Romero's prophetic activity proclaiming, "this award means we recognize the merits of the martyred archbishop, that we honor him with the best means at our disposal, and that we want his presence to remain alive and efficacious. But above all it means a commitment to do in our university way what he did in his pastoral way" (Ellacuria 1985, 167). For Ellacuria, to do the work of justice in a "university way" meant that the university should "serve the people" (ibid., 650) The university is not fundamentally to serve the small population within its gates but the vast majority of the people, the mass of humanity outside its gates.[7] With great rigor, Ellacuria and his companions at the UCA pursued the role of the university in service to the people, applying the tools of academic insight and discourse to the complex world in which they were living for the benefit of those on the margins. As Dean Brackley (2004, 28) explains:

> As legitimate and necessary as they might be, neither the search for truth in general nor the training of professionals constitutes the chief

goal of the university. Rather, its reason for being is the liberation of the poor majority of El Salvador and, through them, of the nation as a whole. . . . The university community responds that the extraordinary poverty and injustice of El Salvador constitute a dramatic negation of truth and reason. Ethically, the university must commit itself to changing this dehumanizing situation.

In this model, the skills of all disciplines are put in the service of citizens in need. In Ellacuria's (1982) own words:

There are two aspects to every university. The first and most evident is that it deals with culture, with knowledge, the use of the intellect. The second, and not so evident, is that it must be concerned with the social reality—precisely because a university is inescapably a social force: it must transform and enlighten the society in which it lives.

. . .

What then does a university do, immersed in this reality? Transform it? Yes. Do everything possible so that liberty is victorious over oppression, justice over injustice, love over hate? Yes. Without this overall commitment, we would not be a university, and even less so would we be a Catholic university.

But how is this done? The university must carry out this general commitment with the means uniquely at its disposal: we as an intellectual community must analyze causes; use imagination and creativity together to discover the remedies to our problems; communicate to our constituencies a consciousness that inspires the freedom of self-determination; educate professionals with a conscience, who will be the immediate instruments of such a transformation; and constantly hone an educational institution that is both academically excellent and ethically oriented.

Ellacuria's vision for justice education calls all the disciplines to work together on behalf of the people. To "analyze causes," "discover remedies," "communicate," and "educate," in order to be "an educational institution that is both academically excellent and ethically oriented." This is the heart of understanding what it means to shape students in "a well-educated solidarity." The problems of the world that divide rich and poor, privileged and oppressed and build walls of exclusion between the races and religions, these problems are complex and require the most sophisticated tools to unmask and undo, to break down and rebuild. It is not enough to send students into service, the university must cultivate with them the tools for dismantling and rebuilding the world.

For Ellacuria and his companions, their call as academics was in service to the people—giving voice to the voiceless with the tools of sociology, theology, and psychology. The university itself took on the role of the prophet. In the view of Heschel (1969, 205): "In a sense, the calling of the prophet may be described as that of an advocate or champion, speaking for those who are too weak to plead their own cause. . . . The prophet is a person who is not tolerant of wrongs done to others, who resents other people's injuries. He even calls upon others to be the champions of the poor." For our companions at the UCA, in the midst of civil war, "it was not their role to support a political party or a particular government or even a particular popular movement. Their task was to judge them and support anything in them which helped bring justice to the people" (Sobrino 1990, 22). These companions were motivated by their commitment to the community which was forged through their walking with the people. As Jon Sobrino describes (1990, 14): "The people's sufferings transformed and purified them, by their hope they lived and their love won their hearts forever."

In coupling the role of the university with the witness of the martyrs of the UCA, we begin to grasp what von Arx (2009) holds out as the real aim of the Jesuit universities' mission of "service for justice": "our universities and colleges are fundamentally about teaching people how to love" Ignacio Ellacuría, Segundo Montes, Ignacio Martín-Baró, Juan Ramón Moreno Amando López, and Joaquin López y López, demonstrated the way that university practice might be forged in love for the people, and out of love to forge a prophetic practice. If we are to teach our students truly how to love, this love will include a prophetic practice of justice.

Once again, the foregoing discussion begs for practical implementation. While the educational vision of Ellacuria and the UCA provides a horizon for imagining our corporate possibilities, the reader might also ask one very specific question to strategize the implementation of this vision. Recalling the words of Barbara Applebaum (2009, 384), "academic neutrality . . . can support oppression by default," the question is simply: Does my work—in research, teaching and programming—actively seek the well-being of "the people" or does my work participate in their injuries by supporting the status quo? To be prophetic institutions, Jesuit colleges and universities require individuals willing to craft their work toward the ends of justice. Embracing the work of the university or college as prophetic will include also a commitment to the martyred.[8]

The Gift of the "Martyrs"

If we pursue the role of the prophet to its end of self-giving love in a world of injustice, we arrive at the state of the martyrs. In Heschel's (1969, 209) words, again, "Justice bespeaks a situation that transcends the individual, demanding from everyone a certain abnegation of self, defiance of self-interest, disregard of self-respect." The martyr is the one who is willing to forego self-interest and self-respect because the vision of human wholeness compels the work of justice even when this will be met by disrespect and the very dissolution of the self. Like companion and prophet, in the work of justice "martyr" stands both in the community and in the university.

The martyr can be found among the crucified people who struggle beneath the structural injustices of minimum wage, a faulty education system, racism, classism, ageism, predatory lending practices, gentrification, and the meritocracy that is our society. In the words of Ignacio Ellacuria (1996, 266): "What is meant by the crucified people here is that collective body, which as the majority of humankind owes its situation of crucifixion to the way society is organized and maintained by a majority that exercises its dominion through a series of factors, which taken together and given their concrete impact within history, must be regarded as sin." The crucified people with whom our students work—in AIDS programs and struggling schools, in soup kitchens and homeless shelters—demonstrate to us the failings of our society as it participates in dehumanization. However, the crucified people are not the recipients of transformation and salvation, they are its agents. The crucified people who continue to live because they have "risen from the Death inflicted on [them]" stand as witness to the power and possibility of resurrection (Ellacuria 1996, 278). Here, the crucified people stand as martyrs, who give their lives in the struggle for a more just world.

In pursuit of justice, the martyr knows that there is a greater calling than what the world currently offers. He or she actively gives her life and life's work to the transformation. We must empower our students to recognize in the underpaid workers, site supervisors, doctors without borders, community organizers, activists and others, those who actively give their lives for the transformation of our world. Insofar as our world drains their life from them in the roadblocks it continues to erect—cuts in funding, ever new challenges to find resources, limits of transformative possibilities—those who give their lives in countless ways for the work of justice align themselves with the martyrs. Just as it will provide tools for recognizing injustice, Jesuit education should empower us to recognize the power of authentic change and rehumanization issuing forth from within the struggle for full humanity engaged by the communities with whom our students work. And so service in the community is to be valued not for what students can *do* but for what they can *witness*: the power of prophecy and the commitment of the martyrs.

As justice education, the role of the martyr within the university might also be recognized. Those who come first to mind, of course, are our companions from the UCA who transformed their research and teaching into action on behalf of the poor. These martyrs were prophetic both within the sphere of the university (challenging us in our own university practices) and in the wider world (challenging the world to bring forth justice for a people). To Jesuit educators everywhere they stand as prophets who insisted that the work of a Jesuit university is to research and struggle on behalf of the poor. To the society in which they worked, they stood as prophets to a world built on the exploitation and silencing of the oppressed. They were companions in the community, and companions of Jesus; following through on his kingdom vision even unto death. The martyr's death is one that can only be understood as a piece of his or her life. For death is not for death's sake, but the death of the martyr has meaning as the culmination of the life so fully engaged in the work of justice as to give itself over to injustice. The martyr stands as negative contrast experience such that in demonstrating the injustice of his or her persecution and death, the fullness of justice stands as horizon in relief. To be a martyr is to follow through on the calling of the prophet; to be a martyr is to be a companion of Jesus to the end.

If the university were to pursue a role as prophet there must be a willingness as well to embrace the outcome of the martyrs. Or, in the words of the 33rd General Congregation, "We cannot carry out our mission of service to the faith and the promotion of justice without paying a price" (Sobrino 1990, 19). Yet, while our institutions may align themselves with prophets and may nurture prophets within their ranks, *as institutions* they are ambiguous prophets at best. Given the self-preserving function of institutions *as institutions*, Jesuit colleges and universities cannot fully give themselves over to the work of being companions to the dispossessed while also maintaining the status of privilege. And because universities do stand on the side of privilege, prophets within the Jesuit network must be willing themselves to pay a price. There will be martyrs whose commitment to justice learning will drain the life from them. Willing to forego prestige, the present systems that reward acclaim will continue to demonstrate the internal injustice the prophet will face. What the institution must not do, however, is martyr its own. In the pursuit of ranking, the institution must take care that the values of the world not overshadow the values of the society for justice. Since the institution cannot stand fully in the role of prophet, the best it can do is protect its prophets. On a practical level, this means encouraging community-based research, activism and service learning pedagogies, but also allowing time spent in the community to be counted as "faculty activity." The university can also promote this work through grants, leave and a valuation of alternatives to publication in the work of activism and social transformation. Finally, Jesuit colleges and universities must actively affirm the commitment to justice in tenure and promotion decisions.

Once again, we arrive at the place where vision must seek implementation, and so the question of how the reader can inform institutional practice emerges. This practical step benefits from the research being done on community-based service learning development at colleges and universities across the country. As such research has shown, faculty may be motivated primarily by experiential learning that enhances student understanding of course material, but they may equally be deterred by institutional practices that do not promote faculty involvement in the community. If Jesuit colleges and universities seek to be recognized as having justice curriculum for a well-educated solidarity, provisions for supporting service-integrated and community-based learning should be given priority attention. In a discussion of factors that promote and deter faculty employing service learning pedagogy, researchers concluded with four very practical steps, one of which articulated what institutions ought to do: "Develop an infrastructure within the institution to support a centralized service learning office to connect potential community partners with the university, provide funding, create incentives to try new approaches, assist faculty with logistical support, and provide developmental instruction to new or potential service-learning faculty" (Abes, Jackson, and Jones 2002, 16). While the practical efforts envisioned throughout this essay have invited the reader to consider his or her personal response, readers are also encouraged to ask questions about how to influence institutional response. If community-based learning and the justice curriculum of service integration is valued at one's home institution, the reader might ask of the administration: What is the infrastructure that supports service learning course development? What funding is available for developing our justice curricula? What incentives can be offered to faculty and staff to engage in the steps outlined in this essay? These structural questions—including support through developing courses and affirmation through promotion and tenure decisions—are the responsibility of both the individual reader and the wider institution.

For those compelled in the work of justice, the institutional accommodations are not motivations but protections. As Abes, Jackson, and Jones have discovered, faculty committed to community-based pedagogy tend to employ this approach regardless of external rewards. Yet, without such protections, if the prophets will continue, there will be martyrs. For in institutions that fail to provide institutional support and affirming rewards, faculty who pursue the justice education will find that their energies are exhausted and their efforts life-draining. But, as Jon Sobrino (2001, 217) writes: "In a world such as ours, full of lies and cruelty, martyrs tell us that truth and love, firmness and faithfulness, and love to the end are possible. And that is good news."

Conclusion: Further and Deeper

DAVID MCMENAMIN

In his landmark speech on the Commitment to Justice in Jesuit Higher Education at Santa Clara in 2000 cited so often in this book, Peter-Hans Kolvenbach expressed his belief that from 1975 to 2000, Jesuit higher education had "made considerable and laudable Jesuit efforts to go deeper and further" in the commitment to the faith that does justice, a commitment that was made explicit in Decree 4 of the 32nd General Congregation of the Society of Jesus. He goes on to say that "implementing Decree 4 is not something a Jesuit university accomplishes once and for all. It is rather an ideal to keep taking up and working at, a cluster of characteristics to keep exploring and implementing, a conversion to keep praying for."

The mention of Decree 4 is not merely coincidental to this book, it is at the heart of it. The conferences that led to and included the 2000 Santa Clara conference and to subsequent conferences at Loyola University, Chicago, John Carroll University and most recently Fairfield University, were all a response to one question, posed at a meeting held in 1998: As the twenty-fifth anniversary of the 32nd General Congregation approaches (in 2000), how has Decree 4 been brought into play in the area of Jesuit higher education?

The contributions to the present book show how that ongoing task has progressed since then and yet, as Dean Brackley indicates in his introduction with a nod to Kolvenbach's earlier statement, we should "harbor no illusions" that the task is completed. If we are to understand that task as continuing to go further and deeper, the comments made here are intended to point out directions and areas of depth that might be followed or explored as ways in which educators at Jesuit colleges and universities might proceed. Two areas suggest themselves for serious consideration as we go forward: in terms of *further*, the concept of "social projection;" in terms of *deeper*, the question of faith as it relates to promotion of justice.

Further

As the contributions in this book as well as the many programs at the various campuses indicate, Jesuit institutions are certainly going further, at least in the geographical sense. Reaching into neighborhoods, countries, and continents that are not our own; sending our students, faculty, administrators and staff on immersions, are certainly valuable for many reasons. But their very existence begs the question of what is accomplished by them other than their educational value for those who participate? This is not to gainsay the value of that objective, but it is to ask how the university projects itself into society to contribute to a just world. The participants in these trips, as well as service learning programs, are certainly transformed by them, but to what extent is the world transformed as a result? In his keynote address at the justice conference hosted by John Carroll University in 2005, Brackley identified "social projection," the way the university or college *projects* itself into its community (local and otherwise) as a measure of how the university works for justice in concrete ways and as one of the higher standards demanded of Catholic education.

We need to be careful in this regard, as the way this is done needs to be in a manner appropriate to the university as university. Brackley describes this as "all those means by which the university communicates, or *projects*, knowledge beyond the campus to help shape the consciousness of the wider society." We might also think of this as the ways in which the university contributes its knowledge and expertise so as to assist the communities in their own work of building more just societies. The danger in even aspiring to such an objective is turning the university into something it is not: a relief organization, a social work agency, a political party or a church. But in the case of Jesuit colleges and universities, it cannot fail to take into account the Catholic and Jesuit identity of the institutions and what that implies—or requires.

In *Ex corde ecclesiae*, John Paul II says that the Catholic university must "demonstrate the courage to express uncomfortable truths, truths that may clash with public opinion but that are also necessary to safe-guard the authentic good of society" (no. 32).

Having extended our reach into Latin America and Africa via the various service and immersion experiences offered, it becomes that much more difficult to carry out and even to conceptualize. But if we are using those trips and projects to educate our students and staff, isn't the obligation to assist those communities in their own endeavors incumbent upon us?

Clearly, this needs to be thought through not only by faculty but also by the institutions as a whole. Research, teaching, future student projects, and institutions' very ways of proceeding are all challenged by this and it needs to be considered as we think not only further but deeper.

Deeper

The above leads to what is perhaps an even more important consideration for the future, the issue of faith as it relates to the university and its work. *Issue* is not an inappropriate word to describe this area demanding exploration, as it is more than merely a consideration or a question.

In Decree 4, the linkage of the promotion of justice to the service of faith is explicit and undeniable. The series of justice conferences that both preceded and followed the Santa Clara conference in 2000 was born of the question of how that decree had been taken up specifically in Jesuit higher education. This is no less true of the 2009 gathering at Fairfield where the present book has its origins.

But a search of the chapters herein will reveal that in comparison to justice the word faith rarely appears. Certainly there are exceptions, but even in those chapters where faith appears with some regularity one finds a particular faith tradition either explicit or presumed. This, too, would seem to be as it should be, at least in some cases. Consider for example the way the Catholic faith and its demands for justice are brought into play in Jeffrey von Arx's essay. How else could an institution that identifies itself as Catholic and Jesuit assess and project its way of proceeding if not against the backdrop of those traditions?

But there is another faith, or faiths, which not only go untouched, but unmentioned: the faith (or faiths) of our students.

As so many disciplines operate under the Weberian fact and value distinction, discussion of faith has been pushed to the periphery of the university's work where it has come to rest in departments of theology or religious studies, and sometimes in philosophy. In the most extreme cases such discussions could be excluded from the students' academic lives entirely and left to the campus ministers. Certainly such discussion is outside the proper range of most disciplines. And as our faculties become increasingly diverse, coming from a wide range of faith traditions or without a religiously defined faith tradition at all, it cannot be expected that faith would enter into their disciplinary work *per se*.

But it is also true that our students come from an increasingly diverse set of religious or faith traditions and it is within the students themselves where the facts and the values do indeed come into contact with each other. Even if, as von Arx has argued, the Jesuit university has a responsibility to inform its students of the Catholic faith in particular, doing that does not necessarily touch the students' own faith or, perhaps more important, their own faith questions.

Making this an even more profound challenge is the fact that we, as Jesuit institutions, are the ones who have made this a problem and who, therefore, have a responsibility to address it. Having taken very seriously the mission of "forming" our students, itself a problematic term for many, of exposing them to the grittiness of the real world, we have multiplied the kinds of immersion and service learning programs and experiences like those described here.

We have as a matter of course put our students in situations that challenge the beliefs they come to us with whether those beliefs have their roots in religious traditions or in nonreligious world views. So the matter of faith is bigger than the question of religion alone. It embraces all that our students believe when they arrive on our campuses; it involves their political and cultural assumptions as well as their religious beliefs.

We teach our students to think critically about all their own beliefs, religious and otherwise, frequently under the rubric that we are challenging them to come to a more mature, deeper, understanding of their own faith traditions. But there is no evidence in the present volume that after we put them in positions that shatter their belief systems we are there to help them pick up the pieces and put them back together or to help them articulate a new expression of their beliefs.

As we are the ones responsible for choosing to educate our students in this way, it would follow that we should also have some responsibility for the aftermath.

We have a responsibility to help students explore the depths of their own beliefs, their own longings, their own conflicts, and their own worldviews. But of course the faculty's very justifiable response to this would be that "we are not trained for that kind of thing, it is outside the realm of my discipline and even if I were inclined to do it I wouldn't know how." At the same time, there are many among us who are quite capable of this and quite comfortable venturing into these waters. We need to hear from them for the benefit of our educational practice.

Some who are versed in the lingo of Jesuit education might see the concept *cura personalis* at work here in a discussion of helping our students address their faith questions, but it might be better characterized by another familiar refrain, "education of the whole person." Even if our aim is education of the whole person, we often approach that whole person piecemeal, and leave it to him or her to integrate the pieces. But if we really believe, as the tradition of Jesuit education would seem to hold, that the person is an integrated whole, our education of these persons needs to be itself more integrated.

How exactly we could meet this responsibility is an open question; but it is a question that demands of us that we take it up. Perhaps such open questions present opportunities for creative responses. Perhaps we need to think about ways in which we can be more interdisciplinary or more collaborative in our teaching, of working with those departments or colleagues who are well able to teach the rest of us, if not actually work together with us in creating courses or programs in such a way that they would by design integrate the academic and the faith dimensions of students' lives.

Faith language is itself an obstacle for many, and perhaps we need to think about the language itself, not abandoning the concept of faith, but expanding our collective understanding of what that term might include. Adding to that word the notion of *the service of* faith does nothing if not further complicate the task. What does it mean to act in the service of faith? It is more than a little bit interesting that one never sees this worded as the service of *the* faith, but always in a formulation that would lead us to think in terms of faith in general, faith more broadly understood than specifically Catholic or even specifically religious.

It is reasonable to suspect that we have seen no work on this question precisely because it is internally controversial, more problematic intramurally perhaps than publicly. But it may be the most necessary of tasks if we are to be able to lay claim to any sort of "uniqueness" or if we are to be able to articulate what makes Jesuit education distinctive qua education. Any institution of higher education can show us the wide variety of ways in which they promote justice, but if we are to be faithful to the heritage our particular institutions claim we must be able to articulate the relationship between that promotion of justice and the service of faith. Finally, if we cannot do this, we will also be left having to admit that the answer to the question posed in 1998 is that Decree 4 only came into play partially at most because Jesuit higher education in North America failed to do the work of a Jesuit university qua university, to think through the very meaning of the faith that does justice.

Notes

1. Beauty Limned in Violence: Experimenting with Protest Music in the Ignatian Classroom

CHRISTOPHER PRAMUK

1. The remaining weeks of the Spiritual Exercises gently teach the retreatant how to do so with one's particular gifts, through the ways of discernment, and above all, through imaginative meditation on the life of Jesus.

2. Carnegie Hall, June 19, 1965; cited in Phil Ochs, *Farewells & Fantasies* (Elektra R273518), liner notes, 31.

3. Ibid., 42.

4. "On the white steed of aesthetic rebellion," Ochs declared in 1966, "I will attack the decadence of my future with all the arrogance of youth" (ibid., 53).

5. I generally present the material that follows in the context of a much broader discussion of possible responses (religious, literary, artistic, etc.) to the problem of suffering and evil, or the theodicy problem. Beyond the examples explored below, there is an enormous body of "protest" or justice-oriented music reaching across historical periods and musical genres, including church hymn texts, which might be explored to powerful effect in the classroom. For a range of possibilities, see James Cone, *The Spirituals and the Blues* (Maryknoll, NY: Orbis, 1972); Josh Dunson, *Freedom in the Air: Song Movements of the Sixties* (New York: International Publishers, 1965); Sing for Freedom: The Story of the Civil Rights Movement Through Its Songs (Smithsonian/Folkways CD, 1992); Marianne Philbin, ed., *Give Peace a Chance: Music and the Struggle for Peace* (Chicago: Chicago Review Press, 1983); Paul Westermeyer, *Let Justice Sing: Hymnody and Justice* (Collegeville, MN: Liturgical, 1998). Though historically the Society's relationship with music is marked by certain ambiguities (e.g., the exemption from singing the Divine Office), by and large Jesuit educators from the beginning have "embraced music's ability to arouse and move the souls of their students." See David Crook, "'A Certain Indulgence': Music at the Jesuit College in Paris, 1575–1590," in *The Jesuits II: Cultures, Sciences, and the Arts, 1540–1773*, ed. John O'Malley et al. (Toronto: University of

Toronto, 2006). A flourishing body of scholarship is advancing the case for a vital renewal of the engagement between theology and the arts in the academy, with particular emphasis in Jesuit circles on the reconciliation of political and aesthetic approaches to theology. Recent ground-breaking studies include Richard Viladesau, *Theology and the Arts: Encountering God through Music, Art and Rhetoric* (New York: Paulist, 2000); Jeremy Begbie, *Theology, Music and Time* (Cambridge, 2000); Begbie, ed., *Beholding the Glory: Incarnation Through the Arts* (Grand Rapids: Baker Academic, 2001); and the slight but shimmering gem by Don E. Saliers, *Music and Theology* (Nashville: Abingdon, 2007). Likewise an enormous body of pedagogical literature expounds the benefits and methods of integrating music and arts into the classroom. For two treatments especially resonant with the Ignatian concern for the whole person (i.e., of teacher and student alike) see Linda Carol Edwards, *The Creative Arts: A Process Approach for Teachers and Children*, 2nd ed. (Upper Saddle River, NJ: Prentice-Hall, 1997), and Edward Knippers, "Toward a Christian Pedagogy of Art," in *Teaching as an Act of Faith: Theory and Practice in Church-Related Higher Education*, ed. Arlin Migliazzo (New York: Fordham University, 2002), 188–209, and references therein.

6. The praise is not a little ironic, given that six decades earlier *Time* had described the ballad as "a prime piece of musical propaganda for the NAACP," and characterized Holiday herself as "a roly poly young colored woman with a hump in her voice," who "does not care enough about her figure to watch her diet, but [who] loves to sing" (Margolick 2000, 74).

7. Lewis Allan (aka Abel Meeropol), "Strange Fruit" (1939); Billie Holiday, *Essential Recordings*, Hip-O Records B0007X9U2Y. For the extraordinary story of Abel Meeropol, a Jewish schoolteacher and musician from New York City, who wrote the song, see "The Strange Story of the Man Behind 'Strange Fruit,'" an audio podcast at http://www.npr.org/2012/09/05/158933012/.

8. The documentary *Strange Fruit,* directed by Joel Katz (San Francisco: California Newsreel, 2002), brings vividly to life not only the song's historical genesis and significance, but also its varied and often contentious reception in different live performance contexts. I would recommend the film for use in college classrooms and church study groups, where it might generate fruitful cross-racial and cross-generational conversations about the history and present challenges of race relations in the United States, especially in view of the historic Obama presidency. For a theological interpretation of the song and its genesis, see Christopher Pramuk, "'Strange Fruit': Contemplating the Black Cross in America," *ARTS* 20, no. 1 (Spring 2009): 12–20.

9. As Margolick notes, Holiday first sang "Strange Fruit" sixteen years before Rosa Parks refused to yield her seat on a Montgomery, Alabama, bus.

10. Cf. Stuart Nicholson, *Billie Holiday* (Boston: Northeastern University, 1995), 112–16.

11. On "negative capability" and "negative space" see Nathan Mitchell, "The Cross That Spoke," in *The Cross in Christian Tradition*, ed. Elizabeth A. Dreyer (Mahwah, NJ: Paulist, 2000), 72–92, at 87. On "negative contrast experience" see Edward Schillebeeckx, *Church: The Human Story of God* (New York: Crossroad, 1990), 5–6; cf. Viladesau, 147–48. The revelatory dimension of a negative contrast experience—as in liturgical or artistic anamnesis—resides in its participatory (not merely passive or objective) dynamic: it is deep, evocative, moving.

12. Both songs draw the empathetic listener into the realm of what feminist theology calls the "abject": "that site of simultaneous fascination and repulsion based on proximity to something that neither maintains the distance of an object nor attains identity with oneself as a subject," Catherine Keller, *Apocalypse Now and Then* (Boston: Beacon Press, 1996), 23, citing Julia Kristeva. The abject sets "on edge," at the eschaton, which is to say, at the edge of rational and otherwise pleasant or normative systems of thought—a privileged locus, as Niebuhr suggests, for grasping Christian revelation. Is this state of being "at the edge" not analogous to the realm of communion envisioned by Ignatius in the various "compositions of place" (e.g., Golgotha; Hell) during the intensely purgative First Week? As the late Jesuit theologian and preacher Walter Burghardt put it, "I do not theologize about the redemptive significance of Calvary; I link a pierced hand to mine," *An Ignatian Spirituality Reader*, ed. George W. Traub (Chicago: Loyola, 2008), 89–98, at 92.

13. To be clear, I am not suggesting a strict, one-to-one identification between the horrors of lynching and the crucifixion of Jesus, especially as Ignatius views the latter in terms of the freely chosen kenosis of God in and through the free self-donation of Jesus. I highlight the term *free* here to underscore the obvious but crucial contrast with lynching, in every case a horrific violation of human freedom, dignity, subjectivity, corporeality. What joins crucifixion with lynching—not rationally, but iconically, where images touch the heart—is the former grasped as God's unreserved solidarity with every person who eventually faces death, but especially those who die in the way Jesus died. What is beautiful is in no way the act of crucifixion itself, but rather that God, in Christ, would choose to "suffer in this way" in solidarity and friendship with human beings, a historical reality that is neither arbitrary nor accidental for Christians. To say it differently, from Jesus' side, as it were, and in the pattern of weeks two and three of the Exercises: What is beautiful in the cross is the life of Jesus that led to it, an intentional life of compassion, self-giving, reconciliation, and mercy, "even unto death."

14. To Holiday's act of memory and resistance we could add many more, most unseen and unsung, a few iconic: a lone Chinese protester standing before an advancing row of tanks in Tiananmen Square; Tommie Smith raising

his fist on the gold medal stand during the 1968 Mexico City Olympics; the Argentinian "Mothers of the Disappeared," dancing in silence for their missing sons, husbands, and fathers. The cause of the Mothers of the Plaza de Mayo was immortalized in the song "They Dance Alone," by British pop artist Sting, as well as "Mothers of the Disappeared" by Irish rock band U2. The Mothers appeared onstage with Sting in Buenos Aires in 1988, and years later with U2; in both cases their missing relatives' photographs were projected on large screens before the audience, and their names invoked in a kind of litany, one by one, as the artist and audience together sang the song. Video footage of these events, extraordinary moments of global solidarity through music, is readily accessible for viewing in the classroom via YouTube.

15. Bruce Cockburn, "If I Had a Rocket Launcher" (Golden Mountain Music, 1984); *Stealing Fire* (True North Records, 1984).

16. In one early interview Cockburn recalls that a lot of people on the Christian scene "got a little nervous when I started talking about politics. . . . [Many] wrote letters urging me, exhorting me, not to lose the way." When asked about the song's reception in America, he says with some amusement, "I did get a few [angry letters] from people who . . . liked the song until they realized it wasn't about the Russians in Afghanistan," "Cockburn Interview," Grand Rapids Press, April 21, 1996, http://cockburnproject.net. In a more recent interview, Cockburn confesses the moral ambiguities and hazards of taking a political stand as a popular artist and Christian: "My hardest fight as a performer has been with myself, to be as clear a conduit as possible for what needs to be said. That's the ongoing struggle. Get my ego and my brain out of the way and let this stuff happen" (March 27, 2002; in ibid.).

17. Compare to Phil Ochs, describing the birth of one of his most criticized songs, "Here's to the State of Mississippi," which includes the lyric, "If you drag her muddy rivers/nameless bodies you will find/the fat trees of the forest have hid a thousand crimes." Ochs explains, "I wrote that song the day nineteen suspects [in the 1964 murder of three civil rights workers] were allowed to go free. It's a song of passion, a song of raw emotional honesty, a song that records a sense of outrage. Even though reason later softens the rage, it is essential that the emotion is recorded, for how else can future generations understand the revulsion that swept the country?" *Farewells & Fantasies*, 73.

18. As in the unforgettable incident during his sojourn to Montserrat in which "a Moor" had, as Inigo believed, insulted the honor due to the Virgin Mary. See the *Autobiography*, Ignatius of Loyola, 74.

19. During the Third Week of the Exercises, Ignatius invites the retreatant to consider how "the divinity hides itself" during the Passion. As Thomas Rausch notes, to fully "get inside" that experience is to enter with Jesus into "the dark night of the spirit. He found himself vulnerable and alone, deserted

by his friends, abandoned even by his God," Thomas P. Rausch, *Who is Jesus? An Introduction to Christology* (Collegeville, MN: Liturgical, 2003), 107.

20. This kind of remembering, of course, resonates deeply in Catholic Christian spirituality and liturgical practice, where the dead are known as the communion of saints, the cloud of witnesses, guiding, interceding, and calling us to account for our actions. Vatican II's *Lumen Gentium* advances a stunning vision of "the pilgrim church" walking in unity with all "the brothers and sisters who sleep in the peace of Christ." Death in no way interrupts the communion between earthly "wayfarers" and those who have passed over, "but on the contrary, according to the constant faith of the church, this union is reinforced by an exchange of spiritual goods" (LG 49). For an expanded discussion, see Christopher Pramuk, "'Strange Fruit': Black Suffering / White Revelation," *Theological Studies* 67 (June 2006): 345–77.

21. November 15, 1984, http://cockburnproject.net.

22. Peter Gabriel, "Biko" (Hit and Run Music, 1980); Peter Gabriel 3 (Geffen Records, 1980).

23. Available on YouTube at http://www.youtube.com/watch?v = iLg-8J xi5aE.

24. "Imagining," writes Antonio de Nicolas, always arises "within social and cultural contexts," and always presses, in its successful transmission and reception, toward "social transformation." In his remarkable study of the "powers of imagining" at the heart of Ignatian spirituality, de Nicolas underscores not only the public or political dimension of all human imagining, but also its transcendent (metaphysical) ground or horizon. "In short, the generative image is also a generative power outside of time. It enters time in the actual act of imagining and transforms time by infiltrating and transforming the public domain made by humans, because it was already there," Antonio T. de Nicolas, *Powers of Imagining: Ignatius de Loyola* Albany: State University of New York, 1986), 70–71. What is "already there" in the artist's and community's powers of imagining—even if implicitly and unthematically in the very cry of protest, solidarity, and pain—is the transcendental horizon of grace, God's revelatory "presence" or "response" to, and through, the human situation, rendered explicitly (categorically) for Christians above all in and through the liturgy. But clearly, as I have intimated throughout this essay, the powers of imagining to move human beings toward justice—the Reign of God; the Beloved Community—may obtain in and through "secular" art forms and rituals no less than through explicitly religious or liturgical ones. This is not to baptize all art (nor every act of liturgy) as beautiful, revelatory, or sacramentally efficacious, since our imaginings, past and present, secular and religious, are always crippled by sin or "concupiscence"; indeed, as an "active" and "synthetic" responding to and re-visioning of the human situation, imagining

"builds scenarios to be tested and painfully rebuilds them when they prove false" (de Nicolas, 70). In the case of the songs explored here, as in the iconic encounter with Christ on the cross, we are talking about the apprehension of a beauty that radically interrupts and challenges "the way things are" and demands conversion. For a lucid and balanced exposition of both the promises and limitations of art and music as theological "text" and "revelatory word," see Viladesau, 123–64.

25. Is this the strangely paradoxical truth that so perplexed Nicodemus, a wisdom that could not be understood, perhaps, until he had seen it play out not only in Jesus' enigmatic words but in the horrific manner of his death? Comparing John 3:1–21 to John 19:38–42, the transformation of Nicodemus suggested in the latter text (and in so few words) is disarming, and almost unbearably poignant.

26. I am grateful to Professor Kane of Regis University for introducing me to Lynch's enormously rich body of thought on the imagination, Christian irony, and education.

27. In a stunning essay that evokes many of the themes treated here, Lutheran theologian Dorothy Soelle suggests that the realization of contradictions (coincidencia oppositorum) within our own being is what "connects our pain with the pain of God," and lay at the heart of biblical and theological hope. Yet naming this experience is difficult: "we must use a different kind of language than our usual one," Dorothee Soelle, "God's Pain and Our Pain," in *The Future of Liberation Theology*, ed. Marc H. Ellis et al (Maryknoll, NY: Orbis, 1989), 326–33. Along with protest music I have used Soelle's writings and the poetry of Abraham Joshua Heschel to explore with students the interplay of divine-human pathos (eros; agape) at the heart of biblical and theological hope. See *Dorothee Soelle: Essential Writings*, ed. Dianne Oliver (Maryknoll, NY: Orbis, 2006); Abraham Joshua Heschel, *The Ineffable Name of God: Man* (New York: Continuum, 2007), including the superb introduction by Edward Kaplan.

28. Cf. Viladesau, 11–58. Trappist monk and spiritual writer Thomas Merton underscores the costly dimensions of such an education in wisdom as it recognizes and seeks to peacefully transform—first of all within oneself—the ego-centered, fear-driven groupthink that passes for "wisdom" in a sharply polarized society. Citing witnesses to nonviolence such as Martin Luther King Jr., Mahatma Gandhi, Dorothy Day, and Jesus himself, Merton writes: "The way of wisdom is no dream . . . and no evasion, for it is on the contrary a return to reality in its very root. . . . It does not withdraw from the fire. It is in the very heart of the fire, yet remains cool, because it has the gentleness and humility that come from self-abandonment, and hence does not seek to assert the illusion of the exterior self," Merton, *Faith and Violence: Christian Faith and Practice* (Notre Dame, IN: University of Notre Dame, 1968), 218.

29. Ochs, *Farewells & Fantasies*, inner sleeve.

30. Metz coins the phrase "mysticism of open eyes" to speak of the follow- ing of Jesus and the spirituality of the Beatitudes, especially the theme of poverty of spirit. Poverty of spirit is a redolent theme in the Christian mystical tradition, and runs like a golden thread through the *Spiritual Exercises*. See Kevin Burke, "A Mysticism of Open Eyes," in *Pedro Arrupe: Essential Writings*, ed. Kevin Burke (Maryknoll, NY: Orbis, 2004), 15–37; cf. Johann Baptist Metz, *Poverty of Spirit* (Mahwah, NJ: Paulist, 1998). No Jesuit has done more to bring these themes to the very center of Jesuit mission and identity than former Superior General of the Society, Pedro Arrupe.

31. The cura personalis so characteristic of Ignatian spirituality implies both patience and persistence with young women and men who are so often, and understandably, driven by more immediate and mundane concerns (Can I get my work done and still go to the game tonight? Can I afford another year's tuition? Will a decent job be waiting for me after graduation?). We distort the call to follow Christ to the degree it comes across as another "should" or "must" in a utilitarian checklist; it ought to feel, rather, like a wondrous invitation, though a costly one—as say, to a wedding banquet. On the challenges of transcribing the preferential option for the poor into a first world context, see Dean Brackley, *The Call to Discernment in Troubled Times* (New York: Crossroad, 2004); and with special attention to interracial solidar- ity and reconciliation, see Christopher Pramuk, *Hope Sings, So Beautiful: Graced Encounters Across the Color Line* (Collegeville, MN: Liturgical Press, 2013).

32. An early draft of this chapter was presented in 2008 at the Third Inter- national Conference on Theological Aesthetics, "Beauty: The Color of Truth," at the Jesuit School of Theology in Berkeley, California. I am especially grateful to the late Alejandro Garcia-Rivera and Jesuit scholar Kevin Burke for their invitation to participate and gracious encouragement of my theological work.

2. Teaching Poverty in America through the Arts

CAROL E. KELLY

1. One spring a young woman who had been raised in migrant farm worker communities and a young man who had been raised in one of the wealthiest families in the country attended the same section of my course.

2. Ice Cube. "It Was A Good Day," *The Predator*. Orig. release 1992, Priority Records. Lyrics available on Metrolyrics.com, http://www.metrolyrics.com/it- was-a-good-day-lyrics-ice-cube.

3. For the complete lyrics to "All That I Got is You" by Ghostface Killah, go to http://www.metrolyrics.com/all-that-i-got-is-you-lyrics-ghostface-kill ah.html.

4. An excellent performance of this scene is available on YouTube, http://www.youtube.com/watch?v = zQXwBQWpl&feature = related.

3. Encuentro Dominicano: Creighton University's Commitment to Education for Transformation

TOM KELLY

1. Becca Harvey, Encuentro Dominicano Alumni, in her reflection on her semester in the Dominican Republic.

2. Maggie Kennedy, Encuentro Dominicano Alumni, in her reflection on her semester in the Dominican Republic.

3. Kolvenbach 2001, "Ignatian Charism," paras. 19–22.

4. Maggie Kennedy, "Life at ILAC," *Encuentro Dominicano Newsletter* (Fall 2009), http://www.creighton.edu/fileadmin/user/encuentro/docs/Encuentro _Newsletter_Fall_2009.pdf.

5. "Mission Statement," Creighton University, http://www.creighton.edu/ministry/ilac/ilacmission/mission/index.php.

6. Ibid.

7. *Strategic Plan for ILAC/CESI, 2006–2009*, Licey al Medio, Santiago, Dominican Republic, 1, translation mine.

8. Ibid.

9. Zach Kesterly and Kali McElroy, "Fondesa," *Encuentro Dominicano Newsletter* (Fall 2009), http://www.creighton.edu/fileadmin/user/encuentro/docs/Encuentro_Newsletter__Fall_2009.pdf.

10. Michael Melaniphy, Encuentro Dominicano alumni, reflecting on his experience in the Dominican Republic.

11. Nick George, Encuentro Dominicano alumni, reflecting on his experience in the Dominican Republic. EDP 361 is the six-credit core class of the program.

12. Marianne Black, Encuentro Dominicano alumni, reflecting on her semester in the Dominican Republic.

13. Liz Kavan, "Curriculum for Life," in the *Encuentro Dominicano Newsletter* (Fall 2009), http://www.creighton.edu/fileadmin/user/encuentro/docs/Encuentro_Newsletter__Fall_2009.pdf.

5. Adopting the Mission of Social Justice in a Political Science Department

JOHN F. FREIE AND SUSAN M. BEHUNIAK

1. It might seem to have made more sense for us to offer SL courses as four-credit courses, but cost considerations and curriculum committee rules

got in the way. An extra credit of teaching means an extra credit of compensation for faculty—in our case about $800. To control expenses, the college limits us to offering only three SL courses per academic year. This means that only six courses can be offered in a typical two-year rotation of our courses despite the fact that a concern for offering students choices led us to develop thirteen SL courses. In practical terms this means that we need the flexibility to offer a course either with or without the SL credit. Under Curriculum Committee rules, the four-credit designation would not allow for such flexibility, but the separate one-credit designation does.

Moreover, we had set a requirement of three, not two, one-credit SL courses, but the road to developing the SL requirement has been a particularly rough one for us to travel as it has been fraught with problems: a lack of resources, conflicts over teaching loads, revisions of courses to fully integrate the experience, student problems with scheduling and registration overloads, the selection of who best to administer the program, and confusion over what is expected of the supervisors at the local sites, our service learning coordinator, our faculty, and our students. Eventually, because of no better reason that exhaustion, we dropped the requirement to two one-credit courses. We also moved SL out of the introductory course altogether because we found it was too much for first year students to handle during their first semester.

2. The college covers the spouses of married people, but because same sex marriage at the time was illegal in New York State, homosexuals were forced to leave the state to be married—something some individuals refused to do. Same sex marriage is now legal in New York State, but the college has not acted to change its policy.

6. Social Justice Themes in the Foreign Language Classroom

MARY L. ZAMPINI AND JOAN KERLEY

1. For the academic year in question, Mary Zampini was the instructor for all of these classes; Jean Kerley was the director of service learning at Le Moyne College and audited the course for both semesters.

2. One of our reviewers recommended that we discuss in more detail the question of whether "the incorporation of social justice improve[s] language abilities and cultural awareness." While we doubt that the incorporation of social justice in and of itself would necessarily improve language abilities, it certainly could improve cultural awareness. A more central question, however (and perhaps what the reviewer intended), is whether the incorporation of service learning improves language abilities and cultural awareness. We agree that this is an important question and should be investigated more thoroughly.

In order to do so, however, one would have to compare the improvement in language ability and cultural awareness of two fairly homogeneous groups of students that receive similar instruction, exposure, and practice opportunities (e.g., two groups of students enrolled in the same course), with the exception of service learning. As mentioned, however, participation in service learning was a course requirement. Thus, we are unable to address this question here.

3. Unfortunately, we no longer have these essays in order to cite some of the answers that were given. This paper evolved as a result of our experiences with service learning; thus, homework assignments were not retained for the purpose of potential research and publication while the course was in progress.

4. We thank an anonymous reviewer for pointing out this issue.

5. This reflection, then, is a result of our service learning experiences of the past few years; we did not use the Spiritual Exercises to help the students in their journaling.

7. Coffee for Justice

SUSAN C. JACKELS, CHARLES F. JACKELS,
CARLOS VALLEJOS, AND MICHAEL MARSOLEK

1. Coffee producers determine when coffee bean fermentation is "complete" by inserting a long straight object such as a tool handle or stick into the fermenting mass and subsequently removing it. Prior to completion of fermentation, the intact mucilage layer is very slippery, and the coffee beans readily slide past each other to fill in the hole as the tool is removed. At completion, however, the mucilage layer is no longer intact, and the beans are not slippery. They experience sufficient friction against each other to maintain the hole formed by the inserted tool for a minute or longer. The fermentation process is then judged to be complete; washing is started as soon as feasible and completely removes the mucilage layer. Fermentation does not actually halt at this point, but, if uninterrupted by washing, continues on to eventually degrade the quality of the coffee.

Although the producer-determined fermentation time of the batches varied from less than ten to nearly twenty-four hours, the large pH decrease generally occurred during the three to four-hour period preceding completion. To facilitate comparison of these fermentation processes, a shifted time coordinate was defined as $t - t_{4.6}$: the total elapsed time in the fermentation tank minus the elapsed time at which pH = 4.6. By definition, this time coordinate is universally zero when pH = 4.6, negative prior to it, and positive subsequently. The pH profiles of the seven batches are presented in Figure 2, where this shift of abscissa permits them to share a common completion point. It is observed that, with this adjustment, the seven curves are nearly overlaid near completion and are quite similar overall.

2. This partnership and collaboration could not have been initiated without the support of Seattle University, specifically sabbatical and travel funds, permission for coursework (Spanish), and permission from the Dean of the College of Science and Engineering to spend time in Nicaragua on the NSF Discovery Corps Senior Fellowship. Also, the culture of Seattle University and in particular the Office of Mission and Identity, the SU Endowed Mission Fund, the SU Nicaragua Immersion Experience and the International Development Internship Program were important in encouraging efforts such as this project. Charles acknowledges the University of Washington Bothell both for sabbatical leave support and for the flexibility in his course assignments needed to conduct several subsequent visits to Nicaragua. Susan acknowledges the support of a National Science Foundation Discovery Corps Senior Fellowship (CHE-0512867) and grants from the Winds of Peace Foundation, Engineers Without Borders, and the Endowed Mission Fund of Seattle University. For essential logistic support and resources while in Nicaragua, the Jackels gratefully acknowledge Catholic Relief Services/Nicaragua, Cáritas Matagalpa, the Association for Agricultural Diversification and Development, the Center of Cooperatives of Multiple Services Aroma of Coffee, and the University of Central America Managua. The hospitality of the model farm *La Canavalia* and of the many small farm families in the Matagalpa region is gratefully acknowledged. Much of this work would not have been possible without the generous contributions of undergraduate students. Civil and Environmental Engineering students Joshua Alcantara, Patrick Cummings, Luis Quintero, and Mike Wynne, participated in the *beneficio* design project. Stephanie Kleven, Scott Fraser-Dauphinee, Jack Chacon, Britt Edquist, Tam Pham, Roberto Rivas, Ervin Garcia, Diana Zelaya, Gema Medina and Maria Castillo are thanked for their assistance in the coffee field studies.

10. Promoting Social Justice: Closing the Gap
Between Rhetoric and Reality

MOLLY B. PEPPER, RAYMOND F. REYES, AND
LINDA TREDENNICK

1. We use the acronym AHANA for African American, Hispanic, Asian, and Native American.

2. We use the abbreviation LGBT for lesbian, gay, bisexual, and transgendered.

3. Campus climate is defined as the cumulative attitudes, behaviors, and standards of employees and students concerning access for, inclusion of, and

level of respect for individual and group needs, abilities, and potential (Rankin 2005).

The campus climate has been defined as the current perceptions, attitudes, and expectations that define the institution and its members. These common attitudes and perceptions have been conceptualized as malleable and distinguishable from the stable norms and beliefs that may constitute an organizational culture (Peterson 1990). Campus climate is the quality of the experiences that students have on campus (Hamilton 2006).

Culture has been defined as the "collective, mutually shaping patterns of norms, values, practices, beliefs and assumptions that guide the behavior of individuals and groups in an institution of higher education and provide a frame of reference within which to interpret the meaning of events and actions on and off campus" (Kuh and Whitt 1988, 13). If culture is an enduring quality, climate may be described as the current manifestation of that culture. Examining the culture and climate of an institution at a particular point in time provides information about the style and effectiveness of the leader and the effectiveness of the organization itself (Sullivan, Reichard, and Shumate 2005).

Four-part framework of an institution's diversity climate: (1) historical legacy of inclusions or exclusion of various racial or ethnic groups; (2) structural diversity (i.e., the numerical and proportional representation of diverse groups on campus); (3) psychological climate (i.e., perceptions, attitudes, and beliefs about diversity); (4) behavioral climate (i.e., how different racial and ethnic groups interact on campus) (Hurtado, Milem, Clayton-Pedersen, and Allen 1998).

4. Questions comprising each scale included:

Perceived personal importance of diversity (scale was 1 to 4 with 1 = strongly disagree and 4 = strongly agree):
I believe that being part of a diverse campus will prepare me for the "real" world.
I think it is important to learn about social groups that are different from my own.
It is important to me that there is a sense of community on campus.
It is important to me that the campus environment is tolerant of diversity.

Perceptions of fair treatment for all (scale was 1 to 4 with 1 = strongly disagree and 4 = strongly agree):
At Gonzaga University, people are treated fairly regardless of their race/ethnicity.
At Gonzaga University, people are treated fairly regardless of their gender.

At Gonzaga University, people are treated fairly regardless of their sexual orientation.

Perceived importance of celebrating diversity (on a scale of 1 to 4 with 1 = not at all important and 4 = very important); students were asked to indicate *how important* it is to celebrate diversity on campus through each of the following:

Events (e.g., festivals)

Programs (e.g., music, theatre)

Workshops

Faculty actions (support/mentoring)

Staff actions (support/mentoring)

Student actions (support/mentoring)

Support services (multicultural services, disability service, etc.)

Student clubs

Campus magazines/newspapers

Guest speakers/presenters (from outside of the campus community)

Campus flyers/posters

Dining hall food options

Campus acknowledgment of a variety of holidays

Campus places to celebrate different faiths/religions

Perceptions of celebration of diversity at GU (on a scale of 1 to 4 with 1 = not at all important and 4 = very important); students were asked to indicate whether diversity on campus is *continuously celebrated* through each of the following:

Events (e.g., festivals)

Programs (e.g., music, theatre)

Workshops

Faculty actions (support/mentoring)

Staff actions (support/mentoring)

Student actions (support/mentoring)

Support services (multicultural services/ disability services, etc.)

Student clubs

Campus magazines/newspapers

Guest speakers/ presenters (from outside the campus community)

Campus flyers/posters

Dining hall food options

Campus acknowledgement of a variety of holidays

Campus places to celebrate different faiths/religions

Experiences; students were asked if they had ever had any of the following negative experiences (yes/no) based on their race/ethnicity, gender, or sexual orientation. Lowest possible score is 0, highest is 21:

Negative or insulting comments

Harassment (stalking, speech, etc.)

Discrimination (prejudice)

Feeling isolated or unwelcome

Offensive language or humor

Not being taken seriously

Discouragement in pursuing your career goals

Open-ended Questions; students were given the opportunity to elaborate on their experiences through these two questions:

Please describe an incident or incidents that illustrate your experience.

Please share any general comments you have about the campus climate community.

11. Opening Remarks to the Jesuit Justice Conference, June 18, 2009

REV. JEFFREY VON ARX, SJ

1. For more details see "The Commitment to Justice in Catholic Higher Education," https://www.scu.edu/ignatiancenter/events/conferences/archives/justice/upload/f07_justice_publication.pdf.

2. Decrees of the 32nd General Congregation, Decree 4, "The Society's Response to the Challenges of our Age," in Documents of the 31st and 32nd General Congregations of the Society of Jesus (St. Louis: Institute of Jesuit Sources, 1977), 411.

3. Fr. Peter-Hans Kolvenbach, "The Service of Faith and the Promotion of Justice in American Higher Education," paper delivered at the Commitment to Justice in Jesuit Higher Education conference, Santa Clara University in October 2000, http://www.loyola.edu/Justice/commitment/kolvenbach.html.

4. Kolvenbach, 9.

5. Ibid.

6. Dean Brackley, SJ, "Justice and Jesuit Higher Education," paper delivered at the Nurturing the Commitment to Justice Conference, John Carroll University, October 13–16, http://www.loyola.edu/Justice/commitment/commitment2005/keynotes.html

7. Kolvenbach, 1.

8. John Paul II. Encyclical Letter "Sollicitudo Rei Socialis" of the Supreme Pontiff John Paul II, Publication No. 205-5. Office of Publishing and Promotion Services, United States Catholic Conference, n. 43 (December 30, 1987), 86–87.

9. Paul Locatelli, SJ, "The Catholic University of the 21st Century: Educating for Solidarity," paper delivered at the Nurturing the Commitment to Justice Conference, John Carroll University, October 13–16, http://www.loyola.edu/Justice/commitment/commitment2005/keynotes.html.

10. Kolvenbach, 4.

11. "Our Mission Today: The Service of Faith and the Promotion of Justice," Decree 4, Documents of the 32nd General Congregation of the Society of Jesus, Jesuit Conference (Washington, DC 1975), 1.

12. Benedict XVI, "Address of His Holiness Benedict XVI," meeting with Catholic Educators, Conference Hall of the Catholic University of America in Washington DC. Thursday, 17 April, 2008, http://www.vatican.va/holy_father/benedict_xvi/speeches/2008/april/documents/hf_ben-xvi_spe_20080417_cath-univ-washington_en.html.

13. Ibid., 4.

14. Benedict XVI, Encyclical Letter "Deus Caritas Est," (December 15, 2005), http://www.vatican.va/holy_father/benedict_xvi/encyclicals/documents/hf_ben-xvi_enc_20051225_deus-caritas-est_en.html.

15. Ibid., 5

16. Ibid., 20n28.

17. Ibid., 21n28.

18. Ibid., 19n25.

19. Kolvenbach, 13.

20. See 32nd General Congregation, Decree 2, note 8, as cited in Kolvenbach, 14.

21. Ibid., 13.

13. Nonviolently Transforming the Road to Jericho

ANNA J. BROWN

1. In fall 2012 Saint Peter's College officially became Saint Peter's University. I will use this designation though at the time that Dr. Martin Luther King Jr. received the honorary doctorate the designation of the school was Saint Peter's College.

2. Art Laffin (2009) writes "The bill [2010 National Defense Authorization Act, signed into law by President Obama and which is the largest of its kind] included $560 for a new F-35 Joint Strike Fighter engine the Pentagon had rejected."

3. Hugh Lacey (2002) gives Ellacuria's reading of the "situated university": "The university, qua university, should not subordinate these [core] values to political, religious, economic or any other values. Nevertheless the university, qua institution, depends on the material, financial and social conditions whose

availability may require the university's cooperation with projects in tension with these values. The central object of investigation is concrete [historical] reality; charting its actual details and variations, analyzing their causes, attempting to identify the range of possibilities that the actually realized permits for the future. Historical reality includes the socially significant phenomena of one's times, those phenomena from which no lives are isolated, and response to which largely defines the moral character of one's times. Truth cannot be pursued in abstraction from complete lives and social relations of the researchers, teachers, students, etc. It must be pursued in dialectical relationship with other values: either those highly embodied in society (e.g., those of the market, private property and consumerism, or those of justice, peace making and solidarity with the poor in Ellacuria's theological perspective, the values of the Reign of God.)".

4. Typically, military service is described as an "act of public service" in our Jesuit college and university website, brochures, and other marketing materials. There may be a certain truth in that but we may wish to think about Dr. King's (1991) description of American forces during the Vietnam War: "They [the Vietnamese] must think of us as strange liberators. . . . They watch as we poison their water, as we kill a million acres of their crops. . . . They wander into the hospitals, with at least twenty casualties from American firepower for one 'Vietcong'-inflicted injury. So far we have killed a million of them—mostly children" (236). Certainly we may wish to think about what kind of service we offer when we see much of what Dr. King described going on in wars that are waged today.

5. Out of the twenty-eight American Jesuit colleges and universities, twenty-six have ROTC programs (Catholic Peace Fellowship 2006).

6. Though this job or payment is not guaranteed even under the provisions of the post 9/11 GI Bill, which states, for example, someone who serves less than three years of active duty will not receive full payment. So, if a student serves only two years active duty and the remainder of his/her time in the Reserves, his/her tuition will not be covered fully (Castor 2001).

7. For example, we may wish to cite the scholarship of Chris Hedges (2010) who explains: "War is brutal. It mocks the fantasy of individual heroism and the absurdity of utopian goals like democracy. In an instant, industrial warfare can kill dozens, even hundreds of people, who never see their attackers. The power of these industrial weapons is indiscriminate and staggering. They can take down apartment blocks in seconds, burying and crushing everyone inside. They can demolish villages and send tanks, planes, and ships up in fiery blasts. The wounds, for those who survive, result in terrible burns, blindness, amputation, and lifelong pain and trauma. No one returns the same from such warfare. And once these weapons are employed all talk of human rights is a farce."

8. In *Empire of Illusion*, Chris Hedges points out: "The US military spends more than all other militaries on earth combined. The official US defense budget for fiscal year 2008 is $623 billion, and by 2010 the Pentagon is slated to receive $700 billion, once funding for nuclear weapons is included in the budget. The next closest national military budget is China's at $65 billion, according to the Central Intelligence Agency" (2009, 144).

9. McCord pulled injured Iraqi children from a van which had been fired upon by US Air Force pilots. For video footage of the July 2007 attack, see "'Collateral Murder': Wikileaks Reveals Video Showing US Air Crew Shooting Down Iraqi Civilians," https://www.commondreams.org/headline/2010/04/05-6.

10. In his 2007 Easter Address, Pope Benedict stated "nonviolence, for Christians, is not mere tactical behavior but a person's way of being . . . Loving the enemy is the nucleus of the 'Christian revolution,' a revolution not based on strategies of economic, or political, or media power."

14. The Ethic of Environmental Concern and the Jesuit Mission

JENNIFER TILGHMAN-HAVENS

1. LEED is an internationally recognized green building certification system, providing third-party verification that a building or community was designed and built using strategies aimed at improving performance across all the metrics that matter most: energy savings, water efficiency, CO_2 emissions reduction, improved indoor environmental quality, and stewardship of resources and sensitivity to their impacts. For more information go to the USGBC website (http://new.usgbc.org/leed).

2. An alliance of more than one hundred environmental, civic, and human service organizations, progressive utilities, and businesses.

3. Superior General of the Society of Jesus from 1965–83.

15. Companions, Prophets, Martyrs: Jesuit Education as Justice Education

JEANNINE HILL FLETCHER

1. Communal Reflection on Jesuit Mission in Higher Education: A Way of Proceeding, Jesuit Conference 2002.

2. I am indebted to my colleagues Sandra Lobo-Jost, Melissa Alvarenga, and Kate Cavanagh in the Dorothy Day Center for Service and Justice at Fordham University for their years of ongoing collaboration which have sustained

numerous insights into Jesuit education as justice education which I attempt to outline in this essay.

3. According to the 2005 Census, only 28 percent of Americans have earned bachelor's degrees, and economic disparity continues to mark the outcomes of education in this country. According to the US Census Bureau "workers 18 and over with a bachelor's degree earn an average of $51,206 a year, while those with a high school diploma earn $27,915. . . . [t]hose without a high school diploma average $18,734" (US Census Press Release, March 28, 2005, http://www.census.gov/Press-Release/www/releases/archives/education/004214.html). The poverty line for a family of four is $22,050 (http://aspe.hhs.gov/POVERTY/09poverty.shtml). Although in our country the structures of education (including higher education) were infused with systemic racism in their creation, the 1954 Brown v. Board of Education decision attempted to legislate an alternative to racial disadvantage in education (and therefore also in wage-earning potential). The actual implementation of this decision was delayed in many parts of our country. Further, in connecting education with geographic location and recognizing the racial disadvantages that accompanied US housing policies up to the mid–twentieth century, actual opportunities to gain a sufficient high school education and therefore a college education have been impacted by continued forms of racial segregation in housing patterns. Educational opportunities, home ownership, and the accumulation of wealth that derive from them intersect with racial exclusion not only in our very recent history, but also impact our nation today. Jesuit economic justice must also be racial justice.

4. For an overview of education in the tradition of "academic, civic and eudemonic" see, Donald W. Harward, "Engaged Learning and the Core Purposes of Liberal Education: Bringing Theory to Practice" Liberal Education Winter (2007): 6–15.

5. See http://www.pisab.org for a description of the People's Institute for Survival and Beyond and workshops it offers.

6. See www.wcwonline.org for this program based at Wellesley College: "The National SEED Project on Inclusive Curriculum, a staff-development equity project for educators, is in its twenty-fourth year of establishing teacher-led faculty development seminars in public and private schools throughout the U.S. and in English-speaking international schools. A week-long SEED summer New Leaders' Workshop prepares school teachers to hold year-long reading groups with other teachers to discuss making school climates and curricula more gender-fair and multiculturally equitable."

7. This vision is in harmony with the founding of public institutions of higher learning in the United States. At these universities, the purpose of establishment was not for personal gain of individual students but for the

collective development of society. Take, for example, the following statements: "The mission of the University is to serve all the people of the state, and indeed the nation, as a center for scholarship and creative endeavor. The University exists . . . to improve the condition of human life" (University of North Carolina chartered 1789; www.unc.edu/about/mission.html). "To teach, to serve and to inquire into the nature of things" (motto of the University of Georgia, founded 1785; www.uga.edu/profile/mission.html). "Princeton in the nation's service . . . and in service of all the nations" (Princeton University's informal motto; http://www.princeton.edu/pub/ph/history/). Stanford University was founded in 1891 to produce "cultured and useful citizens" (http://www.stanford.edu/about/history/).

8. The six Jesuits of the UCA named above were targeted and murdered on their own campus in the midst of civil war November 16, 1989. While the martyrs of the UCA stand as prophetic witness to the possibilities for members of a university to serve in a prophetic role, the question of what justice demands of Jesuit institutions in the United States remains a live one. The posture of the prophet is to submit all interests to the greater good of the Kingdom of God. As private universities in the meritocracy of North America, it is unclear whether Jesuit institutions are in a position to adopt the posture of the prophet, foregoing status and self-interest which structures US systems of higher education seem to demand. As members of the Jesuit institutions, we do ourselves a disservice if we do not recognize the limits of the institution as prophet or deny the privileges we enjoy as part of privileged institutions which *does* seek its own well-being. The tension with which we pursue our mission (of excellence and justice; prestige and an option for the poor) renders Jesuit institutions ambiguous prophets, at best.

References

1. Beauty Limned in Violence: Experimenting with
Protest Music in the Ignatian Classroom

CHRISTOPHER PRAMUK

Daley, Brian. 1988. "'Splendor and Wonder': Ignatian Mysticism and the Ideals of Liberal Education." In *Splendor and Wonder: Jesuit Character, Georgetown Spirit, and Liberal Education*, edited by William J. O'Brien, 1–21. Washington, DC: Georgetown University.

Evdokimov, Paul. 1990. *The Art of the Icon: A Theology of Beauty*. Redondo Beach, CA: Oakwood.

Griwkowsky, Fish. 2002. "The Mouth that Roared." Interview. *Edmonton Sun*, March 27.

Harrington, Richard. 1984. "The Long March of Bruce Cockburn: From Folkie to Rocker, Singing About Injustice." Interview. *Washington Post*, October 19.

Hellwig, Monika. 2008. "Finding God in All Things: A Spirituality for Today." In *An Ignatian Spirituality Reader*, edited by George W. Traub, 50–58. Chicago: Loyola.

Ignatius of Loyola. 1991. *Spiritual Exercises and Selected Writings*. Edited by George E. Ganss. New York: Paulist.

Kane, John. 2009. *Passion, Polarization, and Imagination: William F. Lynch, SJ, and Spirituality for Public Life*. Unpublished manuscript.

Lynch, William. 1973. *Images of Faith: An Exploration of the Ironic Imagination*. Notre Dame, IN: University of Notre Dame.

Margolick, David. 2000. *Strange Fruit: Billie Holiday, Café Society, and an Early Cry for Civil Rights*. Philadelphia: Running Press.

McGregor, Arthur, ed. 1990. *Bruce Cockburn: Rumours of Glory: 1980–1990*. Ottawa: OFC Publications.

Metz, Johann Baptist. 1997. *A Passion for God: The Mystical-Political Dimension of Christianity*, edited by J. Matthew Ashley. Mahwah, NJ: Paulist.

Nicholson, Stuart. 1995. *Billie Holiday*. Boston, MA: Northeastern University.

Niebuhr, Reinhold. 1949. *Faith and History*. New York: Scribner's.

O'Meally, Robert. 2000. *Lady Day: The Many Faces of Billie Holiday*. New York: Arcade Publishing.

Sobrino, Jon. 2003. *Rethinking Martyrdom*. London: SCM.

———. 1994. *The Principle of Mercy: Taking the Crucified People From the Cross*. Maryknoll, NY: Orbis.

Time. 1999. "The Best of the Century." December 31.

2. Teaching Poverty in America through the Arts

CAROL E. KELLY

Badaracco, Joseph L., Jr. 2006. *Questions of Character: Illuminating the Heart of Leadership Through Literature*. Boston, MA: Harvard Business School Press.

Barker, Joel Arthur. 1992. *Future Edge: Discovering the New Paradigms of Success*. New York: William Morrow.

Beegle, Donna M. 2007. *See Poverty Be the Difference*. Communication Across Barriers.

Dominguez, Virginia R. 2006. "Seeing and Not Seeing: Complicity in Surprise." Understanding Katrina, June 11. http://understandingkatrina.ssrc.org/Dominguez/.

Dyson, Michael Eric. 2010. *Come Hell Or High Water: Hurricane Katrina and the Color of Disaster*. New York: Perseus Book Group.

Egan, Kieran. 1988. *Primary Understanding*. New York: Routledge.

Ehrenreich, Barbara. 2001. *Nickle and Dimed*. New York: Henry Holt.

Frank, Robert H., and Philip J. Cook. 2003. "Winner-Take-All Markets." In *Wealth and Poverty in America*, edited by Dalton Conley. Malden, MA: Blackwell Publishing.

Gans, Herbert J. 1995. *The War Against the Poor*. New York: Basic Books.

Harrington, Michael. 1962. *The Other America, Poverty in the United States*. New York: MacMillan Company.

Iceland, John. 2003. *Poverty in America*. Berkeley: University of California Press.

Katz, Michael. 2003. "In the Shadow of the Poorhouse: A Social History of Welfare in America." In *Wealth and Poverty in America*, edited by Dalton Conley, 225–53. Malden, MA: Blackwell Publishing.

Kolvenbach, Peter-Hans, SJ. 2000. "The Service of Faith and the Promotion of Justice in American Higher Education." http://www.scu.edu/ignatiancenter/events/conferences/archives/justice/upload/f07_kolvenbach_keynote.pdf.

Levitan, Sar A., Garth L. Mangum, and Stephen L. Mangum. 1998. *Programs in Aid of the Poor*. Baltimore, MD: Johns Hopkins University Press.

Wilson, William Julius. 1997. *When Work Disappears*. New York: Vintage Books.

Parks, Suzan-Lori. 2001. *Topdog/Underdog*. New York: Theatre Communications Group.

Shipler, David K. 2006. "Monkey See, Monkey Do." *Shelterforce Online* 145 (Spring). http://www.nhi.org/online/issues/145/monkeyseemonkeydo.html.

Smith, Adam. 1976. *An Inquiry into the Nature and Causes of Wealth of Nations*. Oxford: Clarendon Press.

3. Encuentro Dominicano: Creighton University's Commitment to Education for Transformation

TOM KELLY

Brackley, Dean, SJ. 2004. *Call to Discernment in Troubled Times: New Perspectives on the Transformative Wisdom of Ignatius of Loyola*. New York: Crossroad Publishing Company.

Kavan, Liz. 2009. "Curriculum for Life," *Encuentro Dominicano Newsletter* (Fall): 4. http://www.creighton.edu/fileadmin/user/encuentro/docs/Encu entro_Newsletter__Fall_2009.pdf.

Kennedy, Maggie. 2009. "Life at ILAC," *Encuentro Dominicano Newsletter* (Fall): 1. http://www.creighton.edu/fileadmin/user/encuentro/docs/Encu entro_Newsletter_Fall_2009.pdf.

Kesterly, Zach, and Kali McElroy. 2009. "Fondesa," *Encuentro Dominicano Newsletter* (Fall): 3. http://www.creighton.edu/fileadmin/user/encuentro/ docs/Encuentro_Newsletter_Fall_2009.pdf.

Kolvenbach, Peter-Hans, SJ. 2000. "The Service of Faith and the Promotion of Justice in American Higher Education." http://www.scu.edu/ignatian center/events/conferences/archives/justice/upload/f07_kolvenbach_key note.pdf.

———. 2001. "The Jesuit University in the Light of the Ignatian Charism." Address to the International Meeting of Jesuit Higher Education, Rome.

4. Teaching Social Analysis through Academic Immersion

GARY K. PERRY AND MADELINE LOVELL

Butin, D. W. 2007. "Justice-Learning: Service-Learning as Justice-Oriented Education." *Equity and Excellence in Education* 40, no. 2: 177–83.

Holland, J., and P. Henriot. 1983. *Social Analysis: Linking Faith and Justice*. Maryknoll, NY: Orbis Books.

McIntyre, A. 2007. *Participatory Action Research*. Thousand Oaks, CA: Sage.

Oakes, J., J. Rogers, and M. Lipton. 2006. *Learning Power: Organizing for Education and Justice*. New York: Teachers College Press.

5. Adopting the Mission of Social Justice in a Political Science Department

JOHN F. FREIE AND SUSAN M. BEHUNIAK

Barber, Benjamin R. 1984. *Strong Democracy: Participatory Politics for a New Age*. Berkeley: University of California Press.

Barber, Benjamin R., and Richard Battistoni. 1993. "A Season of Service: Introducing Service Learning into the Liberal Arts Curriculum," *PS: Political Science and Politics* 26: 235–40.

Charney, Ruth Sidney. 2002. *Teaching Children To Care: Management for Ethical and Academic growth, K-8*. Greenfield, MA: Northeast Foundation for Children.

Calero, Luis, F. 1994. "A Christian University at the Service of the Poor." In *From Power to Communion: A New Way of Being Church Based on the Latin American Experience*, edited by Robert Pelton, CSC. Notre Dame, IN: University of Notre Dame Press.

Colby, Anne, Thomas Ehrlich, Elizabeth Beaumont, and Jason Stephens. 2003. *Educating Citizens: Preparing America's Undergraduates for Lives of Moral and Civic Responsibility*. San Francisco: Jossey-Bass.

Correspondents of *The New York Times*. 2005. *Class Matters*. NY: Henry Holt.

Crabtree, Robbin D., David Alan Sapp, and Adela C. Licona. 2009. *Feminist Pedagogy: Looking Back to Move Forward*. Baltimore, MD: Johns Hopkins University Press.

Davis, James W. 2005. *Terms of Inquiry: On the Theory and Practice of Political Science*. Baltimore, MD: Johns Hopkins University Press.

Ellacuría, Ignacio, SJ. 1982. "Commencement Address, Santa Clara University," *Santa Clara Today*, October, 12. http://www.scu.edu/Jesuits/ellacuria .html.

Finkel, Donald L. 2000. *Teaching with Your Mouth Shut*. Portsmouth, NH: Boynton/Cook.

Finkel, Steven E. 1985. "Reciprocal Effects of Participation and Political Efficacy: A Panel Analysis," *American Journal of Political Science* 29: 891–913.

Freire, Paulo. 1970. *Pedagogy of the Oppressed*. New York: Continuum.

Gorham, Eric B. 2000. *The Theater of Politics: Hannah Arendt, Political Science, and Higher Education*. Lanham: Lexington Books.

hooks, bell. 1994. *Teaching to Transgress: Education as the Practice of Freedom*. New York: Routledge.

Kolvenbach, Peter-Hans, SJ. 2001. "The Service of Faith and the Promotion of Justice in American Jesuit Higher Education." In *A Jesuit Education Reader*, edited by George W. Traub, SJ, 144–62. Chicago: Loyola Press.

Lane-Garon, Pamela S. 2002. "Classroom and Conflict Management: Rethinking Teacher Preparation for Ethical Practice." Paper presented at the Annual Meeting of the Association of Teacher Educators, Denver, CO.

Markus, Gregory, J. Howard, and David King. 1993. "Integrating Community Service and Classroom Instruction Enhances Learning: Results from an Experiment." *Educational Evaluation and Policy Analysis* 15: 410–19.

McClurg, Lois Gail. 1998. "Building an Ethical Community in the Classroom: Community Meeting." *Young Children* 53: 30–35.

Miroff, Bruce, Raymond Seidelman, Todd Swanstrom, and Tom De Luca. 2010. *The Democratic Debate: American Politics in an Age of Change*. Boston, MA: Wadsworth.

Palmer, Parker. 2007. *The Courage to Teach: Exploring the Inner Landscape of a Teacher's Life*. San Francisco: Jossey-Bass.

Pateman, Carole. 1970. *Participation and Democratic Theory*. Cambridge: Cambridge University Press.

Shedd, Joseph. 2002. *Results of the Survey of the Relation Between SCH and Class Time*. Washington, DC: Institute for Higher Education Policy.

6. Social Justice Themes in the Foreign Language Classroom

MARY L. ZAMPINI AND JOAN KERLEY

Abbott, A., and D. Lear. 2010. "The Connections Goal Area in Spanish Community Service-Learning: Possibilities and Limitations." *Foreign Language Annals* 43, no. 2: 231–45.

Abes, E. S., G. Jackson, and S. R. Jones. 2002. "Factors That Motivate and Deter Faculty Use of Service Learning. *Michigan Journal of Community Service* 9, no. 1: 5–17.

Arrupe, P. 1973. "Men for Others: Education for Social Justice and Social Action Today." Paper presented at Tenth International Congress of Jesuit Alumni of Europe. Valencia, Spain, July 31. http://onlineministries.creighton.edu/CollaborativeMinistry/men-for-others.html.

Battistoni, R. M. 2002. *Civic Engagement across the Curriculum: A Resource Book for Service-Learning Faculty in all Disciplines*. Providence, RI: Campus Compact.

Beebe, R. M., and E. M. DeCosta. 1993. "Teaching Beyond the University: The Santa Clara University Eastside Project: Community Service and the Spanish Classroom." *Hispania* 76: 884–91.

Bennet, J. M. 2008. "On Becoming a Global Soul: A Path to Engagement during Study Abroad." In *Developing Intercultural Competence and Transformation*, edited by V. Savicki, 13–31. Sterling, VA: Stylus Publications.

Bloomgarden, A. H., and K. A. O'Meara. 2007. "Faculty Role Integration and Community Engagement: Harmony or Cacophony?" *Michigan Journal of Community Service* 13, no. 2: 5–18.

Brackley, D. 2005. "Justice and Jesuit Higher Education." John Carroll University: Jesuit Justice Conference. October 14. http://www.loyola.edu/Justice/commitment/commitment2005/keynotes.html.

———. 2004. *The Call to Discernment in Troubled Times: New Perspectives on the Transformative Wisdom of Ignatius of Loyola.* New York: Crossroad.

Bringle, R. G., and J. A. Hatcher. 1996. "Implementing Service Learning in Higher Education. *Journal of Higher Education* 67: 221–39.

Eyler, J., and D. Giles, Jr. 1999. *Where's the Learning in Service Learning?* San Francisco: Jossey Bass.

Eyler, J., D. Giles, Jr., C. M. Stenson, and S. J. Gray. 2003. "At a Glance: What We Know about the Effects of Service-Learning on College Students, Faculty, Institutions, and Communities, 1993–2000." In *Introduction to Service-Learning Toolkit: Readings and Resources for Faculty.* 2nd ed., 15–19. Providence, RI: Campus Compact.

Freire, P. 2000. *Pedagogy of the Oppressed.* New York: Continuum.

Fleming, D. 1978. *The Spiritual Exercises of St. Ignatius: A Literal Translation and a Contemporary Reading.* St. Louis: Institute of Jesuit Sources.

Galura, J., P. Pasque, D. Schoem, and J. Howard. 2004. *Engaging the Whole of Service-Learning, Diversity, and Learning Communities.* Ann Arbor, MI: OCSL Press.

Hellebrandt, J., and L. T. Varona, eds. 1999. *Construyendo Puentes (Building Bridges): Concepts and Models for Service Learning in Spanish.* Washington, DC: American Association for Higher Education.

Kolvenbach, P.-H. 2000. "The Service of Faith and the Promotion of Justice in American Jesuit Higher Education." Address given at Jesuit Justice Conference, Santa Clara University, October 6. http://www.loyola.edu/Justice/commitment/kolvenbach.html.

Osborn, T. A. 2006. *Teaching World Languages for Social Justice: A Sourcebook of Principles and Practices.* Mahwah, NJ: Lawrence Erlbaum Associates.

Savicki, V., ed. 2008. *Developing Intercultural Competence and Transformation.* Sterling, VA: Stylus Publications.

Tonkin, H., ed. 2004. *Service Learning across Cultures: Promise and Achievement.* New York: International Partnership for Service-Learning and Leadership.

7. Coffee for Justice

SUSAN C. JACKELS, CHARLES F. JACKELS,
CARLOS VALLEJOS, AND MICHAEL MARSOLEK

Association for Science and Information on Coffee. 2006. Informal group discussion at 21st International Scientific Colloquium on Coffee. Montpelier, France.

Avallone, S., J.-P. Guiraud, B. Guyot, E. Olguin, and J.-M. Brillouet. 2000. "Polysaccharide Constituents of Coffee-Bean Mucilage." *Journal of Food Science* 65: 1308–11.

Bacon, C. 2005. "Confronting the Coffee Crisis: Can Fair Trade, Organic and Specialty Coffees Reduce Small-scale Farmer Vulnerability in Northern Nicaragua?" *World Development* 33: 497–511.

Brown, G. H. 2004. "Making Coffee Good to the Last Drop: Laying the Foundation for Sustainability in the International Coffee Trade." *Georgetown International Environmental Law Review* 16: 247–80.

Catholic Relief Services. 2009. *Fair Trade Fund Support of Nicaraguan Coffee Farmers: A Case Study*. Baltimore, MD: Miller, Kelly. http://www.crsfairtrade.org/wp-content/uploads/2009/09/Nicaragua-case-study-FINAL.pdf.

———. 2006. *2006 Annual Report*. Baltimore, MD. http://crs.org/about/finance/pdf/AR_2006.pdf.

International Coffee Organization. 2003. *Impact of the Coffee Crisis on Poverty in Producing Countries* (International Coffee Council document 89-5). London. http://dev.ico.org/documents/icc89-5r1e.pdf.

Jackels, C., and S. Jackels. 2006. Coffee Fermentation Kit and Method. US Patent Application No.US20060204620, published September 14. Washington, DC: US Patent and Trademark Office.

Jackels, S., B. A. Edquist, T. N. Pham, C. F. Jackels, R. R. Rivas, and C. Vallejos. 2008. "HPLC and Test Strip Analysis of Bioacids Produced in Fermented Coffee Mucilage on Small Farms in Nicaragua." Paper presented at the 235th American Chemical Society National Meeting, New Orleans, LA, April 6–10.

Jackels, S., and C. F. Jackels. 2005. "Characterization of the Coffee Mucilage Fermentation Process Using Chemical Indicators: A Field Study in Nicaragua." *Journal of Food Science* 70: C321–25.

Jackels, S., C. Jackels, C. Vallejos, S. Kleven, R. Rivas, and S. Fraser-Dauphinee. 2006. "Control of the Coffee Fermentation Process and Quality of Resulting Roasted Coffee: Studies in the Field Laboratory and on Small Farms in Nicaragua during the 2005–2006 Harvest." Proceedings of the 21st Meeting of the International Association of Coffee Science, Montpellier, France.

Jackels, S., C. Lopez, C. Jackels, R. Rivas, S. Kleven, S. Fraser-Dauphinee, and C. Vallejos. 2010. "Successful Experiences in Research between the University of Central America Managua, Seattle University, and Coffee Farmers of Matagalpa, Nicaragua." In *Innovations in Nicaraguan Universities*, edited by F. Aleman, H. Medrano, A. Norgren, A. Reyes, and S. Scheinberg, 102–6. Managua, Nicaragua: Consejo Nacional De Universidades.

Marsolek, M. D., P. Cummings, J. T. Alcantara, M. Wynne, L. Quintero, C. Vallejos, and S. C. Jackels. 2012. "Wastewater Treatment for a Coffee Processing Mill in Nicaragua: A Service-Learning Design Project." *International Journal of Service Learning in Engineering* 7, no. 1: 67–92.

Martinez-Torres, Maria Elena. 2006. *Organic Coffee: Sustainable Development by Mayan Farmers*. Athens, OH: Ohio University Press.

Olle, D., Y. F. Lozano, and J.-M. Brillouet. 1996. "Isolation and Characterization of Soluble Polysaccharides and Insoluble Cell Wall Material of the Pulp from Four Mango (*Mangifera indica* L.) Cultivars." *Journal of Agricultural and Food Chemistry* 44: 2658–62.

Oxfam International. 2003. *Mugged: Poverty in Your Coffee Cup*. Oxford: Oxfam International.

Ubben, S., S. Jackels, and C. Jackels. 2010. "Nicaraguan Campesino Coffee Roasted under Different Conditions and Analyzed Using Gas Chromatography and Principal Component Analysis." 239th American Chemical Society National Meeting. San Francisco, CA, March 21–25.

United Nations Development Programme. 2002. *Report for Nicaragua*. Managua, Nicaragua. http://www.undp.org.ni/idh2002/index.htm.

United States Agency for International Development. 2003. *Improving Lives through Agricultural Science and Technology*. Washington, DC: US Agency for International Development. http://transition.usaid.gov/our_work/agriculture/improving_lives7-03.pdf.

Wagner, C. S., I. Brahmakulam, B. Jackson, A. Wong, and T. Yoda. 2001. *Science and Technology Collaboration: Building Capacity in Developing Countries?* Santa Monica, CA: RAND Corporation.

8. Personal Transformation and Curricula Change

SUZANNE HETZEL CAMPBELL, PHILIP GREINER,
SHEILA GROSSMAN, ALISON KRIS, LAURENCE
MINERS, AND JOYCE SHEA

American Association of Colleges of Nursing. 2008. *The Essentials of Baccalaureate Education for Professional Nursing Practice*. Washington, DC: AACN.

Angelo, Thomas A., and K. Patricia Cross. 1993. *Classroom Assessment Techniques: A Handbook for College Teachers*. 2nd ed. New York, NY: John Wiley & Sons.

Bean, John C. 1996. *Engaging Ideas: The Professor's Guide to Integrating Writing, Critical Thinking, and Active Learning in the Classroom*. San Francisco: Jossey-Bass.

Brookfield, Stephen D. 1995. *Becoming a Critically Reflective Teacher*. Hoboken, NY: John Wiley & Sons.

Campbell, S. H., and K. Daley, eds. 2009. *Simulation Scenarios for Nurse Educators: Making it Real*. New York, NY: Springer Publishing Company.

Cox, Milton D. 2004. "Introduction to Faculty Learning Communities." *New Directions for Teaching and Learning* 97 (Spring): 5–23.

Facione, Noreen C., and Peter A. Facione. 1992. *CCTDI: The California Critical Thinking Disposition Inventory*. Millbrae, CA: California Academic Press.

Facione, Peter A. 1992. *The California Critical Thinking Skills Test. A College-level Test of Critical Thinking Skills*. Millbrae, CA: California Academic Press.

Fink, L. Dee. 2003. *Creating Significant Learning Experiences: An Integrated Approach to Designing College Courses*. Hoboken, NY: John Wiley & Sons.

Kolvenbach, Peter-Hans. 2004. "The Service of Faith and the Promotion of Justice in American Jesuit Higher Education." In *Jesuit Health Science and the Promotion of Justice: A Invitation to a Discussion*, edited by J. V. M. Welie and J. L. Kissell, 49–65. Milwaukie, WI: Marquette University Press.

Siegel, Daniel J. 2007. *The Mindful Brain: Reflection and Attunement in the Cultivation of Well-being*. New York, NY: W. W. Norton.

Tervalon, M., and J. Murray-Garciá. 1998. "Cultural Humility versus Cultural Competence: A Critical Distinction in Defining Physician Training Outcomes in Multicultural Education." *Journal of Health Care for the Poor and Underserved* 9, no. 2: 117–25.

Zull, James. 2002. *The Art of Changing the Brain: Enriching the Practice of Teaching by Exploring the Biology of Learning*. Sterling, VA: Stylus Publishing.

9. Doing Well by Doing Good: The Application of Ignatian Principles to Legal Education

DAVID C. KOELSCH

Aschenbrenner, G., SJ. 1972. *Consciousness Examen*. Chicago: Loyola Press.

Barkan, Steven M. 1993. "Jesuit Law Schools: Challenging the Mainstream." *Conversations on Jesuit Higher Education* 3, no. 1 (Spring).

Brand, J. 2001. "Disciplinary Perspectives: Jesuit Law Schools and the Pursuit of Justice." *Conversations on Jesuit Higher Education* 19, Article 6.

Breen, J. 2007. "The Air in the Balloon: Further Notes on Catholic and Jesuit Identity in Legal Education." *Gonzaga Law Review* 43: 41.

Brown, P. 2009. "Ethics as Self-Transcendence: Legal Education, Faith, and an Ethos of Justice." *Seattle University Law Review* 32: 293–310.

Bryce, C. M. 2009. "Teaching Justice to Law Students: The Legacy of Ignatian Education and Commitment to Justice and Justice Learning in 21st Century Clinical Education." *Gonzaga Law Review* 4, 577–606.

Chemerinsky, E. 2008. "Rethinking Legal Education." *Harvard Civil Rights Law Journal*, 43, 595–98.

Dinovitzer, R.,and Garth, B.. 2009. "Lawyer Satisfaction in the Process of Structuring Legal Careers." *Law and Society Review* 41, 1–50.

Ellacuria, I., SJ, "Religious Task Force on Central America and Mexico." http://papers.ssrn.com/sol3/papers.cfm?abstract_id = 2058694.

Fagin, G., SJ. 2002. *A Dream Confirmed: Ignatian Discernment and Decision Making*. New Orleans, LA: Loyola Press.

Fleming, D., SJ. 2008. *What is Ignatian Spirituality?* Chicago: Loyola Press.

Gilmore, H. 2009. "To Failure and Back: How Law Rescued Me From the Depths." *Florida Coastal Law Review* 10, no. 4 (Summer): 567–619.

Glesner, B. A. 1991. "Fear and Loathing in the Law School." *Connecticut Law Review* 23: 627–68.

Kalscheur, G., SJ. 2007. "Ignatian Spirituality and the Life of the Lawyer: Finding God in All Things—Even in the Ordinary Practice of the Law." *Journal of Catholic Legal Studies* 46, no. 7: 211–58.

Kalscheur, G., SJ. 2009. "The Law School Must Embody a Special Culture." *Conversations on Jesuit Higher Education* 35, Article 9.

Krannich, J., J. Holbrook, and J. McAdams. 2009. "Beyond 'Thinking Like a Lawyer' and the Traditional Legal Paradigm: Toward a Comprehensive View of Legal Education." *Denver University Law Review* 86: 381.

Krieger, L. 2002. "Institutional Denial About the Dark Side of Law School, and Fresh Empirical Guidance for Constructively Breaking the Silence." *Journal of Legal Education* 52: 112–29.

Kronman, A. 2005. "Can the Ordinary Practice of Law Be a Religious Calling?" *Pepperdine Law Review* 32: 439.

Marlow, G. 2008. "It Takes a Village to Solve the Problems in Legal Education: Every Faculty Member's Role in Academic Support." *University of Arkansas at Little Rock Law Review* 30: 489.

McCaffrey, A. 2003. "The Healing Presence of Clients in Law School." *William Mitchell Law Review* 30: 87–95.

Moore, A. 2007. "Contact and Concepts: Educating Students at Jesuit Law Schools." *Gonzaga Law Review* 41: 459.

Morrissey, D. 2004. "Bringing the Messiah Through Law: Legal Education at the Jesuit Schools." *St. Louis University Law Journal* 48: 549.

Nussbaum, S. 2008. "No Man Can Serve Two Masters: A Student Perspective on Jesuit Legal Education." *Gonzaga Law Review* 43: 631.

Pang, C. 2009. "Eyeing the Circle: Finding a Place for Spirituality in a Law School Clinic." *Willamette Law Review* 35: 241.

Perry, J. 2009. "Therapeutic Pedagogy: Thoughts on Integral Professional Formation." *Review of Jurisprudence U.P.L.R.* 78: 167.

Rose, H. 2001. "From the Field: A Law School Professor's Perspective on Justice." *Conversations on Jesuit Higher Education* 19, Article 10.

Rothstein, L. 2008. "Law Students and Lawyers with Mental Health and Substance Abuse Problems: Protecting the Public and the Individual." *University of Pittsburgh Law Review* 69: 531.

Scholla, R., SJ. 2004. "Fides Quaerens Iustitiam Socialem: A Jesuit Law School Perspective." *Loyola Los Angeles Law Review* 37: 1209–32.

————. 2002. *Fordham: A History and Memoir.* New York: Fordham University Press.

Shaffer, T. 1996. "Legal Essay, The Profession as a Moral Teacher." *St. Mary's Law Journal* 18: 195.

Silecchia, L. 2000. "Integrating Spiritual Perspectives with the Law School Experience: An Essay and an Invitation." *San Diego Law Review* 37: 167.

Toben, B. 2009. "The Added Value and Prerogatives of a Law School with a Faith Mission." *Journal of Legal Education* 59: 158.

Uelmen, A. 2004. "An Explicit Connection between Faith and Justice in Catholic Legal Education: Why Rock the Boat?" *University of Detroit Mercy Law Review* 81: 921.

Welch Wegner, J. 2009. "Reframing Legal Education's 'Wicked Problems.'" *Rutgers Law Review* 61: 867.

Young, W., trans. and ed. 1959. *Letters of St. Ignatius of Loyola* Chicago: Loyola University Press.

10. Promoting Social Justice: Closing the Gap Between Rhetoric and Reality

MOLLY B. PEPPER, RAYMOND F. REYES, AND LINDA TREDENNICK

Book, H. E. 2000. "One Big Happy Family. The Emotionally Intelligent Organization." *Ivey Business Journal* 65, no. 1: 44–47.

Breslin, J. B., SJ. 1990. "The Dialogue between Faith and Culture: The Role of Campus Ministry in Jesuit Higher Education. In *Promise Renewed: Jesuit Higher Education for a New Millennium,* edited by M. Tripole, SJ, 73–84. Chicago: Loyola Press.

Dumville, J. C. 1995. "Business ethics: A Model to Position a Relative Business Ethics Decision and a Model to Strengthen Its Application." *Employee Responsibilities and Rights Journal* 8, no. 3: 231–43.

Hamilton, K. 2006. "Toxic Campus Climates." *Diverse: Issues in Higher Education* 23, no. 8: 32–35.

Hill, R. E., and L. S. Baron. 1976. "Interpersonal Openness and Communication Effectiveness." *Academy of Management Proceedings*, 408–11. Boston, MA: Academy of Management.

Horine, L. 1990. "The Johari Window—Solving Sport Management Communication Problems." *Journal of Physical Education, Recreation and Dance* 61, no. 6: 49–51.

Hurtado, S., J. F. Milem, A. R. Clayton-Pedersen, and W. Allen. 1998. "Enhancing Campus Climates for Racial/Ethnic Diversity: Educational Policy and Practice." *Review of Higher Education* 21, no. 3: 279–302.

Locatelli, P. L., SJ. 2009. "A Justice of Faith. Kindling New Fires at the Frontiers." *Explore* 12, no. 1: 8–11.

Luft, J. 1969. *Of Human Interaction*. Palo Alto: National Press Books.

Matthews, G., R. D. Roberts, and M. Zeidner. 2004. "Seven Myths about Emotional Intelligence." *Psychological Inquiry* 15: 179–96.

Mueller, R. K. 1981. *The Incompleat Board: The Unfolding of Corporate Governance*. Lexington, MA: Lexington Books.

Nicolas, A., SJ. 2009. "Companions in Mission: Pluralism in Action." Keynote at Loyola Marymount University Mission Day. Los Angeles, CA. February 2.

Peterson, M. W., and M. G. Spencer. 1990. "Understanding Academic Culture and Climate." In *Assessing Academic Climates and Cultures*, edited by W. G. Tierney, 3–18. San Francisco: Jossey-Bass.

Rankin, S. R. 2005. "Campus Climates for Sexual Minorities." *New Directions for Student Services* 111: 17–23.

Schein, E. H., and W. G. Bennis. 1965. *Personal and Organizational Change through Group Methods*. New York: Wiley.

Shenton, A. K. 2007. "Viewing Information Needs through a Johari Window." *Reference Services Review* 35, no. 3: 487–98.

Sullivan, L. G., D. L. Reichard, D. Shumate. 2005. "Using Campus Climate Surveys to Foster Participatory Governance." *Community College Journal of Research and Practice* 29, no. 6: 427–43.

Wessler, S., and M. Moss. 2001. *Hate Crimes on Campus: The Problem and Efforts to Confront It*. NCJ 187249. Bureau of Justice Assistance Monograph. US Department of Justice. http://www.ncjrs.gov/pdffiles1/bja/187249.pdf.

Whittaker, M., and A. Cartwright. 2000. *The Mentoring Manual*. Brookfield, VT: Gower.

Witherell, C., and N. Noddings. 1991. *Stories Lives Tell: Narrative and Dialogue in Education*. New York: Teachers College Press.

12. Transforming Ourselves in Order to Transform the World

KENT KOTH, LÊ XUÂN HY, AND T. DAVID HENRY

American Community Survey. 2007. United States Census Bureau.

The Decrees of General Congregation 35. 2008. Washington, DC: Jesuit Conference of the United States.

Derman-Sparks and the Anti-Bias Curriculum Task Force. 1989. *Anti-Bias Curriculum: Tools for Empowering Young Children*. NAEYC No. 242.

Nicolás, Adolfo. 2008. "Mission and the University: What Future Do We Want?" Speech delivered at Escuela Superior de Administración y Dirección de Empresas, Barcelona, Spain. Translated by Mark Lester, Augsburg College, Nicaragua.

Privett, Stephen A. 2009. "Travel Abroad is as Eye-Opening for Administrators as It is for Students." *Chronicle of Higher Education,* May 28. http://chronicle .com/article/Travel-Abroad-Is-as-Eye-Ope/44418/.

Rucker, Victoria. 2010. *The Seattle University Youth Initiative: A Comprehensive Look at Our Neighborhood.*

Seattle Public Schools. 2009. Bailey Gatzert School Annual Report. http:// www.seattleschools.org/area/siso/test/anrep/anrep_2009/226.pdf.

Seattle Youth Violence Prevention Initiative. 2008. *Overview.* http://www.seattle .gov/neighborhoods/education/youthInitiative/do   cs/080910PR-Youth Violence.pdf.

13. Nonviolently Transforming the Road to Jericho

ANNA J. BROWN

Ali, Ahmed, and Dahr Jamail. 2008a. "Iraqis Running Out of Water in Rising Heat." *Antiwar.com,* May 10. http://antiwar.com/ips/aali.php?articleid = 12398.

―――. 2008b. "Iraqis Still Left in Dark." *Anti-War.com,* February 16. http:// www.antiwar.com/ips/aali.php?articleid = 12372.

―――. 2008c. "Iraq Unemployment, Too, Becomes an Epidemic." *Antiwar .com,* February 5. http://www.antiwar.com/ips/aali.php?articleid=12398.

Arrupe, Pedro, SJ. 1980. *Justice with Faith Today.* Edited by Jerome Aixala. St. Louis: Institute of Jesuit Sources.

Baxter, Michael. 2004. "Just War and Pacifism: A 'Pacifist' Perspective in Seven Points." *Houston Catholic Worker Newspaper* (May–June). http:// www.cjd.org/paper/baxterpacif.html.

Berrigan, Daniel, SJ. 2004. *Testimony: The Word Made Fresh.* New York: Fordham University Press.

―――. 1998. *And the Risen Bread: Selected Poems, 1957–1997.* Edited by John Dear, SJ. New York: Fordham University Press.

―――. 1982. "What Is Yet Lacking?" *Catholic Worker* (August): 1.

―――. 1968. *Night Flight to Hanoi: War Diary with 11 Poems.* New York: MacMillan.

Blimes, Linda, and Joseph Stiglitz. 2009. "Adding Up the True Cost of War" *Common Dreams,* July 7. https://www.commondreams.org/view/2009/07/ 07-7.

Brackley, Dean, SJ. 2009 "November 1989 Remembered." *Catholic Worker* (October–November): 2–4.

Burnham, Gilbert. 2006. "The Human Cost of War in Iraq: A Mortality Study, 2002–2006. Cambridge, MA: Center for International Studies. http://web .mit.edu/cis/pdf/Human_Cost_of_War.pdf.

Castor, Oskar. 2001. "Post 9/11 GI Bill: A Sure Bet? Maybe . . . Maybe Not?" http//:www.afsc.org/youthmi (site discontinued).

Catholic Peace Fellowship. 2006. "The Moral Compass of Benedict XVI: Where Will His Commitment to Peace Lead Us?" *Sign of Peace* 5, no. 1 (Spring). http://www.catholicpeacefellowship.org/nextpage.asp?m=2462.

―――. 2006. "Saint Ignatius Loyola and ROTC: A Report from Jesuit Campuses." *Sign of Peace* 5, no. 1 (Spring). http://www.catholicpeacefellowship.org/nextpage.asp?m = 2459.

Crews, Robin. 2009. "Peace and Justice Studies Programs as Transformational Education in (All) Jesuit Colleges and Universities." Paper delivered at *Justice in Jesuit Higher Education Conference: Transforming the World and Being Transformed.*

Galleymore, Susan. 2009 *Long Time Passing: Mothers Speak about War and Terror.* New York: Pluto.

Gill, Lesley. 2007. *The School of the Americas: Military Training and Political Violence in the Americas.* Durham, NC: Duke.

Hedges, Chris. 2010. "The Pictures of War You Aren't Supposed to See." *Truthdig,* January 4. http://www.truthdig.com/report/item/the_pictures_of_war_you_arent_supposed_to_see_20100104/.

―――. 2009. *The Empire of Illusion: The End of Literacy and the Triumph of Spectacle.* New York: Nation.

Human Rights First. 2003. "The Iraq Refugee Crisis: An Overview." http://www.humanrightsfirst.org/our-work/refugee-protection/iraqi-refugee-crisis/overview/.

Juhasz, Antonia. 2005. "Bush's Economic Invasion of Iraq." http://archive.truthout.org/article/antonia-juhasz-bushs-economic-invasion-iraq.

King, Martin Luther, Jr. 1991. *A Testament of Hope: The Essential Writings and Speeches of Martin Luther King, Jr.* Edited by James M. Washington. New York: Harper Collins.

Lacey, Hugh. 2002. "Ellacuria on Dialectic of Truth and Justice." Office for Mission Effectiveness, Villanova University. http://www3.villanova.edu/mission/peace/lacey.htm.

Laffin, Art. 2009. "$680 Billion Military Budget an Affront to God, the Poor" *National Catholic Reporter.* http://ncronline.org/news/peace-justice/680-billion-military-budget-affront-god-poor.

Mainichi Daily News. 2009. "52% of US Soldiers Wounded in Iraq, Afghanistan Diagnosed with TBI." July 23. http://archive.truthout.org/072609Z.

Merton, Thomas. 1996. *Passion for Peace: The Social Essays.* Edited by William Shannon. New York: Crossroads.

National Priorities Project. 2013. "Trade-offs." http://costofwar.com/tradeoffs/.

O'Neill, Patrick. 2001. "The Ethics of War." *National Catholic Reporter,* October 5. http://www.questia.com/library/1G1-79339762/the-ethics-of-war.

Phillips, David. 2009. "Casualties of War, Part II: Warning Signs." *Gazette*, July 28. http://www.gazette.com/articles/html-59091-http-gazette.html.

Pope Benedict XVI. 2006. "Message of His Holiness Pope Benedict xvi for the Celebration of the World Day of Peace." http://www.vatican.va/holy_ father/benedict_xvi/messages/peace/documents/hf_ben-xvi_mes_20051213_ xxxix-world-day-peace_en.html

———. 2007. "On the Revolution of Love." February 18. http://www.vati can.va/holy_father/benedict_xvi/angelus/2007/documents/hf_ben-xvi_ang _20070218_en.html.

Social Justice Secretariat. 2003. "War is a Defeat for Humanity." http://people .sju.edu/~jgodfrey/IraqWarSJ.

Steiber, John, and Ethan McCord. 2010. "An Open Letter of Reconciliation and Responsibility to the Iraqi People" *Reader Supported News Service*. April 17. http://readersupportednews.org/off-site-opinion-section/54-iraq/1515- An-open-letter-of-reconciliation.

Solomon Amendment. 2000. http://www.yalerotc.org/solomon.html.

von Arx, Jeffery, SJ. 2009. "Jesuit Justice Conference: Opening Remarks." Jesuit Justice Conference 2009: Transforming the World and Being Transformed. June 18. http://www.fairfield.edu/about/adm_just_conf09.html.

Williams, Linda. 1998. "When Jesus Said 'Love Your Enemies' . . ." *On Earth Peace*. http://www.onearthpeace.org/faith-legacy/bumper-stickers-buttonsstickers/lyrics-when-jesus-said-love-your-enemies.

14. The Ethic of Environmental Concern and the Jesuit Mission

JENNIFER TILGHMAN-HAVENS

Barclay, Eliza. 2008. "Climate Change Fueling Malaria in Kenya, Experts Say." *National Geographic Magazine*, January 9. http://news.nationalgeographic .com/news/2008/01/080109-malaria-wa rming.html.

Brundtland, Gro Harlem. 1987. *Our Common Future*. New York: Oxford University Press.

Creyts, Jon, Anton Derkach, Scott Nyquist, Ken Ostrowski, and Jack Stephensen. 2007. "Reducing Greenhouse Gas Emissions: How Much At What Cost?" US Greenhouse Gas Abatement Mapping Initiative Executive Report. McKinsey & Company.

Czerny, Michael, SJ, ed. 1999. "We Live in a Broken World." *General Congregation Document 35*, Decree 20. Rome, Italy.

Davis, Kingsley. 1973. "Zero population growth: the goal and the means." In *The No-Growth Society*, edited by Mancur Olson and Hans H. Landsberg. London: Brown, Knight, and Truscott.

Fitzgerald, Paul. 2009. "Finding God in all Things: An Ignatian Ethos for Sustainability." Lecture presented at Seattle University, Seattle, WA, May 12.

Fitzgerald, Paul. 2009. "The Theology of Sustainability." *Explore* 12, no. 2 (Spring): 10–15. http://www.scu.edu/ignatiancenter/publications/explore-journal/archive/upload/explore_spring2009_final.pdf.

The Holy Bible: New International Version. Genesis 1:31.

Ignatius of Loyola. 1991. *Spiritual Exercises and Selected Writings.* Edited by George E. Ganss. New York: Paulist Press.

Kenney, Brad. 2008. "Green Spot: Stonyfield Farm: A Culture of Leadership." *Industry Week.* January 8. http://www.industryweek.com/articles/green_spot_stonyfield_farm_a_culture_of_leadership_15585.aspx.

Kolvenbach, Peter-Hans. 2000. "The Service of Faith and the Promotion of Justice in American Jesuit Higher Education." Address presented at Santa Clara University, Santa Clara, CA, October 6.

Laitner, John A. 2009. "The Positive Economics of Climate Change Policies: What the Historical Evidence Can Tell Us." Report Number E095. Washington, DC: ACEEE. http://aceee.org/research-report/e095.

Matson Laura. 2008. The Higher Education Sustainability Officer Position and Salary Survey. Lexington, KY: Association for the Advancement of Sustainability in Higher Education.

Olin, John C. 1992. *The Autobiography of St. Ignatius Loyola.* New York: Fordham University Press.

Oliver, Rachel. 2008. "Rich, Poor and Climate Change." *CNN.com.* February 18. http://edition.cnn.com/2008/BUSINESS/02/17/eco.class/.

Oxfam International. N.d. Oxfam in Bangladesh. http://www.oxfam.org.uk/what-we-do/countries-we-work-in/bangladesh.

Pope John Paul II. 1991. Encyclical Letter *Centesimus Annus*, 36: AAS 83, 838–40.

Pope John Paul II. 1997. "L'Osservatore Romano." Address to participants in the Environment and Health convention. March 24. (English edition, April 9.)

Price, Karen. 2008. "What is Sustainability." http://seattleu.edu/sustainability/define.aspx.

Society of Jesus. 2008. General Congregation 35 Decree 3. Rome, Italy.

———. 2006. "Regional Sustainable Development: A Plan of Action." Portland, OR: Society of Jesus Oregon Province.

Sundborg, Stephen. 2008. "The World Comes to Seattle University." Speech given at Seattle University Convocation, Seattle, WA. September 17.

US Conference of Catholic Bishops. 1991. "Renewing the Earth: An Invitation to Reflection and Action on Environment in Light of Catholic Social Teaching." Washington, DC.

Vidal, John. 2008. "Global Warming Causes 300,000 Deaths a Year, Says Kofi Annan Thinktank." *Guardian*, May 29. http://www.guardian.co.uk/environment/2009/may/29/1.

15. Companions, Prophets, Martyrs: Jesuit Education as Justice Education

JEANNINE HILL FLETCHER

Abes, E., G. Jackson, and S. Jones. 2002. "Factors that Motivate and Deter Faculty Use of Service-Learning." *Michigan Journal of Community Service Learning* 9, no. 1: 5–17.

Applebaum, B. 2009. "Is Teaching for Social Justice a 'Liberal Bias'?" *Teachers College Record* 111, no. 2 (February): 376–408.

Beirne, C. 1996. *Jesuit Education and Social Change in El Salvador.* London: Routledge.

Brackley, D. 2004. *The University and Its Martyrs: Hope from Central America.* San Salvador: Centro Monsenor Romero Universidad Centroamericana.

Chubbuck, S. 2007. "Socially Just Teaching and the Complementarity of Ignatian Pedagogy and Critical Pedagogy." *Christian Higher Education* 6: 239–65.

Ellacuría, I. 1996. "The Crucified People." In *Systematic Theology: Perspectives from Liberation Theology,* edited by Jon Sobrino and Ignacio Ellacuria. Maryknoll, NY: Orbis.

———. 1985. "Editorial" *Estudios Centroamericanos* 40 (March): 167–76.

———. 1982. "Commencement Address." Santa Clara University. http://www.scu.edu/Jesuits/ellacuria.html.

———. 1980. "Editorial" *Estudios Centroamericanos* 35 (July–August): 649–54.

Heschel, A. J. 1969. *The Prophets.* New York: Harper Torchbook.

Howard, J. 1998. "Academic Service-Learning: A Counternormative Pedagogy." *New Directions for Teaching and Learning* 73 (Spring): 21–29.

Howard, J. 1993. "Community Service Learning in the Curriculum." In *Praxis I: A Faculty Case Book on Community Service Learning,* 3–12. Ann Arbor, MI: OCSL Press.

MacDonnall, J. 1995. *Companions of Jesuits: A Tradition of Collaboration.* Fairfield, CT: Humanities Institute, Fairfield University.

Sobrino, J. 2001. *Christ the Liberator.* Maryknoll, NY: Orbis.

———. 1990. *Companions of Jesus: The Murder and Martyrdom of the Salvadoran Jesuits.* London: Catholic Fund for Overseas Development.

Von Arx, J. 2009. June 18) "Opening Remarks" Jesuit Justice Conference, Fairfield University. June 18. http://www.fairfield.edu/about/adm_just_conf09.html.

Young, I. M. 2000. "Social Difference as a Political Resource," In *Inclusion and Democracy,* 81–210. New York: Oxford University Press.

Contributors

REV. JEFFREY VON ARX, SJ, has been president of Fairfield University since 2004. Previously he was chair of the History Department at Georgetown University and dean of Fordham College at Rose Hill.

SUSAN M. BEHUNIAK is professor emerita of political science, Le Moyne College. She is known for her teaching, scholarship, and faculty leadership, all tied to social justice issues.

DEAN BRACKLEY, SJ, was a prophetic voice for solidarity and social justice. He went to El Salvador immediately after government military forces murdered six Jesuits and two women in the San Salvador University Dormitory, in 1989.

ANNA J. BROWN is chair of the Political Science Department and director of the Social Justice Program at Saint Peter's University.

LISA SOWLE CAHILL is the Monan Professor of Theology at Boston College. She researches social ethics, feminist theology, and bioethics. She also served as president of the Catholic Theological Society.

SUZANNE HETZEL CAMPBELL is director of the School of Nursing at University of British Columbia, Vancouver, Canada.

MARY BETH COMBS is associate professor of economics at Fordham University, where she specializes in economic history. Her research on nineteenth-century married women's property rights has been published in a number of economic journals and edited volumes.

JOHN F. FREIE is professor emeritus of political science, Le Moyne College, and has written extensively on democracy and community. With

Susan Behuniak, he was corecipient of the 2006 Le Moyne College Social Justice Award.

PHILIP GREINER is a professor at SDSU and specializes in community-based participatory research.

SHEILA GROSSMAN is professor of nursing at Fairfield University where her research focus is critical patient care.

T. DAVID HENRY is a former member of the Society of Jesus and has served as facilitator of five faculty/staff local immersions at Seattle University.

JEANNINE HILL FLETCHER is associate professor of theology, faculty director of service learning at Fordham University, and member of the Northwest Bronx Community and Clergy Coalition.

LE XUAN HY is associate professor of psychology and adjunct associate professor of pastoral theology and directs the Institute for Human Development at Seattle University.

CHARLES F. JACKELS teaches chemistry at the University of Washington where he promotes the application of scientific methods to interesting environmental, societal, and philosophical questions.

SUSAN C. JACKELS teaches chemistry at Seattle University and is involved in campus service learning. She studies coffee chemistry, especially processing on farms and in the remediation of flavor defects.

CAROL E. KELLY, MA (Columbia University), is assistant professor in Matteo Ricci College at Seattle University specializing in arts, humanities, and interdisciplinary social science.

TOM KELLY is associate professor of theology at Creighton University. From 2005 to 2007 he was academic director of Encuentro Dominicano, Creighton University's study abroad program in the Dominican Republic.

SR. JOAN KERLEY, FMSJ, was the first director of service learning at Le Moyne College. She currently serves on her religious congregation's leadership team in Worsley, England.

DAVID C. KOELSCH is associate professor and director of the Immigration Law Clinic at the University of Detroit Mercy School of Law. He also was named Outstanding Immigration Law Professor by the American Immigration Lawyers Association.

KENT KOTH is the director of the Seattle University Center for Service and Community Engagement and the Seattle University Youth Initiative.

ALISON KRIS is associate professor at Fairfield University where her research involves the relationship between nurse staffing levels and patient outcomes.

MADELINE LOVELL is an associate professor in the Department of Anthropology, Sociology, and Social Work at Seattle University. She has been active in disaster relief work.

MICHAEL MARSOLEK teaches environmental engineering at Seattle University. He utilizes coffee projects to engage students in practicing real-world engineering and helping farmers in Nicaragua.

DAVID MCMENAMIN directs Boston College's PULSE program, and teaches in the philosophy department. He has been a member of the National Steering Committee on Justice in Jesuit Higher Education since its inception in 2002.

LAURENCE MINERS is professor of economics at Fairfield University. His research focuses on microeconomics.

REV. DAVID J. O'BRIEN, SJ, Holy Cross Loyola Professor of Roman Catholic Studies, retired in 2007, after forty years' teaching American-Catholic history and Catholic social and political thought.

MOLLY B. PEPPER is an associate professor of management at Gonzaga University. She has a PhD in business administration from Arizona State University.

GARY K. PERRY is associate professor in the Department of Anthropology, Sociology, and Social Work at Seattle University. His area of expertise is urban sociology

CHRISTOPHER PRAMUK teaches theology at Xavier University and is the author of *Hope Sings, So Beautiful: Graced Encounters Across the Color Line* (Liturgical, 2013).

REV. STEPHEN A. PRIVETT, SJ, is president of San Francisco University. He has received both criticism and praise for his social justice practices.

RAYMOND F. REYES is the associate academic vice president and chief diversity officer for Gonzaga University. He has a PhD in educational leadership from Gonzaga University.

PATRICIA RUGGIANO SCHMIDT is professor emerita of education, Le Moyne College. *Practicing What We Teach: How Culturally Responsive Classrooms Make a Difference* (2011) is her recent book with Althier Lazar, St. Joseph's University.

JOYCE SHEA is an associate professor at Fairfield University School of Nursing. Her research relates to identity, self-recovery, and community living for those with severe mental illness.

JENNIFER TILGHMAN-HAVENS is associate director of the Office of Jesuit Mission and Identity at Seattle University. A graduate of Notre Dame and Boston College, she focuses on social responsibility and organizational change.

LINDA TREDENNICK is associate professor of renaissance literature at Gonzaga University. She has a PhD in English from the University of Oregon.

CARLOS VALLEJOS teaches chemistry at the University of Central America Managua. He studies coffee because of its importance for Nicaragua and the educational opportunities for students.

MARY L. ZAMPINI is associate professor of Spanish at Le Moyne College. Her areas of specialization include second language speech production and perception.

Index

The Crucifix seen on the cover of *Transforming Ourselves, Transforming the World* is the steeple of the Roman Catholic Church in Soufrière, a small fishing village in Dominica. This Caribbean nation deals with great economic poverty supported by their strong spirit. In 2002, Rev. Donald Maldari, SJ, initiated the Le Moyne College Dominica Service-Learning Project. Eight groups of students and faculty have learned important life lessons from the island population, while serving beside them; many come away transformed. They change their areas of study and find new insights concerning the meaning of justice in developing nations.

— How does the university practice solidarity & then
how do the students participate in the
university's broader framework/practices
of solidarity?

— what if they chose a service side ^(as soph's) that they
continued w/ for the next two years? or
at least in a significant way for a whole
year — Bırıhe scholar model.

— S.L. as "lab" courses

⟶ competitive b. w/a
difference — how ss?

Who our students b/cm
        fac.   do
How our universities proceed

1. what do we think of the 4 characteristics
plus the above.

2. Reflect on & write a grad et grad statement
    · what should your student /read like @
    Graduation — "They should... be able to...
                        feel &
                        have experience